T0334226

GODFATHER OF THE MUSIC BUSINESS

GODFATHER
OF THE MUSIC BUSINESS
MORRIS LEVY

RICHARD CARLIN

University Press of Mississippi / Jackson

www.upress.state.ms.us

The University Press of Mississippi is a member
of the Association of American University Presses.

Photos courtesy BenCar Archives except as indicated.

First printing 2016

∞

Library of Congress Cataloging-in-Publication Data

Carlin, Richard, 1956–
Godfather of the music business : Morris Levy / Richard Carlin.
pages cm — (American made music series)
Includes bibliographical references and index.
ISBN 978-1-4968-0570-6 (cloth : alk. paper) — ISBN 978-1-4968-0571-3
(ebook) 1. Levy, Morris, 1927– 1990. 2. Sound recording executives and
producers—United States—Biography. I. Title.
ML429.L485C37 2016
781.64092—dc23
[B]

2015027997

British Library Cataloging-in-Publication Data available

CONTENTS

PREFACE

Why are you writing a book about *him*?
—Eddie Brigati

Eddie Brigati gave me a long, cold stare after I told him I was writing a book about Morris Levy. Like many of the people I interviewed, Brigati had strong opinions about Levy and his operations. And like many people I interviewed, he could not understand why anyone would want to dig into the dark story of one of the music industry's most polarizing figures.

Both beloved and feared, Morris Levy cast a long shadow on the world of popular music from the bebop era through the birth of rap. As a founder of Birdland in late 1949—the premier progressive jazz club in New York City—Levy was also among the first to promote a racially integrated club on Broadway, and helped build the careers of jazz greats from Count Basie to Dizzy Gillespie and Maynard Ferguson. Once he established his own label, Roulette Records, he represented the old guard of scrappy record producers who shaped the early years of jazz, R&B, and rock 'n' roll by signing acts that the major labels would not touch. Early on, Levy recognized the value in songs that most viewed as disposable fluff (at best) or vulgar teenage pulp (at worst), scooping up copyrights and master recordings from his peers, building an empire based on a bet that these songs would continue to be performed for decades to come.

However, Levy also represented the darker side of the paternalistic system of music production that came of age in New York City after World War II. Artists were paid a minimal fee up front, but rarely saw royalties for their songs. Levy was not averse to listing himself as a "coauthor" of songs that he recorded, and insisted that his artists publish their work with one of his many related companies, thus taking an extra share of every penny earned. He was a ruthless competitor, skirting the edges of the law—if not completely ignoring them—when it came to enforcing his ownership rights. He was loath to pay artists and used his physical size and intimidating manner as a means of scaring off those bold enough to enquire about their money. Many of these were common practices among the entrepreneurs who recorded R&B, jazz, and rock 'n' roll in the years immediately following World War II. But Levy unquestionably was among the most egregious offenders, while he lacked many of the redeeming qualities—such as a deep understanding and love of the music—of his peers.

Stories about Levy are the stuff of legends, often told by music industry veterans as examples of how business was conducted in the "good old days." In retrospect the humor in Levy's gruff retorts—"You want royalties? Go to England!"—makes him appear to be at least aware of his own duplicity. However, many who tell these stories recall being truly frightened by Levy's words at the time, and there are many tales of beatings and other rougher treatment of those who questioned the executive's manner of doing business. Decades later, the truth is difficult to unwind; but the preponderance of the evidence shows that Levy could veer from lovable to dangerous in the wink of an eye. Only the strong survived in his world, and he grudgingly admired most those who stood up to his harangues.

Whenever anyone writes about the fifties and sixties music scene, questions of exploitation of artists arise. Some forgive the record producers, saying it was standard industry practice to pay pitiful royalty rates and charge all expenses against future earnings, as well as using various schemes to underreport actual sales figures. Despite the fact that some of the independent label owners—such as Ahmet Ertegun at Atlantic or Bob Weinstock at Prestige—were often enthusiastic lovers of R&B, blues, and jazz, many had no qualms about taking the lion's share of profits from their businesses and sharing as little as possible with the artists who made the actual records. Of course, Levy took these practices to a new level of dishonesty. Ruth Brown—who spent decades trying to get an accurate accounting of her royalties from Atlantic Records—aptly described the situation when she compared Atlantic's Ahmet Ertegun with Levy, saying when you recorded for Roulette you expected "statutory rape," but with Atlantic it was more like "date rape."[1]

Levy took the shady practices of the music industry and developed a series of clever new ways to pocket his artists' income. Besides adding his name to countless compositions, he charged every penny of expenses he possibly could justify (and many that he could not) against artist royalties. He played the role of legal advisor, manager, label owner, and music publisher for many of his artists, a clear conflict of interest. He licensed his own recordings for reissue on his budget labels, without paying royalties to the artists, which was legal under the terms of his contracts but morally questionable. He bullied his artists into recording his own copyrights, so he could make extra money from his publishing. Ultimately, Levy cared little about developing his artists; he merely wanted to make a quick buck off their work. For this reason, many who worked with him still seethe, decades later, when his name is mentioned. "I want to go with you and piss on his grave," David Brigati told me—Eddie's brother and once a member of Joey Dee and the Starliters, a band that Levy recorded—with a look that indicated he was dead serious in this mission.

Another reason Levy's story has attracted scholars and fans alike is his ties to the Mob. The Mob's infiltration of the entertainment business was part and parcel of the lives of pop artists and those who exploited them throughout this period. Levy worked in a world where it was impossible to avoid mobsters; he began in nightclubs where the Mob literally controlled almost all aspects of the business, from the tablecloths that were used in the clubs through the vending machines placed in them and the liquor and food that was sold. He never denied knowing leading mafiosos; he even bragged about these ties, perhaps to puff up his own importance and power. Nonetheless, the question remains how much he was in bed with them. It seems that—like many other victims of the strong-arm tactics of the Mob—Levy found himself relying more and more on the Mob for funding his operations, and ultimately found himself in a position where he had little choice but to do their bidding. It is difficult to untangle how much he was a mere front man or co-conspirator with these lifelong associates.

This is a story of the music business in all its ugly glory. It is also the story of individuals struggling to survive, where mere pennies could separate a successful operation from bankruptcy. Levy was a man full of contradictions, like the world he inhabited. It is my hope to illuminate a small corner of that world to show how it came to grow and thrive, but also how it ultimately was impossible to sustain. Morris Levy is both hero and anti-hero of his own life story, representing both the glory and the infamy of the pop music world.

ACKNOWLEDGMENTS

Like many others, I was exposed to the incredible story of Morris Levy through the writings of Fredric Dannen, first in an interview feature in *Rolling Stone*, and later as part of his seminal book, *Hit Men*. Dannen was among the first to make a compelling case for how the music industry took advantage of artists, with Levy serving as an inspiration for many of its darkest practices. Reporter William Knoedelseder, who covered the trial that ultimately saw Levy's downfall in the mid-eighties, is the second key source on Levy's operations. In a series of articles in the *Los Angeles Times*, Knoedelseder traced a complex web surrounding an ill-fated sale of remaindered records by MCA that involved Levy and his cohorts. This was expanded in his important book, *Stiffed*, one of several studies of MCA's ties with the Mob.

Several writers and friends have been key in helping me understand the story of Morris Levy. John Broven, the author of *Record Makers and Breakers* among other important works, has been very helpful, providing leads and other material, along with memories of his interviews with industry insiders like Hymie Weiss. Stan Soocher, author of *They Fought the Law*, graciously provided introductions to several in the legal and music business communities who I was subsequently able to interview. Tim Riley gave me an introduction to Richard Foos of Rhino Records, who generously told me about his negotiations to purchase Roulette Records from Levy. Foos in turn introduced me to his partner at Rhino, Harold Bronson, and Bob Emmer, who conducted the negotiations for Rhino to purchase Roulette. Both were extremely helpful in reading the manuscript and offering suggestions for further leads. Aurin Primack, son of Morris Primack, one of the original investors in Birdland, shared generously his time as well as two video interviews that were conducted with his father during the 1990s that provided fresh information about the club and its operations. Chuck Rubin gave a lengthy and revealing interview about his entire career and his many tangles with Morris Levy over artist rights. Brad Fisher spoke to me at length about his father, Howard Fisher, and his role at Roulette, along with his own impressions of Morris Levy and various others who worked at the label. Brad's mother, Marilyn, and his sister, Gail, were also very helpful in commenting on the manuscript. The family also provided some photos for use in the book.

Joel Selvin kindly provided unpublished interview materials that he conducted with industry insiders along with two revealing unpublished interviews with Morris Levy in his possession. He offered good advice on how I could approach the story, for which I am very grateful. Bud Powell biographer Peter

Pullman directed me to Aurin Primack and offered a candid assessment of Levy's and Oscar Goodstein's roles in Powell's career. Michael Zager told wonderful stories about the disco-crazed seventies and his production work for Roulette. Attorneys Paul Walker and Ira Greenberg gave me insights into the music publishing business; Greenberg was particularly helpful on details of the "Why Do Fools Fall in Love?" litigation.

Jazz bassist Bill Crow shared his memories of Birdland and the jazz world of the fifties. Retired record distributor George Hocutt explained how the record distribution business worked and shared his memories of dealing with Levy in the seventies and eighties. Photographer Chuck Stewart spoke of the early days of Roulette and generously provided a photo of Duke Ellington at Birdland for this book. Neil Sedaka gave insights into the Jewish social culture of the 1950s, including the mambo craze, and his own dealings with Levy. Rupert Surcouf, ex-manager of the Meters, shared a story regarding Levy's bootlegging activities. Ted Hershorn helped me navigate the Rutgers University Jazz Archives and also provided information on Norman Granz. The Brigati brothers, Eddie and David, provided pithy commentary on their association with Levy. Dick Hyman shared his memories of playing at Birdland. Showing that Levy remains a controversial character to today, some others spoke to me under the condition of anonymity.

Among those who provided editorial guidance and advice, I am particularly indebted to Dick Weissman, who read an early version of the manuscript and provided helpful comments. Dick kept an eagle eye out for stray tidbits about Levy, directing me to the memoirs of performers like Nile Rodgers, which I might not have found on my own. Larry Sandberg similarly provided a critical reading that helped me focus the text. Ed Berger provided information related to his interviews with Teddy Reig in preparation for Reig's autobiography. Bob Porter provided contact information for several of the individuals who I was able to interview for this text. Marcie Werner aided in my attaining access to Levy's trial transcripts and related materials. Kenneth Kimery at the Smithsonian American History Museum's archives pointed me toward relevant interviews with jazz performers. Salvatore Gigante kindly provided a photo of his uncle for use in this text. Thanks to Craig Gill at the University Press of Mississippi for his faith in this project and support as I was working on the manuscript.

Many offered guidance in how to evaluate the memories of different informants, who often gave conflicting accounts of the same events; I am particularly indebted to Jim Elkins, Joel Selvin, John Edward Hasse, Ken Bloom, Ben Bierman, Atesh Sonneborn, Thom Holmes, Albin Zak, my brother Bob Carlin, and others who have conducted aural histories and grappled with this question. My wife Jessica Myers conducted genealogical research and provided much-needed encouragement and support, tirelessly listening over five years to anecdotes about Morris Levy and the music business.

GODFATHER OF THE MUSIC BUSINESS

1

Beginnings: From the Bronx to the Royal Roost

I was smart, I was hard-working, and I was a tough kid.
—Morris Levy

Morris Levy was born to a working-class Jewish family in New York City's Harlem on August 27, 1927. His father, Simon Levy, was originally from Greece and
immigrated to the United States in 1912; he was preceded by a brother, Morris,
who came in 1909 and settled in Brooklyn.[1] Simon may have joined his brother
Morris in operating a small grocery in Brooklyn. In March 1921, Simon wed the
former Rachel Rodrigues, who was born on May 18, 1896, in Andrinople, Tur-
key, and came to the United States in November 1919.[2] A son named Zachariah
(named for Simon's father, he was later known as Irving) was born on December
3, 1922, followed by another child (who died before Morris's birth), and finally
by Morris five years later. However, tragedy struck soon after when Simon died
of pneumonia in 1928, a disease that regularly ravaged the slums of New York in
the early twentieth century. Simon's brother Morris had four children himself,
so he may not have been able to offer any aid to Rachel or her family.

Following Simon's death, the family moved to the Bronx. According to Morris, his mother was ill-equipped to support him and his brother; Zachariah
was temporarily placed in an orphanage while Rachel Levy struggled to cope.[3]
Rachel suffered from an assortment of ailments, including such severe lockjaw
that she had to have her front teeth removed in order to eat,[4] and thus was
unable to hold a regular job. Initially she worked as a sewing machine operator, a common occupation for first-generation Jews in the city. However, as
she became increasingly disabled, she found work on a piecemeal basis, clean-
ing apartments and doing chores. Her two sons were mostly left to fend for
themselves.[5]

Like many other immigrant families during the Depression years, the Levys
were driven onto relief, a source of embarrassment to the young man. "When
we got the [welfare] check on the first of the month," he boasted years later, "I
used to mail it back to the state, or the city, or whoever the fuck it was."[6] (This
is highly unlikely, as no family was in a position to turn down aid, particularly

the Levys.) Desperate to be self-sufficient, he began shining shoes at the age of nine. Like many others, he found school boring and a waste of time when he really wanted to be supporting himself and his impoverished mother.[7] By the mid-thirties the family was living in a small apartment in a tenement in the West Bronx. At age seventeen Zachariah was working as a printer's apprentice, having dropped out of school after completing the sixth grade.[8]

When Levy hit adolescence, he had already achieved a formidable physique: he was tall (nearly six feet) and muscular. Levy managed to stay in school through at least junior high school.[9] However, the tipping point for him came when he experienced what he considered to be a grave injustice. Although he did well on a math test, the teacher required the entire class—most of whom had failed the exam—to spend their homeroom time doing extra math work. Still bitter decades later, Levy said this teacher "had no business teaching school. [She] . . . must have been seventy-five years old, never got fucked in her life." After she demanded that all be punished because of the poor performance of a few, Levy challenged her, asking, "What about those who *passed* the test?" According to him:

> She looks at me and says, "Levy, you're a troublemaker. I'm gonna get you out of this classroom if I have to take your family off home relief." And I got up—I was a big kid—took her wig off her head, poured an inkwell on her bald head, and put her wig back on her fucking head. Walked out of school and said, "*Fuck* school." Never really went back to school after that. I was sentenced to eight years to [reform school] by the children's court . . . This bitch had no fucking *humanity*.[10]

In another telling of his story, Levy said that following this incident he ran away from home to Florida to avoid serving time in juvenile detention. He claimed to have effectively covered his tracks by getting "my school records destroyed. I had someone apply for a transfer to another school, and the old school gave them my records to take to the new school—and they made them disappear. So *I* disappeared as a student in the U.S."[11] Whether Levy was so well connected as a teenager that he could pull off this stunt is unknown; but in any case he never completed his formal education, seeing little value in kowtowing to tyrants like this teacher.

While in Florida, Levy may have landed his first job working in a nightclub. At the time, nightclubs were mainly financed and controlled by "criminal elements" that kept a hand in every level of their operation, from the checking of hats and coats to the serving of drinks to the booking of entertainment. A common entry-level position for a young man on the make was to serve as a hatcheck boy. Prior to the early twentieth century, men kept their coats and hats with them on the backs of their chairs or on wall hooks. The idea of checking your hat at the door was unknown until an enterprising individual—different names have been floated for the man who first came up with the idea[12]—approached one of New York's tonier restaurants and suggested that, in return for paying an annual fee, he would operate a hatcheck concession for them. All he asked for in return was the ability to collect tips from the patrons. Even though the initial concession fees were in the $2,000–$3,000 range, and tips were in the range of a dime or so per customer, the profits were enormous and various groups—both legitimate and semi-legitimate—began bidding for control of these concessions in every major U.S. city.

According to a 1911 article in the *New York Times*, hatcheck boys could earn a pretty good wage and were given other perks, including dress uniforms—although the concessionaires had special reason to insist that they wear these pocketless outfits:

> The [hatcheck concessionaires] . . . employ ignorant Greek boys and sometimes Russians [i.e., Jews], because they are cheap and cheeky. They get from $25 to $30 a month, with their uniforms, and the Captain, who has a confidential job, gets $60 a month and sometimes a small share of the profits. The clothing of the boys is made without pockets, so that they cannot conceal any money they receive and the duty of the Captain is to keep a lookout and see that they do not hide coins away in their shoes, under the carpet, or any other likely place of concealment to the detriment of his employer.[13]

An enterprising hatchecker could work his way up from cloakroom boy to captain to being his own boss through scraping and saving (as well as the occasional pocketing of tips). And Levy was enterprising; by age fourteen he was working his way up the hatcheck ladder.

After working in the checkrooms, Levy graduated to working in another semi-legitimate business that flourished in New York's nightspots: darkroom boy. His first job was the at the Ubangi club, when he was sixteen. He relates: "The camera girls would go around clubs taking flash photos. You were in a room in the back of the club, and you got the negatives, and you developed 'em and had 'em ready in 15 minutes for the customers."[14]

Even as a teenager, Levy was well aware of who the true powerbrokers were in the clubs: "When I was 14 or 15 I worked for people that were in the Mob because they were the people that owned the clubs. They liked me because I was smart, I was hard-working, and I was a tough kid."[15] Levy noted that the fact that he "associated" with mobsters was hardly unusual; their presence as nightclub operators was universally acknowledged, and winning their favor was the way a smart young man could get ahead: "In those days, even the judges and politicians would kiss [the mobsters'] ass. . . . They'd want to be seen with these guys.

Entrance to Atlantic City's Dude Ranch, August, 1948. Note how you would enter through the cowboy's legs! This is one of the clubs where Levy helped manage photo and hatcheck concessions, in the period 1946–48.

If you wanted to be somebody, you came in contact with them."[16] It was during this time that Levy probably met Morris Gurlek,[17] who had his own concession business.[18] Gurlek remained a personal mentor and financier for many of Levy's projects until his death in 1970.

Being street smart and tough were key qualifications for a young man working his way up from the very bottom. Levy possessed these skills by the boatload, and impressed his bosses with his work ethic:

I became good at the darkroom. I advanced with the people who I worked for and became a head guy, setting up darkrooms around the country. We had the rights to a lot of clubs. In Atlantic City, there was Babette's, the Dude Ranch, the Chateau

Teddy Reig, ca. 1948, when he was working as a producer for Savoy Records. Photograph by William Gottlieb, courtesy the William Gottlieb collection/Library of Congress.

Renault. In Philadelphia, there was the Walton Roof, the Rathskeller, Frank Colombo's. In Newark, it was the Hourglass; in Miami there was places like the 600 Club, the Frolics Club, the 5 O'Clock Club. New York itself had two hundred nightclubs, probably.[19]

Many of these clubs had notorious reputations and were regular targets of law enforcement. Their activities present a veritable checklist of criminal and semi-criminal activities. Babette's, operated by Dan Stebbins and named for his wife who led the floor show, was a target of a federal probe into illegal gambling in the 1930s;[20] it featured a yacht-shaped bar and a "trapdoor [leading to] the roof and a descending stairway for quick getaways."[21] The colorful Dude Ranch featured a huge, thirty-foot tall cutout of a cowboy on its façade; guests entered by walking through its legs.[22] The Rathskeller was the subject of several raids, in 1945 for employing underage bartenders and a year later for presenting an "obscene" act.[23] The FBI claimed that Miami's Frolics Club was operated by notorious Jewish gangsters Morris Barney Dalitz (a.k.a. Moe Davis) and Louis Buchalater, who ran illegal gambling operations in nightclubs across the country from their base in Cleveland, Ohio.[24] Levy's education involved interacting with this entire cast of characters, many of whom served as informal role models for his later business dealings.

Levy's progress up the nightclub career ladder was temporarily interrupted—as was the case for many in his generation—by World War II. Perhaps in anticipation of his eighteenth birthday exposing him to the draft, Levy enlisted in the navy in March 1945 and went on active duty a month later working as a hospital apprentice on Long Island. (Levy's brother Irving also served in the navy, enlisting earlier in the war.) His service ended after only five months when he received an honorable discharge because of "the dependency of [his] ill mother."[25] All in all, Morris avoided the danger of going overseas, and could still maintain his contacts in New York City while he was in service.

During the war, servicemen on leave flooded New York City, seeking entertainment of all kinds. Clubs that had been struggling to survive were suddenly minting money. As Teddy Reig—a self-described "jazz hustler"—recalled: "The fleets would dock and the sailor and army guys were all over. Add to them everybody else who had made it here by bus or rail, and the *locals* were ready for them. It was a place to *score*, to make a living. You could get any f—king thing, do any f—king thing. The music was the icing on the cake, but for that you had to go to 52nd Street."[26]

It was a boom time for everyone who fed off of the nightclubs, from operators like Reig to musicians like the young jazz performers who were developing bebop. And it all began on a block-and-a-half strip of run-down tenements. 52nd Street became known as "Swing Street," and from the mid-thirties through the end of World War II it was the heart and soul of New York's jazz scene. The 52nd Street clubs were all whites-only, despite the fact that they predominantly featured black jazz musicians.[27] World War II, however, would bring changes to the way the races intermixed. Although the army was segregated, blacks and whites mixed more freely while overseas than they had at home, each exposing the other to a variety of different musical styles.

After the war, the older clubs on 52nd Street featured some of the bop players for a while, but their clientele was drifting away to the newly growing suburbs. Meanwhile, the high "minimums" set for drinks—and the pushy waiters who demanded that patrons continue to spend their cash—alienated their original audience. Many clubs dropped jazz in favor of less-expensive-to-produce and easier-to-market girlie shows, earning the street a new nickname, "Strip-ty Second Street." The strippers and prostitutes—known as "B-girls" in contemporary

Royal Chicken Roost photo holder, ca. 1948. Patrons would be photographed when attending the club by house photographers, and could purchase prints mounted in a sleeve like this.

slang—often came up with unique acts to build their audiences. One stripper, Lili St. Cyr, was famous for her reverse striptease, starting out naked in a bathtub and ending fully clothed; another, known as Zorita, specialized in stripping while handling a snake.[28] In 1948 *Time* magazine lamented: "Swing was still there, but it was more hips than horns. Barrelhouse had declined. Burlesque was back. . . . in place of swing bands they had installed . . . strip-teasers in net brassieres. . . . There was little jazz left on 52nd Street."[29] It would take a new type of nightclub to reflect bop's high energy.

Although the exact chronology is unclear, after his service Levy was working again running photo concessions in New York and looking for opportunities for advancement. It is not known if he had any interest in jazz, but he was interested in making money, and jazz was big business in the postwar club scene. Levy heard about a nightclub/restaurant that was just about to close, a low-cost eatery known as Topsy's Chicken Shack, which had a prime location on Broadway just north of 47th Street. Levy says that he interested some of his original patrons—including the mobsters who had employed him in the hatcheck business—to purchase the restaurant in early 1947.[30] For a finder's fee, Levy was given a small piece of the club, but more importantly a substantial cut of the hatcheck concession. Levy was only nineteen years old at the time. The new nightclub was christened the Royal Roost and opened in March 1948.

Although in his telling of the story Levy did not mention who his partners were in operating the Roost, from contemporary accounts it is clear that the club was primarily the brainchild of Ralph Watkins. Watkins was a jazz saxophonist turned club owner who had previously managed the famous club Kelly's Stable on 52nd Street. Described as a "Jewish Rex Harrison" because of his love of all things English, including bespoke tailored suits,[31] Watkins was originally a saxophone player who graduated to running jazz clubs and managing artists. From the late 1930s through his induction into the army in 1943, Watkins successfully promoted singers like Billie Holiday, pianist Art Tatum, and swing bands at Kelly's Stable. For financing he partnered with George Lynch, the owner of the La Salle Cafeteria—a local hangout for club owners and musicians known for its inexpensive food and easy access to drug dealers—who took over the club after Watkins went off to war. On his return, Watkins was surprised to find the place overrun with "B girls—that's short for shady ladies."[32] Looking for a new place to do business, he became a partner in the Royal Roost.

According to a pre-opening announcement in *Billboard*, the club was being closely watched because it was the first jazz venue to venture off of 52nd Street onto Broadway, "the Main Stem."[33] The opening night act, Jimmie Lunceford's Orchestra, failed to draw crowds; Watkins blamed one of New York's "worst blizzards" on the failure of patrons to crowd the club. Over the next few months, Watkins tried everything to build an audience for the club. According to *Down Beat*: "He tried novelty bands, rhumba bands, jazz trios, cocktail trios, hot combos, piano teams, single names, vocal stars, instrumental jazz award winners, the big Jimmie Lunceford band, and even offered [Harry Truman's daughter] Margaret Truman a job, which got the spot a lot of publicity but no customers."[34] Things were looking bad for Watkins and his investors.

And then along came two promoters and fans of a new jazz phenomenon, bebop, who went by the colorful names of Symphony Sid and Monte Kay. Sid (born Sidney Tarnopol, he later used the name Torin) was already a well-known New York area deejay who was an avid fan of the new jazz being played in the city's clubs. Promoter Monte Kay (born Fremont Kaplan) was a second-generation Jewish immigrant who became known around the city's jazz scene for trying to pass himself off as black due to his olive-toned skin. Monte was the youngest of five sons[35] and was raised in relative comfort, and showed an early interest in black culture and particularly jazz music. Since the early forties, Kay had been producing concerts in any space he could rent, mostly fraternal halls and other small auditoriums; bebop was not yet well known, and only a small group of cognoscenti could be relied on to show up for these concerts. Finally, Kay landed a major booking in May 1945 for Dizzy Gillespie at a well-known

52nd Street jazz club, the Three Deuces. Kay began to worry that he would not have a sufficient audience, so he offered to give deejay Sid a 50 percent cut of the proceeds from the show in return for his publicizing it on the radio. Its great success cemented their relationship, and they subsequently produced other jazz shows, including a celebrated concert featuring Gillespie and Charlie Parker at Town Hall a few months later.

Tired of working with the 52nd Street club owners—Kay complained they had developed "a real clip-joint attitude,"[36] forcing patrons to constantly order drinks if they wanted to continue to listen to the music—the duo began looking for appropriate spots to stage bop shows on Broadway. In Levy's telling of the story, Sid and Kay approached him about staging a bop concert at the Roost; in Watkins's telling, Levy is not mentioned at all. In any case, Watkins agrees that it was Kay and Symphony Sid who brought bop to the club. In Watkins's words, "I didn't know a thing about the new jazz," and it is likely that Levy knew even less. Monte and Sid offered to take Tuesday night—when the club was usually closed—and book in bop acts in return for the admission fee of ninety-nine cents plus a small percentage on the sale of drinks.[37] Watkins was amazed when "such a crowd showed up that we had to call the cops. It turned the spot into a progressive jazz joint."[38] According to Levy: "There was a line up the block. We had Dexter Gordon or Charlie Parker or Miles Davis. They did two nights a week, and then it grew to three nights a week, then six and seven nights a week.... It was really fabulous."[39] By August 1948 the club was a major success.[40]

The Roost attracted a hip, young crowd to hear the latest in jazz. The club also drew sightseers and novelty hounds interested in gawking at the latest sensation in music and fashion. By September 1948, the uninitiated spectators were so numerous that Watkins distributed a free brochure introducing them to bop's musical and hipster language:

> The squares who enter the Royal Roost these nights (co-owner Ralph Watkins admits that some do) are handed a brochure illuminating the mystique of be-bop. Sample excerpt from the pamphlet, titled What Is Bop?:
>
> "If you feel something when you hear be-bop, you feel something because something is there." Dig?
>
> And: "The dominant, tonic, and the other diatonic chords in most cases are altered by adding the 6th, 9th, 11th and 13th ... However, Neapolitan, French, German and Italian sixths are used extensively in an altered form."[41]

The bemused *Billboard* correspondent concluded the brief notice with: "Oo-bop-sha-bam plus oo-pa-pa-da equals ool-ya-koo. See!!!"

The Roost's layout would be widely copied. Besides the normal table seating area and bar, the club installed bleacher seating, fenced in next to the bar, to hold underage fans who were too young to be served alcohol, as well as those who simply wanted to hang out without paying the necessary minimum for drinks beyond the ninety-nine-cent admission fee. Although Watkins originally was concerned about charging anything at the door, he was gratified to find that it did not affect attendance and often nearly covered the costs of booking the acts.[42] For his underage patrons, Watkins installed a soda fountain in the club; he claimed that it sometimes took in more each night than the regular bar.[43] The Roost heavily promoted its connection with bop, taking the nicknames "The Metropolitan Bopera House" and "The House that Bop Built."

Things were going very well at the Royal Roost through early 1949, so well that its managers started to look for a larger space. According to Levy, his original partner (presumably the unnamed Watkins) failed to cut him into the new deal that involved opening a lavish new restaurant/nightclub on the second floor of the Brill Building at 49th and Broadway, to be called Bop City. The space previously had been the home to several well-known clubs, including the Paradise, Hurricane, and most recently the Zanzibar. Although significantly larger and more expensive to operate (rent alone was quoted as being $35,000 a year), Bop City mirrored the unusual admission policies and seating arrangements of the original club.[44]

The African American newspaper the *New York Age* covered Bop City's opening night, focusing on its integrated staff and celebrity audience:

> Over 300 celebrities, bop-lovers, music lovers, and the generally curious were able to push, squirm and pack themselves into the huge [room] . . . but over twice that many were unable to gain admittance . . .
>
> In keeping with the tone of the place, owner Ralph Watkins saw to it that his waiters, a big, interracial crew, were dressed exactly as you'd expect a waiter to be dressed at a palace of bop, and they looked interesting if not completely authentic in big, flowing polka dot bop bow ties. Outside of Ella Fitzgerald, the greatest performance was that put in by the audience, the greatest mixture of humanity this side of the Casbar [*sic*]. Celebs came to ogle each other, beautiful dames came to be ogled, and the rest of 'em just came to ogle, period.[45]

On the same page, the paper announced that the Royal Roost was switching its policy from presenting "be-bop shows to fast-moving revues, featuring all-Sepia chorus lines."[46]

Watkins had grand plans for Bop City, including installing a formal stage and hiring such class acts as modern dancer Katherine Dunham, known for incorporating Caribbean and African influences in her dance works aimed at an art-loving audience. He also was thinking of franchising the Bop City name and formula in other cities.[47] While Watkins was moving into the big time,

Levy was left to manage the Roost. Unable to compete with the better-funded Bop City enterprise to attract acts, he soon had to close the club. It looked like Levy's brief career as a nightclub manager was about to end—but, ever the street fighter, Levy was not willing to accept being snubbed by Watkins and his partners. Instead, he looked for a new opportunity that he discovered in another soon-to-be-closed nightclub located further up Broadway at 52nd Street. This would become home of the most famous jazz club of the era: Birdland.

Lullaby of Birdland: The Making of a Hipster's Paradise

Whenever I played a low A, [the] speaker enclosure vibrated . . . causing a loud buzzing
noise. When I reported the problem to Morris Levy, he said, "'Don't play that note."
—Bill Crow

In 1949 Levy opened Birdland, a trendy nightclub featuring the hottest new music, bebop. Opening night featured Charlie Parker and Dizzy Gillespie, among other jazz luminaries; regular customers included writers Norman Mailer and Jack Kerouac; the bar space attracted down-on-their-heels students, drifters, and jazz freaks, while the more expensive tables, requiring a full cover charge, brought in haute society.

Levy was not the only one abandoned by his original partners at the Royal Roost when they opened Bop City. Monte Kay and Symphony Sid were mentioned in the press as joining Watkins at the new club to book the acts. However, they had a falling out with him soon after it opened. Kay was so depressed he said that "as soon as the ax fell on me, I went across the street to [a] little club . . . and got very drunk."[1] According to Levy, Kay approached him shortly after the Bop City debut with a proposition to open a new club. Levy found a space that had previously been occupied by a nightclub called the Clique.

Despite many claims that Birdland was named in honor of Charlie Parker, it is more likely that it continued in the tradition of the fowl-based names of Topsy's Chicken Shack and the Royal Roost.[2] The Charlie Ventura bop-flavored recording of the same name released in early 1949 may have also been an inspiration; the opening harmonized scat vocal gave it a hip, modern sound.[3] For jazz fans, the name would indicate that the club would feature the new style of bebop without directly stating it.

The exact identity of the club's original financial backers is shrouded in mystery. Two of Monte Kay's brothers, Joe and Sol Kaplan, were the original applicants for the club's liquor license, which was initially denied by the city's Alcohol Beverage Commission.[4] According to the Kaplans, they had already booked the talent for a projected September opening night, and spent $8,000 redecorating the club.[5] However, the licensing bureau was unmoved, saying "anyone who

The Primack family celebrate at Birdland, ca. 1951. L to R: Aurin, Morris, Jeanne, and Harriet. Courtesy Aurin Primack.

proceeds with decorating a room and hiring of talent without knowing whether the liquor license was forthcoming has only himself to blame."[6] *Down Beat* more ominously said that—given their failure to get an operating license—"chances are [the club] won't open at all."[7]

Having missed their original opening date, the club's promoters scrambled to find someone who had a "clean" background and the cash needed to pay for a liquor license. An unlikely investor was brought to the table by a shadowy figure named Dave Rosenbloom, said to be involved in at least one of the 52nd Street clubs. Rosenbloom had a childhood friend named Morris Primack, who had lately cashed out of his family's lumber business.[8] Primack had the cash and the "clean" name, so he was selected to apply for the license. His son, Aurin, recalls some burly-looking police inspectors visiting the family apartment to check out Primack and to make sure he had no nefarious associates. Word came back from the liquor board with provisional approval, so a new opening date of December 15 was planned. However, when Primack and his lawyer went to pick up the license at the end of November, the clerk had a surprise for them:

> I went up with my lawyer to the liquor board and asked for the license and why they were withholding it and so they said it may take a month or so or a little more but we would definitely get it since everything was OK. Then my lawyer came out and told me that I had to pay $3000 under the table if I wanted to get the license immediately. Since we were going to open, I had to pay the $3000, and we got our license.[9]

Opening night at Birdland, Dec. 1949. L to R: Red Rodney, Lester Young, Hot Lips Page, Charlie Parker, and Lenny Tristano. Courtesy Aurin Primack.

Although rarely documented, this demand by city officials for additional pay-offs was not unusual.

When *Down Beat* announced the new opening date for Birdland, the two "operators" were listed as Irving Levy and Morris Primack.[10] Perhaps Kay and Morris Levy were keeping a low profile because of their previous failure to obtain a liquor license. Over the years, both Irving Levy and Primack seem to have played a variety of roles at Birdland as needed. All agree that Morris Levy was the front man who booked the acts and also kept the club's silent partners (i.e., mobsters) happy.[11]

Besides the named investors, there are several other accounts of who may have been behind-the-scenes investors in the club. Levy acknowledged that his old employer in the hatcheck business, Morris Gurlek, provided key seed money. There were also rumors that a well-known mobster, Joseph "Joe the Wop" Cataldo, invested in the operation.[12] Cataldo owned several nightspots, including Pastor's Club in Greenwich Village and the Camelot Supper Club—located across town from Birdland and a known "wise guy hangout"[13]—and was a major dealer in illegal narcotics.[14] The FBI dubbed him "a top NYC hoodlum," a dubious honor. Some sources say Levy and Kay bought from Cataldo the lease to the space, previously occupied by the Clique, which had itself experimented with a jazz policy for a while during 1948.[15]

Birdland finally opened on December 15, 1949, with an all-star concert featuring Parker, Lester Young, a Dixieland band, and the young singer who Levy claimed to have discovered at the Royal Roost, Harry Belafonte. Showing their ambitions to make Birdland the definitive jazz club, Levy and Kay put together a program that was a kind of mini-history of jazz, from Dixieland to the latest bop. The opening night was a sellout, and more importantly a critical success. John S. Wilson, writing in *Down Beat*—the jazz bible of the era—lauded the concert not only for its historical significance but for the quality of the music:

> A little imagination was applied to the presentation of jazz in a night club and, wonder of wonders, it resulted in not only good entertainment but good music. . . . Show is called A Journey through Jazz, and it turned out to be just that. With Bill Williams, an unfrocked disc jockey, doing the commentary, it covered the Dixie of the '20s, the swing of the '30s, the bop of the '40s, and the ultracool, or whatever it's going to be called, of the '50s.
>
> So far, so good. It's a nice idea and anybody can get up and talk about the history of jazz. But the real kick to the presentation is the fact that when the samples of each type of music are offered, the guys offering the samples are the kingpins, or damned close to it, of their period.[16]

Birdland struggled during its first months of operation. The new club faced the same challenge as the Royal Roost; Watkins's Bop City was better funded and could outbid Levy for the best talent. Finally, Levy and Kay came up with a counterstrategy:

> We . . . came up with a Machiavellian move against Bop City. Every time we reached for an act, they would get it. So we went to the big booking agents and said, "You've got a band we want: Amos Milburn and his Chicken Shackers." Which really don't belong in a jazz joint. We picked another band that played tobacco barn dances. And they said, "We'll get back to you." And being that we tried to book those two bands, they grabbed 'em and put 'em into Bop City. We got ahold of Charlie Parker. So we sort of stunk out their place and got tremendous good will at our place. From that point on, we drove Bop City into the ground.[17]

Born a street fighter, Levy's take-no-prisoners approach to his nightclub competition would continue throughout his career managing Birdland. Levy's tactics worked; Watkins tried introducing a revue format to attract new customers to Bop City, but the upshot was the club quickly closed, as *Down Beat* reported in its December 1, 1950 issue.[18] Watkins was unable to support the overhead of a larger space.

Perhaps because Birdland was still struggling, Levy was also involved in other businesses during this time, including running a bookie operation. Police officers arrested Levy and an unnamed partner at Levy's apartment on May 5, 1950, when Levy was found with "a sheet of paper bearing names of race horses, amounts wagered, [and] identity of players." Levy told the officers that he and his partner had "just started in business—we're here three days." Levy was fined $250 or thirty days in jail when the case came to court about a year later.[19] Shortly after this incident, Levy's mother died on June 23, 1950.[20] On August 25 Levy married his first wife, Patricia Byrne. She was already active in nightclub management, and would help Levy run Birdland during its first years.

Birdland was a subterranean place; it was located in a basement underneath a Broadway storefront. A simple awning with the name on each side led you to the club's entrance. Oddly enough, a uniformed doorman stood there, as if he were guarding a Park Avenue apartment house, holding open the door for those willing to descend into the jazz world below. Patrons entered down a steep staircase, stopping at the first landing before a small ticket window where a comely ticket girl collected the admission fee. As writer Rob Mariani recalled, even the ticket taker had a special aura:

> I remember thinking the first time I stepped up to it to buy a ticket that the woman behind the glass was the most exotic, beautiful creature I'd ever seen. She had big soft black eyelashes, a white flower in her hair like Billie Holiday, and when she handed me my ticket I noticed her fingernails were long and pink like flower petals. Her perfume wafted through the window's speech hole and mingled with the smoky beer smell coming up from the bar.[21]

Another flight down was the club itself. As you entered, you passed under a crudely hand-lettered sign that read: "Welcome to The Jazz Corner of the World. Through these doors pass the most." (Some say the sign painter ran out of space, although others noted that "the most" was hipster language for the hippest, coolest customers.) Originally, playing on the Birdland name, Levy had installed bird cages hanging from the rafters complete with finches and a Mynah bird, but the birds soon succumbed to the thick smoke and dim light of the club; the birds also had the annoying habit of dropping the husks of their birdseed on patrons' tables.[22] A saxophone-tooting bird sporting a nifty tuxedo and up-swept tail was used in the club's original advertisements and programs. The jazz critic Leonard Feather found the entire bird motif slightly distasteful:

A bird motif was maintained in a manner that later seemed, in sober retrospect, slightly debatable. There were finches and canaries hung around the walls, an aviary in back of the bar, and a so-called "fortune-telling bird" that took quarters from customers. Even the invitations to the opening were provided by homing pigeons carried around . . . to the various newspaper and magazine offices. New Yorkers were somewhat baffled, during the next few days, to see birds flying out of the windows of the Time and Life Building, the *New York Journal-American* and other vantage points; all were returning to their stations carrying capsules in which were the folded acceptances. (No birds were lost.)[23]

Like the Roost, admission was only ninety-nine cents initially, with a minimum charged at the bar and tables. Next to the bar was a "bullpen" where underage patrons could watch the proceedings without access to alcoholic drinks or paying the minimum. This cramped area attracted a motley crew of patrons, mostly young college students or those just out of school. It was separated from the posher seating area and bar by a fence that kept the riffraff properly corralled. The tables attracted the more upscale patrons, along with "friends" of the club and other luminaries, who enjoyed a less obstructed view and more breathing space. Backstage there was a small kitchen along with a service bar and an office/bandroom. Dividing the space were the back stairs where, before and after performing, musicians and staff would often hang out.

Birdland was noted as a place where musicians and music lovers could simply hang out, without worrying about having to keep buying drinks or food. Even at the more expensive tables, Levy maintained the policy that listeners were allowed to linger without being harassed by the staff, as Leonard Feather noted:

> There was a need for this type of jazz club, where people can be sure that the bouncer won't shove you against the bar to make you buy another drink the moment your glass is empty. There's no business-hustling atmosphere; no matter how long you sit at a table, nobody gives you a dirty look. And no matter how big or expensive the shows may be, Birdland has never gone in for a policy of raising the admission price where there's a big name artist.[24]

Levy took the unusual (for the time) stance that Birdland would be open to both blacks and whites, with a low admission price ensuring that young fans as well as the more well-to-do society types could attend the club. The African American newspaper the *New York Age* celebrated the club because of its open policies, saying it was helping to desegregate the music world.[25] The *Age's* reporter noted that even the head waiters reflected the club's policy, with one being black and the other white. Levy hosted fundraisers for the NAACP on several occasions, both at the club and at other venues.

Birdland became a popular hangout for musicians when they were not working, to check out what their competitors were up to, to sit in with a band, or to just gossip and meet with friends. During the daytime when the club was not in use, the management would allow select musicians to use it as a rehearsal hall or to work up their acts. Management also never dictated to the performers what they should play. Just the fact that black musicians were given the chance to perform on Broadway—New York's premier entertainment thoroughfare—was unheard of before Birdland opened. As Morris Primack recalled: "The thing that I really didn't know and appreciate was that a lot of these people who came at that time had no place to go and play on Broadway. I know when we hired Erroll Garner he was so appreciative that we gave him his chance, that we brought him up to a higher bracket, which surprised me. I wasn't cognizant of the problems that black people had."[26]

The African American press regularly cited Birdland as a model club, one where musicians were treated well regardless of their race. The staff, too, was largely African American, and most staff members remained with the club for years, enjoying the prestige and regular pay that their positions offered. Morris Primack's son, Aurin, recalled that the management and staff often ate dinner together before the club opened, giving a family feeling to the operation.[27] When Birdland waiter Jimmy Bowman purchased a brand new 1956 Cadillac—supposedly the first purchased in New York City that year—it was duly reported in *Jet* magazine. The unnamed columnist wryly noted, "His boss drives a Ford."[28]

The African American newspaper the *Pittsburgh Courier* lauded Birdland for its integrated policy, which was highly unusual for the day: "White Southerners, venturing North, who express the slightest objection or protestation in the truly democratic policy at Birdland, are asked out quietly, gently, firmly, and emphatically. There are probably fewer racial incidents in Birdland than in any similar spot in the country."[29]

One of the best-loved annual events in the early years of Birdland was a charity baseball game that pitted the Count Basie band against the Birdland staff. The game was held in Bear Mountain State Park as a benefit for the Police Athletic League. Aurin Primack remembered that, besides the Birdland staff, the game attracted precinct cops and also several less-savory types who were associated with the club. He has a particularly vivid memory of his father asking one beefy-looking gentleman who he called "Mr. Swats" to help young Aurin unload a big metal container of potato salad from the back of their car. "Mr. Swats" was the nickname of mobster Dominic Ciaffone,[30] who became a key partner in Roulette Records.

The annual games were so popular that they attracted notice in the African American press. In the 1955 outing, the band was pitted against "the bop palace's personnel in a crewcial [*sic*] Basie-ball game." Pee Wee Marquette pitched for Birdland, which also "include[d] seven players named Morris," a nod to the many partners named Morris in the operation. Joe Williams had "the distinction of throwing out the first nonbopper."[31] This humorous notice was obviously a product of Birdland's PR department, but it rang true of Basie's own accounts of genial horseplay between his band and the Birdland staff.

From the start, Birdland attracted a wide swath of New York society. Gossip columnist Dorothy Kilgallen regularly attended, if only to report on the comings and goings of the artsy set; Earl Wilson also reported on the activities of the musicians and stars at the club, as did African American gossip columnist Izzy Rowe. Glamorous stars like Ava Gardner and Elizabeth Taylor showed up when they were in town; Gardner particularly enjoyed hearing Miles Davis.[32] In 1958 novelist Kingsley Amis came to hear Miles play, drawn by the trumpeter's reputation as a brooding master of cool jazz. The black-interest weekly magazine *Jet* regularly reported on the doings at Birdland, often focusing on the fistfights and brawls begun by the angry wives of jazz musicians who confronted their husbands' lovers when they encountered them at the club.[33]

Although many nostalgically recalled Birdland as a place where bebop giants performed for an audience of high-society actresses and club hoppers, there was another regular clientele that packed the audience. Drug dealing and prostitution were rampant at Birdland and in the surrounding bars, cafeterias, and drugstores, and police raids were frequent. In 1951 a New York State commission investigated drug use in New York City's nightspots. One prostitute recalled how different acts at Birdland would attract drug dealers specializing in different products; the Spanish acts, like Machito's Cubans, tended to attract cocaine dealers, while the boppers' drug of preference was heroin.[34]

While drug stores and cafeterias were catering to a broad range of users, the clubs tended to attract a more sophisticated crowd. There was an admission charge to attend a club, plus if you wanted to sit in a preferred table or booth, you had to spend additional money on food and drink. So Birdland attracted users, among both its performers and audience, and sellers, using everything from lower-priced narcotics to the more "upscale" heroin and cocaine.

Unlike the Cotton Club in the late twenties and thirties, which relied on lavish floor shows and beautiful girls to pull in the crowds in addition to its talented house bands, Birdland only featured music, with a sparsely decorated stage featuring an awning-like overhang that could barely hold a small ensemble. The stage was so small that the piano had to be placed on the floor when a larger band appeared, replacing the front row of tables. The ceiling was so low that drummers had to be careful not to swing their sticks too high. Although

Pee Wee Marquette with deejay Bob Garrity posing with the Gretsch "Birdland" model drum kit. Courtesy Aurin Primack.

the sound system was primitive, the sound quality in the room was said to be exceptional; even the bar denizens, who could barely see, were treated to a full sonic experience.

The simplicity of the setup was part of the place's unfinished charm. However, Levy was enough of a showman to realize the crowd craved something exotic along with the hip music, so he hired an emcee who became emblematic of the club's image as part hipster paradise and part freak show: Pee Wee Marquette.

Marquette was born William Crayton Marquette in Montgomery, Alabama. By the early thirties, he was working as the "band mascot" for a popular Nashville, Tennessee–based dance band led by Francis Craig, which worked local hotels and broadcast regularly over the powerful station WSM. Exactly how Marquette got from Nashville to New York is not known, but by 1941 he was emceeing at the popular nightclub Zanzibar, where he occasionally joined in the act as a comic singer. When the Zanzibar closed in 1949, its location was taken over by Ralph Watkins's new club, Bop City, and Marquette became the emcee there.[35] However, by 1951 notices appeared indicating that Marquette was now working at Birdland, where he would gain his greatest fame.[36] A midget who stood 3'9" inches tall, Marquette became Birdland's voice, as he announced all the acts and kept order on stage. His costume varied from clownish near–minstrel show attire—a ringmaster's felt jacket with an oversized bowtie—to formal wear for more auspicious occasions. He was famous for his raspy, high-pitched voice, malapropisms and mispronunciations, and strange speech rhythms. As Bill Crow recalled:

> Pee Wee's voice was high-pitched and brassy. . . . He frequently slipped into the dialect of Montgomery, Alabama, his birthplace. He would climb laboriously onto the Birdland bandstand, pull the microphone down to his chin and shout officiously:
> AND NOW, LAYDUHS AND GENTLEMEN "BIRDLAND" THE JAZZ CORNAH OF THE WORLD, IS PROUD TO PRESENT, THE ONE AND ONLAH . . .[37]

Crow also recalled that the diminutive announcer carried an adjustable butane lighter that he used to light the large cigars that he puffed on as he announced an act. Marquette would light a cigarette for a customer by dramatically adjusting the height of the flame to compensate for his own short stature: "It was an unnerving experience in a dark nightclub to put a cigarette in your mouth and have a two-foot flame suddenly shoot up from waist level with Pee Wee leering hopefully at the other end."[38]

Mariani described Marquette as purposely misusing the microphone, reveling in creating feedback, hiss, and other comical effects, while announcing each act in his "shrill voice that would rattle the ice cubes in your glass."[39] Among his many annoying habits, Marquette would leave the microphone at his level, so when a bandleader came on stage he would have to grapple with it to bring it back to the right height. It is said that once Dizzy Gillespie comically walked across stage on his knees in order to speak directly into the microphone following Pee Wee's introduction.

As part of his job as emcee, Pee Wee would announce the names of each performer—for a price. He demanded that sidemen and even featured performers tip him before they appeared on stage. If not, he would mispronounce or mangle their names—if he acknowledged them at all. Mort Lewis, then manager of the Dave Brubeck Quartet, recalls how Pee Wee would treat those who refused to tip him:

> Every act that played [at Birdland], the musicians had to give [Marquette] fifty cents and he would announce their names as he introduced the band. Dave Brubeck gave him fifty cents, Joe Dodge gave him fifty cents, and Norman Bates gave him fifty cents. Paul Desmond refused to pay one cent. And when Pee Wee Marquette would introduce the band, he'd always say, in that real high-pitched voice, "Now the

world famous Dave Brubeck Quartet, featuring Joe Dodge on drums, Norman Bates on bass," and then he'd put his hand over the microphone and turn back to Joe or Norman and say, "What's that cat's name?" referring to Paul. Then he would take his hand off the microphone and say, "On alto sax, Bud Esmond." Paul loved that![40]

Bobby Hutcherson recalled how Pee Wee mispronounced his name throughout his first week playing at Birdland until he paid him a five-dollar tip out of his wages. After paying up, he was amazed by how "that five dollars completely changed everything, because all of [a] sudden, everybody heard that there was this new kid in town and he's playing four mallets with a sextet at Birdland, on the stage and he's only nineteen-years-old, and 'boom' everything started."[41]

Lester Young summed up most musicians' attitudes toward Pee Wee when, fed up with the midget's insistence that he pay him for the privilege of announcing his name correctly, he quipped, "Get out of my face, you half-a-motherfucker."[42]

Marquette could be considerate of some performers. When cool jazz vocalist Jeri Southern appeared at Birdland in the mid-fifties, her sotto voce singing was difficult to hear above the usual crowd banter and noise. To quiet the crowds, Marquette left cards at each table stating:

> Cognoscenti of the Birdland Arts are hereby importuned to forgo requesting of *vins et viands* during the recital of Miss Jeri Southern to effectuate the maximum benefits from her volatile variations in vocalization. There will be a hiatus of service, seating and side issues during Miss Southern's renditions, with full restoration of such facilities following the *denouement* of her inimitable delineations. (French words italicized by *moi*.)[43]

Marquette's mock formality in this announcement is in keeping with the minstrel tradition of black performers parodying the highfalutin style of white presenters.

The second colorful character who was a regular at Birdland was radio deejay and announcer Symphony Sid, the self-named "Mister Hip" who was a major exponent of bebop. Beginning in 1951, Levy sponsored a regular live broadcast from Birdland on Friday nights from midnight to 4 a.m., with Sid alternating records with live performances. Initially Sid worked remotely, but soon a special glass booth was constructed at the back of the club to house him, where he sat under bright lights as if he were in a display case. Sid's booth was such an attraction among the bleacher crowd that "those kids would press against the window watching the show until I thought the whole booth would collapse," according to the deejay.[44]

Sponsoring Sid's radio broadcast was a canny move on Levy's part; in the days before radio signals were more closely regulated, late-night broadcasts

Frank Sinatra, boxer Ezzard Charles, Symphony Sid, and an unknown woman in the small glassed-in booth that served as Sid's
broadcast studio in Birdland, in 1953. Courtesy Aurin Primack.

from New York's stations could be heard through a vast area, from the Midwest
to the South, even to ships crossing the Atlantic. By 1955 *Billboard* reported that
Levy was "buying multi-hour segments over WINS and WOR radio," and also
covering the union fees that enabled the musicians to appear on these broadcasts.[45] Sid's broadcasts would help make Birdland a destination for tourists
from around the country and across the globe.

Sid's radio patter was a mix of old-time vaudeville jive, relentless shilling
for his sponsors (including half-price clothiers, jazz record shops, and flea-bag
hotels), and his own take on contemporary slang (he has been credited with
coming up with bopper's slang expressions like "kooky," although these things
are hard to trace). Among the devoted listeners to Sid's monologues was the
nascent beat author Jack Kerouac, who picked up some of his own jazz-inflected
prose rhythms from listening to Sid's patter.[46] Ross Russell recalls Sid's improvised advertisement for a funeral home: "When fate deals you one from the
bottom of the deck, fall by the Sunshine Funeral Parlors. Your loved ones will be
handled with dignity and care, and the cats at Sunshine won't lay too heavy a tab
on you. Now, I'd like to play a request . . ."[47]

Another devoted listener to Sid's late-night broadcasts was a young Stokely
Carmichael, who was turned on to African singer Miriam Makeba while still a
junior in high school through the deejay's broadcasts. Carmichael compared Sid
to the black R&B deejay Jocko, saying Sid was more "erudite . . . he addressed an
adult rather than a youth audience. . . . I learned a lot from Sid." The fact that Sid
recognized Makeba as an important artist with links to American jazz deeply
impressed Carmichael, who had never heard an African performer before.[48]

Sid's radio mike was wired directly into Birdland's PA, so his relentless patter could be heard by the club's late-night denizens. Supposedly, on opening night when Charlie Parker was on the bandstand, Sid called out that a "caller from the Bronx" wanted to hear the bop great blow "White Christmas"; Parker obliged with a "big, buttery, luscious" version.[49]

In August 1953 Sid was replaced on the Birdland broadcasts by deejay Hal Jackson, among the first African American deejays. The *Pittsburgh Courier* approvingly noted that this was "the first time a Negro has had a six-hour show nightly on any major network affiliate." The broadcast was carried live from midnight to 6 a.m. every night on WABC. This was a brave move for the early fifties and was in keeping with Levy's open policy to black and white audiences.[50] Sadly, ABC cancelled Jackson's contract by early December "despite being roundly applauded for its democratic principles" in hiring the African American deejay, according to the *New York Age*. Poor ratings were given as the reason for firing Jackson and cutting back the broadcast to just one hour.[51]

Performing on the cramped stage at Birdland was not the most comfortable experience. How Count Basie fit his sixteen-piece band into the club is something of a miracle. Bassist Bill Crow recalled how the band was squeezed onto the bandstand, while Basie led the band from his piano on the floor.[52] Crow was playing with vibraphonist Terry Gibbs's band at Birdland opposite Basie. He described the rather crude "stereo" sound system that Levy had installed supposedly to improve the sound quality when larger groups like Basie's performed there:

> A pair of speakers were hung, one at each side of the Birdland bandstand, but only the front microphone was connected to both channels. The piano mike went to the left speaker and the bass mike went to the right one. When more mikes were added for larger groups they were split between the two channels. The music sounded balanced to anyone sitting at a table between the two speakers, but at the bar and in the bleachers the left one predominated.
>
> Since the speaker that carried the bass mike was across the bandstand from where bass players usually stood, it took me a while to notice that whenever I played a low A, something in that speaker enclosure vibrated in sympathy, causing a loud buzzing noise. When I reported the problem to Morris Levy, he said, "Don't play that note."[53]

Levy also cut corners when it came to the club's house piano. Jazzman Billy Taylor served as house pianist in the early fifties and was dismayed by the condition of the instrument. He later recalled how he convinced Levy to purchase a better instrument:

I said [to Morris Levy], "Look the piano has been going for a while so this might be a good time to get a new piano." So he said, "Well what kind of piano should I get?" So I said, "Steinway." He said, "Well that's very expensive, isn't it?" We had a long conversation about it. . . . the way I finally sold him on it is I said . . . "You are aware of the value of a Cadillac right?" He said, "Of course." So I said, "If you buy this year's Cadillac and you keep it for four or five years and then you want to sell it as a second hand car as opposed to an Oldsmobile or a Chevy . . . you can get much closer to your investment right?" He said, "Yeah sure, it's a Cadillac." I said, "That's my point. This is a Steinway."[54]

Another key figure in Birdland's operations was Oscar Goodstein, the club's long-suffering manager. Before joining the Birdland staff, Goodstein had worked as "an auctioneer, a metallurgist, an insurance salesman, a deck hand on a tugboat, and just before his Birdland debut was manufacturing oil burners."[55] An amateur pianist, Goodstein visited Birdland early on when Bud Powell was performing, and immediately was hooked on jazz:

I had the misfortune, or good fortune, call it what you want, to go down to Birdland one night. I paid the big ninety-eight cents to get in. And who was on the stand but Bud Powell . . . I enjoy[ed] what he was doin', but [didn't] understand him. He was playing a riff within a riff within a riff. [He] played very little melody—if I strained, every now and then I heard the melody—then I realized, My God, this is a different kind a music than I ever heard in my life. I went back the next day. And the next day. And I decided . . . I'm gonna get into this business.[56]

It is not surprising that, after being drawn to Birdland by hearing Bud Powell perform, Goodstein would form a long relationship with the pianist—perhaps as a front for Levy. It began in 1953, when Powell was institutionalized for psychological problems. To secure his release for performances at Birdland, Goodstein appeared in state court to vouch for the musician and became his de facto guardian, overseeing his finances.

Goodstein was in a powerful position to take advantage of the often mentally frail pianist, as many contemporary critics noted. Writer Maely Daniel Dufty wrote a stinging condemnation of Goodstein's arrangement, noting that "Goodstein had . . . an ideal set-up [as Powell's manager]. . . . All he really needed was some real talented 'boys' he could sell to himself and his boss/and or partner [i.e., Levy] at the price he sets in his double function as buyer *and* seller."[57] In Goodstein's defense, Powell was often uncommunicative and difficult; could fail to show up for a date or leave halfway through a set; and was easily set off by even one drink.

Nonetheless, Goodstein took strong control over Powell's life and career. Alfred Lion, the president of Blue Note Records, who recorded Powell on several occasions during this period, related how Goodstein ensured that Levy's needs were met: "Morris Levy insisted that everything [Powell] recorded had to be written out because they had all the publishing rights. So the bass player George Duvivier wrote out Bud's tunes. We rehearsed at Birdland that afternoon. And Goodstein was there making sure that Levy got the written music."[58] In 1956 Powell finally freed himself from Goodstein's direct control, although Goodstein would reenter his life again and again through Powell's death in 1966.

Although the club was purportedly named for him, Charlie Parker was hardly a regular performer there. After his appearance on opening night, he appeared a few times over the next year or so. His most notable appearance was when he played accompanied by a small string section in July 1950. Parker was promoting his recent recording *Bird with Strings*, with the accompaniment arranged by pop producer Mitch Miller, hardly a fan of bebop. Many jazz critics felt that the string setting was not ideal for Parker, leading him to play in a much more restrained style. An anonymous reviewer in *Down Beat* complained "His tone [is] a flat, monotonous, squawking thing, and his work in general appears to have no relationship to what is going on around him."[59] Jerry Wexler, later a producer for Atlantic but then working as a staff writer for *Billboard*, agreed that the album and Birdland performance did not represent Parker's best work: "The fans ate it up, but it's a fair guess Parker will have to expand and vary his program if he hopes to sustain audience interest after the novelty wears off. More and different arrangements, a vocalist, a few unvarnished, swinging numbers with the chamber group and solo with the rhythm section should be added."[60]

The idea of a dedicated bebopper playing with classical musicians accompanying him fascinated both the jazz and "long-haired" crowd. Billy Taylor—who was subbing at the last minute for Parker's usual pianist Al Haig—commented that "The opening night was a smash! . . . People absolutely loved it."[61] Levy later bragged, "It was the biggest and most important week we'd had."[62] Oscar Goodstein also gave Levy credit for the show's success: "Morris Levy has always had a unique faculty, a sixth sense of timing. He knew Bird with Strings would be perfect for the club."[63]

The club did so well in July that they brought back the "Bird with Strings" show a month later, enjoying equal success. About the August appearance Dorothy Kilgallen reported: "there are lines of patrons outside the club . . . and box office receipts have tripled since Charlie introduced his long-hair variety of bop."[64]

In July 1951 Parker lost his cabaret card due to his drug use, which meant he was unable to appear in any New York nightclub, and had to scramble for work wherever he could find it. He did occasionally appear at Birdland but only as a "guest" sitting in with another group (a way to sidestep the law), but in general was absent from the club's roster. Parker was able to get his card reinstated in early 1953 and subsequently appeared in late June 1953 at Birdland, but was so unreliable that he was "banned" from performing in the club going forward. Throughout the period of his banishment, Parker begged for a second chance, according to Goodstein, who quoted him saying, "Let me right my wrongs. I'm really straight this time, for good. Give me a chance to show what I can do—put me in for just a week. You'll never regret it."[65] The management finally relented after a year and Parker returned again with strings in August 1954 for what was to be a three-week engagement. Parker showed up to perform wearing orange Bermuda shorts, suggesting that anyone else wearing Bermuda shorts should be given free admission.[66]

Shortly before the fourth night of the engagement, Parker was drinking in a backstage party celebrating his thirty-fourth and singer Dinah Washington's thirtieth birthdays. When he came on stage, he called for "East of the Sun," but after the introduction began to play "Dancing in the Dark."[67] Even though he was at fault, Parker angrily told the string players to leave, and was himself then fired from Birdland. Realizing that, per union rules as the bandleader, he was on the hook to pay the musicians for the entire engagement, Parker went home and attempted to commit suicide by drinking a bottle of iodine. He was committed to Bellevue State Hospital, a mental institution, where he spent the next two weeks.[68]

Parker's last appearance at Birdland has become legendary due to his onstage falling out with pianist Bud Powell. Powell may have been hired by Birdland manager Oscar Goodstein for the date, as he was anxious to find the pianist work. It is unclear whether Goodstein was aware that Powell and Parker had a longtime rivalry, with Powell feeling that Parker was given more credit for the innovations of bebop than he deserved. Whoever put together the group, the players were at odds almost immediately; one musician who witnessed their performance said, "I don't think I ever saw a group on any bandstand with more internal friction and less mutual love."[69] Nonetheless, the opening performance went well according to Charles Mingus, who was also on the date. However, the next night was when the trouble between Powell and Parker occurred. Years later, Mingus recalled:

> The second night Bud Powell is very unruly. Bird is late. The set starts off with me and [drummer] Art Blakey. [Trumpeter] Kenny Dorham is late, also. Charlie comes up to the bandstand and tells us to hold everything. He then calls a tune and starts counting a tempo and Bud plays a different tempo. This goes on a second time. "Come on, baby," Bird says to Bud; he goes over to the piano to set the tempo for him.
>
> After intermission, Bud starts doing the same thing again. Bird walks off in disgust, and proceeds to get drunk...

The rest of the evening was no better than the first two sets. . . . Oscar Goodstein and Charlie had words. Oscar ordered him out. Bird reminded him who he was talking to and strode out, only to return later, walk up to the bar, put a wet cheek next to mine, and say, "Mingus, I'm goin' someplace, pretty soon, where I'm not gonna bother anybody."[70]

Parker's comment to Mingus turned out to be prophetic, as he died the following Saturday.

When Birdland celebrated its fifth anniversary in 1955, its owners had reason to be proud; where the average jazz club closed within a few months (or at most a year or two), Birdland had endured. Larger, more posh clubs had tried to duplicate its success and had failed. Even though it was associated with a new and, for many, foreign-sounding music, Birdland consistently drew appreciative audiences and the best performers in jazz. The African American press lauded the club for consistently offering work to black artists at a time when few venues were able to do so: "the club has provided the most consistent outlet for Negro talent in the big city. Modern jazz advocates and other musicians have long been able to count on a date at Birdland when few other spas would put them on their bandstands. It has been a mecca for top Negro performers in the jazz field."[71] Levy was honored at a special dinner given by the *Courier*, an African American paper, in Detroit in mid-1955 for opening "a proving ground for musicians on Broadway."[72]

Birdland was so successful that in mid-1955 the club was expanded to accommodate more patrons: "With its jazz stars tearing the house down, they not only had to call out the cops to hold the crowds in check, but also the carpenters, who are now taking the walls down to make [room] for the overflow patrons. When the carpenters complete their digging, the hepcats will be able to continue their digging from sixty extra seats."[73]

At the height of its success, Birdland employed thirty-one people, including: "ten waiters, four bartenders, three cashiers, two busboys, two porters, a ticket seller and ticket taker . . . The payroll runs between $2500 and $3000 a week."[74] The cost of booking artists was also steadily rising through the fifties:

With the musicians' union scale [in 1961] up to about $132 per sideman and double for the leader, even a show featuring nothing but two flat-scale quintets would run to over $1500 a week, but in an expansive mood Birdland has been known to stretch as high as $7500 for a strong program. Billy Eckstine, at the height of his career, once got $6500 for a week's work, a figure that did not include the supporting show.[75]

Although these figures sound impressive, the sidemen made very little; drummer Don Lamond lamented that his pay came to only $18.00 a night when he was working with Stan Getz's band at Birdland, playing from 10 p.m. to 4 a.m. every night.[76]

Variety attributed Birdland's success to the fact that the "spot has skirted some typical jazz spot pitfalls and the club has gained a corollary rep for being straight and clean. So much so, that Birdland has been an extracurricular classroom for several college jazz courses, including that of Dr. Marshall Stearns of New York U."[76] Stearns was among the first academic jazz historians, and his imprimatur gave the club a whiff of respectability that jazz venues rarely enjoyed. How "straight and clean" the club was is a question of debate; as the fifties wore on and the sixties began, the club would become increasingly noted for incidents of racial tension and violence that would overshadow its musical reputation.

3

Jazz Entrepreneur: 1949–1957

Morris may have been a gangster but he was a man of his word.
—John Levy

The success of Birdland inspired Levy to expand his operations into just about every aspect of a musician's career, including recording, composing, publishing, concert promotion and production, and management; why share any of these income streams with outsiders? By 1957 Levy's many holdings and cross-interests in the jazz and pop music worlds led jazz critic Ralph J. Gleason to call him a "music octopus," whose tentacles reached deeply and dangerously through the pop music scene.[1]

Early on in his operation of Birdland, Levy discovered almost by accident the value of owning the publishing rights to the music performed there. In a story he told to several interviewers, Levy related how he was told that he had to pay a fee to ASCAP for any copyright material performed at his club:

> I was in my club one night and a guy comes in from ASCAP [American Society of Composers Authors, and Publishers, a performing-rights agency] and said he wanted money every month. I thought he was trying to shake me down. I wanted to throw him out. And then he came back and said he was going to sue. I said, get the fuck outta here. I went to my lawyer and says, What *is* this guy? He keeps coming down, he wants money. My lawyer says, He's entitled to it. By act of Congress, you have to pay to play music. I said, Everybody in the world's gotta *pay*? That's a hell of a business. I'm going to open a publishing company.[2]

What Levy suspected as a Mob shakedown was actually the law of the land. ASCAP had been founded in 1909 after composer Victor Herbert had heard one of his compositions being played by the house band at one of New York's most popular restaurants. Through a series of lawsuits and legislative battles, ASCAP was formed as a way to collect "performance rights" payments from restaurants, bars, nightclubs, and other places where music was played publicly for profit, and to distribute the monthly fees to composers based on the popularity of their songs.

"Lullaby of Birdland" sheet music by George Shearing,
released by Levy's first publishing company, Patricia Music.

Levy's experience running hatcheck and photo concessions had taught him an important lesson: There was big money to be made out of the nickels and dimes. Although each individual transaction might be small, the aggregate amounts could be large; plus, being cash businesses, the money that flowed through was difficult if not impossible to trace. Levy quickly realized that owning the music that was played in his club would give him an extra hit of income. He began with the nightly radio broadcast from Birdland, which he sponsored. He decided that the show should have a signature theme song, and reasoned that it should be played to introduce each hour of the broadcast. Since the show was aired from midnight to 4 a.m. each night, that gave Levy four performance royalty hits a night.

Originally, Levy found someone to write a theme, and gave it to house pianist George Shearing to play. Shearing was not too enthusiastic when he saw the score:

> Morris wanted me to record a theme . . . and he sent the music to me. It wasn't much good, and so I called Morris and said, "Look, I can't relate very well to this theme you sent me, why don't I write one for you?"

He was immediately on the defensive. He said, "I'll bet you'd like to write one, because you have your own music publishing company, haven't you?" . . .

But . . . that wasn't actually the reason I didn't want to record Morris's song. It just wasn't very good. So I said to him, "The reason I want to write a tune is so that I can feel comfortable about playing it."

"Well," he came back with, "we would feel comfortable about you recording a tune that we own."

So I suggested a compromise. I said, "Okay, I'll give you the publishing rights, but I'll keep the composer's rights."[3]

Shearing's wife, who ran his new publishing company, was not very pleased when she heard that he had given up half his income to Levy; but being his employee and faced with having to record a second-rate tune and make nothing, Shearing figured he had made the best deal possible.[4] Thanks to its constant repetition on Birdland's local radio show, "Lullaby of Birdland" became an immediate hit, and was widely covered by other jazz musicians. Not only did it bring in a steady income for Levy, it helped further promote the mystique of Birdland as the center of contemporary jazz performance.

Levy's first publishing company was named Patricia Music, after his then-wife Patricia Byrne. He took on as a partner Phil Kahl (born Kolsky), who had strong experience in managing music rights. An ex-hairdresser, Kahl had previously worked for Walt Disney Music,[5] joining the firm right after it was founded. It represented all of Disney's lucrative film songs, and gave the young man entrée into the entire world of music publishing. By this time he had taken on the name "Kahl" perhaps as an attempt to hide his immigrant roots. In 1953 Kahl joined Patricia Music as general manager; at the same time Levy and Kahl formed a separate firm, Kahl Music, as a partnership. Kahl remained active in Levy's businesses through the fifties and into the early sixties, and was probably also responsible for introducing his brother, Joe Kolsky, to Levy, who had previously worked in the family business wholesaling fruits and vegetables.

Levy and Kahl did not focus on jazz compositions alone; they recognized the growing popularity of R&B and early rock 'n' roll, and began snapping up the publishing rights held by other small label operators. Eventually, they created a web of companies operating under various names that owned some of the most important copyrights in fifties popular music.

One part of the music business that Levy mostly avoided was artist management. Although often it appeared that Levy played the role of manager, he claims he never took a manager's commission and only advised performers who he considered to be friends. Levy said he had experimented with managing artists in the early fifties but found dealing with temperamental artists not to his liking:

Cover of Birdland All Stars brochure from the first tour, 1955.

I was managing an act, and they would call me at four in the morning, "We've got a flat tire in North Carolina." I said, "What the fuck do you want me to do about a flat tire in North Carolina?" Another act called me up and says, "We ain't got the star dressing room in the Howard Theater in Washington." ... I says "Fuck this shit." It's like a pimp, managing acts.... If I'm gonna manage an act, it's for nothing. I'll help out friends.[6]

Levy did make one big move to become involved in a talent agency in mid-1955. *Billboard* reported that he was "negotiating for a fair-sized piece of the Gale Agency," and noted that this would extend his "interest into virtually every facet of the industry."[7] Gale was a major agency booking R&B and jazz groups, led by Moe Gale, who had previously managed the Savoy Ballroom. Irving Siders—who was working for Gale as a booking agent—told the FBI how he initially partnered with Levy to purchase 40 percent of the agency, with Levy putting up $20,000 himself and $20,000 for Siders, with the proviso that if they were successful Siders would pay him back; if not the loan would be forgiven. Siders said the deal went south when Levy began immediately pressing him to repay the $20,000, and within a few months Siders negotiated with Moe Gale to buy out Levy's portion.

Moe Gale told the FBI that he was originally willing to take Levy on as a partner because "he considered [Levy] to be an energetic young man with good business sense . . . [Gale] said that it did not work out because he and LEVY were unable to agree on the methods of conducting their business and because he also had heard rumors that LEVY was connected in some way with the 'rackets.'" However, Gale told the FBI that he himself had "never [seen] anything which would confirm these rumors."[8]

Another way to build the Birdland name and gain important contacts across the country was Levy's decision to organize several Birdland tours, beginning in 1955.[9] A key inspiration for Levy was the great success that Norman Granz enjoyed with his Jazz at the Philharmonic concerts, tours, and recordings from the late forties and early fifties. Granz was among the first postwar entrepreneurs to realize the potential in handling all aspects of a jazz performer's career— from management to touring and bookings to recording and publishing. While the two shared many similarities, they were also in many ways polar opposites, particularly when it came to their interest in the music business. Granz was a crusader who believed black musicians were unfairly treated by the music business and deserved better; he was politically a leftist and never really enjoyed the rough-and-tumble of commercial music. While not entirely uninterested in his artist's welfare, Levy's main interest was building his own musical empire. He had no problem being a player on the music scene, enjoying the opportunity to maximize his earnings through all legitimate (and not-so-legitimate) means.

Levy was also a fierce competitor, and Granz's success must have inspired his natural tendency to try to beat—even eliminate—his competition. According to the *New York Age*, Levy made a $1,000 bet with Granz that he could fill Carnegie Hall with a jazz show one night before the scheduled New York opening of the 1952 Jazz at the Philharmonic premiere.[10] The concert staged by Levy in November 1952 featured Duke Ellington, Billie Holiday, Charlie Parker, and Ahmad Jamal; the two Friday night shows were nearly sold out, and Levy was said to have grossed $21,000, a tidy sum. A similar show was held in Pittsburgh a week later, and based on that success Levy announced his plans for a Birdland All Stars package tour.[11]

Perhaps due to this rivalry, Granz became a partner in a new club, the Bandbox, which opened in 1953. The club's owners tried to best Levy by locating the Bandbox literally next door to Birdland; they also charged no admission (beating Levy's ninety-nine-cent price), and offered a dance floor open all night long.[12] However the Bandbox faced a similar fate to Bop City; with a larger seating capacity, it could not support itself strictly through jazz bookings, and it closed within a year of its opening.

The first extended Birdland tour was organized to occur in early 1955, to mark the fifth anniversary of the club. The tour featured leading jazz performers including Sarah Vaughan, Count Basie's orchestra, George Shearing's quintet, pianist Erroll Garner, sax player Lester Young, and Latin bandleader Candido.[13] Many of the regulars from Granz's Jazz at the Philharmonic tours participated in this show, including most notably Count Basie and Lester Young, perhaps a sign of Levy's ambitions to steal Granz's acts. It is also noteworthy that Candido was part of the tour, reflecting Levy's recognition of the attraction of jazz and Latin dance music to similar audiences. The tour began at the nightclub itself, followed by almost a month on the road. According to Levy, it grossed a quarter of a million dollars through its twenty-four performances across the country.[14]

John Levy (no relation), originally a bass player who became the manager of George Shearing's quintet,[15] recalled negotiating a better fee for the group. He objected to Levy's guarantee of $5,000 a week, saying that was the same amount the group made playing Birdland. In John Levy's opinion: "Morris was a fair guy. 'If the tour's a success, I'll give you a bonus,' he agreed."[16] Although aware of Morris's coarser nature ("[he] was a real 'dis, dem, dose' kind of guy"[17]), he trusted his word.

When the tour was over, John Levy went up to Morris's offices to collect the bonus the group was promised. Levy's secretary told him that Morris was in Florida and she had no knowledge about a bonus. Nonetheless, John Levy trusted that Morris would honor his verbal agreement: "I wasn't really worried. Morris may have been a gangster but he was a man of his word."[18] It took a year to catch up with Morris, but eventually he paid the $1,000-a-week bonus to the agent. For Morris Levy, his word was his bond, particularly for an artist like Shearing who was a regular at Birdland.

Headliners on the Birdland tours were accorded some special treatment by Levy. Count Basie and the other stars were given extra space on the tour bus. At the end of the tours, Levy lavished presents on the participants, including engraved commemorative watches. This kind of special treatment was unheard of among most pop promoters of the day. While the tours were grueling—with as much as 500 miles to be driven between dates—Levy seemed to care enough to spend some extra money keeping his stars happy.

Levy also traveled with the Basie band on at least one of the tours. Basie recounts in his autobiography how Levy participated in the off-hours hijinks of the band while they were touring. "By the time of the Birdland tours, the band was . . . divided into two groups that were always challenging each other in the games we used to play on the road," Basie recalled:

On one side there were the little guys . . . and they called themselves the Midgets. And the others, the big guys . . . were known as the Bombers. . . . Well, Morris Levy was classified as a Bomber, and he was having a ball with all of the games and pranks, and when the tour went out to Kansas City, Morris went around to the novelty stores and bought up a supply of water pistols for the Bombers to attack the Midgets. . . . [However] Sonny Payne found out where Morris had his supplies stashed, and . . . stole them for the Midgets.[19]

Using their newfound weapons, several of the midgets chased Levy, who tried to escape their fire, but slipped and fell under the band bus, breaking his arm. Basie continued:

The minute the Birdland people back in New York [heard about it], they started burning up the telephone wires . . . and Morris had to explain that it was all part of a game. Because as soon as he said that the Midgets were chasing him, they thought he was talking about a mob trying to cut in on the business. . . . [Levy's] business associates in Chicago were ready to put somebody on the next plane to Kansas City to help him take care of the situation. But Morris said it was all in fun and the joke was on him.[20]

This humorous account is the only indication in Basie's autobiography that the bandleader was aware of Levy's ties with the Mob.

Like Granz had done before, Levy added to his contracts an important clause that mandated all Birdland tour shows be open to ticket buyers regardless of race.[21] This was a particularly daring move considering the tours included stops in major Southern cities. Levy was also protecting his investment in the tour, reserving the right to keep the guarantee if the show was cancelled due to any racial strife. *Variety* attributed Levy's motivations partially to a genuine desire to fight discrimination, but also inspired by commercial considerations, in that the jazz audience itself tended to be the most open to integrated performances:

The jazz field is regarded as particularly important because its audiences are generally in the teens and 20s group . . . The "Birdland" backers apparently figure that they can give the cause of integration a tremendous boost because it affects the age groups now regarded as the prime battleground. It's figured that if the teens and 20s fall in line with the Supreme Court ruling in that matter on a voluntary basis, the strife will diminish considerably in all age groups.[22]

Promoters like Granz and Levy recognized that jazz musicians played together regardless of racial differences. As *Variety* commented, "Sight of Negro and white tootlers working together in the same outfit is not uncommon."[23]

Dizzy Gillespie, Broadway star Nanette Fabray, and singer Harry Belafonte share drinks at Birdland. Birdland was unique in that white and black patrons could intermix freely. Courtesy Aurin Primack.

These musicians often were unhappy playing in segregated venues. Levy was brave to take this position at a time when segregation was still very much in place in the entertainment world. Nonetheless, the *Courier* noted that "none of the promoters have objected to the desegregation clause to date."[24]

By the early fifties the Birdland name was so valuable that Levy sued two clubs, one in Chicago and one in Washington, D.C., for using the name. His success in these lawsuits led him to come up with the idea of officially franchising the Birdland name. Local owners could benefit from the association, while Levy would gain a franchiser's fee as well as establishing a regular touring route for the acts that he managed.[25] Whether there were any takers for this offer is unclear, although Levy opened a branch of Birdland in Miami in December 1953. Levy insisted that the club be open to all, regardless of race. *Jet* magazine proudly reported:

When Birdland opened its canopied doors on ultra-swank Miami Beach, Jim Crow went out the back door. Negro and white jazz fans sat side by side in mixed groups for the first time in Florida's history. The club admits all patrons without color

Advertisement for Teddy Wilson and Wild Bill
Davidson appearance at The Embers.

restriction. Such toppling [of] racial barriers in the South—along with enticing salaries—are encouraging previously reluctant Negro performers to accept more night
club engagements below the Mason-Dixon line.[26]

Opening act Erroll Garner was paid $1,700 a week, a princely sum for the time.
In the photos accompanying *Jet*'s coverage, a white doorman was shown smiling
as he admitted two black patrons, including Garner's wife.

Following his success at Birdland, Levy saw an opportunity to open a more
upscale club on New York's East Side to feature a smoother form of jazz. Levy
buried the hatchet with Ralph Watkins to partner again to open a new club in
1951 called the Embers. It was considered a gamble to open a jazz club in the
neighborhood where residents were fairly conservative. Levy correctly figured
that this bold move would attract both press coverage and at least curiosity
seekers. Nonetheless, he hedged his bets by employing mostly lighter jazz performers. Acts featured at the Embers tended to be either piano soloists like Garner, known for his mildly jazzy playing, or smaller combos. The emphasis was
as much on the plush décor and fine food as it was on the listening experience.
Billboard noted that the Embers "plays modern jazz combos, but on a smooth,
rather than a wild kick."[27]

Levy cleverly located the club across the street from the posh El Morocco
nightclub, which attracted New York's most glamorous nightclub goers. By 1957,
when Levy issued the album *Dorothy Donegan: At the Embers*, the anonymous
liner notes writer could joke about the club's notoriety in relation to El Morocco:

"So important has The Embers become in the history of American jazz that the hipsters tell the tourists that El Morocco is the spot across the street from The Embers. Of course, the squares still say that The Embers is 'that place across the street from El Morocco,' but there's no point in arguing with squares . . ."[28]

Some musicians enjoyed the tonier atmosphere at the Embers as well as the more comfortable playing conditions. Trumpeter Buck Clayton recalled a gig that he played shortly after the club opened: "The Embers was one job that it seemed to me I should be paying the management for having such a good time every night. The room was ideal for jazz. It was a long room with very soft lights, a nicely lit bandstand and, at the rear, a huge fireplace with the glowing embers that gave the club its name."[29] Stars who hung out at the club, according to Clayton, included Jackie Gleason, José Ferrer and his then-wife Rosemary Clooney, Art Carney, Tallulah Bankhead, Peggy Lee, and Sylvia Sims. "They were all jazz-conscious," Clayton recalled.

Others were less impressed with the stuffy audience at the club. Bassist Bill Crow found the East Side café crowd to be less interested in the music than the hip audience at Birdland: "They wouldn't come in unless you had a headliner like Erroll Garner . . . and they would sit there and talk real loud through all the music. It was just more like a fashionable thing to do to go to that club."[30]

Although partners at the Embers, Watkins and Levy remained rivals on the New York club scene. After Bop City closed, Watkins attempted to take progressive jazz upscale by opening Basin Street, which was located close to Broadway and to Birdland. It opened with a "regular night club policy" in mid-1953, but switched after six months to present only jazz, a "sudden and unexpected move," according to *Billboard*. Levy and Watkins tried to work out an arrangement that would benefit both Birdland and Basin Street, but could not come up with an agreement; "in spite of protracted talks," *Billboard* reported, "Basin Street is battling Birdland and vice versa, both for talent and for each other's patronage."

Levy's final foray into the nightclub world came in 1958 when he took over the East Side space that had previously been occupied by the posh club Versailles, which was shut after the owners were charged with owing $350,000 in back taxes.[31] Levy's named partner was again Morris Gurlek, but New York City police believed that other partners were Mafiosos Frank Carbo (a key player in the Mob's control of boxing) and John "Johnny Bathbeach" Oddo (a Colombo family leader).[32] Phil Kahl, Levy's partner in publishing, was also named as a co-owner by the contemporary press.[33] Renaming it the Roundtable, Levy had the place decorated in "King Arthur Motifs," a step down from the more subtly elegant décor of the former tenant. The physical layout of the club was unusual; it consisted of a series of circular levels like an upside down funnel, with a central, circular performance space. In this way, the Roundtable name referred to its circular design as well as recalling the shape of a phonograph record.

Society columnist Mel Heimer attended the opening night festivities to report on the "names" in attendance. Heimer looked down his nose at Levy's background as a "saloon" owner: "Morris Levy, who at 30 has parlayed a couple of saloons called the Embers and Birdland into a million dollars, is opening another new one called The Roundtable, and you have assured him you will come and lend a little class to the premiere . . . [However as] you look around at the quietly milling throng and decide that maybe Morris didn't need your class after all." Heimer noted that Mickey Mantle, dance king Arthur Murray and his wife, and TV host/jazz fan Steve Allen all graced the opening. The entertainment included pianists Count Basie and Teddy Wilson. However, Heimer expressed disappointment at the general low-key proceedings: "Oddly, the hilarity is at a minimum. The customary noise and babble that accompany any such gathering of big names is missing. . . . No one drinks champagne from a slipper. No one gets up and dances on a table. There isn't even a pleasant little fistfight." Heimer reported he was home in bed watching television by ten thirty, ending his column with the sarcastic note: "It was a very glamorous evening. Wasn't it?" Heimer obviously viewed Levy as an upstart in New York's toney nightclub world. During the evening's entertainment, Heimer observed Levy standing "nervously in the corner" eyeing the performers. Heimer sniffed, "Levy's first million has not acted as a tranquilizer, obviously."[34]

The emphasis in the Roundtable was more on fine food than on jazz, although jazz acts did perform there. Levy's old patron Morris Gurlek managed the club. Bill Crow recalled how Gurlek was suspicious of single women frequenting the club, perhaps afraid of facing charges by the police of allowing prostitutes to work there:

> I told [jazz singer] Dave Lambert's daughter Dee that we were going in there behind Mel Torme and she said, "Oh I love Mel Torme," and I said, "Well, why don't you come up one night? I'll treat you to a show." So she agreed and I went to make a reservation and they said we don't take reservations for single women. And I said, "She's not by herself; she's going to be with me." And they said, "Not when you're on the bandstand." I said, "Well, what's your problem?" And they said, "Well we don't want any hookers in here." And I said, "What do you do if your wife wants to come down here," and [Gurlek] said, "I wouldn't let my wife in a place like that." And I had to tell her that she couldn't go.[35]

Levy's experience promoting the Birdland tours gave him entrée into another part of the music industry: the local deejays who spun the records and could turn an unknown act into a major hit maker. At the time, deejays were just coming into their own as a cheaper alternative to hiring live musicians to play music on the air. By the mid-fifties, radio stations realized that these on-air personalities could be as popular as the music they played. The jocks began hosting local shows by visiting artists, making a steady stream of extra income for themselves and their employers. Meanwhile, the local record distributors soon realized that the deejays served as a gateway between the hundreds of weekly releases coming into the stations and getting a particular record played on the air. It made sense to sweeten the deal for the deejay to favor one disc over another, either by cutting them into the publishing income (listing the deejay as a coauthor of a song) or by giving out-and-out cash payments in return for play (later dubbed "payola").

Levy quickly realized that the best way to promote his touring show was to hire local jazz and R&B deejays to serve as emcees for the show. Not only could he legitimately pay them for their time, they would naturally have an interest in seeing that the show was successful, so they would plug it on the air during their normal broadcasts. Sometimes the radio stations themselves were cut in as "co-producers" of the shows, earning a small percent of the profit in return for the free promotion. It was a win-win situation for everyone. Moreover, it enabled Levy to build a network of friends in radio across his touring routes, laying the groundwork for his entry into record promotion and production.

It is probably through these associations that Levy became aware of a young deejay named Alan Freed who was shaking up the airways in Cleveland.[36] From an early age, Freed's ambition was to be on the radio, and he pursued this dream doggedly through a series of jobs after leaving college and briefly serving in the army in the early forties. After a series of radio jobs, Freed was working in Cleveland by the early fifties. At first, he was playing the usual mix of early fifties pop along with other commercial music on his show. However, local record dealer and small label distributor Leo Mintz, whose clientele was primarily Cleveland's African American population, approached Freed offering to sponsor the show in return for the jockey playing the latest R&B releases. Unaware of the popularity of these records, Freed at first rejected the idea, thinking that he would lose his audience and perhaps his time slot. Mintz eventually prevailed and Freed began introducing R&B into his show, which quickly propelled him to the top attraction in local radio. Soon thereafter, he adopted a new on-air personality perhaps inspired by the recording "Moondog Symphony," howling as records played, ringing a cowbell and thumping on a phone book to emphasize the "big beat" of the records he liked best.[37] The *Moondog Show* became a major hit, and Freed soon extended his popularity by coproducing and emceeing a live stage show, the Moondog Ball, in 1952, credited by some as the first rock 'n' roll show. Twenty-five thousand fans showed up to an arena that seated 10,000; without reserved tickets, some fights broke out, giving a black eye to the young musical style.

Freed's radio show was picked up by a small station in Newark, New Jersey, in 1953, giving him a toehold in the New York market. A concert emceed by

Freed in Newark attracted landmark crowds, showing the growing popularity of R&B in the New York region—and the potential for the music to generate big money for concert promoters. *Billboard* estimated the crowds at over 11,000, with about 20 percent of the audience being white—a significant number in the period when most R&B concerts drew only small audiences outside of the African American audience.[38] It also attracted the attention of New York radio station WINS, then struggling to build listenership. Bringing the popular deejay to New York was the obvious solution.[39] On his arrival in New York, Freed soon was either introduced or reintroduced to Levy, who quickly made moves to ingratiate himself with the important deejay.

Soon after bringing his Moondog persona to New York, Freed hit an unexpected roadblock. A blind street singer named Louis Hardin, who had already recorded under that name, sued Freed for infringement. Hardin appeared in court like a biblical prophet, wearing long robes and appearing every bit the street person that he was. Nonetheless, because he could show he was using the Moondog name years before Freed adopted it, Hardin won an injunction against Freed. WINS was anxious to put the case behind them, so they urged Freed not to appeal. Levy recalled a meeting where they discussed a new name for the Moondog radio show: "Alan was having a few drinks and bemoaning the fact that he had to come up with a new name. To be honest with you, I couldn't say if Alan said it or somebody else said it. But somebody said 'rock and roll.' Everybody just went, Yeah, *Rock and roll.*"[40]

Still smarting from the incident with Hardin, Freed and Levy formed a corporation together to copyright the term "rock and roll."[41] Although much has been made about this move over the years as a brazen attempt to cash in on a new musical style, Freed more likely just wanted to avoid future lawsuits. As the term increased in popularity, Levy realized that it would be impossible to police it and, even if they could, their claim to have originated the term probably would not hold up in court.

Soon after coming to the city, Freed asked Levy to produce a local live show like the ones he had previously hosted in Cleveland. The deejay probably lacked the finances and connections to book a hall in New York and looked to the more experienced Levy to put up the cash and handle the details. Levy agreed to split the proceeds fifty-fifty with Freed. However, he soon realized that Freed was not above selling more than 100 percent of his ventures: "About five days [after they made their agreement], the manager of WINS says, 'Moishe,[42] we have a problem. Alan Freed's been in town a week now, and he's already given away a hundred and twenty percent of himself!' He had a lot of talent, but he was also a little *nuts.*"[43]

Perennially in need of cash, Freed would often make overlapping deals with several different people to fund his many side ventures, as Levy would witness many times. Levy also believed that Freed was lured into business arrangements with many less-than-savory types, ruefully noting that "he had to be protected from people who would play up to him ... he had his needs and his weaknesses. One of these was to be told how great he was. If people did that, they could get to him."[44] WINS already had in place in their agreement with Freed a stipulation that they would take a percentage of any income the deejay earned by hosting live shows; in the end, Freed and Levy negotiated a deal whereby WINS would be given 10 percent of any profit from their live shows.

Slowly, Levy expanded from being Freed's partner in concert promotion to being his manager, partnering with him in all his activities beyond deejaying, including music publishing and eventually proposing that they start a record label together. Oddly, in October 1955, *Billboard* announced that Gaetano (aka "Tommy"; "Corky"; "the Big Guy"; "The Galoot"[45]) Vastola was Freed's manager. Vastola—a known member of New Jersey's DeCavalcante gang, as well as the second cousin of Dominic Ciaffone[46]—was another reputed mobster who would be an early investor in Roulette Records. Vastola was an intimidating figure; Ciaffone said, "This kid could tear a human being apart with his hands."[47] Levy claimed that he met Vastola through Ciaffone, and originally hired him to work "as a bouncer in a couple of clubs I owned. . . . And then later on he was trying to get into the business, so he worked with me on shows that I did with Alan [Freed]." Levy said he also gave Vastola "some acts to manage."[48] As late as 1958, Vastola was cited in the trades as being Freed's manager.[49] Whether Levy was fronting for Vastola when he claimed to be Freed's manager, or Vastola was protecting Levy's investment in Freed, is unknown. The Galoot certainly had the muscle to keep would-be "friends" of Freed from gaining access to him.

R&B shows were not the easiest sell to local ballrooms, which were leery of the bad publicity that might occur if crowds got out of control. The music itself was under attack for its sexual lyrics (*Variety* magazine stuffily tagged them "leer-ics"[50]), heavy rhythm, and "juvenile" appeal. An unspoken subtext was the fears of white and black audience members mixing freely, with white teens being negatively influenced by their interaction. The only hall Levy could find for the first Freed show was at the St. Nicholas Arena located on the corner of West 66th Street and Columbus Avenue. A run-down ice rink converted to a boxing hall, the arena was located north of New York's prime entertainment district. Drawing a large crowd to this off-the-beaten-path location would be a struggle. The show was produced under the new name of a "Rock 'n' Roll Ball," although much of the press still referred to the music played there as R&B. According to Levy, Freed made just six brief announcements on air before the show to solicit advance ticket sales; almost immediately, $38,000 in advance sales flooded in. Levy was stunned: "I says, 'Oh my God. This is crazy.' Well, it was two of the biggest dances ever held. The ceiling was actually dripping from the moisture. It was raining inside the St. Nicholas Arena. I'm not exaggerating."[51] It was estimated that the audience was nearly evenly split between white and black teens, one of the early indications of the crossover appeal of R&B music and Freed himself.[52]

The industry journal *Cash Box* reported that the show

> had to be seen to be believed. A total of about 12,000 people jammed the hall on both nights. When we say jammed we must add that the word hardly describes the solid mass that stood for five hours to see the wonderful r&b show that Freed had arranged. Seen from above, the enthusiastic teeners seemed to be jelled into one swaying body with thousands of heads. That they adored Freed was evident from the uproarious welcome with which they greeted his appearance. . . . A finale that lasted about half an hour was rocked in the atmosphere of a revival meeting. With Joe Turner at the mike and Fats Domino at the piano the entire troupe returned to the stage for a closing that was without parallel. Singers and instrumentals danced, dancers and singers grabbed instruments and instrumentalists and dancers sang. Alan Freed and his lovely wife, Jackie, jitterbugged and the kids went wild. An exhausting but thrilling experience.[53]

The success of this first show gave Levy the leverage needed to book a better hall for the next Freed revue. Not able to convince the owners of Manhattan's Paramount Theater—where Frank Sinatra had left bobbysoxers swooning in the mid-forties during his appearances there—he booked the next best location in the chain, the Brooklyn Paramount. Located in the then still thriving area of Flatbush Avenue, the lavish movie palace was among New York's finest. *Billboard* announced the booking with the unusual headline "Deejay Freed Opens B'klyn Para to Flesh," indicating the novelty of having a live stage act being presented for a week at a theater usually devoted to films.[54] (Live acts were a staple of movie houses in the twenties and thirties, but by the fifties most stage shows were gone from major theaters.)

Usually, the Paramount kept half of the ticket income over $30,000 in return for a guaranteed payment of $15,000 to the promoters, a fairly health sum for the time. Cannily, Levy negotiated different terms, forgoing the guarantee in return for an escalating portion of the box office that would reach 90 percent if the gross topped $60,000. The Paramount's owners—having never seen a show gross anything near that high—were happy to accept his offer. Freed, however, was more skeptical and was furious that Levy made this deal. Levy said:

> Alan stopped talking to me, because people had steamed him up that I sold him down the river by not taking a guarantee. As a matter of fact, one big agent bet me

a case of Chivas that we're gonna get killed. Well, we opened up the first day, and there's lines in the streets, and the pressure's so great at the door that we start to cut out the movie. Alan and I pass each other in the hallway. I says, How's it goin', Alan? He makes a face. I says, Hey, Alan, let me ask you a question. You want to sell your end now for twenty thousand? He says, What do you mean? We're making *money*? I says, Alan. And I told him what we're gonna make for the week. And he started talking to me again.[55]

In those days, it was common to have six or seven performances a day before each showing of the movie. However, no one came to see the movie with Freed in the house; instead, the film was used to clear the house between shows, as a means of moving in the next crowd of teenagers. Many of the kids booed loudly during the showing of the film.[56] Levy noted that the crowds got so large that they stopped showing the film during their week's run. *Cash Box* reported that the total take for the week was $178,000, topping the previous record holders, Jerry Lewis and Dean Martin, who took in $147,000 at the Manhattan Paramount.[57] Freed must have been overwhelmed himself by the response, as *Cash Box*'s reporter noted: "As we approached the theatre, hundreds were milling about and the crowd was almost completely around the 2½ block area. . . . The lines were four abreast. . . . . During his broadcast from backstage . . . [Freed] had to tell his audience to stop coming to the theatre that evening because of the jamup."[58]

Variety remarked on how well-behaved the audiences were, despite being primarily teenagers and racially mixed: "Despite the surcharged excitement of the audiences, mostly juvenile and never more than 20 or 25% colored, there was no shagging in the aisles . . . The remarkable thing about the audience behaviorism, to [Gene Pleshette, manager of the Paramount], was the 'all-day fanaticism' but it never took the shape of anything worse than that they all wanted to sit down front.'"[59]

Freed and Levy would produce several more shows in Brooklyn. The *New York Times* reported that their Easter 1956 show grossed $204,000 over ten days and their following Christmas revue racked up $180,000 over eight days. The shows attracted wide press attention, with the Easter show rating a half-page photo of the cheering teens in the audience in a *Life* magazine feature on the popularity of the new rock music style. Not surprisingly, while praising the music's danceability, the *Life* reporter raised questions about its "suggestive and occasionally lewd" lyrics.[60] Nonetheless, these were record-breaking takes for the theater, and Levy and Freed's portion of the gross was far more than any previous promoter/artist team had been able to negotiate.

Levy explained how he could predict which would be the major acts months before each show:

Deejay Alan Freed ca. 1959. Courtesy Photofest.

We'd watch the charts, the records, and I'd try to [book] them. In other words, if we had a show coming over Easter, I'd try to look at records that were breaking in November [by] new groups, and they would be top ten, and I would buy them for $1250, $1500 a week in November ... [Their] managers would be happy to [make this deal] because Alan was going to play the records from November to Easter.[61]

By predicting future hit makers based on early chart action, Levy saved thousands of dollars in booking fees. He had the additional leverage of being able to promise that Freed would push the group's releases in advance of each show, thus ensuring that a would-be hit became a real chart topper.

The duo's successful shows in Brooklyn enabled Levy to score his biggest coup, a booking at the Manhattan Paramount for the Alan Freed Rock 'n' Roll Show during the Washington birthday week in early 1957. And while the movie was often an afterthought, in this case the performances were complemented all week by the premiere of the latest Alan Freed movie, *Don't Knock the Rock*. The result was throngs of teenagers crowding New York's Times Square, the heart of the entertainment district, attracting coverage in "respectable" media like the *New York Times*. The crowds began gathering as early as 4 a.m. for the opening of the box office that was scheduled for four hours later; the box office was continually busy with new ticket buyers through 1 a.m. the following morning.

All in all, over 15,000 teens saw one of the six stage or seven movie shows on the first day, with a total take of $29,000, a record for a single day at the theater. This record attendance occurred despite the fact that kids seated in the second balcony "stamped their feet so vigorously . . . that firemen became alarmed and sent for inspectors from the Fire and Buildings Departments at 5 PM. The management cleared three-fourths of the 1600 youngsters from the second balcony as a precautionary measure." It wasn't until 8 p.m. that the balcony was reopened when it was deemed safe.[62]

Freed's previous Brooklyn shows had been timed to occur during major school holidays (Easter and Christmas) so that he could maximize his audience. His concern in coming to midtown was that the shows were scheduled for a time when most teens were in school and he was afraid that adults would not let their teenage children go out on school nights. His fears turned out to be ill-founded, as the attendance all week was strong for all the shows. The financial arrangement was amazingly generous: the Paramount kept the first $50,000 in admissions, but then Freed and Levy took 90 percent of the take above that. Admission prices began at $1.50, but increased as the day went on, so that the charge reached $2.00 at 10 a.m. and $2.50 after 2 p.m.[63] According to ledger notes that Freed kept, his take from the show was almost $109,000.[64]

In a review headlined "Frenzy and Furor at the Paramount," the *New York Times* critic assessed the show:

> A so-called "rock 'n' roll" musical program opened yesterday on the Paramount's screen and stage. And somehow . . . the roof stayed on. . . . this spectator watched the stage platform rise from the pit, as the entire, chanting audience mounted seats. . . . The stage portion . . . was obviously what the spectators had come for, and they thumped it on down with the whole performing gang.
>
>   And O-Daddy-O, those cats had it! Anybody above 30 who elects to brave the Paramount's new program may find himself amid a composite of a teen-age revival meeting and the Battle of the Bulge. And O-Daddy-O, with a slight case of St. Vitus dance, compliments of the house—if it's still standing.[65]

The stunning success enjoyed by Freed and his meteoric rise to fame and power in the New York pop music scene was not lost on Levy. Clearly there was big money to be made on the new teenage music. Levy was well positioned as a publisher, artist manager, promoter, nightclub operator, and tour manager, but he lacked one key ingredient for maximizing his profits: a record label. His success with Freed gave him the financial ability and the inspiration to go into the record business big time. This would become the focus of his energy in the years to come.

4

Breaking into the Record Business: 1955–1957

You want royalties? Then go to England!
—Morris Levy

Although Levy was enjoying great success with Birdland, his growing music publishing empire, and the Birdland tours, the dream of starting a label was one he would pursue through the 1950s, culminating in his successful launching of what would become his major business interest for the balance of his career: Roulette Records.

Levy's attempts to establish his own record label began as early as 1950 when he briefly formed a partnership with Bob Weinstock to form the Birdland Records label; a handful of 78s were issued, but the label folded and the masters went to Weinstock, who used them to establish his new jazz label, Prestige. By the mid-1950s Levy was in a better position to find a new partner to get into records. With Birdland booming and shows already being broadcast on radio every night, it made sense to take advantage of the opportunity to release live recordings from the club. A live recording captures all the excitement of the show itself, and there are no studio costs. Just as Granz had entered into a deal with Mercury Records to handle his "Jazz at the Philharmonic" live show recordings, Levy made a deal with RCA Victor to issue a series of "Live at Birdland" LPs. Unlike Mercury, still a relatively small independent, Victor was a powerhouse in the recording industry, the most successful of the "big three" (the others being Columbia and Decca). The PR value for Birdland alone was enormous, and Levy also could collect revenue as producer of the recordings and publisher of any original compositions performed on the records.[1]

Levy's deal with Victor was officially announced in September 1955. It was said to be for a six-year arrangement that would produce a minimum of four LPs each year under a Birdland imprint. As part of the RCA deal, *Billboard* noted that Levy would "make available" unsigned acts that appeared on his Birdland tours, and hoped that "within two years his tours will feature Victor talent exclusively."[2]

Birdland label 78 ca. 1950 by Stan Getz. The original Birdland label released only a handful of 78s.

Among the first releases Levy arranged with RCA was a record of major jazz artists playing their versions of "Lullaby of Birdland"—Levy's first copyright and the signature tune for his nightclub and road tours. The album was issued in December 1955 and quickly racked up impressive sales, selling over 10,000 copies in its first three weeks on the market, "without benefit of company promotion," according to *Billboard*.[3] One of the disc's biggest supporters was Levy's own Patricia Music, which snapped up 400 copies itself, undoubtedly to give away as a means of promoting its publishing rights as well as to support Levy's new arrangement with RCA. This auspicious beginning inspired RCA to mount a full-fledged promotion effort for the disk and boded well for the partnership.

Victor issued a series of albums in the Birdland series over the next few months, but these did not achieve as great success as either the label or Levy was expecting. Jazz's popularity was fading under the onslaught of rock and R&B. Within a year Levy was unhappy with his association with Victor. Perhaps he felt his percentage of the take was too small and, despite its marketing muscle, Victor was doing little more than he could do as an independent to sell the Birdland discs. Perhaps Levy thought he could continue to work for Victor while separately pursuing his own recording interests on the side. Whatever the case, the six-year deal was over before it had run its course and Levy was again looking for a new label as a home for his acts.[4]

While making his deal with RCA, Levy was keeping his eye on another potential business partner, label owner George Goldner, who was establishing himself as a major force in R&B and doowop. Like Levy, Goldner was a second-generation Jewish American who was attracted by the new musical sounds emanating from New York's nightclubs, although the music that initially caught his ears had a distinctly Latin tinge.

After World War II, Goldner established a small garment business. However, his true passion was the time he spent at night at the Palladium and other clubs. The Palladium was a hot spot for Latin dancing and music. Ironically, its main customer base was the children of Jewish immigrants living in Brooklyn and the Bronx. Neil Sedaka recalled the place as full of hot young Jewish women, all moved to a frenzy by the seductive beat of the Latin bands.[5] These fans gained a Yiddish-inspired nickname: mamboniks. According to future nightclub owner Norby Walters: "A mambonik was a *trombenik* who loved mambo—*trombenik* being a Yiddish word for a bum. A knockaround guy. It was a badge of who we were, you know?"[6] Goldner was a true mambonik. An avid dancer and fan, Goldner longed for a way to participate in this exciting new culture. In 1948 he found his point of entry through establishing a new Latin music label. Goldner's transformation into entertainment mogul had begun.

Goldner found a partner in one of the best-known deejays promoting the new Latino music, Art "Pancho" Raymond, who also worked as an announcer at the Palladium. Like Goldner, Raymond was born Jewish, and began his career as a deejay working at a small Paterson, New Jersey, radio station, filling in wherever he was needed. As he recalled several decades later: "One day I was asked to do a half-hour Latin-music program in the middle of the day, . . . Using my high school Spanish, I began the program with 'Muy buenas tardes, queridos amigos, como están Ustedes?' The station manager heard me and called me into his office. He said, 'I want you to do the show every day. Use the [Spanish] accent. It's cute.'"[7] The show eventually was named *Tico Tico Time* after a popular Latino hit of the era. Not surprisingly, when they joined forces in 1948, Raymond and Goldner named their fledgling label Tico Records, linking themselves to both the popular radio show and the hit song.

Having a successful deejay with many connections in the Latino music world as a partner showed that Goldner had the savvy to succeed in the record business. Not only could Raymond introduce him to the best acts, he could plug their records on the air and at any personal appearances he made as an emcee.

While other deejays made similar arrangements for themselves, the ethics of such deals were somewhat questionable, and radio station owners were often none too pleased if they discovered their deejays profiting off their radio shows. In fact, some sources say Raymond lost his job hosting *Tico Tico Time* because of his association with the label.[8]

In the fast-and-loose world of the independent recording scene, many performers were happy to record for whoever would foot the session bill and pay the union fees. If the majors—Columbia, Victor, or Decca—took an interest in a specialty act like a Latino band, it was often on a one-off basis. Tico was able to record two of the most prominent Latino bandleaders, Tito Rodriquez and a young up-and-comer named Tito Puente. Many Palladium patrons were more interested in the scene—the hot music, the gyrating bodies, the exotic, Latino atmosphere—than in specific bands. Recognizing this trend, in the early fifties Goldner shrewdly marketed his records by issuing a series of mambo albums, called *Volumes*, into which he packaged previously released 78s. These albums allowed the hip mamboniks to recreate the Palladium atmosphere at home.

At some point around 1950, Goldner bought out Raymond's share in Tico. This strain on the small label, whose finances were probably shaky at best, was probably the beginning of Goldner's endless search for investors—or people at least willing to give him a quick loan to keep the operation afloat. At this time, the record business was primarily a cash business; a small label had to pay an independent pressing plant up front to get his product made, and then had to wait to collect the proceeds once the records filtered through the rather baroque system of distribution from record label to independent distributor to store owner. Not only were there many chances along the way for profits to disappear, there was also the fear that at the end of the day much of the "sold" product would be returned—as the entire industry worked on the unwritten guarantee that any unsold product could be returned to the producer for credit. Pressing plants could easily run off extra copies of a record to sell out of the "back door" directly to distributors without the knowledge of the label's owner. Independent distributors were fly-by-night operations themselves, often chasing cash owed to them by the many small record store accounts and jukebox operators they served. A small label like Tico had to wait months to be paid, having little leverage with those who had purchased their product; meanwhile, they had to be able to continue to finance sessions in order to release new material.

Goldner also suffered from an addiction to gambling. One industry insider told me that he was so heavily addicted that he tried to cure himself by joining Gamblers Anonymous, only to quit when he began betting on whether an odd or even number of attendees would attend the next meeting.[9] Levy said gambling led to Goldner's downfall: "He liked horses. He always needed money. Any degenerate gambler needs money all the time. It's like being a junkie, isn't it? It's

George Goldner (right), ca. 1960, receiving a Silver Record award for sales of his Gone and End labels in Canada. Goldner would soon sell these labels, as he did his previous ones, to Levy. Courtesy Ace Records Ltd. Collection.

a shame, because George knew music and knew what could be a hit. But if he was worried about the fifth race at Delaware and working the record at the same time, he had a problem. George was a character, and a victim of himself."[10] As long as the hits kept coming and Goldner could scrape up the funds to press his new releases, Tico could at least survive.

And then in 1953, Goldner branched out from Latin music to a new area, forming Rama Records to pursue the growing world of R&B, leading to a new level of success—but also increasing vulnerability. Ironically, he may have become aware of the popularity of R&B through his association with Latin musicians and clubs; *Billboard* reported in April 1954 that Latinos were one of the key new audiences entranced with the R&B sound.[11] A local Harlem doowop group, the Crows, came to Goldner's attention through an agent named Cliff Martinez, who heard them perform on the famed Amateur Night at the Apollo

Theater. Martinez introduced the group to a pianist/vocalist/songwriter named Viola Watkins, who worked up some material for them to record. The group's baritone, Bill Davis, wrote a ballad called "I Love You So," and Watkins and the group worked up an uptempo song, "Gee," to be its flip side. At the recording session, Goldner contributed the idea of adding to the basic song a hook repeating the song's title, "Uh uh uh oh gee-ee," which became its signature; for this contribution, he naturally claimed coauthorship of the song.[12]

While the song was purportedly written in six minutes by Watkins, the recording sounds like it was made even more quickly. Typical of the other New York area small labels, Goldner used the cheapest possible studios and hired session musicians who may or may not have any familiarity with the music that they were playing. Constantly eyeing the clock, Goldner undoubtedly would accept just about any performance that did not feature an obvious flaw—such as a total breakdown in the singing or accompaniment—for his master take.

The success of "Gee" was both a blessing and a curse for Goldner. He had to quickly press records to fill the unexpected demand, but then had to wait months, at best, to get payment from the distributors who handled the disk. Not surprisingly, the success of "Gee" led Goldner to experience a cash crunch. His most valuable asset was the publishing rights he held in the song, along with his authorship credit. Goldner immediately sold the copyright for what was reported to be "a lot of money" by the industry papers to a company called Meridian Music—which just happened to be one of many fronts for Morris Levy's publishing empire. This was the beginning of Goldner's long association with Levy, who also took a piece of Goldner's company in return for promoting the disc.[13] Not only did Levy gain the copyright, he mysteriously became an author of the song, replacing Viola Watkins as Goldner's coauthor.[14]

Goldner tried his best to duplicate the lightning-in-a-bottle success of "Gee" with the group, but several followup singles went nowhere. He tried to take the group directly into the Latino market where he had his greatest presence by having them record the improbably titled novelty song "Mambo Shevitz," satirizing a radio jingle for the Jewish wine maker.[15] Goldner even started a new label named Gee in honor of his big hit (or perhaps because his first and last names both began with the letter "G").

One of the first groups signed to Gee was the Cleftones, who had the first Gee release with their song "You Baby You" in December 1955. After recording the single, the group was called down to see Goldner at his offices. When they arrived, they were surprised to see sitting at Goldner's desk a large man who they had never met before: Morris Levy. Along with Levy were two tough looking characters, Tommy Vastola and his associate Johnny Roberts. Levy announced to the group that these men would be their new managers. Vastola was also given a co-author credit for "You Baby You."[16]

Gee Records label, ca. 1956, for Frankie Lymon and the Teenagers.

A month before Goldner launched the Gee label, *Billboard* announced that he was taking on a partner in his Rama label: Joe Kolsky, Phil Kahl's brother. Denying the obvious connection, Goldner told *Billboard* that "outside of seeing Phil's brother make good," Levy and Kahl were not in any way involved in the deal. Nonetheless, *Billboard* noted that "the Kahl-Levy publisheries have obtained first call on all original material sliced on the Rama label."[17] The article stated that the deal was unrelated to Goldner's Tico label, of which he was to remain sole owner. However, almost immediately notices in *Billboard* clearly indicated that Kolsky was involved in all of Goldner's operations.

This deal set the stage for many more to come in which Levy would begin by purchasing an interest in a competitor's operation and then eventually swallow them whole. He preferred to invest rather than to make loans to those in distress, which proved to be in the long run a smarter strategy. Putting an associate into the business—in this case Joe Kolsky—enabled Levy to monitor his investment and also to further lay the groundwork for eroding the original owner's control. In many ways this basic strategy paralleled how mobsters infiltrated legitimate businesses. First, the cash-strapped business operator would come to the mobster as a lender of last resort. The loan was given at often exorbitant rates so that the owner was almost guaranteed to default. Once default occurred, the business itself could be seized or at least coopted to the lender's benefit.

Record companies like Goldner's had little or no physical assets. They did not own their own pressing plants or recording equipment; their artists were rarely under an exclusive recording contract, so once they hit it big they could easily be snapped up by the bigger, more legitimate labels; their inventory was essentially held by third parties (such as distributors) who were not always quick to pay; and their offices were rented spaces that they filled with the most basic furnishings. What Goldner had was a good ear for music and luck in discovering some potentially hit-making acts. Banks, however, do not make loans based on a producer's ears. At least Levy was in the music business and would understand how a small operation like Goldner's worked. Goldner may have believed Levy would leave the creative end of the business to him to manage. As it worked out, however, this was not the case.

Shortly after Kolsky joined the firm, Goldner released a record that would turn out to be his greatest success to date. It featured a group of teenagers from upper Manhattan. Auditioning as the Premiers, the singers performed one of their own compositions, called "Why Do Birds Sing So Gay?" The group consisted of lead singer Herman Santiago, first tenor Jimmy Merchant, baritone Joe Negroni, bass Sherman Garnes—and the newest and youngest member of the group, thirteen-year-old second tenor Frankie Lymon. The song was originally written by Merchant and then adapted by Santiago to better fit his vocal style and range. Hearing the group, Goldner recognized that Lymon was the vocal standout, besides possessing a natural magnetism that would make him a star. He suggested that Lymon take over the lead from Santiago and retitled the song "Why Do Fools Fall in Love?"

As was typical of the era, Goldner wasted no time getting the group into the studio, hiring saxophone player Jimmy Wright to work out the instrumental arrangement and play a solo on the record; Wright also suggested that the group rename themselves the Teenagers. While the recording was made in spring 1955, Goldner sat on it for months, busy putting out songs by more established groups that were more likely to hit. Finally, in January 1956 the record was released, and much to everyone's surprise, it sold over a hundred thousand copies in its first three weeks of release.[18] The record was credited to "The Teenagers with Frankie Lymon," with Lymon's name printed in larger type; the song was credited to Lymon-Santiago-Goldner on the original release, but as soon as Goldner realized he had a major hit on his hands, he dropped Santiago's name from the label credit and—most importantly—left it off the copyright registration. Although the group members were probably just happy to have the record finally released and to unexpectedly find themselves major stars, the implications of Goldner's exploitation of this copyright would resonate over the following decades.

Perhaps with an eye to taking over Goldner's record businesses, Levy used his association with RCA to chip away at Goldner's most valuable assets: his best-selling artists. As an enticement to unsigned artists, Levy bragged he could guarantee "up to 20 weeks a year work at Birdland and featured billing on the Birdland tour"[19] for any act willing to sign with RCA. Among his first recommendations to RCA, Levy convinced Tito Puente, the popular Latin bandleader and percussionist, to sign with them. He claimed that he was unaware of the importance of Puente to Goldner and was just doing Puente a favor by referring him to the larger and better-distributed label;[20] Goldner, on the other hand, was particularly angered by losing one of his key acts. It is highly unlikely that Levy was totally unaware of the mischief he was creating by depriving Goldner of one of his major breadwinners. Levy may have been using Puente as a means of increasing pressure on Goldner to sell out or at least take him on as a partner in his labels, which in fact would occur in 1957 when Roulette was formed.

In addition to investing in Goldner's operations, Levy was pursuing other opportunities to establish his own label or at least to take on an existing one. A tempting target was the record label associated with the first club that he managed, the Royal Roost, owned by Teddy Reig and Jack Hooke. The label was founded in 1949 by Reig in association with Ralph Watkins and several investors; within a year, Reig and promoter Jack Hooke were running it on their own. The label enjoyed some success through the mid-fifties, particularly when Reig had Stan Getz band member and guitarist Johnny Smith record the standard "Moonlight in Vermont" in 1952. Dedicated to releasing advanced jazz—its motto was the grandiose "The Music of the Future," aligning the enterprise with bop's forward-looking aesthetic—the label began suffering when R&B records began replacing jazz on the charts. Hooke later admitted that they were always short of cash and anxious to find surer financial footing.[21]

Levy first made a play for ownership of the label in mid-1955. The deal called for Levy to invest $50,000 for a half-interest in the label, with Hooke and Reig continuing to run it.[22] One new source for recordings would be live recordings from Birdland, presumably the same shows that Levy was marketing to Victor. While this was announced as a complete deal in June 1955, it never reached fruition once Levy made his agreement with Victor that August. Obviously for Levy the Victor deal had much more upside, as he probably was paid an advance by RCA for the rights to the Birdland material, rather than himself having to invest in the Roost venture. Roost's footprint was miniscule compared with Victor's, and Levy was able to achieve much more by aligning himself with the major label.

Phil Kahl, Morris Gurlek, and Morris Levy, ca. 1958. Photo courtesy Photofest.

However, as the Victor deal was coming to a close, Levy reopened discussions to purchase the Royal Roost label in fall 1956, as *Billboard* reported: "Outside of the operating capital Levy could contribute to a young disk business, the operator's many-faceted enterprises provide a wide assortment of inducements for unaffiliated talent. For example, as bait for signing a disk contract, he is in a position to offer the artist a certain number of weeks work at Birdland or a spot on the bill of the annual Birdland stars tour."[23] While Levy eventually purchased Roost, it would not be the main focus of his recording activities.

In early 1957 Levy finally was able to put together his own label, Roulette Records. To do so, he assembled what he felt was the perfect team of partners to be the owners/operators of the new label: his old friend from the hatcheck world, Morris Gurlek, to oversee the label's funding; Alan Freed, the most successful deejay in the country, who seemingly could make any song a smash hit; producers Hugo Peretti and Luigi Creatore (a.k.a. Hugo and Luigi), who had established themselves as hit makers at the fledgling Mercury label; George Goldner, who would bring with him the masters from his Tico, Rama, and Gee labels; Goldner's partner, Joe Kolsky, along with his brother Phil (Kolsky) Kahl, both of whom were associates of Levy's and looked after his interests; and an entertainment lawyer named A. Halsey Cowan. However, Levy quickly asserted himself as the alpha dog in this pack, consolidating his position by eliminating potential rivals while integrating the label into a web of interrelated music businesses.

The Roulette story begins with a short announcement that appeared in early 1957 in *Billboard* magazine:

> Roulette Records is the designation of the latest addition to the Tico-Gee-Rama diskery operated by George Goldner and Joe Kolsky....
>
> "We have so much new talent that needs special exposure and promotion that a new label was necessary," Kolsky said. A complete line is contemplated, and pop and rhythm and blues records. Later it will enter the LP field ... Joe Derashio has been added to the a&r staff, and will cut sessions for Gee and Rama as well as Roulette. He will also supervise jazz dates.[24]

Oddly, Morris Levy's name is conspicuously absent from this announcement, although he was very much involved with the founding of the new label; why his name was omitted is a mystery.

Meanwhile, the real partners in Roulette were already engaged in shifting allegiances, with the wily Levy silently pulling the strings to achieve his goals. The first to drop out was Alan Freed, who was given a 16 percent interest in the new label in return for a $1,600 investment, to encourage him to promote the records.[25] Levy discovered to his chagrin that the unpredictable Freed immediately sold part of his interest to other, less desirable investors, ones that would fall outside of Levy's control: "[Freed sold his stock] to some wiseguys from around town.... And I got hold of Alan, and I said, [']Gimme back my fucking stock. Here's your contract with the shows, but we're not partners no more.[']"[26] According to Levy, Freed held the stock only for a month.[27]

In March 1957 a short notice appeared in *Billboard* announcing the Levy-Freed split. When asked whether there was any acrimony that led to the split, Freed sarcastically responded, "We're just going to ... silently steal away into the night."[28] Freed also said he was selling the copyrights held by his music publishing firm, Jackie Music, to Levy. The article further illuminated the Roulette deal that collapsed, stating that Freed was going to have a 50 percent stake in the new label (not 25 percent as Levy later claimed). Freed gave the reason for his leaving Roulette as his being "not in accord with some of the policies of the company." The egotistical deejay wasted little time making his future plans known, stating that he was "expect[ing] to start his own record company" shortly, although just two weeks later in a second *Billboard* notice he was "deny[ing] rumors" that he

would be entering the record business on his own.[29] He outlined a busy schedule, including more live shows, tours, and feature films, and also announced that
he was establishing his own publishing firm to be run by Jack Hooke.

Hooke believed that Levy resented Freed leaving him, claiming that when
Freed announced that he was hiring him to run his firm, Hooke was approached
at

> a bar where I hung out, [some] guys pulled me aside and said, "Listen you stay away
> from Alan Freed or you're dead." Turned around and walked out.
>
> So I called Morris and said, "How the fuck could you do this? You know me, you
> know my wife?"
>
> [And Morris said] "I didn't do it, I swear, Jack, I didn't do it." And possibly he did
> not do it, because this is how things work[ed]. The next thing I know I got a call
> from a rival mob. "Jack, you're in trouble. People looking to kill you. Why don't you
> let us come in with you?" I took them in. Gave them the 15% the other people were
> getting. Now, as I learned many years later, they went to each other and said, "Listen,
> you back off, I'll get the 15% and I'll split it with you."[30]

When asked about Hooke's involvement with Freed, Levy claimed Hooke
was just a "gofer" who "reported to me" but then decided he'd do better on his
own: "Hooke was looking [out] for himself. He got a little bold.... [and thought]
he would do better with me not there because I would hold him down to what
he was ... With me gone, he'd start to influence [Freed] with playing some songs,
he'd be the connection to get to him ..."[31]

Despite Freed's declaration of independence, by the end of May Levy and
Freed buried the hatchet, recognizing the mutual benefit of renewing their
working relationship. In a *Billboard* notice headlined "Freed-Levy Team Back
in Harness,"[32] Freed reversed his earlier position, stating: "Disc jockeys have no
business being in the record and publishing fields.... jockeys can't be fair to all
record companies and publishers when they're in the same field themselves."
The article featured a long list of deals negotiated by Levy for Freed going forward, including a new TV show on ABC that Levy would executive produce.
It also ended with a cryptic mention of "mutual interests" of Freed and George
Goldner that might be affected by the reunion with Levy, perhaps hinting at the
fact that Goldner had approached Freed about forming a new record company
to challenge Levy and his partners. Goldner was quoted as being "surprised and
shocked" by the news that Freed and Levy had reunited, but denied that he had
any "mutual business interests" with the disc jockey.[33]

Indeed the hapless George Goldner would also be quickly eliminated from
the founding membership of the new Roulette label. Exactly what happened is
unclear, although some believe that Goldner's gambling habits and his constant

need for cash led him to quickly sell out his shares in the enterprise. Goldner's daughter, Linda, however, claims that the always independent operator just couldn't adapt to working for the strong-willed Levy:

> Morris went to a lot of trouble to create an atmosphere to attract George to go into business with him.... [George] was very self-assured and never thought he would have a partner disagreeing with him in reference to studio budgets or spending money on the road when he promoted their records. No one was going to dictate an opinion to George, including Morris Levy.[34]

While Linda felt that Levy had "deliberate[ly] set up" her father to grab his labels, Levy simply stated to author Fredric Dannen that "George got disillusioned and we bought him out."[35] Levy went so far as to say that he formed Roulette "because George kept telling me I didn't know nothing about the record business, and it aggravated me. And I says, [']Okay, now I'm gonna form a record company that *I'm* gonna run.[']"[36]

When interviewed by the FBI in 1961, Goldner told the agents that the reason he left Roulette was because he "and LEVY differed as to their methods of obtaining recording artists.... LEVY was interested in signing well known artists and paying a great deal of money in order to sign them, whereas GOLDNER was more interested in signing unknown artists and using certain recording techniques in attempting to turn out hit records."[37] Goldner was to be given $250,000—not an insignificant sum—for his labels and publishing along with his share in Roulette; he quickly used the down payment to establish two new labels, Gone and End, announcing his intention to set up shop in mid-April 1957.[38] As of 1961, he was still receiving "monthly payments of $1000 from Planetary Music" for his share of Roulette.[39]

Losing Goldner and his ear for pop music could have been a fatal blow to the fledgling label. However, Levy had been canny enough to hire the creative team of Hugo Peretti and Luigi Creatore (known as Hugo and Luigi) to work at Roulette. The duo would be responsible for the label's initial productions. Hugo and Luigi were cousins and first-generation Italian immigrants, raised in New York's Hell's Kitchen. After World War II, the duo found work writing commercial jingles. After producing a few children's records locally, they were hired by Irving Green, who operated a record-pressing plant in Chicago, leading him to start his own label, Mercury Records. Hugo and Luigi were hired to produce children's material for Mercury and to join the then small New York office the label maintained above an auto dealership. They graduated to heading A&R for the label's pop stars.

Despite producing top ten hits for Mercury, the duo were kept on a small retainer by Green, who reluctantly raised each of their salaries from $75 to $125

Hugo and Luigi shown on the picture sleeve for their single "Cha-Hua-Hua," 1958. This kind of novelty number was a specialty of the producing and performing duo.

a week following the #1 hits "Tweedle Dee" and "Dance with Me Henry" that they produced for Georgia Gibbs. They travelled to Chicago to plead for more compensation, but Green was unmoved by their arguments.[40]

Levy kept his eye on the charts and was aware of Mercury's growing presence as a pop label. He would, in fact, raid Mercury's list to help build Roulette in its early years, taking from them jazz-pop vocalists like Sarah Vaughan and Dinah Washington, among others. Aware of Hugo and Luigi through both their recordings and his meetings with the duo to push them to record his copyrights, Levy opened the door to a deeper partnership, as Luigi explained:

> [Levy] came up one day and said, "Look when you guys get tired of being [at Mercury] . . . not making any money, I'll back you for a record company." So we didn't pay any attention, because we had the chart action, too. Now after a while, we were

sitting there and not doing what we wanted to do. I said to Hugo, "What about this guy Morris Levy?" He said, "I don't know about him, Morris has a reputation as kind of connected, you know, the hoodlums, I don't know about that." I said, "That's a lot of crap; people, rumors, and stuff. The guy is a guy; let's talk to him."[41]

According to Luigi, Levy offered the duo a "50 percent" interest in the new label, while he would provide the capital, although the duo did actually put up a small amount of money for their stake. By this point, it seems that Levy had already sold more than 50 percent of the label to Freed, Goldner, his associates Morris Gurlek, Joe Kolsky, and Phil Kahl, not to mention any silent partners who also may have been funding the operation. With the constantly changing status of the principals, it is hard to keep an exact count, but one wonders if Levy was pulling the age-old scam of selling more than 100 percent of the firm.

At least at first, Hugo and Luigi were pleased to be associated with Roulette. Asked to guest write for Dorothy Kilgallen, the duo took over her "Voice of Broadway" column on October 26, 1957, although the actual writer for the column was likely a PR agent. The duo bragged about the "kicks and rewards" they had enjoyed "since becoming artists and repertoire chieftains at Roulette Records." Among the artists they bragged about signing were jazz singer Pearl Bailey and comedian Milton Berle, who successfully pitched to the duo an album of his mother's favorite songs. Berle brought along "his usual massive entourage, the 32 musicians with their instruments, and the 20 vocalists" to the studio. The producers were impressed with Berle's comfort at the microphone: "Berle went to the podium, with sleeves rolled up, and via an eighteen hour session interrupted only by coffee breaks, the entire album was completed in fine style."[42]

Levy had ulterior motives in recording Berle. He used Berle's celebrity to help Roulette break into the lucrative department store market. As an independent label, it was hard to sell directly to the big stores. Levy recalled: "Roulette couldn't get records into major department stores, which would only stock product from the majors. We made a record with Milton Berle, when he was hot on TV, and gave him to department stores for nothing on a personal appearance tour if they'd stock the records which opened them up to us."[43] As always, what appeared to be altruistic on Levy's part—covering the costs for Berle to make in-store appearances—was part of a plan to help him expand his business.

Hugo and Luigi noted their "proudest moment" at the young recording company came when Levy

secured the rights to the tapes of the unforgettable conductorless concert staged at Carnegie Hall on Oct. 27, 1954, by the NBC Symphony, for years conducted by the immortal Arturo Toscanini. It was presented shortly after Toscanini was forced into retirement in April of '54, all proceeds to keep the orchestra alive . . . Levy, successful with pop recordings of all sorts, burned to expand into the classical field, contacted the powers-that-be . . . and made an offer for the tapings. . . . All three of us feel we'll never top the peak of honor we reached when we secured the rights to produce the Toscanini benefit concert so all the world can enjoy it.[44]

It is hard to picture Levy "burning" with desire to present classical music on Roulette. Undoubtedly this play for long-hair respectability was part of his over-all strategy of building a label to compete with the majors.

The quick elimination of Goldner from being Roulette's house A&R director and the elevation of Hugo and Luigi had a profound impact on the records that Roulette produced in its first year. Just compare Goldner's slapdash but highly effective production of "Why Do Fools Fall in Love?" with how Hugo and Luigi shaped Frankie Lymon's followup recordings. Where Goldner's record had the immediacy of a hot New York summer's night, Hugo and Luigi went for a more smooth, fifties-era pop style that was already showing its age in the nascent rock era. They chose the old standard "Goody Goody" for their first Frankie Lymon and the Teenagers production (although the Teenagers were actually absent from the track itself, forecasting the demise of the group as Roulette pushed Lymon forward as a solo attraction). The song was composed in 1936 with lyrics by the pop-jazz master Johnny Mercer and music by Marty Melneck; by 1957 it was already over two decades old, a lifetime on the pop charts. In Hugo and Luigi's version, the track opens with blaring horns, and Lymon belts out the lyrics as if he were a pint-sized Frank Sinatra. The backing vocalists were as far removed from doowop as possible, sounding more like the Four Freshmen than the four Teenagers. The producers replaced the teen angst of Lymon's vocal on "Fools" with the kind of generic belting that was more suited to a nightclub than a hoppin' teen spot.

Although the recording is far more professional-sounding than Goldner's lo-fi productions, it did little to further the career of Lymon, who lost his teen following without gaining an "adult" audience. Luigi recognized that the track was hardly rock 'n' roll, but nonetheless was thrilled with the results: "We came up with 'Goody Goody' with really a swing band arrangement; it had nothing to do with rock 'n' roll. It was great and he *did* it great. . . . he just got up and sang, and his arms would go. He just had it, a natural gift."[45] The song only reached #20 on the charts, a big fall from the strong showing of "Fools." Frankie's follow-ups were equally disappointing aesthetically and commercially.

Levy justified Roulette's focus on Lymon over the rest of the group by noting that Lymon "was the talent" while the other Teenagers "meant very little to me." Further, according to Levy the group members were squabbling over who would be featured in their live performances:

They started fighting among themselves and they wanted everything split equal. They wanted to start doing solo numbers in their act, the appearances, and none of them had the talent for it. . . . There was nothing personal in what I did there. . . . Any agent today, any record company, if they had the same act, if they were fighting among them[selves], if he'd got half a brain up his ass, they're going to pick Frankie Lymon.[46]

Sadly, by focusing on Lymon, Levy essentially destroyed both the group's appeal and Lymon's potential career. The group itself may have collapsed based on the internal conflicts among its members. Lymon was starting to skip appearances to chase women and use drugs, which certainly did not help.

Roulette's first major hits had nothing to do with Hugo or Luigi, but rather came through purchasing a master from a smaller regional label, a not uncommon practice at the time. The regionals would often record local acts, and when the records starting "breaking" locally, they'd try to hawk them to a larger outfit. Lacking the clout to promote a disc on the national level, it made sense to sell out and take a cut of the profits from someone who did. Roulette charged out of the gate with two major hits in the then-popular rockabilly style, Buddy Knox's "Party Doll" and Jimmy Bowen's "I'm Stickin' with You." The two songs were drawn from a single released on the small Triple D label out of Texas by a local group known as the Rhythm Orchids featuring rhythm guitarist Knox and bass player Bowen. Recorded by Norman Petty at the same studio where Petty shaped the sound of Buddy Holly and the Crickets, the sound is thin and trebly; unable to deal with a full drum kit in his primitive studios, Petty had the drummer pound out the rhythm on a cardboard box. Nonetheless, the record got some airplay outside of Texas, and Roulette quickly scooped up the rights. Sensing that they had two potential hits on their hands, Roulette released each song individually, one credited to Knox and the other to Bowen, as they were the lead vocalists on each song, respectively. While neither song was hardcore rockabilly and the recording and performances were rather primitive, both singles benefited from Roulette's national presence and promotion. "Party Doll" reached #1 and the somewhat tamer "I'm Stickin' With You" reached #14.

According to Bowen's memoirs, Levy flew the group to New York to record flip sides for the two singles, using George Goldner to produce the sessions (who was still involved with Roulette at the time). Knox was so nervous that Bowen ended up singing lead on both songs, so for the B-side of the Buddy Knox single Goldner "pumped up the echo . . . so high on my voice that you could hardly tell it wasn't Buddy, though my voice was deeper and less twangy," according to Bowen.[47]

Just as Hugo and Luigi changed the sound of Frankie Lymon from teen doowop star to mainstream crooner, they would also shape Buddy Knox's

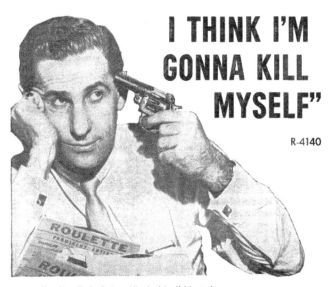

This Is **JOE KOLSKY**, Executive Vice-President of Roulette Records

He's so excited about the new **BUDDY KNOX** record

he says, "If This Isn't A Hit

I THINK I'M GONNA KILL MYSELF"

R-4140

Keep Your Singles Business Alive (and Joe Kolsky, too)

A sound bet . . . buy

ORDER THIS BUDDY KNOX SMASH NOW!

Trade ad promoting Buddy Knox's latest hit. It ironically shows sales executive Joe Kolsky holding a gun to his head.

followups to the successful "Party Doll." They chose an odd pop song called "Hula Love" for his next single. While the producers more or less preserved the rockabilly group's style on the recording of "Hula Love," the backing singers were clearly studio professionals, cooing and oohing in the style of the plain-vanilla pop of the day that was at the opposite end of the spectrum from the rough-edges of rock. It must be admitted that even on "Party Doll," Knox's brand of rockabilly was hardly in the fire-breathing mold of masters like Jerry Lee Lewis or even the surefooted pop of Buddy Holly.[48] However, Hugo and Luigi's production was typically popish and, along with the poor choice of material, doomed Knox's and Bowen's future recordings to oblivion. Assigning Hugo and Luigi to work with both artists was a disaster, as Bowen noted: "They weren't the best match for our sound, not to mention our unschooled, instinctive way of doing things. . . . Hugo and Luigi failed to draw out of us the raw magic that

Petty had captured in Clovis. We should have insisted on going back to re-create whatever it was that excited Morris [Levy] in the first place."[49] Levy was most excited by the money-making potential of their original recordings, not their rockabilly style. So it is not surprising that he was not concerned with recreating that sound on the group's Roulette releases.

Setting the pattern for future Roulette artists, Levy's aversion to accounting accurately for record sales led to him alienating these young hit makers. While the Rhythm Orchids were hardly a stable group—merely a couple of kids who started to play together for college dances on a lark—both Knox and Bowen had the talent to be groomed into long-term artists. However, Levy lacked the musical knowledge to recognize that it was their raw, rockabilly style that gave them their appeal; and he was so tight with money that after initially spending freely to bring the group to New York and sign them to Roulette, he nickeled and dimed them on their royalties. As Bowen recalled:

> Our deal with Morris was for 2 percent of 85 percent of gross sales. Despite considering Morris a friend and mentor, he had this irritating aversion to paying royalties. "You want royalties?" he was fond of saying. "Then go to England!" . . . We were counting on very big royalty checks, even with 45s selling for 98 cents. I knew "Party Doll" had sold 1.2 million singles, and "Stickin'" was up to 900,000. But the royalty statement reflected payments on only 600,000 copies of "Party Doll" and 300,000 copies of "Stickin'." Even we knew that the difference between royalties on 2 million records and royalties on less than 1 million was a good chunk of change.

The group originally signed contracts that gave Levy control of their "record, publishing, management, and agency." This arrangement could be challenged by a shrewd lawyer because it posed a clear conflict of interest—or at least Bowen thought he could use this threat to negotiate a better deal with Levy. He went to the Roulette offices to confront Levy with this problem. "Is that all that's botherin' ya kid," Levy said to Bowen: "With that he opened a desk drawer and pulled out a thick stack of papers. 'This here is your management contract,' he announced and ripped that sucker in his large thick hands, tossing the ripped deal in the trash. Then he looked back to me and asked calmly, 'Now, anything else I can do for you?'"[50] Bowen limply replied, "I think that'll actually do it for today," quickly hightailing it out of Levy's office.

Bowen and the Orchids' guitarist Donnie "Dirt" Lanier next visited the musician's union. Initially a union official told them that it would support them in escaping the onerous terms of their Roulette contract; but mysteriously a day or two after their visit the same official told them that their contract was valid. Several lawyers they visited also initially expressed interest in representing them until they discovered that they had to deal with Levy.

Their last chance to escape Roulette came from a character who Bowen in his memoirs describes as "Tommy V."; this was Gaetano "Tommy" Vastola. Vastola had already worked with Levy and Alan Freed, and was hardly a disinterested party. Bowen was unaware of this potential conflict of interest when Vastola told him that "he was going to take [the group] to MGM, a major label that paid legit, and get us $50,000 to sign and 7 or so percent—a much better deal than we had. 'I can handle Levy,' he said. 'I'm not scared of Moishe.'"[51]

What followed came straight out of a gangster movie. Vastola arranged for a meeting at a lawyer's office. Bowen showed up for the meeting (Knox was out of town serving a stint in the ROTC, while Lanier was ill) to represent the group; Levy and Vastola showed up each "flanked by two immense guys with overcoats." A mysterious third character, "Sonny," arrived last and entered the office. (Although Bowen does not identify who this is, it may have been John "Sonny" Franzese, an underboss in the Colombo crime family.) Bowen entered the office and found Sonny behind a desk, taking the part of the judge, with Levy's men on one side and Vastola's on the other, each prepared to argue why they should "own" the Rhythm Orchids. Levy's argument was simple: "I signed these kids, spent thousands on 'em, we got a contract"; Vastola countered "Yeah, but Moishe ain't payin' 'em proper, ya see, he ain't takin' good care of these kids." After hearing both sides, Sonny rendered a verdict: Levy would keep the act.

Bowen's experience with Levy and Roulette was so unsettling he knew there was no point in confronting Levy further. Years later, reflecting on his experiences, he balanced both the good and bad after effects of having begun his career under Levy's domination:

> Morris got our masters and publishing for a total of $8,000. "Party Doll" was probably worth $400,000 in publishing alone. If we'd have been more experienced we would have kept the publishing and made a lease deal for the masters. But we didn't have a strong negotiating position: No one else wanted our masters. All the majors had passed on us or not responded. Dot Records even sent a letter saying "Party Doll" was obscene.
>
> What was obscene was the amount of money Morris Levy made off us. Yet without Morris . . . we'd have likely never had our No. 1 hit record.[52]

This conundrum was at the heart of the 1950s pop business: Without operators like Levy, the Orchids would never have enjoyed the success that they had. But, because they were signed to Levy, they were not able to enjoy the financial rewards that they should have gained from that success.

The Orchids finally found a young lawyer hungry enough to represent them, named Marty Machat. He in turn brought to the table a brilliant young accountant named Allen Klein—who would earn a reputation in the coming years as

Jimmie Rodgers publicity photo, 1961.

one of the industry's shrewdest and toughest negotiators, winning unheard of deals for the Rolling Stones and the Beatles. In late 1958, Klein met with Levy and had no problem getting him to admit he owed the Orchids a considerable amount in back royalties; the biggest problem was getting him to pay. Levy said he would pay them back over four years; when Klein threatened to sue, Levy countered, "I'll tell the judge I'm a little tight but that I'll pay it out to you." Realizing that suing would just cost him more time and money—and likely lead to the same outcome—Klein accepted the terms. Levy had a soft spot for young Jewish hustlers like himself, and recognized in Klein a kindred soul. The two remained close for the remainder of Levy's life.[53]

Hugo and Luigi brought in the next major star to Roulette, a singer they had originally auditioned for Mercury named Jimmie Rodgers. Rodgers was working as a professional entertainer in small bars and clubs mostly around his native Seattle when the duo found him in the mid-fifties.[54] Mercury had initially approved their recording Rodgers, but then decided they had enough "boy singers" and the artist was never signed. Now that they were at Roulette, the producers brought Rodgers into the studio, and he had an immediate hit with the folk-styled song "Honeycomb," which reached #1 on the pop charts in late 1957.[55] When working in Nashville, Tennessee, Rodgers had heard the song performed by another local singer and added it to his act; it was the first song he sang when auditioning for Roulette in mid-1957.[56]

Rodgers's contract with Roulette was typical of the onerous terms that pop singers faced at the time. The agreement's terms specified that:

"Jimmy" [sic] Rodgers would record at least eight record sides for the defendant [i.e., Roulette Records and Morris Levy], the compositions to be chosen by defendant. Plaintiff was restricted from making recordings for anyone else during the term of the agreement and for five years thereafter. Defendant was to pay plaintiff royalties in the amount of three percent (3%) of ninety percent (90%) of the "retail list price of double-faced record sold in the U.S. and paid for." . . . Defendant would charge against plaintiff's royalty account the entire cost of the recording sessions and any advance made by defendant to plaintiff.[57]

In short, Rodgers was made an exclusive artist with Roulette for the term of the agreement plus five years, during which period all expenses would be charged against future royalties. Royalties would be calculated at a pitiful 3 percent rate on 90 percent of the records sold (this was left over from the days of 78s, when "breakage" of returned shellac discs typically ran about 10 percent of all sales). At a time when "double-faced records" generally retailed for around seventy-five cents, the artist stood to make about two or three cents royalty per record sold. Levy justified this by saying: "We used to sell a record for 35 cents [to the distributors]. . . . [Today people say] 'Oh, isn't it terrible, they used to pay three cents a record.' Well, goddamn it, what did they want us to pay? We sold the records for 35 cents and gave 300 free on a thousand."[58] To keep his distributors happy, Levy claimed he had to ship 1,300 records for every 1,000 ordered (throwing in 300 free)—so was actually netting about 27 cents a record on each sale. However, even accepting this royalty rate, most artists did not see regular statements or payments from Roulette (or most other independent labels at the time), undermining Levy's argument that his terms were fair.

In 1988 Rodgers finally sued for nonpayment of royalties. Roulette countered that they had spent $26,000 on Rodgers and only recouped $20,000 in royalties over the 3 decades that his records were available, despite his scoring several top ten hits, so the singer owed *them* $6,000! After the lawsuit was filed, Roulette conveniently discovered that there was another $14,000 due, supposedly because of earlier miscalculations, so offered to pay $8,000 to the singer to settle the case; Rodgers asserted that he was owed significantly more than that and opted to continue the suit.

One of Rodgers's lawyers who took Levy's depositions in the 1988 case says that Levy claimed that recording artists of that era typically did not earn much in royalties, but their success on the charts enabled them to make a good living performing on the road. Thus, the record company—which Levy asserted took all the risk—was rewarded through sales of singles, while the artist would benefit from this success through live appearances, which did not benefit Levy.[59] However, this argument had several flaws. Because Levy also controlled Rodgers's publishing, he benefited from live performances of the songs on radio or television, not to mention that Levy certainly had a hand at least in arranging Rodgers's initial tours. And live performances drove record sales, so Rodgers was lining Levy's pockets without earning any royalties himself.

"Honeycomb" is a typical Hugo and Luigi production, opening with a male chorus chanting the song's title, and oohing and aahing throughout behind Rodgers' light country-flavored vocal with the addition of an occasional rockabilly hiccup. To add interest, each verse modulates in key, and hand-clapping and a light cymbal beat give the song a sprightly rhythmic drive. The song ends dramatically with a break in the rhythm, Rodgers singing the last note in falsetto, and the male chorus responding with the final harmonized "Honeycomb." This was a period when folk-styled songs were charting big, and Rodgers's natural warmth and the smooth production undoubtedly contributed to the song's success.

For a followup, Rodgers recorded "Kisses Sweeter than Wine," another folksy number. Believing it to be a traditional folksong, Roulette claimed the publishing rights and began heavily promoting the song. The song was in fact a hit for the folk group the Weavers in 1951, and was based on a song that the African American guitarist Huddie Ledbetter (a.k.a. Lead Belly) adapted from a traditional Irish folksong; group members Lee Hays and Pete Seeger further reworked the song. The Weavers' publisher, Howie Richmond, copyrighted the song under the names of Paul Campbell and Joel Newman, two fictitious cover names.[60] When Richmond heard about Rodgers's cover of the song, he informed Levy that he already owned the copyright and that it was not a traditional piece that Roulette could exploit for its own profit. Richmond ribbed Levy over the misunderstanding that year at the annual BMI dinner, where the song was honored as a major hit. As he accepted the award, Howie quipped, "I'd especially like to thank the boys at Roulette, who worked on the tune just as hard as they might if it had been their own."[61] Levy, who hated losing a copyright to anyone, must have been seething that he had helped Richmond line his pockets by having Rodgers record the song.

Rodgers scored a few more hits while at Roulette, but his career faded in the early '60s as pop music styles changed. While living in Los Angeles in 1967, Rodgers's career was cut short following a mysterious incident involving an off-duty police officer. Driving erratically, Rodgers was pulled over by officer Michael Duffy early on the morning of December 1. What happened next is a mystery; Duffy claims Rodgers stumbled and fell after getting out of his car, fracturing his skull, while Rodgers claims he was beaten by Duffy along with two other officers who were called to the scene. Supporting Rodgers's claim was the fact that Duffy had been previously suspended for using a blackjack to subdue a juvenile suspected of driving while intoxicated.[62] Adding to the mystery, the officers left Rodgers unconscious in his car, where he was later discovered by his musical conductor, Eddie Samuels, who had been following Rodgers in a separate car.[63]

Rodgers later sued the city and the policemen turned around and sued him for defamation of character; eventually, all charges were dropped, and Rodgers was awarded a $200,000 settlement by the city in 1973 to avoid further legal liability.[64] The singer never fully recovered from the head injuries resulting from this incident—including losing his voice to spasmodic dysphonia—although in 2010 he returned to performing in a limited way after a period of surgeries and therapy.[65]

Some have suggested that the assault on Rodgers was connected with his attempts to collect royalties from Roulette for his early hit recordings, although no evidence has been offered to support this suggestion. Rodgers noted that he knew better than to challenge Roulette's accounting:

> I got along with [Roulette] alright. But, they never paid anybody. I had an accoun-
> tant go ahead and go over all their books. They owed me at that time, probably a
> million dollars or more. . . . I had management and accountants go in there and
> they found so many sets of books that it's impossible to figure out what they really
> owed. So, we left the company and the company went on selling my records. . . . I
> had absolutely no contact with them until 1967, and I left them in 1960. We had no
> words, no problems. I didn't sue them. I didn't go after them. I didn't do anything. I
> knew their reputation. I knew it wasn't a smart thing to do.[66]

When Rodgers sued Roulette and Levy for underpayment of royalties in 1988, he lost on most counts due to the statute of limitations.[67]

5

Roulette on the Rise, Birdland in Decline: 1958–1965

Morris Levy, a lean muscular New Yorker . . .
now heads a music empire of staggering proportions.
—Ralph J. Gleason

From the start, Levy intended Roulette to be a "major" record label, not just another fly-by-night operation like so many other New York–based outfits. This meant going beyond issuing singles to break into the growing album market. By May 1957 the label announced its first twelve LP releases, forecasting that among Roulette, Tico, Rama, and Gee they would issue a hundred albums by the following fall. Emulating RCA and the other major labels, the roster of initial releases ranged from full albums from Buddy Knox and Jimmy Bowen (repackaging their hit singles) to a calypso album from the harmony trio the Playmates, easy listening orchestral music from bandleader Henry Jerome, and a selection of 1920s-era pop songs from "canary" Bonnie Alden.[1]

Roulette also made a splash by releasing all of its albums in what it called "Dynamic Stereo" along with standard mono. Stereo was still new in 1957, and not many people owned phonographs that could play stereo recordings; even the major labels were not yet widely releasing stereo albums. Levy had shown an interest in high fidelity early on, installing a stereo sound system at Birdland in the mid-fifties. All of the live recordings that he oversaw at Birdland were made in stereo, which was highly unusual for jazz recordings of any kind.[2] One of Roulette's initial releases was a Dynamic Stereo demonstration record, the kind of thing high-end audio enthusiasts could use to show off the potential of their stereo systems.

Levy's album packages were also far more upscale than Goldner's previous labels or operators like Hy Weiss at Old Town—his most immediate competitors. Levy printed full-color covers with high-quality photographs and included album notes on the back, rather than ads for other releases, as Goldner had typically done. He used noted jazz photographer Chuck Stewart—an African American photographer who was beloved in the jazz world—for most of his initial releases. Stewart showed unusual sympathy for his subjects, creating memorable cover images for Levy.

At the close of its first year of business, Roulette took out a splashy eight-page "advertorial" in *Billboard* to trumpet their astonishing success. Among other claims, the firm asserted they had sold over a million copies of "Party Doll" and nearly a million of "I'm Sticking With You" "before installing office furniture." By year's end, they had over 100 employees "including field personnel" across the country. And they bragged of having signed major talent including Pearl Bailey, Count Basie, and Milton Berle, as well as developing new talent like Jimmie Rodgers. They held their first national sales meeting in November, where supposedly "one of the distributors proclaimed, 'Roulette will be the next major company in the record industry,'" with the crowd responding with "sustained and spontaneous cheering."[3] By year's end, the label had released "24 albums, eight EP's and about 50 singles. Nine of those singles—about 20 per cent—had hit the charts."[4]

The advertorial included a month-by-month description of the year's successes followed by brief biographies of the key artists on the label as well as of the "executive talent that boomed Roulette." Levy's biography is typically hyperbolic while at the same time being fairly light in details:

> Morris Levy is a young man with experience beyond his years. It is hard to pin down his special talent other than to say that he approaches every job to be done with a prodigious energy that is in direct contrast to his outward quiet demeanor. . . . He has achieved success in a rough, tough field that separates the men from the boys. . . . It was not by mistake that Morris Levy was chosen president of the Roulette organization.[5]

While obviously a PR piece, the biography hints at Levy's reputation as a streetfighter (having succeeded in a "rough, tough field") and his ability to "get the job done"—including a willingness to succeed by any means.

The pop acts brought in enough income to support the fledgling label, but Levy's first love remained jazz. He retrieved the Birdland series albums he had previously licensed to RCA in September 1957 as the basis of building Roulette's jazz listings; in September 1958 he finally purchased Roost Records from Teddy Reig (who was already working as a producer at Roulette), taking over its back catalog.[6] But the real prize for Levy was in signing Count Basie to a five-year deal on his new label. Levy was particularly close to Count Basie, who he hired in the early fifties as a regular performer at Birdland, featuring the band on his Birdland tours. In a review of one of Basie's successful engagements at Birdland, an African American critic noted: "The number one Basie fan at Birdland is, of

Count Basie playing at Birdland, ca. mid-fifties.
The club was so small that Basie's piano had to be
placed on the floor so the band could fit on the
stage. Courtesy Aurin Primack.

course, Morris Levy, the owner of the spot. In the past, he just brought the Count
in for his own kicks and the few dollars he made. However since that beginning
the crew has developed into one of the most popular in the country and now
Levy can't even get a seat in his own place to hear the band he adores."[7] Levy
made more than a "few dollars" off of Basie's band through his many appearances at Birdland. Nonetheless, this piece of puffery genuinely reflects Levy's
feelings about the band, despite its smell of a PR man's pen.

According to some people—including Basie himself—Levy was central in
reviving Basie's band after he had to temporarily disband his group in the early
fifties. By guaranteeing Basie regular work at Birdland, Levy lay the groundwork
for the resurrection of the band. Levy's partner Morris Primack recalled: "Basie
only had a 6-piece band when we first booked him. . . . So Morris Levy made
him an offer: He could get his big band [back] together. [In return,] he's got to
play Birdland Easter, 4th of July, and Christmas at Birdland. And any other time
he's out of work he could come to Birdland."[8]

Basie's first appearance at Birdland with his new big band came in summer
1952. The bandleader was particularly appreciative of the exposure the gig gave
him as well as the chance to work in the new band:

It's always good for a new band to have a chance to settle down somewhere and play
in one place night after night for a while. . . . And you couldn't wish for a better spot
than Birdland. You were back in the Apple, and you were right on the main stem

[Broadway], right where everything was happening. You couldn't beat that kind of exposure, and the people running Birdland, from Morris Levy himself right down to the washroom attendants, were all for us.[9]

Basie credited Levy with the idea of booking a big band into the otherwise cramped quarters of Birdland: "Morris Levy himself was the one who came up with the idea of having me come into Birdland with a full band. Before that I don't think they had used anything but combos, mostly stand-up groups. . . . Morris was very pleased with the way everything turned out. Business was good, and we got a few favorable write-ups. . . ."[10] The constant exposure and assurance of regular income kept the band's personnel relatively stable and allowed Basie to develop a new approach that would ensure that his band remained popular for decades to come.

Bass player Bill Crow—who was friendly with several members of the Basie band and a regular performer and audience member at Birdland—relates that the band members looked at the gig as both a stable source of income and as a means to stay close to home, as most lived in the greater New York area: "Most of the guys were New Yorkers and the band was just happy to have a spot they could come back and play."[11]

By 1955 the African American press was running regular notices of how the band was thriving at the nightclub, consistently drawing sellout crowds during its regular engagements. The *Pittsburgh Courier* reported: "Not since he came on the scene several swingcades ago has the mighty maestro met with so much approval."[12] The paper followed up after the engagement, noting that Basie's band set a house attendance record during its two-week stay.[13] The Basie band became so closely associated with Birdland that each new engagement was announced with a simple placard: "Basie's back."

One of Basie's more unusual bookings in the mid-fifties probably came through Levy's ties with deejay Alan Freed. Basie's band was hired to appear as a regular on Freed's CBS radio show, *Rock 'n' Roll Dance Party*. However, the engagement was less than successful; the show's sponsors complained to the network that "their teenage sons and daughters didn't like the program whose ratings had been slipping because Basie 'was simply not rock and roll' . . . and he didn't have that beat."[14] Basie was dropped from the broadcast, although he claimed in an interview with *Down Beat* magazine that in fact he "asked to be released": "I knew after the first week that this wouldn't work out. I just don't think we fit into that kind of program. I think it's a real cute show if [Freed] has a band that knows how to play that rock 'n' roll. But we don't fit in any kind of way." Another reason Basie may have been miffed was that Freed had tried to get Basie to use his arrangements rather than play from his normal book. Freed may have hoped to earn royalty payments for the use of his musical settings.

Levy was determined to bring Basie to Roulette. He called on Teddy Reig, who besides being hired to produce jazz acts at Roulette was a longtime close associate of the Basie band, to help him win over Basie:

> When I went over to Roulette in 1957, Basie used to drop in to see how I was doing. Morris Levy noticed how strong the relationship was and kept pestering me to get Basie to sign with Roulette. Basie was with Verve at the time, and Norman Granz was always very good to him. So I told Morris, "He ain't leaving Norman, and I ain't getting in the middle." But Morris wanted him desperately, and he put together a fabulous offer. Basie was very honorable about it, and insisted on giving Norman a chance to meet the offer.... To Norman's credit, he accepted the situation with Basie very graciously. He couldn't match Levy's offer and parted on friendly terms with Basie.[15]

Basie's manager Willard Alexander also played a large role in bringing the bandleader to Roulette. A major powerhouse at the booking agency MCA, Alexander represented many major jazz acts, having taken on Basie in 1936.[16] Although "managed" by Alexander, Granz became an informal manager/career advisor to Basie from the time he signed him to his label in 1952. Alexander had tried to extract as much money as he could when Basie signed his original contract with Granz; now, with the contract up, he pushed for more money, using Levy's offer as a negotiating point. Granz held no bitterness, telling Albert Murray, Basie's biographer, years later: "I think that Willard just felt he wanted to get the best deal he could. Levy was always trying to get Basie, and so Basie went with Roulette. I think that was the only time Basie and I came close to having any differences."[17] In his autobiography, Basie treated very lightly the switch from Granz to Levy, suggesting that Granz had left the business to spend more time in Europe and that Basie's leaving Verve to join Roulette came as a natural result. Granz had been grumbling about the record industry and possibly selling out for years but in fact did not make a permanent move until 1962, when he finally sold Verve. It may be that Basie misremembered the sequence of events.[18]

Basie's move to Roulette aroused considerable rumors in the jazz world that something more sinister must have motivated him to leave Granz. In fact, the occasion of Basie joining Roulette was what inspired Ralph J. Gleason, the jazz critic for the *San Francisco Examiner*, to write his now famous article "Morris Levy, Music Octopus." In it he speculated that Levy's ownership of Birdland, his music publishing holdings, and his new record label gave him unique and perhaps unfair leverage with those musicians who he sought to sign:

> Some weeks ago the jazz world was rather startled to learn that Count Basie had switched recording companies. After some five years' association with Norman Granz, Basie has signed with Roulette.

During Basie's association with Granz he ... had the two biggest hits of his career—in terms of sales, anyway. So it must have been something pretty strong to make him change.

What it actually was no one will ever know, I suppose, but it easily could have been the same reason that made pianists Bud Powell and Phineas Newborn Jr. switch from RCA Victor to Roulette, and singer Jeri Southern switch from Decca to Roulette.

The power that caused all these changes ... is Morris Levy, a lean muscular New Yorker who some five years ago was operator of the hatcheck concession at Birdland, New York's leading jazz night club,[19] and now heads a music empire of staggering proportions. Through direct control or via subsidiaries or affiliated companies, Levy controls Birdland (and can guarantee bands like Basie a three-month booking in New York each year) ... several publishing companies ... and four record companies. ...

Rumor has it that many, many more artists will end up in the Levy combine. ... With the double guarantee of Birdland bookings and concert tours, it's a strong persuader.[20]

Gleason was no friend of Levy's. He hinted that Levy was taking advantage of jazz acts who could ill afford to turn him down, lest they lose a major source of their income. Describing Levy as "lean" and "muscular" was shorthand for his alleged Mob ties, or at the very least indicated that Gleason felt that Levy could easily intimidate performers like Basie into signing with him. Gleason's own bias is clear; he viewed Granz as a friend to jazz musicians who supported them through his Jazz at the Philharmonic tours and recordings, while Levy was pictured as an opportunistic predator.

Gleason further speculated that Levy's stealing Basie from Granz would inspire an "out-and-out war for attractions" between them. This inspired Granz to write to the editor of *Variety* (which had reported on Gleason's article) claiming that the breakup with Basie was amicable:

Without going into details of why Basie left Verve, it was simply that Basie's asking price for us was uneconomic since we already had 12 LP albums of Basie ... Our split was amicable. ...

I don't think there will be any special competition between Roulette and Verve, certainly not any more than exists between any two record companies, and, in fact, possibly much less, because my company is guided by my tastes, and my tastes are radically different from the tastes of the people who run Roulette.[21]

Granz never mentions Levy by name in his response, although one can read more than a slight edge in his response that his tastes are "radically different" from "the people" at Roulette. The subtext is that Granz viewed himself as motivated by his love of jazz, while Roulette was motivated by profit.

George Avakian, a jazz fan and producer for Columbia who was close to Basie and other jazz musicians, also believed there were more sinister forces at work that influenced Basie's move to Roulette. Avakian and others claimed that Basie had run up considerable debts betting on horses and that, in return for bailing him out, Levy was able to get Basie to perform regularly at Birdland for a lower-than-usual fee. Trumpeter Clark Terry was among those who blamed Basie's financial problems on his gambling habit:

> Basie had lost his ass playing horses and his band had broken up [ca. 1950]. He'd blown so much bread on those ponies that he was working his behind out of debt. While doing so, the cats whom he owed said, "You can run your band for salary, and we'll take so much every week of your bread to get you back up to par." He had problems like that all his life. Teddy Reig, who worked as a liaison between Basie and the record man Morris Levy, he had practically taken everything, he almost owned Basie's band.[22]

According to Avakian, Levy used his leverage over Basie to bring the band to Roulette, taking de facto control over all aspects of his career. Avakian bitterly noted: "Levy made money for [Birdland] not the musicians. . . . He was best at his forte; strong-arming artists to work cheap—like Count Basie, who borrowed money from him and ended up working many weeks a year at Birdland for peanuts."[23]

Tony Bennett's recollections support Avakian's belief that Basie was in debt to Levy: "Levy was a classic ruffian who wheeled and dealed any way he could. He was notorious for scamming artists, and unfortunately Bill Basie was a gambler who ended up borrowing a lot of money from Levy. . . . It was rumored that after a while Basie was simply put on the payroll, like the rest of his band, and never got a cent of the royalties from his compositions or recordings."[24]

Basie's gambling habit was hardly a secret in his band or the broader jazz community. Gossip columnist Izzy Rowe ran a short notice teasing Basie after the Yankees lost the World Series to the Brooklyn Dodgers in 1955: "Count (Yankee fan) Basie had Joe Williams singing 'The Game that Got Away' that fateful final series night. The bar next door to Birdland had a huge newspaper headline pasted up, 'Basie Rocks Band to Pay Off Bets.'"[25]

Famed jazz critic Gary Giddins summed up the widespread rumor that Levy had a special hold over Basie when he cryptically commented that "Roulette Records made Basie an offer he could not refuse"[26] to bring him to the label, hinting at the label's tie to the Mob and perhaps Basie's indebtedness to it.

Cover for *The Atomic Count Basie* album, 1957.

Roulette announced the signing of Basie and singer Joe Williams in the September 9, 1957, issue of *Billboard;* the article stated that, wasting no time, "Basie's first LP for Roulette . . . will be cut this week."[27] This first album turned out also to be the most significant album that Basie recorded while at Roulette. Producer Teddy Reig had the idea of pairing the band with a single arranger for this album, Neil Hefti, who had already been writing for the band. The album's packaging was particularly striking. It featured a picture of an atomic bomb blast in a hot red tint, with the letters of the name BASIE in caps above the mushroom cloud, appearing to be flying out from the force of the explosion. At the bottom of the cover, the words "$E=MC^2$—COUNT BASIE ORCHESTRA + NEIL HEFTI ARRANGEMENTS" furthered the metaphor that this album would shake up the jazz world. (On later pressings, the words "The Atomic Mr. Basie" were added to the side of the cover in case the buyer missed the connection.) The presence of new blood in the band—particularly trumpeter Thad Jones and sax player Eddie "Lockjaw" Davis—and Hefti's innovative arrangements made for the most exciting Basie album in years. While Basie usually played a subdued role as a pianist in the band, his piano playing was featured on "The Kid from Red Bank," showcasing his laidback, minimalist style. Perhaps most shocking to longtime fans was that Basie's famous three-note piano tag was only heard at the end of one number on the album ("Splanky"). Many critics consider it the single best album by the later Basie bands and it is often cited as being among the greatest jazz albums of all time.

On the next Basie album, Reig hired arranger Quincy Jones to handle all of the tracks. Jones had been working as an arranger for many jazz bands and vocalists in the fifties. He learned an important lesson early on from Morris Levy about music publishing that would stand him in good stead when he was asked to work on Basie's new Roulette album:

> Morris Levy had found a way to split the publishing rights between him and a partner. . . . [so] in 1954 I got involved with my own publishing company, Silhouette Music. . . .
>
> So then when Morris Levy [said in 1957], "What're we gonna do about the publishing on the second Basie album?" I could say, "We're not gonna do anything about it. I have my own publishing company." Morris came back with "Now you're getting smart, kid." So I figured I was on to something. . . . He said, "Publishing is where it's at. All I want is to own 20,000 copyrights that pay two dollars a quarter from record sales—that's $160,000 a year." It's an incredible business.[28]

Levy clearly understood how pennies from each recording could add up to big money; his 1950-era take of $160,000 would be nearly $3 million in today's money.[29]

Levy continued to hire the best arrangers and give Basie star treatment on the label, even though jazz albums did not bring in as much income as pop singles. The full-scale promotion of Basie culminated in 1961 in celebration of the twenty-fifth anniversary of the band. In a full-page advertisement run throughout October 1961 in *Billboard* magazine—under the headline "There's Plenty of Silver in Count Basie's Silver Anniversary Sales Program"—Roulette announced a major promotion tied to the anniversary. The word SILVER was printed separately in open letters, the background filled with coins, just in case the dealer missed the point that this was to be a major money-making opportunity for both the label and retailers.[30] In a box to the side of the main advertisement was a "personal message" from Morris Levy, expressing the label's "pride" in producing the albums of "one of the greatest living jazz legends of all time." The ad promised "one of the most massive promotional programs ever offered the record industry . . . backed by sensational advertising and publicity." The promised support included "D.J. service," a thinly disguised promise of at the very least special treatment for deejays who favored the new Basie releases. Timed for the anniversary, Roulette ambitiously released three albums: a two-record anniversary set featuring new recordings of classic Basie hits of the thirties and forties; a second accompanying singer Big Joe Williams; and an album of the Basie band with strings.[31] When the ad was repeated later in October, the Levy boxed letter was replaced with a "free goods" offer giving the dealer one Birdland jazz series album for every two purchased and was amended to include the new Count Basie releases, perhaps a sign that this new product was not moving as quickly as Levy had hoped.[32]

Whether it was a combination of poor sales for Basie's later albums or Basie's own growing need to separate himself from Levy, their relationship abruptly ended in mid-1962 when Basie re-signed with Verve Records, now owned by the entertainment company MGM. A short announcement appeared in *Jet* magazine:

> While declaring that "Count Basie has never at any time been on salary to (Morris) Levy or anyone else," Willard Alexander, booking agent for Count Basie for 23 years, confirmed reports that Basie has cut close ties with Roulette Records and Birdland. . . . Alexander said that Basie will now appear at the Jazz Gallery and Basin St., instead of exclusively at Birdland, and that he will probably sign a contract with MGM Records that will include "recording and movie deals."[33]

Alexander's announcement may have been inspired by Dorothy Kilgallen, who reported frequently on Levy and Roulette. Kilgallen had posed this provocative question in her May 13, 1962, column: "Just asking: Is it true that Count Basie has sold his band to Morris Levy and is working on a straight salary from the impresario?"[34] Kilgallen's column appeared in newspapers across the country and must have angered Alexander, who bristled at a public acknowledgment of Basie's alleged indebtedness to Levy.

Basie himself treats the move very lightly in his own autobiography. He said he left Roulette in order to make an album with Frank Sinatra, who had long wanted to record with the band. Sinatra had just founded his own label, Reprise, and Basie was now "at the end of [my] longtime deal with Roulette," so they grabbed the opportunity to work together.[35] The Reprise recordings were made with the permission of MGM/Verve as part of Basie's signing agreement with them. Some believed that only Sinatra—with his alleged Mob ties—had the clout to enable Basie to break from Levy.

Not only was Basie leaving Roulette, he would no longer perform at Birdland. Basie commented, "Birdland had gone through some changes and it really wasn't the same kind of club anymore."[36] On the occasion of his first show in New York outside of Birdland in March 1962, Basie gave an interview to the

New York Post. The reporter noted: "For 11 years, Basie played Birdland . . . and nowhere else in New York. His habits suddenly have changed, but he would rather not talk about it."[37] For whatever reason, Basie was silent as to the reason he broke all ties with Levy.

Basie moved his annual Christmas show in 1962 to Basin Street East, a club operated by Levy's ex-partner Ralph Watkins. As it turns out, Birdland was not long for the world anyway, and jazz soon faded as a drawing card for New York's nightspots. Like many other big bands, Basie would struggle during the sixties to keep his band going in the face of the popularity of rock 'n' roll. Although Basie broke off his relationship with Levy, he continued to work with producer Teddy Reig until Reig's health deteriorated in the late sixties and he retired.

Another early signing to Roulette was Bud Powell. Although he recorded an album in 1957 for the label—which at Levy's suggestion was to be all covers of pieces associated with Charlie Parker—it went unreleased at the time. Powell was mystified as to why Levy would want him to record a saxophonist's tunes, suggesting instead that they cut an album of Art Tatum's material, but Levy thought that would not be sufficiently commercial.[38] Leaving New York to live for several years in Paris, Powell returned to the city in 1964, when he made an album for Roulette shortly before his death.

Levy signed other Birdland favorites to Roulette, pulling many artists from Mercury when their contracts came up for renewal. Some say he offered attractive signing bonuses; others said that he was able to bring artists to Roulette thanks to his association with Birdland; others hint at more nefarious reasons that several artists left Mercury to join Roulette from 1960–62. Mercury's A&R director Jack Tracy thought there was something strange about the number of artists leaving all at once: "A number of the black artists left Mercury and other labels to go to Roulette—why they went, I don't know. But somebody knows something. . . . There were no big screams of protest that I heard from anyone. They just accepted that they went to Roulette because of Morris Levy. All I can say, Roulette all of a sudden assembled a big roster of black artists."[39]

It is possible that there were business links between Irving Green, owner of Mercury, and Levy. The FBI's investigation of Levy's operations in 1964 turned up some tantalizing hints at ties between Mercury and Levy's other operations. Following a discussion of Favorite Music, one of Levy's many publishing holdings, the investigating agent noted: "The record further reflect that both [redacted] and [redacted] are affiliated with Mercury Records." Later in the same report, the investigator notes the existence of a separate company, "Mercury Record Sales Corporation," that shared officers (names redacted) with Roulette.[40]

Whatever their motivations to come to Roulette, Levy did not stint on his jazz artists. Sarah Vaughan had several pop hits at Mercury during the mid-fifties thanks to producers Hugo and Luigi, but generally the sophisticated bop-influenced singer had stronger appeal to the hardcore jazz audience than to pop music fans. When she came to Roulette in 1960, Teddy Reig was put in charge of her sessions. Despite his gruff exterior, Reig understood what was needed to make the sometimes prickly singer—she was nicknamed "Sassy" because of her fiery temperament—most comfortable in the studio. Reig arranged a nightclub-like atmosphere for her 1961 album *After Hours*, according to guitarist Mundell Lowe, who played on the session: "We recorded it in about three and a half hours, from six to nine-thirty, in a single evening. Teddy Reig brought tables, food, and drinks to the studio. . . . Every song was recorded in one or two takes. . . . Reig later told me that it was the only album that she ever made [for Roulette] that made money."[41]

Many feel that Vaughan's work for Roulette was among her best recordings. However, Vaughan and her husband-manager C. B. Atkins were unhappy with the sales of her records. By 1961 they were convinced that "either Roulette . . . is not promoting . . . Vaughan's records in the proper way or else they are not paying her the royalties on all her records which were sold."[42] Vaughan returned to recording for Mercury in 1964.

Dinah Washington also got the star treatment when she left Mercury to join Roulette. Once Mercury heard that she was leaving, they rushed her into the studio to cut new material and also to recut her old hits, to preclude Roulette's doing so. This allowed Mercury to keep releasing material well into her Roulette contract. Nonetheless, Roulette made the most of signing the popular singer. Whereas Mercury had done little promotion for the singer, Roulette took out full-page ads in *Billboard* and other industry journals. Her debut Roulette album *Dinah '62* sold well, as did its first single, "Where Are You?"[43] Levy booked her into Birdland that June for a two-week run to promote her new status as a Roulette artist, although he paid her only $2,500 a week (her normal rate was $3,000). Nadine Cohodas, Washington's biographer, speculates that the deduction was either because as a Roulette artist she was required to give the club a preferential rate, or perhaps because she was appearing in her hometown and thus had no travel expenses.[44]

Washington enjoyed playing at the club and considered Levy to be a friend. In 1956 she described her relationship with Levy to *Tan* magazine: "Morris and I are old friends who know what it's like to be poor. Years ago we used to share our wealth to buy sandwiches, things were that tough. The years have changed all that, but Morris has remained the same, a smiling, generous easygoing guy who doesn't take advantage of people and is never happier than when he's helping."[45]

Washington died at age 39 in 1963 at her home in Chicago of an overdose of sleeping pills. Immediately following her death, her seventh husband, pro football player Dick "Night Train" Lane, came to New York to collect royalties due to her from Levy. Levy at first tried to avoid seeing him, but his staff lawyer advised him that it would be unwise to pretend to be out of the office. While Levy often took a hard line with those who came seeking royalty payments, Lane, a large and muscular man, left the office with a check. It seems that the physically intimidating Levy had met his match.[46] Roulette quickly exploited the singer's back catalog following her death, rushing two memorial albums into stores, as did her previous label, Mercury.

Using the clout of his connection to Birdland, Levy was able to build an impressive roster of jazz artists from Roulette's founding in 1957 through the early 1960s. As he had allowed labels like Atlantic and Blue Note to record live albums at his club, he was not above asking for reciprocal treatment in the form of the loan of their leading performers for special Birdland album releases. In July 1960, Teddy Reig approached Nesuhi Ertegun of Atlantic Records to arrange to record John Coltrane as part of Roulette's Birdland series. Typical of the back-of-the-envelope kind of deals that were made during the period, Ertegun responded on July 28 with a letter outlining the terms that were acceptable to Atlantic:

1. Only one side of an LP could be released, and it would be part of Symphony Sid's "Birdland" series on Roulette.
2. The LP must say "by arrangement with" or "by courtesy of" Atlantic Records.
3. Roulette must allow Atlantic to record one of Roulette's artists at a future date.[47]

On September 8, the recording session took place while John Coltrane was in Los Angeles, and had nothing to do per se with Birdland. Nonetheless, Roulette issued an album of the material, with Coltrane on the first side and trumpet player Lee Morgan on the back, titling it *The Best of Birdland, Volume I*. It is unknown whether Atlantic ever "borrowed" a Roulette artist for a recording of its own.

This album might have been created out of Levy's frustration with trying to record Morgan, who he had signed to Roulette about this time. Morgan had made a major impact in the mid-fifties, first with Dizzy Gillespie's big band and then with Art Blakey's Jazz Messengers. His records for Blue Note and Vee-Jay in the later fifties were fairly successful, as well as his appearances at Birdland, which is probably why Levy signed him. However, Levy had trouble getting him into the studio to record. Morgan's life was chaotic during this period, due to his increased drug use, and—after a mysterious incident outside the Apollo Theater in 1961, in which the trumpeter was attacked and sustained damage to his teeth—he returned to his native Philadelphia for a while and stopped performing altogether. The Birdland album was probably issued as a means of getting something out of his contract until he could be coaxed back into the studio. Apparently this never happened, because in 1963, Alfred Lion—the owner of Blue Note—asked Levy if he would release Morgan from his contract so he could record for him. Levy was said to reply, "You can have him . . . I can't get him in the fucking studio."[48] There was one proviso: Levy insisted on handling the publishing on anything that Morgan recorded for Blue Note. As it turned out, this was a canny move; Morgan's next Blue Note session yielded the major soul-jazz hit, "Sidewinder." (Morgan's biographer speculates that Levy may have used his clout with black deejays to promote the record, because it was Morgan's first major hit.[49]) Levy always managed to profit off his contracts, even if indirectly through his publishing empire.

Another jazz project that came to Levy in the early sixties was Randy Weston's *Uhuru Afrika* album. An unusual piece for the time, it was a multi-part suite that Weston composed with Gigi Gryce, and would require a large studio ensemble to record. Weston was under contract to United Artists, where he had some success, but UA was unwilling to pay for the sessions for what was likely to be a hard-to-sell record. Weston turned to Sarah Vaughan's manager/husband C. B. Atkins, who arranged for him to meet with Morris Levy at Roulette. Levy was willing to pay for the sessions, but the deal nearly broke down because— as usual—Levy wanted to control the publishing for the compositions as well. However, Gigi Gryce was one of the few black musicians of the time who had his own publishing company and refused to give up the rights. Levy threatened the duo by saying, "You guys are never gonna work Birdland again; forget about it." Nonetheless, the sessions were completed and the album released.[50]

Levy would also support fledgling groups through hiring them for an extended run at Birdland while also signing them to Roulette. One person who benefited from this double-barreled support was trumpeter Maynard Ferguson, who beginning in 1956 was able to keep his big band financially afloat thanks to Levy. Initially known as the Birdland Dream Band—because it fulfilled Ferguson's dream of forming a contemporary big band—the group played an extended six-week appearance at the club. The success of that first engagement led Levy in 1958 to make Ferguson an offer he truly could not refuse: in return for signing with Roulette, Levy guaranteed the band sixteen weeks a year at Birdland, a considerable commitment. As Ferguson recalled some decades later, the Birdland gigs provided "enough [money] to keep the band together."[51] Like many other artists, however, Ferguson became disillusioned with the deal when he realized that, despite strong album sales, he was not earning much in royalties from his recordings. When he confronted Levy in 1962 about the missing money, Levy was reported to say, "You're working twelve weeks a year at Birdland, so?" as if the payment for the gigs made up for the lost record revenue.[52] Ferguson embarked on an ambitious recording schedule to finish out his

Birdland, jazz corner of world, gives visiting drummers use of its spectacular GRETSCH green and gold set

"Most of the drummers playing the club use Gretsch drums anyway," so as a convenience to them, Birdland has a Gretsch outfit on hand at all times. "And what an outfit", says Oscar Goodstein, Manager of the famous New York jazz mecca. "The Gretsch green and gold drums alone are worth the price of admission." The Birdland Model drums are finished in Cadillac Green pearl with gold plated metal parts. If you're in New York City, be sure to drop in to Birdland for some of the country's finest sounds. For more details about these drums and other favorite Gretsch models played by consistent top winners in the national drummer popularity polls—write FRED. GRETSCH, Dept. 60 Broadway, Bklyn. 11, N.Y.

Here *(listed alphabetically)* are a few of the star drummers who regularly play Birdland. They all agree "Gretsch Broadkasters—greatest drums I ever owned."

Louie Bellson	Philly Joe Jones
Art Blakey	Mel Lewis
Kenny Clarke	Sonny Payne
Jimmy Cobb	Charlie Persip
Chico Hamilton	Max Roach
Elvin Jones	Art Taylor

Birdland MC Pee Wee Marquette, Birdland Mgr. Oscar Goodstein and Gretsch Broadkasters.

THE FRED. GRETSCH MFG. CO. 60 Broadway, Brooklyn 11, New York

Gretsch Drum Night is celebrated in this advertisement featuring Birdland club manager Oscar Goodstein and announcer Pee Wee Marquette at the drum set.

contract with Roulette, and Levy ended up with enough material to continue to release albums of the band through 1964.

Levy was always looking for new ways to promote Birdland and to use the club as a source of material and artists for Roulette. In 1957 he was approached by Gretsch Drums' artist relation director Phil Grant, who wanted to sponsor a "Gretsch Drum Night" at Birdland to celebrate the firm's seventy-fifth anniversary in 1958. Gretsch would pay for the drummers and Levy would hire the other musicians. Gretsch also issued a special Birdland edition drum set finished in "Cadillac Green" for the occasion.[53] The event was so successful that it was held annually from 1958 through 1963. The April 25, 1960, evening featured drummers Art Blakey, "Philly Joe" Jones, Charli Persip, and Elvin Jones. Levy released two albums on Roulette drawn from that night; on the stereo versions of the records, the liner notes indicated which drummer was playing in each channel. Blakey insisted that the drummers play together on at least one song, "El Sino," exchanging breaks so you could hear the differences in their styles. Elvin Jones noted that this exchange could only have happened at Birdland; at larger theaters, their managers probably would never have allowed them to perform together.[54]

With Roulette taking more of his time, Levy left Birdland more or less on its own to be run by longtime manager Oscar Goodstein. The late fifties saw a steady decline in New York's nightclub business. Part of Birdland's original allure was the combination of characters—from jazz hounds to low-level gangsters to would-be hipsters to movie stars—who frequented it. However, as the fifties wore on, several events at the club showed that the balance between those seeking a taste of the underworld lifestyle and those actively participating in it was tipping increasingly toward the rougher crowd. As the jazz fans aged, they were less likely to spend time late at night in a smoky midtown nightclub; they were increasingly leaving the city at 5 p.m. for their homes in the comfortable and safer suburbs. Meanwhile, stars like Marlon Brando who had been regulars at Birdland were spending most of their time out west making movies rather than hanging out after hours on Broadway.

Another problem for the clubs was that jazz musicians and patrons attracted drug dealers, and the dealers would attract the attention of the police. The owners had a financial stake in keeping drug users and dealers out of their clubs; if drug use was found in a club, its license would be revoked.[55] Nonetheless, many dealers patronized the clubs for just the reason that their customers were easily accessible on the premises. Nightclub historian Robert Sylvester quotes "one bop club operator," who sounds suspiciously like Morris Levy, who described how he approached this problem: "We hired hard guys who knew almost all the pushers. One night we took seven pushers into the office and, one by one, busted open their heads. The word soon got around. The pushers rarely go near a bop club these days."[56] Birdland investor Morris Primack recalled how they had to regularly check the musicians for drugs: "We used to periodically go through everything that they brought into the place. And we'd confiscate a lot of stuff." He noted that the police "knew how to shake you down" when it came to enforcing the drug laws.[57]

While there were ongoing problems that could lead to trouble with the law, it was more often minor scuffles between the musicians—mostly black—and the cops or club's bouncers—mostly white—that could escalate into serious violence at almost any moment. While the club was fully integrated, attitudes of both the police and the club's employees toward black performers and patrons were not always in line with the open-door policy. The patrons were not always conscious of what was happening on the street level, where musicians were often hassled by cops for hanging out between sets. Charles Mingus witnessed a fight between a cop and Max Roach in late 1952 or early 1953, saying that Birdland's bouncers held Roach while the cop hit him.[58] Mingus also related how he saw Irving Levy push musicians down the club's stairs when they were late to begin a set, yelling "Get down the stairs, Nigger."[59]

The year 1959 marked a turning point in the history of the club and for Morris Levy personally. His brother Irving was tending bar early on the morning of January 26 while the Urbie Green Big Band was performing. At around 2:30 a.m., Irving approached a woman who he thought was a prostitute and asked her to leave the club; the man who was with her—who turned out to be her husband—objected to Levy's insinuation that his wife was a hooker. A scuffle ensued and the man pulled a knife, stabbing Levy. Levy staggered from the bar into the tiny service room/kitchen behind it, collapsing and dying there, out of sight of the audience and musicians. The man and woman ran upstairs to leave the club, but were calm enough that they stopped to reclaim their hats from the hatcheck girl on the landing. The club's patrons and other employees were unaware that the stabbing occurred for a while, and even after the club was cleared a news photo showed crowds milling outside smiling as if nothing unusual had occurred that morning.

Green's saxophonist Hal McKusick described the killing:

> I had just started my alto sax solo when we heard a fight start near the bar. We could hear shouting and scuffling but the bandstand lights were in our eyes and we couldn't see what was happening. . . . As the scuffle continued, we went into our finale—"Cherokee"—a real wild arrangement. A woman yelled. Some glasses crashed. We finished the number, left the stand and learned Irving was dead.[60]

The AP ran a sensational report of the event, headlined "Jazz Provides Background for Death."

In the immediate aftermath of the killing, several theories were floated as to why Levy was targeted. The police initially stated that Irving might have been mistaken for his brother, Morris; the two were similarly built, tall and muscular, and both had dark hair. As the local newspaper *Newsday* reported, the police said: "Morris Levy had been [previously] involved in scuffles with patrons. In one instance, he threw out a man who had cut his ear with a knife. In the other, he was flung through a glass doorway by a customer. Police refused to disclose the reasons for the fights."[61]

A later report stated that Levy's ear was cut in a "scuffle" with patrons over the paying of a bill on the night of December 8, 1958.[62] Both New York's

Irving Levy in a World War II–era photograph from his stint in the navy, released by United Press International following his murder at Birdland in 1959.

Amsterdam News and the industry magazine *Variety* reported that "the body of a longshoreman was found lying outside on the street in front of the club" on the same date.[63] The FBI were told by an informant of a stabbing of an unidentified man that occurred at Birdland "some months before Irving Levy was killed." According to this informant: "After his recovery he was summoned to a 'meeting downtown.' At this meeting [the man] was told that this stabbing was to be forgotten and nothing further was to be done. . . . John 'Bathbeach' Oddo and 'Swats' Mulligan [a.k.a. Dominic Ciaffone] were present at this meeting."[64] Oddo was another mobster who the FBI believed was involved with Levy's enterprises, although they were unable to make a solid connection between the two. There was no further coverage in the press or in the FBI files concerning any of these incidents and if they were related to Irving Levy's murder.

Five days after the murder, the *New York Times* identified Irving Levy's slayer as Lee Schlesinger and the woman his wife Terry. Schlesinger was a small-time thief and his wife was convicted of being a prostitute, among other offenses,[65] so Irving Levy's belief that they were working Birdland was not totally unreasonable. Schlesinger had an extensive record, with six arrests for "weapons violation, forgery, attempted robbery and grand larceny," according to the *Times*. His most recent brush with the law occurred the previous September when he shot a tavern manager named Dominick Manfro in Yonkers, New York. Manfro had been a lightweight boxer before entering the bar business. He was running away from Schlesinger after the two had dined together on the evening of September

12 when Schlesinger shot him. Miraculously, Manfro survived; Schlesinger was charged with "felonious assault and violation of the Sullivan Law" (carrying an unlicensed concealed weapon) and was out on bail when he stabbed Levy.[66]

The rumor in the jazz world was that Schlesinger was a Mob hitman who had mistakenly killed Irving Levy thinking that he was Morris. This rumor gained some credence at least among rival gang leaders; in a secretly recorded conversation made in 1984, Joe "Joe Bana" Buonanno, a Gambino crime boss,[67] repeated the story that the hitman mistook Irving for his brother. According to Buonanno, Levy "tried to sever his relationship with the Genovese LCN Family" following Irving's murder, but "that Levy could never succeed in doing so 'without the okay of who he works for.'"[68] However, Buonanno also said that Morris Levy fled to Israel after the incident, which does not appear to be the case, so it is unclear how reliable his testimony is.[69]

Gossip columnist Earl Wilson helped spread the rumor that Irving's death was a Mob hit, speculating in his column that, "Despite the hunt for local guys and gals in the Birdland murder, some detectives insist that ... Zachariah [Irving] Levy was slain by out-of-town professional killers who have now touched off a bloody war among the people who live and live it up after dark. The war could extend to the middle west, say some informants."[70] Wilson gives no information on who his "informants" were, and his other notices about the Birdland murder showed he was hardly sympathetic to the club or its patrons. In his January 30, 1959, column, just three days after the murder, he ran this brief sarcastic note: "B-way Crack: The Birdland murder was perpetuated by a music-lover!'"

Certainly, Schlesinger's background and previous convictions give credence to the possibility that he was a professional hitman. The September incident with bar owner Manfro is especially curious. The Mob was active in the ownership and operation of many bars and clubs throughout the New York area, as well as the careers of many small-time boxers, so it is not much of a stretch to suppose that Manfro was fronting for the Mob as the "owner" of the Yonkers bar when he was shot. Schlesinger may have offered to take him to dinner as a ruse to set him up for the shooting.

In the Levy case, Schlesinger claimed that he was acting in self-defense after Irving confronted him and his wife. It is worth noting that the clubs were very careful at this time to keep prostitutes off the premises. They could easily be subject to extra police scrutiny and possibly even lose their operating licenses if they were suspected of being fronts for prostitution. As a result, any unaccompanied woman was likely to be a subject of suspicion; jazz musician Bill Crow notes that single women were prohibited from sitting at the bar at many jazz clubs and even musician's wives were barred from attending the clubs alone.[71] If Schlesinger's wife was indeed alone when Irving first saw her in the early hours of the morning of the 26th, it would not have been unusual for him to insist that she leave.

Schlesinger was convicted of second-degree murder and sentenced to life in prison in December 1959.[72] The motivation for the slaying was not investigated in any depth, nor was any mention made at the trial that Schlesinger had intended to kill Morris Levy. Decades later, Levy said that Irving was "killed by a pimp in revenge for ejecting a hooker from the club."[73] Tommy James claims that Levy took personal vengeance on Schlesinger, telling him: "I fucking took a knife and stuck it in his fucking stomach and twisted it . . . until his guts fell out."[74] However, there's no evidence that Levy personally "took care" of Schlesinger; it is most likely that this colorful description was meant to put the fear of God into James, who was often fighting with Levy over unpaid royalties. In an interview conducted shortly before he died, Levy claimed he could not even remember the name of the man who killed his brother.[75]

Nonetheless, Irving's murder must have had an impact on Morris personally. One reporter noted—not surprisingly—that Morris was "shaken and shocked and almost unable to follow a reporter's questions" and was "glassy eyed" on the day of Irving's funeral.[76] Dorothy Kilgallen reported at the end of January that Morris "has been under doctor's care ever since the funeral of his murdered brother Irving."[77] She followed up in mid-February, noting that Levy had been "little help to the police. He claims he can't identify the suspect currently under arrest and has no idea why the alleged killer would have slain Irving."[78] Finally, she reported on February 23 that Levy had left New York to "get away from the Broadway scene" for a visit to Miami. (Miami would become a second base of operations for Levy in the early sixties.) If Irving's murder was in fact a botched Mob hit, Levy may have left the city waiting for things to cool down. As late as that March, Kilgallen was reporting that her sources were "predicting that Morris will unload some of the companies that made him head of Broadway's most colorful music empire" in the aftermath of the shooting.[79] In fact, Levy was looking for new investors to help keep Roulette and his other holdings afloat, but had no intention of giving up most of his extensive holdings.

The shooting attracted widespread attention in the New York City tabloids, and was quickly picked up by major news organizations across the country. Lurid headlines associating jazz with murder did little to burnish the image of the music, its fans, or Birdland. UPI described Levy's killer as "a hopped-up jazz enthusiast," a description that many papers incorporated into their headlines.[80] While the hint of danger that was always present at the club was attractive to its mostly white, middle-class patrons, actual murder was not something that clubgoers hoped to see. Along with the changing demographics in the city, this spelled the beginning of the end for clubs like Birdland.

Strangely, Birdland remained open on the Monday after the killing; Herbie Mann performed on what was traditionally an open jam session night. A *Newsday* reporter interviewed both patrons and musicians performing on that night,

Miles Davis after his beating while standing outside of Birdland with one of the arresting police-men. Courtesy Getty Images.

and most seemed unmoved by reports of the murder. A musician told him that the murder "perhaps makes it a little hard to swing tonight, but that would be deep in the subconscious. It's not like it was a close friend or relative."[81] The reporter concluded his report with this film noir touch: "In this sanctuary, a murder turns no heads. It is slick and hard, it is the city, it is Birdland."[82]

A different reporter for the *Amsterdam News* tried to get employees to talk to him but was given the cold shoulder: "'What stabbing?' was the stock answer to any query. 'Nothing happened here last night.'"[83] This reporter speculated that the State Liquor Authority or the police might be inspired by the killing to investigate the club and perhaps pull its license, not to mention the impact on the club's patrons, who might be more wary of attending the club. The reporter ended his article on an ominous note as well: "The Jazz Corner of the World could well become the Siberia of the Jazz world in the future."[84] Perhaps in response to these articles, the club closed on Tuesday and Wednesday nights.

The shooting brought increased scrutiny to the club and its patrons by the New York City police. Any club with a non-segregated policy that brought black and white audience members together was bound to attract some attention, as blacks were not regulars in the Broadway district. A black man hanging out with a white woman on the street would certainly be noticed by the cops—which is exactly what happened one night later in 1959 to trumpeter Miles Davis.

In August 1959, Davis was performing at Birdland where he had often appeared during the fifties. During a break, he went upstairs to the street and mingled with some fans, including several white women. A beat cop tried to break up the crowd, ordering them to clear the sidewalk. At the time, the cops had a broad mandate to keep clear commercial thoroughfares like Broadway. When Davis responded that he was appearing at the club and merely getting some fresh air, a scuffle broke out, and one of the cops struck Davis in the head with a billy club. Davis suffered a mild concussion along with bruises and cuts.[85] As Davis recalled: "A crowd had gathered all of a sudden from out of nowhere, and this white detective runs in and BAM! Hits me on the head. I never saw him coming. Blood was running down the khaki suit I had on."[86] (Always a sharp dresser, Davis was particularly annoyed that his fancy suit was covered with blood.) Davis was arrested and held overnight on $1,000 bail for "disorderly conduct and simple assault."[87] Dorothy Kilgallen reported the incident a day after it occurred, slamming the police for brutality, which Davis dryly noted in his autobiography "was somewhat helpful to my cause."[88]

Being charged by the police with a felony could seriously damage a jazz performer's career, because it could lead to the suspension of his cabaret card. Without a card, a musician could not legally be employed by a nightclub in New York. The clubs often worked in collusion with the police to "clear up" these matters, but performers as varied as Billie Holiday and Thelonious Monk suffered severe damage to their ability to support themselves due to the hassle of losing their cards. Davis was using a provisional card at the time, "because of a record of previous arrests—a 1954 Los Angeles charge of suspicion of violation of narcotics laws and a 1955 Rikers Island sentence on a warrant charging nonsupport."[89] Nonetheless, he was able to return to performing at Birdland within weeks of the incident in mid-September, according to New York's *Amsterdam News*: "because his attorneys . . . were able to reduce charges lodged against him. . . . if a felony had been committed, a narcotics charge, or any charge involving morals . . . he would not have been able to return so soon to Birdland . . ."[90]

It took several months for the incident to be investigated by a Special Sessions Court, which concluded that the officer "may well have been guilty of misguided zeal and not a deliberate violation of law, in placing the defendant under arrest for disorderly conduct, a charge later dismissed in the Magistrate's Court."[91] How the Court could characterize a blow to the head hard enough to require stitches as "misguided zeal" is a mystery. The white judges undoubtedly reflected the general community attitude that jazz players were ne'er-do-wells and any policeman confronted by one like Davis who refused a simple order to clear the sidewalk would be justified in detaining him. Davis was cleared of both the disorderly conduct and felonious assault charges brought against him. While his lawyer threatened to sue the city for damages, George Hoefer wrote in *Down Beat* that Davis preferred to go no further: "Miles does not wish to push the City too far, feeling that even though he might win his damage suit, he would then become a target for the police who would be out to nail him for any charge they could find or drum-up . . ."[92]

Besides the musicians, the club owners were often harassed by police. Aurin Primack remembers sitting with his father in Birdland's office when several "big guys" from the NYPD's 54th Precinct came in to pick up their monthly envelope of cash—a none-too-subtle payoff that guaranteed that the club and its patrons would not be hassled too much by the cops.[93] There were myriad rules under which the clubs operated, some of which were fairly arcane; a fairly simple trick pulled by undercover policemen was to order a drink at one minute past midnight on a Saturday night when the "blue laws" went into effect. Depending on how closely the bartender was watching the clock, a fine could be levied for serving alcohol after hours. For this reason, when musicians hung out backstage after hours, drinks were given out free of charge rather than risk a problem with the licensing board.[94]

In May 1960, another incident underscored the growing tension between blacks and whites that was infecting the usually racially harmonious atmosphere at Birdland. The Ghanaian ambassador to the UN stopped by the club and was invited to demonstrate some traditional drumming on stage. On this particular evening, Art Blakey was appearing with his Jazz Messengers as well as Buddy Rich and his group. Blakey took offense when Rich joined the Ghanaian on stage to play with him. Although "no blows fell . . . tempers were short, and words were sharp."[95] An AP report stated that Blakey was angry because he was not asked to pose for a PR photo with the Ghanaian drummer, as Rich was.[96] The fact that Rich was a white swing-era drummer who was known for his onstage theatricalism may have annoyed Blakey, who felt he better represented the African heritage in his music.

Another incident with the police occurred in 1962 when the African-born drummer Babatunde Olatunji was appearing at Birdland. According to a report in the *Pittsburgh Courier*:

> During a flash crackdown on narcotics in the downtown area, Olatunji was roughed up by police as he was leaving Birdland, where he was starred [*sic*] at the time. . . .
> Attempts were made to squelch the incident after Olatunji's identity was revealed but it was too late. The drummer did not press the case but gained a new understanding of race relations in America although he had been in the country over ten years.[97]

Olatunji was attacked close to the spot where Miles Davis had his run-in with the police just a few years earlier.

The combination of the demands of running a major record label along with the murder of his brother led Levy to withdraw from day-to-day involvement with Birdland. For a period from about 1960–61, Goodstein also ceased working at the club and old partner Morris Primack—who had been working for Levy at his other clubs the Embers and the Roundtable—was brought back in to run it. Primack claimed that neither Levy nor Goodstein "could be known as" operators of the club, intimating that they had alienated many of the musicians who performed at the club.[98] He said that Levy brought in another "partner" to revive the club. Primack explained that Birdland was suffering from a common problem facing nightclubs, requiring a quick infusion of cash:

> Almost every business on Broadway had to collect a 10 percent tax. And in order to stay open . . . most of the [club owners] used that money up [rather than paying the tax]. So the nightclubs would owe a million dollars or half-million dollars . . . [so] they'd make deals with the IRS. Like if you owed say a hundred thousand dollars and if you would pay $50,000 or $40,000 immediately, they [would] wipe out [your tax debt] and you'd start afresh. When this other fellow came in and took over, Birdland was $10,000 behind. And this other fellow had paid this to keep Birdland open, but he wouldn't take it unless I ran the place.[99]

Goodstein returned to operating the club by late 1962, when Primack left in disgust. It was becoming impossible to book the kind of acts that made Birdland famous, plus the atmosphere in the club was changing, said Primack: "You couldn't get anybody to appear. Any decent musician . . .there was so many tours, and so many concerts going on, that people we were paying $1000 to . . . were making $10,000, $25,000 in a night. . . ."[100]

In June 1964, Goodstein filed for bankruptcy as a means of trying to salvage the business, with over $100,000 owed to creditors, about a quarter of which was owed to Goodstein himself.[101] In October 1964, the *Pittsburgh Courier* reported that Johnny Gray was named Birdland's new manager, the first African American to manage a Broadway nightclub. Gray had worked as a general factotum for singer Sarah Vaughan through the fifties. The *Courier* bragged that he worked his way up at Birdland from his original position taking tickets.[102] However, Gray's run as manager was short-lived; by early 1965 the club had shut its doors.

6

Wise Guys with a Peppermint Twist: 1957–1961

Roulette was a small subsidiary of a vast international mega-conglomerate . . . whose board of directors and shareholders met at clam bars in Brooklyn, Las Vegas, Naples, and Palermo
—Bob Thiele

After the excitement of the first years and the launching of the label, Roulette's management faced the same challenges that many small independent labels encountered. Levy dreamed of creating another RCA, launching ambitious recording programs in R&B, pop, and jazz initially and quickly adding classical, soundtracks, and adult pop music by the end of the fifties. He moved quickly from producing singles to full-scale album production, with an ambitious release schedule. Roulette was seemingly able to release more material more quickly than many of its smaller rivals, but ultimately the same challenges would arise that plagued all independents: the need to produce a large amount of inventory well in advance of being paid by customers; the challenge of fighting pirated copies and illegal sales; and holding on to key talent, including staff producers and hit recording artists. It did not help that Roulette's creative staff—the producers who handled the artists—quickly became aware that the company's offices were being used for more than merely running a record label.

While Levy had an appreciation for jazz, he did not possess the ear for R&B or teen pop that George Goldner did. His first hires to cover these markets, the producers Hugo and Luigi, were themselves oriented more toward mainstream pop. Whether under the instruction of Levy or because of their own musical taste, their productions for artists like Frankie Lymon sanitized the music to such an extent that it lost its appeal to teenage listeners while failing to "cross over" into the adult market. While Levy had substantial contacts through Birdland in the jazz world, he did not have similar ties to the unknown teens who were developing doowop and R&B out in New York's streets.

Although Hugo and Luigi were not attuned to the teen market, they were talented producers capable of handling a range of artists. So it came as a blow to Roulette when at the end of its first year of operations, the duo was snatched away by major label RCA. Their immediate replacement, Joe Reisman, came from RCA's A&R department; it may be that Levy insisted on this talent swap in a behind-the-scenes deal with RCA. The fact that Levy did not block their departure—in fact seemingly encouraged it—also would indicate that he had some motivation to let them go.

Initially Luigi suggested to RCA's general manager, George Marek, that he purchase the label along with hiring the producers: "I said, 'Why don't you buy Roulette; then we'll come. We'll make money, all the guys will make money there, and everybody will be happy. We would leave, [and] we'll bring you the tapes of Jimmie Rodgers, everything that we have. It's an asset, and we will be running it.'"[1] While Marek was interested, he ultimately told the duo that RCA's lawyers rejected the idea because they feared the government would block any merger because it would create a monopoly in the market. It may be that RCA was still smarting from its earlier deal with Levy, or was suspicious of his alleged Mob ties.

Meanwhile, Levy had renegotiated Hugo and Luigi's original percentage of ownership in Roulette, noting that since he had acquired Goldner's labels and also established a separate distribution business, they would do better having 10 percent of the bigger operation rather than 50 percent of Roulette alone. As Luigi later lamented, "It was not that great an idea as time went by."[2] When the duo left Roulette, Levy repaid them for their initial investment of $1,000. It either did not occur to Hugo and Luigi that they should have shared in some of the increase in value that their share was now worth based on the hits that they produced while working for the label or they were so grateful that Levy released them from their obligation to Roulette that they did not complain. In any case, they left to work their magic at RCA, and Levy had to find a replacement fast if he wanted to continue to have pop hits.

Luigi never saw any evidence of Mob involvement at Roulette, and indeed in the beginning there may have been little evidence of any outside interference with the label's operations. Countering the common rumor, Luigi noted: "Roulette was struggling; we struggled. I know what we made and what we didn't make. And after we left, Roulette was struggling and didn't make it as a company, really. If [Levy] had been connected with the mob, they would have supplied him with all the money he needed, and they would have made it . . . If we had to struggle here and you're connected, what's going on?"[3]

While Hugo and Luigi may have been blissfully ignorant of any Mob presence at Roulette in its initial year of operation, as the hits started to dry up and the label continued to need cash to continue operating, the presence of less savory types became more obvious on a day-to-day basis to the legitimate staff working at the label.

In a move to bring in additional capital to the label, Levy took initial steps to take the company public in September 1959. Levy petitioned the Securities and Exchange Commission to issue 330,000 shares at $3.50 per share to raise money for construction of a recording studio, new office space, and "working capital."[4] He planned to move the label from the rather seedy neighborhood of 10th Avenue—where most independent labels were located at the time—to lavish new offices on Broadway, again to emphasize that Roulette was a major player in the business. The cost would be half a million dollars, a hefty sum. Many in the industry felt that Levy was taking on a huge liability, and in fact it turned out to be so, particularly after the SEC turned down Levy's request. This left Levy in a bind, according to gossip columnist Izzy Rowe:

> [There has been] a report that Roulette Records' future is in jeopardy. Denied the right to float a big stock issue, Morris Levy ... has a $1,000,000 building[5] on hand on Broadway for the company, which may never get open, but will have to be paid for. A heck of a nice guy, he made quite a splash in the music and recording business, but it would seem his dreams ran away with his cash and fogged his business logic.[6]

The company somehow came up with the cash and eventually moved into four floors of offices on Broadway and 50th Street, which would be the home for all of Levy's enterprises through the rest of his career. The new building was capped with a neon sign that read "Roulette Records—Home of the Stars," with its hit makers' names emblazoned in lights.[7]

As early as late 1957, Levy and his partners were interested in bringing in fresh capital to the label—if not to sell it outright. To pump up interest, Levy probably planted items with Dorothy Kilgallen. In March 1958, she reported that he had turned down an offer of "two and a half million dollars ... by 20th Century Fox" for Roulette, adding: "His taking price is $3,000,000, and he seems to think he'll get it."[8] This seems highly unlikely; Levy may have merely been trying to impress his peers with his business acumen. *Billboard* added that Levy was also talking with Columbia Pictures about a possible sale of his labels.[9] At the time, the major studios were looking to invest in record labels to enter into the pop music market. ABC-Paramount had purchased Dot Records from independent owner Randy Wood, known for its hits with Pat Boone, and Warner Brothers was also looking to either purchase or start its own label. Kilgallen also reported that Frank Sinatra looked into the possibility of buying Roulette in September 1960 (at the time, Sinatra also spoke with Norman Granz about possibly purchasing Verve). However, within a week following Kilgallen's announcement, the deal fell through.[10]

One new partner did enter the picture at this time who had great impact on the Roulette story: Dominic Ciaffone purchased 5 percent of Roulette Records on April 22, 1958.[11] The following January, Ciaffone was hired as a part-time employee at Roulette, supposedly to oversee relations with rack jobbers who sold Roulette product to smaller record shops.[12] Ciaffone, a.k.a. Swats Mulligan, was a New York mobster with a long history in the Genovese gang. In addition to investing in and setting up an office at Roulette, he served as business manager for the New York Radio Union Local 1010 of the International Brotherhood of Electrical Workers, overseeing the union's contracts with radio and TV stations.[13] Ciaffone would prove to be a poisonous presence at the label. His involvement with Roulette attracted the attention of the IRS, as well as local New York City and FBI investigators who were curious as to the relationship between the Mob, unions, and record labels.

Roulette's problems with the government began in the late fifties and early sixties during the so-called payola scandals. While the practice of the "$20 handshake" was well-known in the record world, by the late fifties the general perception was that the entire practice of paying for play was getting out of hand. At first, the independent labels viewed payola as a means of leveling the playing field, because they could not compete with the marketing clout of the major labels; but as deejays became increasingly greedy, it became clear that they would continue to up the ante for their services.

Deejay Alan Freed was particularly egregious in this practice. He famously insisted that Atlantic Records pay for a swimming pool at his new suburban home, but then snubbed the label when it was suggested that he ought to favor their discs in return for this lavish gift. Reportedly, Atlantic chief Ahmet Ertegun asked Morris Levy to intercede; Levy supposedly said to Freed, "Why are you doing this to Ahmet and Jerry [Wexler, Ertegun's partner at Atlantic]? They're nice guys." Freed responded, "I just have to prove to them that they don't own me because they bought me a pool." Levy thought Freed's cavalier attitude was foolish at best. In addition, Freed was milking Atlantic out of $600 a month and giving little in return. When times got tough for the label, Wexler begged the deejay to keep playing their records: "One day I met [Freed] and said, 'We can't keep up the payments—Can you carry us for a while?' He said, 'Gee, I'd love to—but it would be taking bread out of my children's mouth.'"[14]

The government was finally goaded into action following the annual meeting of deejays in Miami in May 1959. The convention was outlandish even by music industry standards, with the *Miami Herald* describing it as an orgy of "Booze, Bribes, and Broads." Roulette threw a lavish all-night barbecue at the event, with music provided by none other than Count Basie. (Levy worked Basie hard; after playing the all-night gig, Basie had to rush back to New York to fulfill an engagement the following night at Birdland.[15]) Roulette was said to have spent $15,000 on the all-night barbecue alone, half of which was used to purchase 2,000 bottles of bourbon.[16] When asked about the high cost of the Roulette party, the hotel's conventions manager quipped to Representative Oren Harris, who chaired the House's investigation into the recording industry in early 1960, that "bourbon costs a little more than eggs."[17] In all about 2,700 deejays attended the convention, and the total cost estimates ranged from $200,000 to $600,000. One trade journal quipped that the attendees "sunned, swam, swizzle-sticked . . . their way through" the meeting.[18]

Besides throwing the all-night barbecue, Roulette rented a suite where deejays could "gamble" on a spinning roulette wheel that magically always seemed to stop on a winning number. Then-deejay Joe Smith (later president of Elektra Records) was surprised by his continuing good luck. "I was a little naïve," he recalled. "I was betting blackjack and losing but they kept paying me. I said, 'But I lost—why are you giving me this stuff?'"[19] Levy was said to have bused in prostitutes from New York with instructions to "talk up" the latest Roulette releases while keeping the deejays company. Unconcerned about the growing scandal, Levy tried to cash in on all of the payola talk, rush releasing a single titled "He Wasn't on the Air Today (Where's My Favorite Disc Jockey?)."[20]

The event inspired lurid reports beyond Miami. Some commentators defended the general practice of payola. Popular columnist Earl Wilson said New York's deejays "are the 'cleanest' in the country. They are mostly well-paid and ethical," further stating that "this deal"—i.e., the practice of payola—was "generally considered a 'good promotion'" by both deejays and the record labels.[21] Small-town editorialists were less sanguine about the incident. Writing in the *Berkshire* (Massachusetts) *Eagle*, George G. Connelly, a professor at Williams College and a local Democratic Party official, fumed:

> Two thousand disc jockeys reveled all night in Miami at a Count Basie bacchanalia, handing the bill of $19,158 to Roulette Records of New York. And this was only the third largest chit picked up by a company that you and I buy records from. At the Count Basie bust, Gov. Frank G. Clement of Kentucky, erstwhile keynoter for the Democrats, addressed the mob though he declined to say how much he got out of the show. What I can't understand is how a Kentuckian, even for payola, could consent to consort socially with Basie.[22]

Connelly's inflammatory language and thinly veiled racism is typical of most press reaction to the event.

The bad PR led to several payola investigations. Most of the New York–based independent labels were targeted, including Atlantic and Roulette. In investigating Freed, New York District Attorney Joseph Stone discovered that Levy held a loan made to Freed that was secured by Freed's Connecticut home. The loan of $8,318 was originally made in August 1957 by Jerry Blaine of Cosnat distributors, a major distributor of independent labels, and subsequently "transferred" to Roulette Records. Mysteriously, Blaine claimed to have returned Freed's payments, including interest, to the deejay after passing the loan on to Roulette. "I don't have any idea what happened to the mortgage after that," he told the New York DA, although he insisted the loan was "strictly a business proposition." Levy's attorney said the loan transfer was "a legal transaction" that was properly recorded by the authorities, further stating to a UPI reporter, in a bit of circular reasoning: "If it was deemed a transaction that was not legal, it would not have been so recorded."[23]

Stone investigated Roulette's books and Levy complained that he "harassed the shit out of me" giving him "plenty of grief" for his involvement with Freed.[24] Stone discovered an additional loan of $10,000 as a third mortgage on Freed's house held by Levy, as well as a separate $10,000 payment made in February 1958 that Levy said was given to Freed to help him pay his taxes. The payment was listed first as a "promotion" fee; when Freed angered Levy it was changed on Roulette's books to a "loan," but subsequently changed back to a "promotion" fee:[25]

> It was no big deal. And at the end of the year, I said to my comptroller, "Take that off the books, we're never going to get it back anyway." And then Alan and I had an argument in February. So I said to my comptroller, "Put it back on the books, fuck him. I'm going to make him pay it." Then about four months later, I said, "Ah, take it off, fuck him." And it's really on the general ledger like that, about five times, on and off and on and off.[26]

In typical Levy style, he relates how he stood up to DA Stone, undoubtedly exaggerating his ability to match wits with his interrogator:

> So he's questioning me. And I says no, it's not payola. I got mad. I got glad. I got mad. I got glad. He says no, it's because he played your record. I said, Not so. He played my records anyway . . . So he said, You're excused. And I says to him, I got something to say. He said, *You're excused.* So one of the jurors said, Let him talk. So what is it? I said, You know, we just had a laugh here about $20,000—which was a lot of money then—and we just had some fun. But you didn't take into account that Alan and I are partners in the rock and roll shows, and we make $250,000 a year each on that. So me giving him twenty or him giving me twenty is really no big deal. Well, he got so mad he said *You . . . can . . . leave . . . now.*[27]

Like the other record executives who testified, the DA gave Levy immunity in return for his testimony, so it was easy for Levy to be cocky. And Levy did have a point that a $20,000 loan was "small potatoes" in relation to the amount of money that he and Freed were regularly dealing with in their many business partnerships.

Besides New York's DA, the House began its own payola hearings, again focusing on Freed. Supposedly, when confronted with the "bribes" he paid to

Freed and being told that he might be compelled to appear before Congress, Levy replied: "[I'd like to know the] date [of] those hearings, because I want to be there." Levy further claimed: "I did a lot of swearing and 'fucking' and 'motherfucking.' I think I persuaded the guy I was completely crazy, a real nut, because I never heard from them [again]. A week before the hearings I called him and said, 'Do you want me to attend?' He said, 'no, no—please no!' So I was never called to the payola hearings."[28]

Levy's bravado performance smells of self-aggrandizement; the possibility of appearing before a Congressional committee must have been daunting, and few label owners looked forward to the ordeal. In this account, undoubtedly Levy was trying to pump up his image as a macho, streetwise recordman.

The Federal Trade Commission (FTC) was also active in pursuing alleged payola violations and brought charges against many of the New York labels, including Roulette. Levy was not about to take these charges lying down, however. In June 1961, he audaciously sent out a letter to every pop deejay and program director in the country inviting them to sign an affidavit that they had never received any payment from Roulette in exchange for playing its records. In this letter, Levy takes the tone of an aggrieved businessman who is simply trying to set the record straight. He addresses the deejays:

> The several investigations and proceedings ... into the historical and traditional conduct and practices of our industry have unfortunately resulted in the casting of odious inferences and unjust accusations on disk jockeys, distributors and record manufacturers alike.
>
> We at Roulette Records are interested in clearing the air and removing the cloud cast upon the integrity of our industry. To achieve our objective we are gathering information in support of our position that the practices and procedures of the recorded music business are fair and free of deception.[29]

With his letter, Levy enclosed "a list of several hundred [Roulette] disks, both LPs and singles," asking the deejays to tick off any item that they had played on the air, indicating the number of times each record was played. Then, they were requested to sign a statement indicating that Roulette had not paid them "monetary or other consideration for playing these records."[30] Levy was obviously trying to build up a file he could use in defense of the charges that might be brought against Roulette by the various payola inquiries. He was also incidentally gathering information from deejays about the records they played, and none too subtly threatening anyone who refused to help Roulette defend itself in the scandal.

All of the hoopla over payola eventually petered out with the various committees and investigations coming to an end without much real action being taken. As just one example, the FTC dropped its investigation of Roulette and other labels on payola charges, stating that "specific statutes have been enacted by Congress which afford adequate protection to the public against the[se] practices . . ." Not surprisingly, the FTC added "The motion is not opposed by respondents," who obviously were let off the hook by the decision.[31] Similar language was used in dropping charges against other labels.

While Levy successfully fought off these investigations, Freed—who had alienated most of his friends in the industry—became the scapegoat for the payola practice. Undoubtedly, many of the independents were pleased by this outcome, as it meant that one of the most egregious practitioners of payola would no longer demand outrageous payments in return for airplay. Levy still wanted to help Freed, despite the ups and downs in their relationship, and so called on old friend and record distributor Henry Stone to help land the deejay a job in Miami, where Stone had many connections with local radio.[32] As late as 1964, a year before his death, a distressed and broke Freed was writing Levy begging him for money, even offering "my share of my song copy rights . . . or whatever else arrangements you wish to make" in return for a cash advance.[33]

Despite all of these distractions, Levy still had a record label to run and needed to fill the void that Hugo and Luigi's departure left in Roulette's pop production department. To keep Roulette competitive, Levy aggressively pursued a number of producers who had experience in the R&B and pop worlds. First, he brought over from RCA orchestra leader/arranger Joe Reisman in early 1959, who had previously been RCA's musical A&R director.[34] Like Hugo and Luigi, Reisman specialized as a producer and performer in mainstream pop, working with artists like Perry Como, and arranging such saccharine hits as "(How Much Is That) Doggie in the Window" for Patti Page. Clearly, Levy would need other talent to help him continue to win hits in the growing teen/R&B markets.

Levy's first attempt to beef up his pop staff came in May 1959 when *Billboard* announced that Nat Tarnopol was joining Roulette.[35] Tarnopol was a notorious producer who guided the career of hit singer Jackie Wilson along with other R&B acts as head of A&R at Decca's Brunswick subsidiary. Wilson's manager was none other than Tommy Vastola. According to *Billboard*, Tarnopol was going to continue recording Wilson at Brunswick while coming to Roulette both to work with established artists, including Frankie Lymon, the Techniques, and Pearl Bailey, and to bring new talent to the label. What came of this arrangement—if indeed it came to fruition—is unknown. There is no evidence that Tarnopol actually produced any recordings for Roulette.

Another successful jazz and pop producer who Levy convinced to come to Roulette was Bob Thiele. Thiele had begun his career as a teenager running his own jazz label, and had achieved great success heading A&R at Coral, a budget division of major label Decca, where he produced, among others, Buddy Holly and Teresa Brewer (who also became his wife). After briefly working for Dot Records, Thiele partnered with talk show host Steve Allen, a jazz fan himself, to start an independent label called Hanover-Signature; one of their first productions was of poet Jack Kerouac reading with a jazz accompaniment. In July 1960, *Variety* announced that Roulette was making a $25,000 loan to the smaller label, with the option to purchase up to 55 percent of the label over the next five years. Thiele was to join Levy in Roulette's offices, but would continue to operate his label separately.[36] By spring 1961, however, Hanover-Signature was no more and Thiele was working full-time in A&R for Roulette.[37]

In his memoirs, Thiele has nothing but positive things to say about Levy and the opportunities he was given at Roulette. He was particularly pleased that Levy had the clout to bring about his dream of producing an album of Duke Ellington and Louis Armstrong performing together. As both were signed to different labels and had different management, Thiele's previous attempts to unite them on disc had been unsuccessful. Levy was the only one who could motivate all the parties to make a deal: "Joe Glazer [the well-known manager of many jazz acts], on behalf of Armstrong, and Duke, both of whom possessed the hardest noses in the music business, unhesitatingly accepted a Levy handshake instead of a contract to proceed with the recording."[38] Levy's word was gold—or at least his connections so strong that he could convince normally tough negotiators to accept his terms.

Thiele also—somewhat unwittingly—brought another hit to Levy thanks to Hanover's sales and promotion manager, Morris I. Diamond. In 1961 Diamond was hanging out at the Bronx record store of Lou Chiccetti, and met many of the fledgling groups that were regular customers there. The duo were particularly impressed by a group called the Tremonts, but were unable to interest any label in taking a chance on them. So, they took them into the studio to record a single, which included a song called "Barbara Ann." Diamond brought it to Thiele, who recommended they license it to Levy. At first, Diamond was happy with the deal, knowing that Levy was a great promoter and could get the record airplay. Levy only paid a paltry $500 advance for the record, which Diamond said just barely covered the cost of making it. When the record took off, Levy offered another $500 advance to the duo to market the record to labels outside of the United States, including the required publishing rights, which they granted him.

Typical of Levy's dealings with rights holders, neither Diamond nor Chiccetti were able to get a statement accounting for all the sales of the song. Instead, Diamond received a call from Levy's lawyer four months after the rights deal was made, who gave him a check for $5,000 but no statement to support the payment. When asked for a statement, Levy's lawyer responded that the duo "should be grateful to get the check and that is how [we'd] be compensated from time to time."[39]

Diamond became even more concerned when a few years later he got a tip from a friend at Capitol Records that the Beach Boys had covered the song and it was going to be released as a single with a major marketing campaign behind it. He tried to get the rights back to the record, arguing that in the "four years Roulette has had … rights we were never given a statement, consequently breaching the basic agreement we had."[40] This carried little weight with Levy or his lawyer, nor could Diamond find another lawyer willing to take on Levy.

By the mid-seventies, Diamond decided to sell his portion of the song, and approached Levy at the National Association of Record Merchandisers (NARM) meeting to make a deal. Levy characteristically offered a paltry sum—$5,000—for all rights. Diamond refused the offer. Later that day, while playing in a friendly poker game with a few industry insiders, Diamond complained about Levy's tight-fisted offer. Levy's marketing manager Red Schwartz, who was participating in the game, ominously warned Diamond to "back off." A year later, Diamond was able to make a deal with Levy's associate Phil Kahl to sell his portion of the song for $25,000—a small sum in comparison to what he believed was due to him (he figured on foreign rights alone he should have been paid over $100,000).

Thiele never had this type of problem with Levy, as he was just an employee at Roulette. However, he became increasingly uncomfortable working at the label, as it became clear to him that something more was happening at Roulette than merely the production of pop records:

A few minutes in the office corridors or reception areas was all anyone needed to be aware that Roulette was a small subsidiary of a vast international mega-conglomerate that never filed with the Securities and Exchange Commission, and whose board of directors and shareholders met at clam bars in Brooklyn, Las Vegas, Naples, and Palermo. … The miasmal hoodlum atmosphere at Roulette Records was so heavily oppressive that it was often difficult for me to concentrate on the musical matters that were my direct and only responsibilities. In fairness, everyone was diligently circumspect about my "civilian" status and left me alone, even though every day I felt I was improbably and inescapably trapped in a grade B gangster epic.[41]

One of the more colorful figures Thiele encountered in the hallways at Roulette was "a domineering, silk-suited, pinky-ringed force of nature" who he knew only as "Dominick." While Thiele claims never to have known his full name, it is clear from his description that this was Dominic Ciaffone. Ciaffone delighted in cooking spaghetti meals for the staff in the firm's kitchen, but he was also obviously a powerful player who was strong enough to unseat Levy from his executive suite when the need arose:

Dominick was, however, no master chef by vocation as was repeatedly apparent on the most dramatically edgy days of all at the Roulette Records offices. On those infrequent occasions, Morris Levy would surrender his imperially appointed suite on the executive floor, and Dominick would commandeer the premises to host intense discussions between imposingly menacing visitors and their ruffian retinues from the Bronx, Brooklyn, New Jersey, and boundaries beyond. I soon came to realize my interesting friend [Dominick] was the supreme court, judge, jury, and irrevocable arbiter who "mediated" all significant disputes involving these "gentlemen of respect" . . .[42]

When Thiele had the opportunity to join ABC Records, he quickly left the employ of Roulette, happy to have escaped from the clutches of Levy's retinue.

Indeed it could be intimidating for a "civilian" who worked at Roulette to find themselves sharing their office space with others who clearly were engaged in less-than-savory work. Roulette's house counsel during this period was particularly surprised one day to find the office next to his being prepared for a new occupant, John Dioguardi, known as Johnny Dio. Dio was a member of the Lucchese crime family, known for helping Jimmy Hoffa gain control of the Teamsters Union in 1956. That same year, Dio was charged with conspiring with five others to have a witness in an upcoming labor racketeering trial brutally attacked when leaving Lindy's Restaurant. Dio's latest stint in prison was for tax evasion; he won parole in 1963 with the proviso that he find legitimate employment. This may have been the reason he was given an office at Roulette Records as an "employee." It is not known how long Dio spent at Roulette.[43]

The presence of the mobsters at Roulette's offices was unnerving—to say the least—to the many who had to pass by their offices to gain access to Levy. Usually, the darker side of the operation was kept under wraps; however, one particularly disturbing incident was witnessed by songwriter Doc Pomus in the late fifties. He told Carl Perkins biographer David McGee of an experience he had one day when he came to the Roulette offices to pitch songs to Levy:

Doc Pomus [was] summoned to Morris (Moishe) Levy's office at Roulette, when Levy was needing new songs for one of his artists (and I do mean HIS artists). Doc arrived early and was waiting in the lobby, in a chair that was directly facing Levy's office, the door to which was open. Inside the office Doc saw two burly boys beating the living hell out of some poor soul, one holding him while the other pounded away, then they would switch positions (I guess to save the wear and tear on their hands). When they had ground him to a bloody pulp they dragged him out of Levy's office, past Doc, and tossed him on an elevator and sent it down. At which point Doc heard Levy call out, "Come on in, Doc!"[44]

Presumably Levy had been present for the beating; his ability to move on quickly to his normal business dealings with Pomus must have been chilling to the songwriter.

Levy either did not realize the impact such behavior had on outsiders like Pomus or did not care. Or perhaps he was intentionally letting possible collaborators know that things could turn ugly for them if they crossed the volatile producer. Another pair of outsiders who witnessed Levy's temper was English producers Simon Napier-Bell (manager of the Yardbirds among other British invasion acts) and Ray Singer. The duo visited Roulette's offices looking for production work sometime around 1969–70.[45] According to Napier-Bell:

> We went together to see Roulette, rumored to be connected with the mafia. People told us not to, but what the hell, we wanted all the work we could get and dealing with the mafia sounded [like] fun....
>
> We were taken to the see the boss—Morris Levy ... His office was long with his desk at one end on a dais. We arrived before he'd finished with his last guest and Morris was standing mid-office. His hands were round the collar of a slightly-built black guy, lifting him off the floor, shaking him furiously. "You fucking black cocksucker. You promised to make me a hit record and you screwed up."
>
> The little black guy was shuddering from top to toe of his shaken body. Then we recognized him.
>
> It was Mickey Stevenson for God's sake. One of the top black producers in the world. He'd written "Dancing in the Street" for Martha and the Vandellas and "What Becomes of the Brokenhearted" for Smokey Robinson. Now he was being shaken to death.
>
> When Morris realized we'd come into the room[,] he let go of Mickey who fell to the floor like an empty sack. While Morris motioned us to chairs by his desk[,] Mickey crawled to the door and fled.
>
> "So you want to make some records for me?" Morris boomed.[46]

Levy was sensitive at least to maintain a pretense of anonymity for some of the less savory associates who worked out of Roulette's offices. Photographer Chuck Stewart recalls being at the offices once when Levy told him: "Now we're going to have a meeting. You can take a photo of me, and this guy, and this guy, but you can't take a photo of that guy or that guy." Not wanting to take any unnecessary risks, Stewart decided to excuse himself entirely, asking Levy to let him know when the meeting was over.[47]

The outcome of the payola investigations was that several agencies—from New York's DA office to the FBI and the IRS—began to more closely scrutinize Levy's many business dealings. The presence of Dominic Ciaffone as an investor/officer of Roulette was not helpful. At the height of the payola investigations, columnist Drew Pearson reported that Ciaffone "has a police record and used to hang out in a Coney Island underworld dive." He also repeated the rumor that the murder of Levy's brother Irving was a Mob hit. Pearson reported that Morris Levy "denied his late brother had anything to do with the rackets, and claimed that Ciaffone had a clean police record since 1929."[48]

In 1961 the FBI began interviewing many of Levy's associates in the music business, trying to ascertain whether Roulette was a Mob front. Most said they knew that Ciaffone had an interest in the label, but either had a positive impression of him or did not know of any alleged ties he might have to the Mob. George Goldner told the FBI that the only evidence that indicated Levy might have Mob connections was the ease with which he was able to raise or borrow money. He noted that most record companies had to pay their suppliers promptly or they quickly went out of business, but Levy had been able to avoid this problem.[49] Irving Siders of MGM Records commented on an "associate" of Levy who worked for him as a "general flunky" in the mid-fifties who seemed to be "quick to give people physical beatings."[50] This may have been Tommy Vastola.

On the other hand, many of the people the FBI interviewed stated that Levy enjoyed boasting of his "mob connections" as a way of puffing up his importance. A one-stop manager said that "LEVY is inclined to be boastful"[51] about having friends in the Mob. A talent agent concurred, saying: "LEVY himself probably encouraged these rumors.... LEVY seemed to be enjoying the reputation that he was a 'friend of racketeers.'"[52] In their opinion, Levy was a braggart who liked to exaggerate his connections as a means of impressing his associates and building his reputation as a tough operator.

Nonetheless, the pretense of Roulette being a legitimate record label began to unravel at about the same time that Levy came under government scrutiny. Two important players, the Kolsky brothers, left the label nearly simultaneously in 1961–62; Joe Kolsky had been the prime marketing force behind Roulette, and Phil Kahl was the key partner in Levy's extensive publishing holdings. Joe left first, announcing that he was forming a new label on his own, Diamond Records, in September 1961. According to press reports at the time, Kolsky's stake in Roulette was purchased by Planetary Music, which was co-owned by Levy and Morris Gurlek. Kolsky himself told the FBI in 1965 that Levy purchased his stock for $100,000, with $10,000 down and forty-five payments of $2,000 due on the 15th of each month.[53] Levy praised Kolsky on his departure, stating "whatever success Roulette has enjoyed . . . is due in a great measure to [Kolsky's] tireless efforts . . ."[54] When Kahl left Levy's publishing companies the following January, he denied that he would be joining his brother at his new label, but a week later it was announced that in fact the two were in partnership.

He also sold out his stake in Patricia and Planetary music publishers and the Roulette label, with Levy directly buying out Kahl's holdings.[55] Levy, Ciaffone, and Gurlek were now the three principal owners of Roulette.

As part of their investigation of the relation between Ciaffone and Levy, Kolsky was interviewed by the FBI in 1965. By this time, Kolsky's relationship with Levy had "cooled," according to the field agent's report, although Kolsky reportedly stated that "he had never known LEVY to be dishonest in any of LEVY's business dealings." Kolsky did admit that Levy had developed "so-called hoodlum associations" through his ownership of nightclubs, but these relations were not reflected in the operation of Roulette: "KOLSKY stated that rumors that Roulette Records was hoodlum controlled were completely false.... He said that in his time at Roulette, he didn't see one shred of evidence of hidden hoodlum interests in the company. KOLSKY pointed out that all incoming and outgoing checks came across his desk, and because of this, he feels he would have known had such conditions existed." When specifically queried about Dominic Ciaffone's role at Roulette, Kolsky disavowed any knowledge of Ciaffone's Mob connections: "In spite of allegations that CIAFFONE is a 'racket guy,' KOLSKY regards him as a complete gentleman. KOLSKY pointed out that CIAFFONE owns about 5% of Roulette on the record and not as a hidden interest. CIAFFONE never participated in company affairs except to offer ideas at meetings concerning company policy."[56]

Kolsky made the argument that if Ciaffone was truly a mobster, his investment in Roulette would have been hidden. It may be true that with the exception of Ciaffone there was no evidence of Mob involvement in Roulette during Kolsky's tenure at the label. Kolsky walks a fine line throughout his FBI interview, not denying Ciaffone's obvious Mob connections, but at the same time asserting that he had no personal knowledge of those connections.

About the time that Kolsky and Kahl were leaving, Levy made an effort to raise money by bringing in a new partner, Horace Grenell (born Greenberg). Grenell had worked his way up in the record business in the late forties and early fifties establishing Young People's Records, which employed progressive ideas about education to records aimed at building music appreciation among the very young, children aged two and up.[57] He also established a label devoted to contemporary American classical music, but had no experience producing jazz or popular music. From running a label Grenell branched out into operating a pressing plant and sound studio, and had done some work for Roulette in both capacities. At one point when Grenell's pressing plant was short of funds, he turned to Levy, who recommended he see Charles "Ruby" Stein, a well-known loan shark described by the *New York Times* as "a dapper Broadway figure."[58] (Stein was associated with the Gambino crime family. He was murdered in 1977 by the rival Irish Westies gang, and his dismembered torso was found floating weeks later in Jamaica Bay.[59]) In 1959 Grenell had to sell out his ownership of the plant—perhaps, his son later speculated, to pay off this and other shady loans.[60]

In an undated "Proposal," a deal was laid out in which Grenell's recording studio, Madison Sound, would become a part owner of both Roulette and Levy's publishing operations.[61] The document appears to have been drawn up sometime in fall 1961, based on its contents. The payment terms for the deal were rather baroque. Madison Sound proposed loaning $200,000 to three of Levy's publishing companies, Patricia, Kahl, and Planetary Music. These companies would in turn loan the money to Roulette as well as forgiving a $1 million mortgage they held against Roulette's masters. The terms for securing Madison's loan were very strict: not only did the three publishing companies co-collateralize the debt, Levy guaranteed it personally through the assets of all of his holdings. Further, a special "sinking fund" would be established in which all of the BMI and ASCAP income due to Levy's companies would be deposited and could be applied to loan payments if necessary.

The board of directors would be divided equally between Roulette and Madison, and no salary increases could be made without "100% board approval, in writing." Madison was "to end up owning 40 percent of all the publishing companies, domestic and foreign, now in existence or to be formed in the future."[62] The purchase price was set at $.01 per share. In the new combined firm, Grenell would be business manager and Levy would deal with "Artists, Disk Jockeys, etc."

The proposal ends with a series of "Miscellaneous Notes" that give further insight into Levy's operations at the time. For example, it is asserted that "irrespective of what financial statements show, the publishing companies have guaranteed annual income." This would seem to be saying that—despite any corporate statements showing losses—the publishing companies were in fact profitable, and that profit was "guaranteed." It is likely that the "guaranteed income" is the rights income that all publishers receive from ASCAP and BMI. Further, the document states that "certain royalties payment figures are not actual," in effect admitting that Roulette did not honor all of its obligations to its artists. Roulette also had "a long-term lease" on its building and so would profit from the rent paid by the music publishing company and Madison Sound, which agreed to move to the fourth floor of the building as part of this proposal. Finally, it was agreed that payroll cuts would be made from $11,000 a week to $3,000.

For whatever reason, nothing came of the discussions for this merger. Grenell's son speculates that perhaps his father got cold feet because of Levy's Mob connections or that his business partner in Madison Studios, Robert Prince, may have backed out. "I'm sure there would have been a demand for money under the table for Roulette," his son remarked, "and I bet Horace . . . couldn't or didn't want to come up with it."[63]

Levy's business practices also came under scrutiny in late 1962 when a complaint was made about payoffs to the campaign fund of officers of New York Local 802 of the American Federation of Musicians. Under this scheme, the incumbent officers collected payments from nightclubs, ballrooms, and record labels in return for preferential rates for the services of the AFM's members, exclusive arrangements whereby bands were barred from playing for competitors, or for overlooking unpaid session fees, according to testimony given to the FBI by a group of union insurgents who were trying to unseat these corrupt officials. One of these men told the FBI that:

> MORRIS LEVY . . . was contacted by him . . . in about April or May of 1961, in an effort to collect approximately forty to fifty thousand dollars which was owed by LEVY to members of Local 802, in connection with recordings they had made for that company. . . . the collective bargaining agreement [requires] that all salaries owed to musicians by recording companies be paid within a two week period, and LEVY had far exceeded this time limitation. LEVY told [name redacted] and [name redacted] not to attempt to pressure him to make these payments since he had friends in local 802 . . . LEVY further advised that he had paid $2,500 to the election fund of the incumbent officers, and . . . was in good standing with the Local 802 officials.[64]

The insinuation was that by making these payments, Levy protected himself from having to pay the overdue royalties.

As part of the investigation, in early 1963 the Assistant US District Attorney for New York subpoenaed the receipt book that was kept for the "Musician's Ticket for Live Music" fund, the group that allegedly shook down the record industry and club owners for payments to keep the incumbent officers in their positions. However, in the end, no evidence could be found of direct payments to the union or its officers by Roulette, and the matter was formally dropped in July 1963.[65]

Levy's tangled web of companies—by this time estimated to include at least thirty publishing, management, and recording operations—attracted the attention of the IRS, particularly since Levy reported making little or no income in any of his ventures. In late 1963, Levy hired an attorney who specialized in tax law—and previously had been working for the New York DA's office, the same office that had investigated Levy during the payola hearings—to help settle the case brought against him by the tax agency. The first thing the new lawyer did was have Roulette's offices swept for bugs—and found that Levy was being recorded, although it was impossible to tell by whom. The lawyer speculated at the time that the bugs were either the work of the FBI, the IRS, or the Mob.[66] A settlement was eventually reached with the IRS for unpaid taxes.

The FBI focused its investigation on Ciaffone's relationship with Roulette. In addition to collecting a salary, Ciaffone acknowledged receiving several loans, including $20,000 from Levy personally in 1961 and $2,000 from Roulette in 1963. The FBI took a special interest in the seeming conflict of interest between Ciaffone's position with the electrical workers union and his work for Roulette. What the investigators failed to realize is that Ciaffone's union work primarily dealt with electricians working on TV and radio broadcasts, not on recording music. Several different investigations were mounted by state and federal agencies between 1961–64, mostly based on the erroneous assumption that Ciaffone or the union were receiving kickbacks for protecting Levy from his workers being unionized.[67] In 1964 investigators spoke with Levy about his relationship with Ciaffone. While admitting that Ciaffone was "a stockholder of Roulette Records, Inc., and also receives wages as a part-time employee of that firm . . . LEVY denied that Roulette Records has a collective bargaining contract with any union."[68] Examination of the union's books verified that Roulette had no business dealings with it.[69] In a summary report, New York's district attorney stated:

> even if it were developed that [Ciaffone] did work full time for the union and had no time to act as a promoter for Roulette, the salary payments he received from Roulette could not in this case be considered illegal payments from an employee . . . because an element is missing. . . . [T]he fact that no known attempts have been made to previously unionize firms engaged in the record producing industry, and the types of electrical businesses previously unionized by Local 1010, there is no indication that this union intends to expand its scope to include Roulette or any other record manufacturing company. . . . [W]ithout this necessary element, there is no violation . . .[70]

Throughout this period of intense scrutiny by various government agencies, Levy was attracting general interest among New York's gossip columnists. In their eyes, Levy had earned himself enough name recognition to compete with the likes of New York's socialites and major Broadway and Hollywood stars. Levy fed into the frenzy by leading a rather hectic romantic life. Following two brief marriages in 1950 and 1954, he began a period of intense womanizing that earned him the nickname of "the Mike Todd of the jazz world," a reference to the well-known Broadway producer and skirt chaser.[71]

From the mid-fifties, Levy began an on-again, off-again romance with "curvy" singer/entertainer Cynthia Brooks, "a lady with a sultry and colorful background," according to Dorothy Kilgallen.[72] A small-time actress and model,

Cynthia Brooks in a wire service photograph during her
advertising campaign to sell pinups photos by mail.

Brooks gained some notoriety in 1957 after running an ad to promote some sexy
pinup photos; as *Life* magazine reported:

> Cynthia Brooks, 23, is very likely the most telephoned girl in the U.S. In 26 cities men
> have been calling and they have all been getting the same sexy answer: "Hello dar-
> ling. I'd love to make your acquaintance with four lovely tempting pictures of myself.
> Just enclose one dollar to cover the cost of handling." ... Some local police have
> questioned her activities and phone companies have cut out her service, but Miss
> Brooks, whose phone pseudonym is Brandy Lee, hopes to stay in business a year ...[73]

Life took the opportunity of running the four photos to show off her curva-
ceous figure. Levy and Brooks wed in April 1958 but by May were separated;
they would subsequently reunite on several occasions, before finally ending
their relationship.

Levy also dated other high-profile names, including actress Natalie Wood and singer Keely Smith (who was married at the time to bandleader Louis Prima). Smith and Levy were often seen around New York in the period April–August 1961 and briefly again that November, when the duo were caught doing "a wild Twist" at Levy's Roundtable restaurant.[74] While the relationship was supposedly serious—with Levy reportedly proposing to the singer—they never made it to the altar and by late 1961 their relationship was on the rocks. Levy married Jean "Nom" Glassell—previously the wife of millionaire Texas oilman Alfred C. Glassell Jr., and a prominent divorcée living at the time in Miami—in February 1962,[75] quickly followed in 1963 by the birth of his first child, Adam, which finally took him out of the gossip headlines. Nonetheless, Levy would continue to be seen around town with a beautiful woman on his arms throughout this and his subsequent final marriage.

While Levy was busily building up Roulette to be a major label—and scrambling for extra funding to achieve his vision—the label itself was not producing many hits after its first successful year. The singles market was a volatile one, and only a best-seller could reap a significant financial reward to a producer who was making at best half of the ninety-nine-cent retail price on every sale. The LP market—aimed primarily at adults—was still a specialty niche; while Broadway cast albums and a few jazz albums sold in significant numbers, most album sales were far smaller than those of hit singles. To be a major label, however, you had to produce albums, and Levy entered the LP market with Roulette quickly after establishing the label in 1957. Over the coming two years, he experimented with several other labels and formats in order to earn a place at the table with Columbia, RCA, and Decca—not to mention Mercury and the other mid-sized independents that were rapidly expanding into all forms of music.

One of his late-fifties new ventures was a budget classical label called Forum Records. Classical recordings from Europe—particularly recorded in Eastern Europe—were already being licensed for US distribution by specialty labels like Vox and Vanguard as well as mid-sized independents like Mercury. In August 1959, *Billboard* announced that the first Forum releases were coming from France, with Levy planning to record "classical works in Europe for Forum himself" along with licensing from other outlets. The aim was to release about fifty albums annually, at budget prices.[76] Although it was initially intended to be solely a classical label, by the early sixties Levy was re-releasing budget versions of Roulette pop and jazz albums on Forum. This established a pattern that Levy would follow throughout his career to milk his catalog in as many ways as he could.

Another odder label that Levy hatched in 1958 was Co-Star Records. Levy was approached by record producer Ray Shaw, who came up with the idea for the series (and may have been a financial partner in the label). These albums were designed to appeal to budding actors (or would-be thespians). They consisted

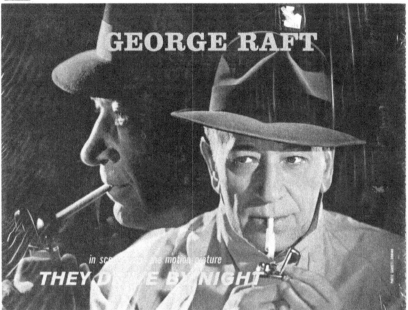

Co-Star Records cover featuring George Raft. The Co-Star label allowed listeners to act along with their favorite stars.

of well-known actors like George Raft, Basil Rathbone, and Tallulah Bankhead reading one part of a special dramatic adaptation of a popular story or play. The listener was supplied with a mimeographed script to supply the "missing" part and thus could enjoy the thrill of acting "along with the stars." Although many were adaptations of existing (public domain) literary works, Levy had special scripts written for two of his singing stars, Pearl Bailey and Jimmie Rodgers. The albums were list priced at $3.98, which was top dollar for 1958 when the first albums were produced.

Besides regular record retailers, Levy attempted to sell the Co-Star releases through toy stores and other non-traditional outlets, subtitling the series "The Record Acting Game."[77] "Anybody can play 'CO-STAR,'" the anonymous liner note author announced. "If you can read the enclosed script, you can play this wonderful new game that is already sweeping the country."[78] "Sweeping the country" was certainly an exaggeration; after the first fifteen albums appeared, the Co-Star label was inactive. The idea of interacting with a phonograph recording was so novel that another feature of the album's liner notes were "simple directions" on how to "play" the game, including the most basic instructions ("remove the script from the envelope . . ."; "place the phonograph needle on the corresponding scene . . ."). Another suggestion was that listeners could tape their performances, creating "a permanent record of your CO-STAR performance." The Co-Star fad failed to materialize, it appears, and the label and idea were quickly mothballed by Levy.[79]

All of these new ventures launched simultaneously must have put a strain on the still-young Roulette operation. In his interview with the FBI, Joe Kolsky noted that after Roulette's initial flurry of success, he was often at odds with Levy, who was constantly pushing for expansion while Kolsky was concerned more about the immediate lack of cash flow. Kolsky noted that the label was saved by an unlikely turn of events in 1961, when they were able to briefly ride a new dance craze, the Twist.

The story of the Twist and its unexpected success among New York's high society is typical of how the music industry coopts the creative work of an artist who himself does not participate in its financial success. The original recording of "The Twist" was made by its composer, R&B singer Hank Ballard, in late 1959 for King Records, an important independent label out of Cincinnati. The song was a moderate success, which brought it to the attention of Dick Clark, the host of *American Bandstand* out of Philadelphia. He had his discovery, Chubby Checker, copy the Ballard recording, which zoomed to #1 thanks to Clark's plugging of the song in September 1960.

The story would have ended there were it not for a small bar in New York City known as the Peppermint Lounge. In 1958 mobster Johnny Biello (a.k.a. Johnny Futto)—a capo in the Genovese crime family—took over management of what had been called the Gang Plank, a seedy bar catering to gay men on West 45th Street; he was already running the Wagon Wheel, another gay bar, down the street. Biello's interest in the bar was in having use of its back room, where he could meet with his associates to manage his loan sharking and gambling enterprises. He renamed the place the Peppermint Lounge. Dick Cami, Biello's son-in-law,[80] suggested that the bar offer as entertainment local rock 'n' roll acts rather than the more usual jazz combos; their main attraction was their willingness to work for peanuts. In October 1960, a group from New Jersey known as the Starliters were hired to play for a weekend and ended up staying as the house band for a little over a year.

Like many of his contemporaries, Passaic, New Jersey–born Joseph DiNicola (a.k.a. Joey Dee) formed several amateur rock bands beginning in his high school years, mostly working small North Jersey clubs.[81] While working this circuit, he met vocalist David Brigati, and the two formed a group that became the Starliters. Unlike many other bands of the era, the group included both Italian and African American musicians—which surprisingly did not attract any special notice even after they achieved fame (although in publicity photos and album covers only the white band members appeared). In early 1959, they recorded one single for Scepter Records, a small label located out of Passaic that achieved its greatest success with the girl group the Shirelles. This single went nowhere, and they were back to scuffling on the bar circuit. While playing one night in Lodi, New Jersey, a New York agent named Don Davis heard them. Dee credits him with landing them the job at the Peppermint Lounge in New York.

The club's audience grew slowly, according to Cami, initially attracting a mix of bikers and bobby soxers drawn to the new rock music. A notice by popular gossip columnist Cholly Knickerbocker that ran in his column on September 21, 1961, mentioned the "chic" new club where "Prince Obolensky" was spotted on the dance floor doing the Twist. The embellishment about the exiled prince was not true, but it did not matter; soon the place was swarming with a mix of New York's high society and Hollywood stars who came to at least watch the goings-on, if not actively participate on the dance floor.[82] Everyone from President Kennedy's sister to Tennessee Williams, the Duke of Bedford, Greta Garbo, and Elsa Lanchester crowded the tiny club. Even *Life* magazine profiled it, running a two-page spread of photos showing the elite crowd.[83]

Most newsmen viewed the dance craze as, at best, fodder for humorous comments about teenagers and their endless appetite for novelties like goldfish eating and eccentric behavior. The AP reflected mainstream "adult" America in describing the Twist as "a sensuous and grotesque dance right out of the jungle." The AP reporter went on to describe the Peppermint Lounge as:

> a hot, jammed, smoky nightmare where 200 customers are jammed on the tiny dance floor or squeezed together at small tables. Men in formal attired and their bejeweled partners vie with sailors, drifters in leather jackets and girls in toreador pants for space to do their stuff. Five musicians on a bandstand blast like fury. They shout and leap like demons on hot coals. On the dance floor, couples gyrate in joyful frenzy.[84]

Suddenly Joey Dee and the Starliters were the hottest band in town.

Naturally, everyone wanted to sign the Starliters to record—but only one record executive had the inside track, thanks to his ties to the Mob owners of the nightclub. On October 25, 1961, Dorothy Kilgallen reported that Levy had scored "a coup" by beating out "seven disc company competitors" to sign Dee to Roulette. "At the same time," she reported, "he bought exclusive rights for the use of the name of the red-hot West 45th Street night club on his album covers. Levy is rushing the initial LP into production, hopes to have it on platter counters . . . within three weeks."[85] Writing about himself in the third person,

Joey Dee (center) in a publicity photo for the low-budget teen film, *Hey Let's Twist*. David Brigati is on left. Unusually for the time, the band featured two black musicians, including their drummer and sax player (not shown).

Dee describes why the group decided to sign with Roulette: "Capitol Records and Atlantic Records approached the group for a contract, but Joey opted to go with Roulette Records which promised to record them 'live' at the Peppermint Lounge and to market a record immediately, as well as to sort out all the other conflicting contracts signed by the group."[86]

Levy had the edge on all other labels as he had both the contacts at the club and the muscle to unravel the tangled agreements that the group had already signed. Besides their previous deal with Scepter, the Starliters also had signed with Capitol before Levy came on the scene, despite Dee's assertion otherwise.

However, Dorothy Kilgallen reported that Levy was able to assert his standing with the group's manager:

> The Starliters' manager, Don Davis . . . says Capitol never filed a contract with . . . the musicians' union, and therefore Morris Levy, head of Roulette, has been given a letter from the president of the union, "recognizing" Roulette as the only disc company with any claim on Joey's services. This also rules out Scepter Records, which Mr. Davis alleges paid the Starliters $20 apiece for their session, which is considerably under union scale.[87]

Levy claimed a special relation with the musicians union and its officers, perhaps thanks to his under-the-table support of their campaign funds. Levy's contract with the group did not stop Scepter from rereleasing the session material that the Starliters had previously recorded for them on an album once the group achieved its fame, but Capitol did not try to hold the group to whatever document they had signed.

The song that launched the group was "Peppermint Twist," which was co-written with producer Henry Glover, the producer of the original "Twist" recording. Glover was a former bandleader who began working in the late 1940s for the notorious Syd Nathan, who owned King Records and several related labels. Nathan knew little about music, but was a canny businessman who set up his own pressing operations as well as recording studio, so he could control all aspects of the records that he produced. Glover helped establish King as a major force in R&B, but typically was shortchanged by Nathan, who watched every penny he spent like a hawk. In 1959 Glover left to briefly form a partnership with Hy Weiss, owner of Old Town Records, a small New York independent.[88]

A year later Glover joined Roulette, where he was assigned to work with most of the label's R&B acts. Unlike Hugo and Luigi, Glover had a good feeling for R&B music, honed through years of performing, producing, and writing songs. The "Peppermint Twist" combines a shuffle rhythm with a catchy chorus opening with "Round and round, up and down . . ." A taste of pop vocal harmonies carried over from the doowop days is heard in the background to the verse, while some of the flavor of the group's stage act is caught during the guitar solo, when group members make some "spontaneous" shout-outs. The group featured some twistin' choreography as part of their act to go along with the song.

The single was an immediate hit, building the Twist craze. It was followed by a live album, which Dorothy Kilgallen claimed was so successful that "[Roulette was] bombarded with orders: it's turning out 40,000 LPs per day but still can't keep up with the demand from all over the United States. . . ."[89] A complete album followed, along with the quickie film *Hey Let's Twist*, all in an effort to cash in on the craze as quickly as possible. In a brief notice headlined "Levy 'Twisting' Lots of Loot Out of Terp Craze," *Variety* reported on Levy's success promoting the song on record and in his nightclubs. The article also reported that Levy appeared "along with an anthropologist and some psychologists" to discuss the meaning of the dance craze on a NBC TV news program in late November 1961. It would be interesting to hear how the gruff-voiced music mogul interacted with these academics.[90]

In the time-honored tradition of payola, George Goldner—once again working with Levy after selling him his Gone and End labels in 1962—took Dee around to visit the major deejays. As Dee recalled:

> I'd get in the limo with Goldner . . . It would be a couple ladies of the evening, hookers, in the back of the limo and we'd drive to these towns. They'd meet with the deejays, give them an envelope with cash in it, allow them their way with the girls in the car, and then go on to the next town. And the next town. And the next town. Our records were played. God forbid they took the money and *didn't* play the records. That's when the baseball bats came out . . . and worse.[91]

Despite the success of the "Peppermint Twist," Dee—like many other Roulette artists—was chagrined when he received his royalty statement. Earning a pittance on each record made, and being charged for all costs including promotional outings like the one he took with Goldner, meant that the artist ending up in debt to the label: "The number one record in the country was 'Peppermint Twist.' I got a royalty check—and it stated that I *owed* Roulette Records eight thousand dollars. I just couldn't get over it. Here I thought I was going to become a millionaire."[92]

Like many other teen acts before them, the Starliters struggled to follow up their initial success. As he had done with Frankie Lymon, Levy tried to promote Joey Dee as a solo act beginning in late 1962, but the attempt to make him a teen balladeer faded quickly. Despite being one-hit wonders, the Starliters managed to extend their stay at the Peppermint Lounge for a little over a year, although much of the gossip columnists had moved on to cover the latest celebrity fads by the end of 1961.

In another effort to milk the Twist craze, Levy signed Bill Haley and His Comets—at one time a major rock act, but by 1962 fairly well washed up as far as hits were concerned—to perform at his Roundtable restaurant with the idea of producing a live album.[93] The result was the oddly titled *Twistin' Knights at the Roundtable*, with a tacky cover photo of a "knight" and his "dame" miming the popular dance. The album opens with a cover of Levy's favorite copyright, "Lullaby of Birdland," while the rest of the tracks are "twistin'" covers of favorites like "Down by the Riverside Twist" and, even odder, "Caravan Twist," based on the

Duke Ellington number. The album did little, however, to revive Haley's career or to line Levy's pockets with more twistin' cash.

Following the success of the New York Peppermint Lounge, Levy partnered with Johnny Biello in opening a branch in Miami in 1961, which was also managed by Dick Cami. Cami appreciated the advice of the more experienced club owner, who helped them obtain prime space for the new operation, and also offered valuable advice in dealing with a classier group of customers. He told Cami not to water down the liquor, a common practice among Biello's seedy establishments. "If some businessman orders Cutty Sark, he's going to know [you've watered it down] as soon as it hits his throat," he warned Cami. "Then he's going to think, 'This guy's a bullshitter.' You've lost him forever."[94] As he did in most of the clubs where he was a part owner, Levy released several albums by Roulette acts recorded live at the Miami club.

Levy maintained a second home in Miami that he purchased around 1960, shortly after the murder of his brother at Birdland. Some of the more amusing items in Levy's FBI files are related to when the Beatles visited Miami during their first American trip the week after appearing on *The Ed Sullivan Show* in 1964. New York deejay Murray the K arranged for the Beatles to stay at Levy's Miami estate, which included a large swimming pool. Although Levy was not using his home at the time, the FBI staked it out during the Beatles' visit and kept tabs on the comings and goings of the new pop stars.

Besides Joey Dee, Levy's most notable rock act came from an Arkansas rockabilly singer who had made a big splash north of the border playing clubs in the Toronto area. Ronnie Hawkins was an energetic stage performer whose band the Hawks specialized in covering the hits of Chuck Berry, Roy Orbison, and other fifties rock and rockabilly acts. They became the house band at Toronto's Le Coq d'Or nightclub in 1959, and were soon drawing big crowds. In summer 1959, they got a gig playing Wildwood, New Jersey, where they soon were outdrawing more established acts and attracting the attention of the major record labels. Mitch Miller was interested in booking the band for Columbia, but Hawkins was more interested when he heard that Morris Levy of Roulette wanted to sign them.

According to Levon Helm—then the Hawks' drummer—Levy sent an emissary to hear the group in Wildwood and invited Hawkins and Helm to come to New York. Hawkins warned Levon to be on his best behavior: "Be polite to Mr. Levy, son. He's Mafia up to his eyeballs." Hawkins knew that with Levy's connections he was sure to do well, telling Helm, "We can't miss with these cats behind us."[95] Wining and dining them at his Roundtable restaurant, Levy quickly convinced Hawkins to join Roulette, and within days they were recording. Signed to produce them was ex-RCA producer Joe Reisman. Reisman did not try to pretty up the band's sound as Hugo and Luigi might have done. Instead, the band was allowed to rip through two of their popular stage numbers for their first single, "Forty Days," Hawkins's shameless rewrite of Chuck Berry's "Thirty Days," and "Ruby Baby." (To his credit, Hawkins at least credited Berry for his contribution to "40 Days.") Other than the addition of some crooning backup singers, "40 Days" featured Hawkins's touring band, including guitarist "Luke" Pullman and pianist Willard Jones, with Helm keeping a steady beat throughout. Where Berry's version had a loping rhythm, Hawkins picked up the speed and evened out the beat to make the song fit a rockabilly aesthetic. Replacing Berry's bluesy vocals with a hiccupy rockabilly lead, Hawkins's singing brings to mind a slightly wilder version of Buddy Holly's trademark style.

The group's followup "Mary Lou" was their biggest hit, reaching #26 on the *Billboard* charts in summer 1959. Producer Reisman added Sam "The Man" Taylor, a well-known studio sax player, to this one, along with some backup singers. Taylor takes the only solo in the middle of the song in his typical honking style. The Hawks' playing is much more subdued on this song. Helm claimed the record sold over three quarters of a million copies. In September 1959, the Hawks made a few records without lead singer Hawkins under the aegis of producer Henry Glover, replacing Reisman. Helm and he quickly bonded over their mutual affection for R&B music. Glover complimented the group, telling Levon that "If you boys ever want to do something by yourselves, I hope you'll talk to me about it first."[96]

Levy did his best to promote the group, booking them into his upscale Roundtable nightclub in 1962, just as the Twist craze was cresting. Hawkins was amused by the high-society crowd trying to master the new dance: "You should see the people . . . They're up on the rafters, up on the tables, some in Levis and T-shirts and some in Tuxedos and minks. It's so crowded a drunk couldn't fall down. I get scared they'll come too close to the bandstand and some of my musicians will get trampled to death."[97]

An unnamed source reported to the FBI that this "new dance craze . . . was evident" at the Roundtable, feeling that this indicated perhaps other "criminal" activities were occurring there, as he also said "there were many . . . members of the hoodlum element present, but he was unable to identify any of them because of the darkness."[98]

Unfortunately, Roulette had little success with Hawkins after his initial minor hits. While Levy had great faith in the artist—telling Hawkins that he was a natural successor to Elvis—Hawkins could not adapt his style to newer trends and also was happier playing for his devoted Canadian fan base. Touring the United States was more difficult, with Levy expecting the group to play many small clubs to promote their releases, often without being paid for their appearances. In an attempt to broaden Hawkins's appeal, Levy had him record an album of traditional folk songs, hoping to cash in on the early sixties folk revival, and a country album devoted to covers of Hank Williams, produced in Nashville. But Hawkins's commitment to both projects was low and Levy was unable to transform him into an album artist. Levy urged Hawkins to stay in New York, but the singer preferred to return to Canada, where he could count on steady, well-paying jobs. "He keeps saying how much he loves Canada," Levy confided to Helm. "It's breaking my heart."[99]

Besides scoring hits with Joey Dee and to a much lesser extent Ronnie Hawkins, Roulette struggled in the early sixties. Count Basie left the label in 1961, and was quickly followed by a number of other jazz stars, including Billy Eckstine and Sarah Vaughan, who returned to Mercury Records, where they had recorded before coming to Roulette. Jazz was no longer charting as it once did, and Roulette had limited success in breaking into either teen pop or R&B. Although Levy had some talented producers like Glover on the payroll, once Joe Kolsky left, he did not have anyone with an overall vision of where the label should go. Instead, Levy was guided mostly by attempts to cash in on novelties and passing fads, rather than carefully building a roster of artists.

7

Doin' the Hanky Panky: 1962–1969

I might fuck you on a contract, but I always keep my word.
—Morris Levy

The early to mid-1960s was a difficult time for most of the independent labels that were founded in the 1950s. The time when you could pick up either a jazz player out of the clubs or a young group off the street, pay them a minimal fee, and take them to the studio for a quick hour or two session to produce a single was coming to an end. Jazz was no longer regularly making the pop charts, and artists were turning to recording entire albums, usually under the supervision of a producer who could shape the music. The major labels—particularly Columbia and to some extent RCA and Decca—had moved in on jazz and were beginning to scoop up the most popular performers, paying them far more money, as well as providing ample studio time. Meanwhile, on the pop music scene, following the payola scandals of the late fifties and early sixties, it was harder to directly influence the charts. Hits increasingly were being created either by canny producers—like Phil Spector, who was developing his Wall of Sound, or Berry Gordy at Motown—or by talented songwriters like Burt Bacharach and Hal David or Jerry Leiber and Mike Stoller. But the single biggest blow to the entire US pop music industry came in February 1964 when the Beatles appeared on *The Ed Sullivan Show*, ushering in the British Invasion. Suddenly, homegrown acts could not get onto the charts.

Roulette's problems were complicated by Levy's almost perverse need to shortchange his acts and the behind-the-scenes producers who could transform them into hit makers. If he did stumble onto a hit-making group or artist, he was so determined to short them on royalty and other payments that he would drive them to take a better deal—which was not hard to find if they had continuing potential. Meanwhile, the low-level Mob activity that was evident in Roulette's offices drove away creative people, who became concerned about being tainted by their association with the obvious illegal activities that were occurring side by side with the more legitimate business. It was one thing for an act to perform at a nightclub where mobsters were closing deals; it was another to face these same gangsters on a day-to-day basis in Roulette's offices. And Levy's ability to throw his weight around with his peers was becoming less meaningful as the next generation of hit makers arose who were not as beholden to him.

Collecting money from Morris Levy struck fear into the hearts of his artists as well as his colleagues in the record business. Levy had no qualms about short-ing his artists, and—depending on their stature within the industry—often took his time to pay off record studios or smaller labels with whom he was doing business. Producer Bob Krasnow—who later founded Blue Thumb Records and ran Elektra for the Warner group—began his career producing local singles. Like many others, he turned to Levy to market one of his records because he could not promote it nationally. Once the record was released, Krasnow did not receive any sales reports—or payment—from Levy, so he travelled to New York to try to collect his money. Bud Katzel—then Roulette's sales director—recalled how Krasnow managed to extract his money from Levy:

> Bob lived in San Francisco in the late fifties, and had a local hit which he couldn't seem to spread. He called his friend George Goldner . . . and George suggested making a deal with Morris. Morris picked the record up and it was a hit single. Of course Bob never saw a dime and couldn't get Morris on the phone.
>
> So he hopped on a plane to New York. Not knowing how "connected" Morris was, he stormed into Morris's office and asked to see him. When told Morris was busy, Bob pushed his way past the secretary, walked right into his office where Morris was sitting with a few Mafiosi looking characters and said, "Morris, Bob Krasnow. Where's my fucking money?"
>
> Morris went into his drawer, pulled out a .38, and said to Bob, "Look you moth-erfucker, I'll give you five seconds to get out of this office or I'll blow your fucking brains out all over this carpet. And furthermore, don't ever let me see your face again." With that, Bob walked out, got as far as the entrance to the building, turned around and went back up to Morris' office. Only this time, he knocked on the door, opened it with only his head sticking through it and said to Morris, "Morris, when you said you never wanted to see my face again, did you mean in New York or the United States?" . . . Morris laughed and Bob got paid.[1]

Despite the fact that in the end Krasnow seemed to be able to laugh off what was a tense situation, it is telling that Levy's first instinct was to try to bully his way out of paying the money that he owed him. Levy seemed to enjoy testing people in this way: those who won his friendship through wit or sheer nerve would be paid; those who ran away in fear lost his respect.

Phil Ramone—later a major pop producer who worked with Paul Simon and Billy Joel—began his career as a partner at A&R Studios in New York, a small independent which Levy sometimes used for Roulette's sessions. Like many other greenhorns in the business, Ramone was given the thankless job of trying to collect money that Levy owed the studio:

> One afternoon my business partners called me in. "Hey—we've got to collect from Roulette. Go over to Morris's office and ask for a check." With all of my youthful innocence I strolled into Morris's office, sat down, and politely explained to him that A&R really needed the twelve thousand bucks that Roulette owed us so we could pay our bills.
>
> Morris was affable and relaxed; we conversed and had a good laugh about the business. Then, Morris called for his secretary. "Bring me the A&R invoice and the checkbook," he asked. He glanced at the invoice, wrote the check, and said, "You do good work—thanks."
>
> On my way back to the studio I unfolded the check and to my chagrin saw that Morris had created his own discount. He'd only paid us eight thousand dollars. When I got back, everyone applauded my courage. What's the big deal? I thought.[2]

Not having experienced his mercurial temper firsthand, Ramone did not realize at the time how lucky he was to be able to collect any amount from Levy.

It seems that the job of collecting money from Morris Levy was a rite of passage for new hires in the music business in the early sixties. Walter Yetnikoff—whose eccentric memoir *Howlin' at the Moon* reflects his reputation as one of the least buttoned-down of all executives who ever ran Columbia Records—recalls his first meeting with Levy after he was hired as a staff lawyer at Columbia. He was sent by his superiors to collect $400,000 that Roulette owed Columbia for pressing its records. Yetnikoff portrays himself as successfully verbally sparring with Levy who—while acknowledging his debt—hurls expletives at the young Columbia executive and dodges his demands for payment. Yetnikoff returned to Columbia without a check, but then reports that a full payment arrived a week later, with a handwritten note from Levy saying: "To bright boy Yetnikoff—I'm not paying because I gotta. I'm paying because I wanna. I'd hate to see you in trouble so early in your career. That'll come later. Moishe."[3] This was the beginning of a long friendship between the two, with Levy referring to Yetnikoff by his Yiddish name of "Velvel" and Yetnikoff reciprocating by calling him "Moishe."

Levy was a man of his word, but his word did not always correspond with the agreements that he signed. According to accountant Ira Hertzog, who worked for Levy in the mid-sixties, he saw no contradiction in signing an agreement to pay one rate while verbally saying he would only pay much less:

> [For example,] a manager says, "I need 10 points [percent of the earnings] on the contract. I'm not going to sign a contract for less than 10 points." Morris says, "OK,

Cover for *At Home with that Other Family*, 1961, Roulette's attempt to cash in on the success of Vaughan Meader's album *The First Family*.

no problem. I'm paying three." Whatever, the contract says 10 points, Morris pays three . . . He didn't care what he signed in the contract. He told them up front. "Good, fine, but I'm going to pay you this. . . ." He wasn't dishonest in that respect. . . . He was very straightforward about it. And he would pay his part, yeah.[4]

Or, as Levy succinctly put it, "I might fuck you on a contract, but I always keep my word."[5]

Levy was a canny businessman and always kept his eye out to jump on the latest pop fads and industry trends. One area that he exploited in the early sixties was the surprising success of comedy albums. The success of artists like Shelley Berman on Verve, Nichols and May on Mercury, and Bob Newhart on Warner Bros. led to a slew of comedians being recorded. One of the most unusual hits of the period was the album *The First Family*, featuring comedian Vaughan Meader, who mastered an imitation of President Kennedy. The album was unusual in that Meader was joined by an entire cast, performing short topical skits in the studio with a live audience. After being turned down by most labels, major and minor, the album was released on the small Cadence label. *Billboard* reported that it broke all sales records following its release in November 1962, setting one-day, week, and month sales records for an LP.[6] By the time that report appeared in late January 1963, the album had surpassed four million copies sold—an incredible sales number for an independently released album to achieve.

Such numbers caught the attention of other label owners—including Levy. Rushing to capitalize on the album's success, Levy produced *At Home with That Other Family*, focusing on Russian leader Nikita Khrushchev. Despite featuring the talent of young up-and-comers Joan Rivers, George Segal, and Buck Henry, the album was an obvious attempt to rip off the successful formula of Cadence's hit. (Other labels were equally shameless, quickly releasing similar efforts including *The Other Family* on Laurie, *The President Strikes Back* on Kapp, and *The Poor Family* on Mercury.) Sales reports for the Roulette knockoff LP from around the country in *Billboard* were decidedly mixed; Roulette's sales director, Bud Katzel, claimed the label shipped 150,000 copies of the album in its first month, perhaps puffing the numbers to help promote the record. In any case, none of the copycat albums achieved anywhere near the success of the original, and all are forgotten today.

With comedy hot, Levy began issuing his own comedy albums—although often without first signing the artists. The comedian Bill Dana had created a comic alter ego named Jose Jimenez for his appearances on Steve Allen's TV show; somehow, Levy obtained air checks of Dana performing his material and rush released an album *My Name . . . Jose Jimenez* right after Dana had signed a contract with Kapp Records. "They actually did that without my permission," Dana recalled in a 2010 interview. "It was a bone of contention and it got a little heavy. I was having these voices call me saying it would be good for me to cooperate with them. It was like a scene from *The Sopranos*."[7] Seeking $175,000 in damages, Dana eventually settled on Levy destroying the master for the album.

Levy was used to issuing live albums culled from recordings made at his clubs, and saw no ethical or moral dilemma in issuing material that he felt he had "paid" for by hiring the performer for the appearance. (Union rules mandated that artists be paid separately for an appearance and a live recording made of that show; however, many label owners ignored the niceties of these rules.) Like many other producers, he also purchased tapes from other sources without the outright consent of the artist themselves. Comedian Don Sherman was the victim of one such deal:

> I walked by Colony Records, a [major New York] record store, and I saw this window full of *Don Sherman at the Playboy Club* albums. And I had no album! I had no deal! Someone said to me, "Well, go talk to them." Then I heard that they were

people that you don't fool around with. I built up the guts. I went up there—in an elevator that opened in the back. That got me nervous right off the bat. [Levy] said that a friend of mine had taped some of my shows somewhere and eventually they were sold to Roulette Records and they put it out. They didn't even bother getting in touch with me.[8]

Levy would repeat this behavior often in the sixties and seventies, buying tapes from dubious sources and then dealing roughly with the annoyed artists.

Another comedian who came into Levy's orbit around this time was Jackie Kannon. Not well remembered today, Kannon combined the "blue" comedy of Lenny Bruce with the insult comedy of Don Rickles.[9] Born in Ontario, Kannon was the son of a cantor, but like Levy he sought success beyond his Jewish heritage. After knocking around on the comedy circuit in Detroit and New York in the late forties, Kannon's big break came in 1961 when he convinced a local printer to produce a satirical coloring book for adults titled *The JFK Coloring Book*; Kannon claimed to quickly have sold 300,000 copies.[10]

In 1961 Kannon recorded his first comedy album for Levy, which was taped in a prison and released as *Prose from the Cons*. (Columnist Earl Wilson said that Kannon quipped about the album that "it won't be released. It'll escape."[11]) As he had done with other creators, Levy proposed a partnership with Kannon. He owned a small room above his Roundtable nightclub that was mostly unused; Kannon was looking for a home club in New York where he could perform regularly. The two went into business together, christening the small space the Rat Fink Room and opening it in September 1963.[12]

The room itself was not the best place to present comedy, or any type of entertainment for that matter. Kannon told a *New York Times* reporter: "Nothing had worked in that room. They had tried everything but they couldn't draw flies. To get there, you've got to climb over belly dancers at the Roundtable. And the room is not a good comedy room because it's L-shaped so that part of your audience is off to your left and other part is around the corner on the right." Kannon concluded that he achieved success because he was able to draw "hip people who have been everywhere and seen everything—they like the informality of the room."[13]

The club was an immediate sensation, attracting a mix of stars and socialites much as Birdland did in the fifties. UPI reported that crowds came nightly to hear what Kannon described as "a new experience in social decadence."[14] Kannon's friend Allan Sherman adapted the western swing hit "Rag Mop" for him to use as his Rat Fink theme song.

The critics were not enamored of Kannon's club or his routines. A typical reaction came from Amarillo, Texas–based columnist Joan Ater. After visiting the club, she panned it, saying: "Jackie Kannon's Rat Fink Room . . . required influence to get in and, once in, we wondered why. Kannon's routine was the 'bluest' it has been my misfortune to hear. Again, the crowded, dingy quarters were jammed despite the enormous cover charge. If this is smart, sophisticated entertainment, I'm glad I'm from the provinces."[15] The height of the Rat Fink Room's notoriety was the period from 1963–66; Kannon and the club lingered on until 1969, when Levy withdrew his support. Kannon worked occasionally thereafter, and died of a heart attack in early 1974.

Just as comedy albums were taking off on the charts in the early sixties, so were albums by folksingers, beginning with the success of the Kingston Trio on Capitol in 1958 and followed by Peter, Paul, and Mary and Joan Baez in 1962. Levy smelled another opportunity in this craze, and signed his own folk trio, the Cumberland Three. The group consisted of John Stewart (later a successful singer/songwriter), John Montgomery, and bass player Gil Robbins (born Rubin; father of actor Tim Robbins). Besides the popularity of the folk revival, semi-historical story-songs were also doing well on the charts. Plus, 1960 saw the one hundredth anniversary of the Civil War, and many labels tried to ride the publicity that it was generating. Levy astutely asked the trio to record two albums of Civil War songs, one featuring songs of the North and one of the South (perhaps hedging his bets that he could appeal to fans of both sides of the conflict). Stewart later recalled, repeating a sentiment expressed by many Roulette artists, that "Morris Levy wanted us to record Civil War songs, and whatever Morris wanted, Morris got."[16]

Despite having Henry Glover on board as a producer, Levy's success with mainstream pop and R&B acts was rather spotty in the early sixties. Meanwhile, George Goldner—who launched several successful groups on his Gone and End labels, including Little Anthony and the Imperials, the Chantels (one of the first girl groups), the Dubs, and the Flamingos—was once again short of cash and sold out his interest in his labels to Levy in July 1962, with Goldner becoming a vice president of Roulette as well as joining their pop A&R staff. Although the arrangement only lasted about a year, Goldner would bring both his back catalog and current contracts along with his solid ear for production to Roulette.[17]

As he had from the very beginning when he bought the masters for Buddy Knox's "Party Doll," Levy often picked up potential best sellers from smaller labels—sometimes by not too subtly applying pressure to the label's owner. This happened to Joe Ruffino, owner of a small New Orleans label called Ric. Ruffino had signed a local singer named Joe Jones. For Jones's first release, he assigned the production duty to a local saxophone player named Harold Battiste. The song was "You Talk Too Much," which featured some funky New Orleans horns accompanying Jones's otherwise middle-of-the-road performance. Ruffino and Battiste took to the road to promote their release to friendly deejays, and the record appeared to be on its way to breaking through nationally. When the two hit New York, Ruffino was summoned to Levy's offices. It turns out that Jones was previously signed to Roulette and had already cut a version of the song for the label, which had never been released, presumably because it was judged to be not commercial enough.[18] It is unclear whether Levy had an exclusive contract with Jones, but nonetheless he threatened to issue an injunction against Ric's release. In what *Cash Box* described as an "amicable decision," as a settlement the Ric master was given to Roulette to re-release.

Battiste told a different story, saying that Levy wined and dined the singer and producer hoping to get Jones to return to Roulette. To make his point, he sent Joe Robinson—a physically imposing man who had worked as a numbers runner in Harlem before marrying popular singer Sylvia Vanderpool of the pop duo Mickey and Sylvia—to the hotel where Jones and Battiste were staying: "Boy I was scared to death. . . . we were thinking, oh man . . . That's the Mafia! [Levy] sent Joe Robinson . . . to make us an offer. They had taken us out to the Roundtable . . . and gave us the royal treatment. They knew Joe Jones was weak for chicks. We told the people at the hotel not to tell anybody we had checked out in case they came looking for us." Jones said that Levy got the master, the publishing rights for the song, and his contract from Ruffino, giving him nothing in return.[19] Ironically, it was Battiste's production that made the song. The Roulette release was a Top 5 hit on both the R&B and pop charts in 1960, a coup for Levy. Unfortunately, under Roulette's producers, Jones was unable to come up with a followup hit.

Jones was not the only regional singer who Levy brought into his growing empire. Levy had cultivated deejays around the country during his days promoting the Birdland tours and working with Alan Freed. This paid off when small labels would enjoy regional hits; friendly deejays or distributors would pass the word along to Levy and he was quick to snap up any product that had the potential to break nationally with a little extra push. One of the many artists who came to Roulette this way was teen pop singer Lou Christie. Christie's dramatic falsetto was reminiscent of another Italian pop crooner, Frankie Valli of the Four Seasons, and like Valli he got his start singing in a doowop group in his native Pittsburgh. He brought some demos of his own songs to a local deejay named Nick Cenci, who produced his first single, "The Gypsy Cried"; Cenci's employer, radio station owner Herb Cohen, paid for the pressing and the two named their label after their last names, Co and Ce. The record began breaking locally, Christie recalled: "It started spreading from Pittsburgh to Ohio to Cleveland to Johnstown, Pennsylvania. Then, it jumped out of San Francisco and started spreading around the country and that was it. Roulette Records picked it up and said I think we got a hit here. And that was the beginning of how I got on Roulette."[20]

"The Gypsy Cried" set the model for Christie's Roulette recordings: opening with a dramatic falsetto introduction, Christie then sang in his normal vocal range during the verses, returning to falsetto for a Frankie Valli–ish reading of "Cry-ai-yi-ai-ai-ai-yi." The backup is pure early-sixties kitschy pop, including cheesy organ and some perky girl background singers. The song reached #24 on the pop charts when Roulette issued it, going gold (indicating a sale of over a million copies). Christie's followup did even better; "Two Faces Have I," released in March 1963, reached #6 on the charts. The two voices, Christie's normal range in the verse and the falsetto on the chorus, complement the "two faces" theme of the song. However, the hits then dried up and Christie's career was temporarily stalled when he was drafted into the army. On his return to performance in 1965, he signed with new management and extricated himself from his deal with Roulette. "I had to fight like hell to get out of the contracts with Morris Levy," Christie said.[21]

Levy had a tendency to view his acts as interchangeable and disposable. While he might purchase a master from an outside producer and then sign the act to Roulette, he did not work with the act to develop a distinctive style and sound, or necessarily promote the work that was produced in the marketplace adequately. One of his biggest missed opportunities in the early sixties came when he picked up a single produced by distributor/small label operator Henry Stone (born Epstein), who operated out of Miami, Florida. Stone ran Tone distribution, one of the largest regional one-stop distributors, dominating the South Florida marketplace. (A one-stop handled many different labels, enabling a record store to buy all its inventory from one source.) He had a keen eye for talent and ran a number of small labels as side businesses to working with independents like Roulette, Atlantic, and Chess. Stone remained a powerful figure on the South Florida scene through the early 1980s, and would work with Levy many times through his career.

In 1962 Stone heard a new duo performing at a Miami club, Dave Prater and Sam Moore. Impressed by Prater's smooth lead singing and Moore's gospel intensity, he produced their first single, "I Need Love," issuing it locally on his Marlin label. Unable to take the record national, he sold the master to Levy. Stone had hired a local musician, Steve Alaimo, to oversee the session for this single, and Alaimo would continue to work with the duo along with Roulette's house A&R man, Henry Glover, after they were signed in 1962. (Alaimo was a popular white performer in Miami who was also managed by Stone; he later gained fame hosting the Dick Clark teen TV show *Where the Action Is* from 1965–66.)

Unfortunately, Alaimo and Glover were unable to decide what direction to take the duo. Some of the songs they cut focused on lead singer Prater as a kind of soulful balladeer ("So Nice") while others bridged the gap between Prater's crooning and Sam's more intense singing (on Alaimo's composition "I Found Out," which starts rather mildly but has a strong gospel coda with Sam ripping it up vocally in response to Dave's lead). While the accompanying musicians were adequate, and the recording quality much better than what Stone achieved on the duo's first single, the overall feeling of these recordings is generic early-sixties pop. More troubling to the duo was Levy's lack of attention to their work; Sam recalled that Levy seemed totally unaware that they were signed to Roulette when the duo went to confront him at his Miami Beach home about the label's lack of support for their efforts:

> Roulette weren't doing anything . . . no promotion, nothing. The records weren't going anywhere. . . . I didn't know what to do. This guy, who was working for Roulette, said, "Why don't you go to Morris and get out of your record contract?" . . .
>
> Morris had a beach house in Miami. Dave and me went to his house and rang the doorbell. A white maid came to the door and gave me and Dave a dirty look. You have to understand that this was the '60s, and we were just starting to depart from color segregation in the buses and restaurants.
>
> "My name is Sam, and this Dave, and we're here to see Mr. Levy." The maid slammed the door in our face. So we rang the bell again and she answered the door and yelled, "You will have to go 'round the side, you're not coming through the house." A very brash woman. We went 'round the side of the house. Morris Levy was sitting on the lawn with a few beautiful girls in bikinis and these tough-looking guys with heavy coats on. Not the sort of clothes to wear in the Florida sunshine, but great for concealing guns.
>
> Morris Levy didn't even know who we were. "Who are you?" he asked. "Mr. Levy, sir, we've come to get our contracts." "What contract?" Morris replied. "We're signed to your label, sir." He calls his secretary to go and get our contracts, and then gives [us] our contracts back. Whilst he's finding our contracts, I start to make eyes with one of the girls. I ask her if she's married. She is, to Mr. Levy. So Dave and I leave the house in a hurry.[22]

It seems unlikely that Levy would just hand them their contracts and let them go; in any case, the duo either left or were dropped from Roulette sometime in 1964.

Ironically, it took the fresh ears of Atlantic Records producer Jerry Wexler—who saw the duo perform in Miami, again at the invitation of Henry Stone—to see the potential in the act. The songs they recorded for Stax/Atlantic have become classics of sixties soul. After they scored their successes at Stax, Levy characteristically dug up his old masters and reissued some of the Sam and Dave material he owned, although these records still failed to make a dent on the charts.

Leader Of The Laundromat
b/w Ulcers

R-4590

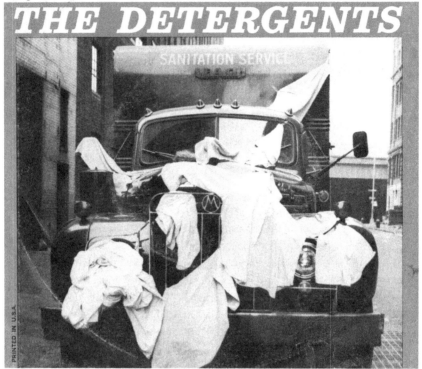

"Leader of the Laundromat," the parody hit that helped pump new life into Roulette in 1965, recorded by the Detergents.

Like many other independents, Levy was not above riding fads or even dipping his toes into the novelty market. Satires of current hits always drew attention from radio deejays and could bring quick cash if not lasting fame to the artists who produced them. One of the more successful Roulette releases of this period was 1964's "Leader of the Laundromat" by the Detergents, a satirical response to girl group the Shangri-La's mega-hit "Leader of the Pack." The overwrought emotionalism of the original was ripe for satire, as was its combination of opening dialogue ("Is she really going out with him?"), sound effects (motorcycle engine sounds; the "off-screen" crash that killed her boyfriend), and teenage fantasy. In the Detergents version of the story, the lovers meet at the laundromat, but he drops her because their laundry comes out "brown"; running away in despair, she is hit by a garbage truck (complete with crash sound effects). Although similar in overall structure, the Detergents were careful to alter the melody and chord progression enough to make it an "original" composition. Nonetheless Jeff Barry, Ellie Greenwich, and Shadow Morton—composers of "Leader of the Pack"—sued the writers of the song, eventually settling out of court.

The songwriters were Paul Vance and Lee Pockriss. The duo's first big score came in 1960 with the novelty hit by Brian Hyland "Itsy Bitsy Teeny Weenie Yellow Polka Dot Bikini." They assembled the group to record "Leader of the Laudromat," including Vance's nephew Danny Jordan (who sang lead vocal), Ron Dante, and Tommy Wynn. They enjoyed enough success that they recorded an entire album (*The Many Faces of the Detergents*) and appeared both under their nom-de-disc and under their own surnames on teen pop TV shows like *Shindig!* and toured with Dick Clark's stage shows through 1966. Dante enjoyed a second brief period of fame in 1969 as lead singer for the cartoon group the Archies and the voice behind the Cuff Links, who had a hit with "Tracy"—also written by Vance and Pockriss.

According to Roulette's then-accountant Ira Hertzog, the success of "Leader of the Laundromat" helped save Roulette at a particularly difficult time for the company financially:

[By 1963] Morris was broke.... [he] had $10,000 left. And we had a promo guy by the name of Red Schwartz. He had a record. We had 10 grand. If you file bankruptcy, you lose it. You might as well buy the record. And the record ["Leader of the Laundromat"] started to make some noise ... It hit the charts. You don't file bankruptcy if you have a record on the charts. And that creates some action ...[23]

Levy also prospered through continuing efforts to milk every last penny out of the catalog of recordings he had built at Roulette and the other labels that he had purchased. His stroke of genius was to recognize that fifties teenagers had matured into sixties young parents and that they were already becoming nostalgic for their carefree high school years and the songs they heard on their transistor radios. At a time when there was no concept of "oldies," Levy launched an LP series titled *Golden Goodies*, mostly drawing on his own recordings. Levy cleverly realized that he could "license" his own back catalog to himself, paying no fee, and thus incurring no obligation to pay the artist a portion of the royalty. Meanwhile, he could continue to collect publishing and authoring fees on any song that he published and/or partially "authored" (often taking an authoring credit in order to take a cut of that income stream). Initially, twelve albums were released in mid-1963. *Billboard* reported that the series was an immediate success, thanks to canny marketing and also many radio promotions.[24] The discount album series would continue to be a staple of the Roulette product line well into the seventies, and Levy would also use it as the basis for developing direct-to-consumer sales through late-night TV ads.

The *Golden Goodies* releases had some unintended side effects. One number featured on the first volume was "Rip Van Winkle" by the Devotions, an obscure vocal group who had recorded in the early sixties for producer Ran Sanchez's Delta label. The record had had some success in 1962 in the New York region, but otherwise was hardly a "golden" oldie. Having purchased the Delta masters, Levy probably threw on the Devotions track as a way of padding out his first *Golden Goodie* release. Surprisingly, the song began gaining traction, with a re-released single version selling 15,000 copies in its first week on release in Pittsburgh. In February 1964, the song reached #36 on the *Billboard* Top 100 charts, and the Devotions—who had already disbanded, with some members unavailable due to being drafted into the army—reformed. They made a few more recordings before finally petering out.[25]

One of the labels that Levy absorbed from Goldner's empire was Tico. Levy maintained it as a separate label, and hired producers with knowledge of Latin music to build the list. Levy also upgraded the quality of Tico's album covers and recordings. When his pop and jazz acts started fading in the early sixties as dependable sources of income, Levy turned to Tico and its dependable—if smaller—market. By 1966 sales on typical Tico releases were in the 25,000 to 50,000–unit range, according to the label's sales manager.[26]

One artist who originally recorded in the fifties for Tico was Tito Puente. Levy arranged for Puente to leave Tico for RCA, with its ability to pay bigger advances; however by the early sixties Puente was dropped by the major label and returned to Tico, now under Levy's ownership. There Puente achieved hits not only on his own but accompanying the powerhouse—and wildly unpredictable—Cuban-born vocalist, La Lupe. Like many other artists, Puente had mixed feelings about his industry mentor. On the one hand, Levy provided solid work for the band during the fifties at Birdland and a home for them on record in the sixties; on the other, Levy expected complete loyalty from his artists, and his ties to the Mob were obvious to musicians like Puente, who spent a lifetime working in clubs owned and operated by many shady figures. Joe Conzo, band member and friend of Puente, recalled:

> To Tito there was nothing middle-of-the-road about Levy—he was either loved or loathed. Tito knew that the record entrepreneur was reputed to be in the employ of the Genovese crime family. Levy wasn't shy about throwing his weight around. Depending on the situation, Levy could come across as either warm, mellow and caring or very much a bully. "If you pissed him off you could get into a hell of a lot of trouble," exclaimed Tito.... [Levy] never mentioned or spoke of his business dealings with Tito. "This was probably why we got along so well. With him and me it was all music. I'm sure I pissed him off once or twice, but we always remained friends. He was always there for me."[27]

Conzo said that Tito often spoke to Levy about his problems in the industry, with Levy reassuring him, "We'll take care of the cock suckers, don't you worry." According to Conzo, Levy sent Puente "a substantial amount of money—five figures" after Puente's mother passed away in 1978 to help him during his period of bereavement.[28] Eddie Palmieri, another Tico artist, took a less rosy view of Levy, realistically assessing his relationship with the recording mogul: "[You] knew that whatever you signed, you signed everything away to [him] one way or the other."[29]

Ironically, one of Levy's biggest pop hits came from Puerto Rican conga player/bandleader Joe Cuba with 1966's "Bang Bang," which introduced mainstream America to boogaloo. Cuba had been on the scene since the fifties and was a regular in New York clubs, playing for both Latino and African American audiences. The band first scored pop success with "El Pito," based on the opening riff from Dizzy Gillespie's Cubop classic "Manteca." The band added lyrics, improbably including the repeated refrain "I'll never go back to Georgia" although, as many critics noted, they had never been south of Houston Street. But their real hit was the infectious "Bang Bang," launched in the New York market by Levy's old friend deejay Symphony Sid, now hosting a Latin music show.[30] The single was a million-seller, an unheard-of success for a Latin band on the pop charts. Another hit, "Push Push Push," followed in similar style.

Levy explained boogaloo's appeal as the perfect marriage of African American soul with Latin rhythms, showing the rapid assimilation of Mexican, Puerto Rican, and Cuban emigrants: "There's a . . . generation of Latin kids in the U.S. who talk perfect English, but who go for Latin sounds. Yet, boogaloo is becoming so popular in other countries that we're now also having to do versions in Spanish for countries where they speak strictly Spanish."

Levy bragged about the growth of the Latin market and Roulette's dominant role in it: "With all of this talk about rhythm and blues, you have about 20 million Latin Americans in the United States starving for Latin music, plus another 400 million around the world who are Latin and moving into the middle-class environment in many countries. . . . We will do 1 million more in business this year than last."

In the mid-sixties, Levy extended his stakes in the Latin market by buying two other leading labels in the field, Alegre and Mardi Gras. Levy bragged that within months of purchasing Alegre he had increased its gross sales by "three or four times" over the previous year.[31] Another appeal of the Latin market was the low rate of returns on Tico sales; unlike pop groups who failed to chart, Levy could count on Tico artists to sell steadily, year in and year out, with little need to remainder his inventory: "The return factor is less than 3 per cent. And your catalog stays good; we've never scrapped a Tico album."[32]

Roulette's PR man, Red Schwartz, confirms that the Tico product sold well and helped keep the company afloat during lean times. He also confirms that Levy protected his product against anyone who dared to try to bootleg it for profit:

> We found someone bootlegging our Tico Record line. I said to the guy, "Are you nuts? Counterfeit Columbia, counterfeit RCA, but don't counterfeit Morris." Anyway, we get the guy in . . . Morris is sitting in the middle [of the room] . . . with his feet up on the desk, leaning back in his chair and never opened his eyes. . . . And there's three guys, they look like the bad boys from *The Untouchables*. . . . [Morris] says, "I wanna know one thing. Who's your partner [in] this operation?" And the kid says, "I don't know what you're talking about." And the guy sitting next to Morris says, "Let me just break one fucking kneecap." And I saw the color drain from the kid's face. I thought he was gonna fall right then and there. He turned ashen white. And Morris said, "I asked you one question—Who's your partner in this operation?" And the kid opened up completely. Morris never opened his eyes all this time. I leaned into Morris and I said, "Morris, don't do anything drastic. The IRS just came in, and besides giving you a clean bill of health, they're refunding about $800,000 to you." He opened his eyes. To make a long story short, [Morris] turned [the bootlegger] in the next day [to the authorities] and the kid got away with a $25 fine.[33]

This bootlegger got off easy; Levy bragged on a separate occasion to *Billboard* "Vox Jox" columnist Claude Hall about how he dealt with another bootlegger copying his product:

> "Over in New Jersey. I got some boys and we went over there and broke a few legs." But later, he said, he heard the same guy was back in business. "So, I got some more boys and we jumped in the car and headed across the George Washington Bridge. About halfway over, we noticed this long black limousine following behind us. When we reached the end of the bridge, we turned around and went home."[34]

Levy was tough, but also shrewd enough not to mess with fellow mobsters.

Levy formed another partnership in the mid-sixties with a record producer named Nate McCalla. McCalla got his start in the record business in the early sixties thanks to label owners Jules and Roy Rifkind, small-time operators similar to Goldner.[35] He formed Calla Records along with record promoter Jerry Shifrin in 1965 (who subsequently left the label in 1968). In August 1966, *Billboard* announced that Roulette had purchased 50 percent of the label's stock and that the operation was moving into Roulette's offices.[36] McCalla served as a kind of bodyguard/collection agent/all-around factotum for Levy. Tommy James described them as physically near twins, both large, tough looking, and intimidating. The Calla label had one big hit in 1966 with the hefty (300-plus pound) J. J. Johnson's "But It's Alright," and also produced singles with other R&B artists until about the mid-1970s with varying success.[37]

Among the first releases on the Calla label was a single by a then 19-year-old singer from Detroit named Bettye LaVette. The song was "Let Me Down Easy," written by a friend of hers, Dee Dee Ford. LaVette described McCalla as "bankrolled" in his label by "underworld contacts" (presumably Levy). Even at her young age, LaVette recognized that McCalla had considerable clout in the business and she felt certain that through his powerful contacts he could make the record a hit. At first, LaVette enjoyed the full support of the label:

> McCalla and his cronies loved me. They gave me an unlimited budget to promote ["Let Me Down Easy"]. They asked, "What TV show do you want to go on?" With their muscle, I had many choices. I said *Shindig!* 'cause that was the only show I knew. If I had been smart like Berry Gordy, I would have said *The Ed Sullivan Show*. Sullivan was the big reason why the Motown acts crossed over in such spectacular fashion. But, still a teenager, I had my mind on teenage shows.[38]

The song reached #20 on the R&B charts but then quickly "vanished," in LaVette's words. She cut a few more singles for Calla (some were also released on Roulette) through about 1967.

Besides his work running Calla Records, McCalla served as an enforcer for Levy in his attempts to collect unpaid bills from distributors and also to thwart the many bootleggers who illegally copied Roulette's releases. According to Tommy James, McCalla helped Levy shut down bootleggers who were illegally copying his records by threatening them with baseball bats, and once confronted a record dealer in Boston who owed Levy money by swinging a mace and chain over his head and demanding that he produce a check—which was quickly written. Nonetheless, a lawyer who represented McCalla described him "as gentle as a Great Dane."[39]

By the mid-sixties, Levy's days as a club owner were behind him; his involvement with Birdland seems to have ended in the early sixties, with manager Oscar Goodstein being primarily responsible for the club's operation until it finally closed in early 1965. Levy continued to have ownership stakes in the Embers and Roundtable, but how much he was involved in running these clubs during this period is unclear. However, Levy did make one last major push in concert promotion in April 1965, returning to the scene of his past triumphs with Alan Freed: Manhattan's Paramount Theater.

The Paramount itself had seen better days as it limped into the sixties. Finally, in 1964 a development group purchased the property with plans to knock down the aging theater and replace it with office buildings. While the details were being sorted out with the city, the hall was shuttered. In 1965 Levy convinced the owners to lease the theater to him to present rock and roll shows there for a year beginning with the Easter season.[40] As before, Levy gambled that the "slow" holiday season would actually be a boon for a teen-oriented show, since many teens would be on school vacation. But instead of booking a rock 'n' roll act to headline the show, Levy turned to a local celebrity/TV host known for his popularity among young adults, Soupy Sales. He filled out the bill with Little Richard, who was making a return to performing rock after having renounced sinful music to become a minister; the British invasion group the Hollies on their first US tour; Shirley Ellis (briefly famous for her novelty hit "The Name Game"); Roulette's own Detergents; and the King Curtis band. The show was an enormous success; the newspapers reported that Sales broke Frank Sinatra's attendance records from the forties. Sales recalled: "We made something like $295,000 in ten days. They were carrying the money out in bushel baskets and cardboard boxes. There were mounted police all over the place. We thought it was a riot."[41]

As was typical for stage shows of the day, the headliner was given the longest time slot, with the other acts performing shorter sets based on their popularity. The stage act was repeated five times a day along with a feature film, so timing was critical to be sure to maximize the number of tickets that were sold. After the first show, Levy realized that the stage show was running long, so he asked everyone to cut back on their act, except Sales—who as headliner was allowed to continue to enjoy his full time allotment. Little Richard was infuriated by Levy's decision and refused to cut back on his performance. According to Sales, when the Paramount's security team attempted to escort him out of the building, Richard held "himself down in the elevator and he said he wasn't going to leave" unless his full time was restored; Levy refused.[42] Richard told a newspaper reporter: "They wanted me to cut my act to six minutes. I take that long just to warm up. It was an insult to me as an artist." Richard told another interviewer: "Me and Morris Levy got into a fight. He got mad at me and Jimi Hendrix [who was touring with Richard as his guitarist at the time] and he told me, 'You'll find yourself floating in a lake.' I never heard that before, so I called him a black dog. And when I said 'black dog,' he leaped up from behind that desk. I didn't know that Morris could jump that high."[43]

Richard threatened to sue for the full $35,000 fee that he was promised for the ten days of performances, even though he was forced out of the show on the second day. Sales claimed that Richard vowed to take revenge against him, hiring gunmen to sit in the balcony of the theater to have him shot during the next performance; he claimed that a "kid with a gun" was apprehended by the police at the time, although no charges were made.[44]

The show was also notable for introducing the Hollies to America. Ever the businessman, Levy also saw an opportunity to invest in the group's trio of songwriters. He paid for studio time for the group to record demos of twenty-five of their original songs and then took Nash and his bandmates out to dinner at his Roundtable restaurant, softening them up with a good meal, liquor, and an enticing belly dancer who performed for them table side. (Nash says that the song "Stop! Stop! Stop!" was inspired by her hypnotic gyrations.) After dinner, he offered Nash, Tony Hicks, and Allan Clarke an unheard-of amount of money—$25,000 each—for the rights to their publishing. This was an offer that was difficult to refuse, as the group was still struggling to get on its financial feet. Nonetheless, Levy's reputation preceded him, and Nash and his writing partners were hesitant to make a deal, as Nash recalls: "Having dinner with Morris Levy was one thing; getting into bed with him was another altogether. We'd heard stories . . . how he put his name on all the records Roulette released . . . But we heard other things that scared the shit out of us. . . . So we weren't willing to sign with him, even for seventy-five grand, even though he was very kind to the Hollies." Nash had successfully wooed Levy's secretary and was sleeping with her during the group's US sojourn; he feared, perhaps not unrealistically, that Levy would have "cut off my dick and put it on a keychain" if he had discovered the affair. Nonetheless, Nash admired Levy's commercial acumen, characterizing him decades later as "a gentleman thug, a great white, one of the early record sharks."[45]

Despite this success, subsequent shows produced by Levy at the Paramount failed to draw crowds. Following the Soupy Sales review, Levy put together a country music show headed by Flatt & Scruggs. While the group had been successful at Carnegie Hall two years earlier—and was riding a wave of popularity thanks to the TV sitcom *The Beverly Hillbillies* and their performance of its theme song—the show itself failed to draw. Levy attributed the failure to the difference in country versus rock audiences: "The country and western [audience] is adult-oriented; and the adults just do not support theater shows like teenagers do." He also blamed the various groups' labels for failing to help promote the show.[46] Levy next booked a Latin music revue (led by Xavier Cugat), which fared slightly better, but the following weeks were disappointing, and after six weeks Levy threw in the towel.

During the mid-sixties, Roulette's fortunes seem to vary from day to day, with contradictory notices appearing in the trade press about the label's future. Perhaps in an attempt to revive the label's glory days, Roulette announced the return of producers Hugo and Luigi to its A&R staff in 1964, in a deal that was purported to include Roulette paying the duo $1.2 million for their publishing and recording holdings.[47] The return of the producers to the label was duly

The Hullabaloos, one of the least successful of the British Invasion bands, who were brought to Roulette by Hugo and Luigi during their second stint at the label in the mid-sixties.

noted by the FBI, who were told by an unnamed informant that the duo's return "will give [Roulette] a tremendous new market in the field of phonographic record production."[48] However, the reunion lasted only about a year and a half, with the producers leaving Roulette in December 1965 and going independent again, taking their publishing interests with them.[49] It is unclear whether they left after discovering that Roulette was no longer a fully functioning label or whether Levy realized that that their production style had become out of date in the face of newer pop acts.

During their brief return tenure at Roulette, Hugo and Luigi signed one of the lesser British Invasion groups, the Hullabaloos. The group took their name from their hometown, Hull, England, a British seaport—just as the Beatles came from another working-class seaside town, Liverpool. Inspired by Beatlemania, the group was adopted by "John Chichester-Constable, Lord Paramount of the Seigniory of Holderness, who took them out of local clubs[,] ensconced them in his baronial home[,] and decided to manage them."[50] Levy marketed them as "England's New Singing Sensation," emphasizing the fact that all four members sang. Never a big act in the UK, they had a minor hit in the United States with their cover of Buddy Holly's "I'm Gonna Love You Too," and recorded two albums for Roulette. At least their records were sparely produced, unlike Hugo and Luigi's more typical heavy-handed productions.

Meanwhile, rumors continued to swirl around Roulette's future. An unnamed informant interviewed by the FBI asserted that Motown was interested in possibly purchasing the label, reportedly investing $800,000 in Roulette in 1964.[51] In August 1965, *Variety* announced that Levy was trying to sell the label for the asking price of $1.75 million, claiming "various labels and interested parties are said to be discussing a deal."[52] At the same time it was announced that Roulette's longtime sales director Bud Katzel was joining Colpix Records. Little did Levy know that he would shortly sign one of the hottest new acts of the sixties, bringing newfound riches into Roulette's coffers.

The artist who saved Roulette from folding entirely in the mid-sixties was Tommy James, whose hit song "Hanky Panky" launched a three-year streak for the artist. Like many other artists, James came to Levy through serendipity. Tommy Jackson (his birth name) began his career in high school with his friends in Niles, Michigan, forming a garage rock band called the Shondells to play at dances and parties. Their music attracted the attention of a local deejay, Jack Douglas, who in 1964 issued their single "Hanky Panky" locally on his Snap label. While sales were strong among local teens, the single quickly disappeared from the shelves and the Shondells graduated from high school and went their separate ways. Jackson performed with another group called the Koachmen following his graduation in 1965 that found work around Michigan and in the Chicago area.

The exact details of how the record was rediscovered a year later in Pittsburgh are unclear. At the time, James said in an interview that a deejay in Pittsburgh known as "Mad Mike" (Mike Metrovich)[53] found a copy of the original Snap single in a cutout bin and began playing it on the air. However, in his autobiography, he says that it was actually a dance promoter named Bobby Mack who found the disc and began playing it at local hops.[54] Either way, facing the sudden success of the record and the demand of local teens to get a copy, a bootleg copy was quickly printed up. In May 1966, it was reported that the record had already sold about 11,000 copies locally; James claims that 80,000 copies were sold in the first ten days. By tracking the Snap label back to Niles, Bobby Mack located Tommy; Mack then signed James to a management contract and within a week arranged to take him to New York to hawk the record to the majors.[55]

Mack's New York connection was Chuck Rubin, a talent agent who managed the group the Happenings, among others; Rubin would later become a major thorn in Morris Levy's side as the head of Artists Rights Enforcement Corporation, which was dedicated to recovering unpaid royalties for early R&B and rock artists. According to James, the trio of Rubin, Mack, and Tommy made the rounds of several labels, including the majors (RCA and Columbia) and several independents. When Mack and Rubin stopped by the Roulette offices, Levy was out of town, so they left a copy of the single for him to review.

In his memoirs, James tells of how Levy quickly asserted his claim to the record and pushed aside all other offers:

The next morning, a frantic phone call from Chuck Rubin got us out of bed in a hurry. He told us that every record company we had gone to see yesterday, the ones that had been so eager to sign us to a deal, had inexplicably called him up to tell him they were going to pass on the record. One of them, Jerry Wexler from Atlantic Records, admitted that he had received a call from Morris Levy, the President of Roulette, who informed him, "This is my fucking record! Leave it alone["] . . . Morris was on a first-name basis with everyone in the music business and, as we later discovered, called each executive the following morning and made it clear that "Hanky Panky" would be better off at Roulette. No one disagreed.[56]

While Levy undoubtedly had the clout to intimidate the independents like Atlantic and Red Bird, it is hard to believe he could stop major labels Columbia or RCA from signing James if they had really wanted to. In fact, Chuck Rubin disputes James's version of these events. He says that Nick Cenci—the Pittsburgh distributor for Roulette who had previously sent Lou Christie to the label—had strongly recommended that Mack make a deal with Levy before they traveled to New York, but that Mack wanted to shop the record around. Rubin took "Hanky Panky" to a producer at Columbia—a young attorney who had no background in music—who passed on the record, despite the fact that it was a major hit in Pittsburgh. Other small labels were interested but their offers were not as good as Levy's, who offered more money upfront.[57] According to James, Rubin justified their signing with Levy by telling him that Roulette desperately needed a hit, saying "nobody knows better how to score hit singles than Morris Levy and Roulette."[58]

Yet another version of this story is told by Roulette's house PR man, "Red" Schwartz. In his telling, he was contacted by a fellow promotion man out of Pittsburgh, Mitch Zinthy, informing him that "Hanky Panky" was getting considerable airplay in Pittsburgh and that "locally looks like it could be a smash." So, Schwartz flew out to Pittsburgh to hear the record; his initial impression was far from favorable:

> I listened to the record and said, "Jesus Christ, biggest piece of crap I've ever heard in my life." [Then] I looked at the charts: Number 3 and number 1. And I found out it had sold about 40,000 so far in Pittsburgh. I made a deal—I offered Bob Mack $10,000 but I picked [it] up [from] record number 1, so I really gave him nothing because I picked up all the money from the initial sales, from [Mack's bootleg release]. . . .[59]

When Schwartz returned to New York to tell Levy about the deal, Levy was annoyed that he paid so much for an obscure record, until Schwartz explained that by picking up the rights to the original single, he in effect offset the $10,000

RECORDED BY TOMMY JAMES AND THE SHONDELLS ON ROULETTE RECORDS

SOMEBODY CARES

Words and Music by Harvey Weisenfeld, Ritchie Cordell and Bo Gentry

BIG SEVEN MUSIC CORP.

75¢

Tommy James and the Shondells shown on the sheet music cover for "Somebody Cares," published by Levy's Big Seven Music.

purchase price with the income of $8,600 that the record had already earned, so the total cost to Roulette was a paltry $1,400.

However and whoever made the deal, in 1966 Tommy James made the trip to New York to meet Levy and to record his first album. James's description of his first visit to the Roulette offices shows how the once plush headquarters—while active as a beehive—was taking on a shopworn look:

> I remember thinking it was not nearly as plush as some of the other [record] com-
> panies we had seen.... Inside the main reception area, there were about a dozen
> small offices down a long, L-shaped hallway. The sound of phones ringing came
> out of every office. There was always a phone ringing in between scattered, echoing
> conversations, and people were constantly moving in and out of offices.... As you
> walked down the hallway different kinds of music—Latin, rock and roll, jazz—came

pouring out of every door. The walls were lined with framed gold records. . . . At the end of the hallway was a large suite with a separate receptionist. *Mr. Levy* was written in raised metal script on a mahogany door.[60]

Levy's office had a back door and private rear elevator through which he could escape when needed.

James's initial impression of Levy mirrored the recollections of others. A big, imposing man who spoke in a throaty New York accent, Levy gave off the aura of an old-time criminal which attracted both respect and, in an odd way, affection:

> Morris Levy looked like the pictures I had seen of . . . Al Capone, except that Morris was bigger and scarier. He was thirty-nine years old but he looked much older. He was very imposing and he talked and laughed in a style that commanded attention and even a kind of reverence. But there was something very likeable about him. He was an average dresser, not flashy, slightly balding, six foot three, and about 230 pounds. He did not have to be at the head of the table or behind his desk for someone to know that he was the man in the room who ran the operation. I could not take my eyes off him.[61]

Roulette's release of "Hanky Panky" was an immediate smash, ousting even the Beatles' "Paperback Writer" from #1 in July 1966, according to *Cash Box*. Interviewed that November, James attributed the song's success to its return to a roots-rock sound:

> It's just plain hard rock, going back to the style of about four years ago. I figure that, with all this talk about music getting more melodious and better, the kids just were glad to hear something simple and easy to understand. "Hanky Panky" is a real blasting number. It was different from the intricate sounds, the intellectually higher level of music of today. The gimmick sounds have been getting out of hand and the kids just found this record a refreshing change.[62]

James may have been obliquely critiquing the baroque arrangement of "Paperback Writer" with its psychedelic touches. But the Shondells' garage-band aesthetic was not unique; the same week they were topping the charts with "Hanky Panky," the Troggs were enjoying Top 10 success with "Wild Thing"—an equally "blasting number."

Having a hit, the Shondells needed an album so they—and Roulette—could cash in on what might be a very fleeting window of popularity. The group was flown to New York and rushed to Bell Sound Studios to work with Henry Glover on creating an album's worth of material. The group put together a mix of James's and their own originals along with a slew of R&B covers.[63] Red Schwartz described the sessions as a rush job, based on the need to cash in on the success of the single: "I had no faith in this group. I'd booked recording time for an album, three hours a night for three nights. . . . They didn't make a hit record on the first album, because it was just too fast."[64] However, when the group had a followup smash with "I Think We're Alone Now," suddenly Roulette had a little "faith."

Unlike other artists who came to Roulette through a master purchase, James was actually taken under the wing by Levy, who became a kind of father-mentor to the young rocker. At first James enjoyed all the benefits that Levy's beneficence could bring: unlimited studio time, creative freedom, excellent promotion that kept his songs on top of the charts. It would take a while for James to start seeing Levy's darker side: his stinginess when it came to accounting for record sales, his paternalistic treatment of artists, and his lack of regard for their feelings about how he handled their professional careers. Levy seemed to have a perverse need to destroy the artists who were most valuable to him, to show them that their success was always contingent on his good will, and that he could send them back to the obscurity from whence they came if he so desired.

Tommy learned this lesson well when he went to see Levy to secure money to cover the expenses of the group's first national tour. In his first solo meeting with Levy, Tommy broached the subject of how the band was going to pay their bills on the road:

> "We're going on the road and we need some cash for expenses."
>
> "What?" Morris would start to get very rough, quickly, "Hotel bills, studio bills, you know how much you guys already cost me? Now you want more? . . . What are you doing to me, kid?" The voice was relentless, booming on and on, rough and threatening. I held firm . . . This was how you did business with Morris.
>
> All of a sudden the haranguing stopped. I had been delivered the lecture for the day and now we got back to business. "Karin [Levy said calling to his secretary] . . . cut Tommy a check for ten grand." That was the way it would always happen. First he would pulverize you, then he would end up giving you the money . . . As I left the office Morris said, "Hey, kid, don't be a stranger. Call every once in a while."[65]

Levy's ability to take both good cop and bad cop roles in his dealings was legendary; he could go from placid to volcanic and then return to being charming within seemingly a blink of an eye. James had to endure many such harangues through his years working with Levy.

Unlike Levy's other acts, James soon realized he would have to be in charge of his own creative direction if he was going to remain a viable act. For their second album, James and the Shondells were irritated that producer Henry Glover was forcing them to pad out the disc with a number of Levy copyrights. James also resented Glover's heavy-handed production techniques, and his attempts "to jazz up [their basic tracks] with a bunch of studio horn players doing schlock arrangements."[66] Soon after, James met songwriter Ritchie Cordell who along with his partner Sal Tramachi had a songwriting contract with Artie Ripp, who ran Kama Sutra Productions (a record label, music publisher, and management house). James liked what he heard, and introduced the duo to Levy. Levy quickly made a deal with Ripp, calling him on the phone and simply stating "Listen, I got two of your writers up here. My artist wants to work with them." "Whatever you want, Mo[i]she," Ripp replied.[67] James took the songwriters' demo of "It's Only Love" to the studio and within three hours had cut his next single. Working with another ex–Kama Sutra employee, Bo Gentry, Cordell next penned "I Think We're Alone Now," which would become one of James's best-known hits of the era and a smash hit in 1967. The Gentry-Cordell-James team was formed as a hit-making machine.

Although Gentry and Cordell were supplying the hits, they were hardly living high off the hog. Like most others who dealt with Levy, they had trouble getting accurate accountings of sales and collecting whatever was due to them. Red Schwartz described the minimalist lifestyle that Gentry enjoyed at the height of his fame; nonetheless, as a typical New Yorker, Gentry worried about protecting even his small number of possessions. Schwartz described picking up Gentry at his apartment:

> There isn't a piece of furniture in the living room. There's a little TV set in the middle of the floor with a pillow that he's leaning on, and he has a mattress in the other room that he's sleeping on. No bed, a mattress. He's watching TV and I looked around. . . . "Come on, let's go, Bo. I'll take you for a ride . . ." He gets up, starts to walk out, and I turn the TV off. He says, "No, no, no. Leave it on. What if somebody wants to rob me? I leave it on, they think there's somebody in here."[68]

As is apparent throughout James's memoir, Levy played the roles of both a surrogate father and a controlling despot with the young star. James credits Levy with helping him skirt several potential legal problems, and even helping him avoid the draft.[69] Levy helped James free himself of his original management deal with Bob Mack, setting him up with a more professional New York outfit. (In rather chilling detail, James tells how he listened through Levy's office door while Morris used his muscle to convince Mack to release James from his contract.[70]) Levy also policed James's relationship with Cordell and Gentry. When James discovered that the songwriters had worked up a song called "Gettin' Together" for Gene Pitney, he angrily asked why they had not given him "right of first refusal" on it. James called on Levy for support; Morris bluntly phoned the songwriters, saying "Get over here right now and bring that record Tommy likes." Although Pitney had already recorded the song for release, Levy simply said "Fuck Gene Pitney," and the song was given to James; it became his seventh gold record.[71] James expresses guilt in retrospect for his behavior at the time, but clearly was willing to benefit from Levy's muscle when he needed to. Eventually, Bo Gentry grew tired of trying to collect money from Levy, and in early 1968 Gentry went to work for rival Laurie Records. Cordell briefly joined him there, but returned in time to help James create the roots rocker "Mony Mony," his next major hit and a return to his garage band sound following the more bubblegum style of "I Think We're Alone Now."

In later years, Levy paid Cordell a flat fee for all his rights in James's hits.[72] Cordell subsequently complained that he had been cheated in this deal, but Levy raised the point that, like many other artists who sold their work to him, Cordell came to him at a low point in his career and needed cash. Levy further claimed that he tried to talk Cordell out of his selling his rights: "I imagine I would feel the same way if I sold something for, say, $20,000 and it was worth $50,000 ten or fifteen years later. But . . . it's like land. Hey, I bought land here [in Ghent, New York, where Levy's farm was located], $200 an acre. It's worth $12,000 an acre here today. Did I screw the guy I bought it off for $200 an acre if that was the going price?"[73]

James next adopted a psychedelic rock sound on 1968's "Crimson and Clover" and the following "Crystal Blue Persuasion," followed by 1969's trippy concept album *Cellophane Symphony*. A second greatest hits album also appeared that year, and James tells the amusing story of how Levy convinced his major distributors to place large advance orders for it:

> Morris . . . drove out to Las Vegas and invited all twenty-eight independent distributors along for a weekend of gambling and hedonism. . . . On Friday night, they all had envelopes shoved under their hotel doors with a hundred-dollar chip in each and Morris's blessing to have a good time. . . . He took care of all the rooms and all the other expenses. On Sunday, with each distributor hung over and probably a little chagrined, Morris announced his firm's intentions. "The New Tommy James Greatest Hits is going to ship platinum." He put his finger on each man's chest and said, "You're taking two hundred thousand copies, and you and you and you, a hundred thousand each, you understand me?" They understood.[74]

James's and the Shondells' careers were cresting, and although he would continue to record for Roulette with the band and then as a solo artist through the early seventies, James was no longer a dependable hit maker. Meanwhile, things were getting dicey at Roulette; in late 1971, Levy and his associate Nate McCalla disappeared from the offices for about six months, according to James, replaced by Levy's old business partner Joe Kolsky.[75] The reason for his disappearance was the unrest among the New York crime families that followed the death of Vito Genovese in 1969 in prison. Levy returned by mid-1972, but by then James's relationship with him had soured. James's new manager reconstructed the sales histories of James's biggest singles by getting a count of how many labels were supplied to Roulette by the printer, asserting that the singer was owed "between thirty and forty million dollars." Such an assertion seems hard to believe, as James was probably earning only three to five cents per single sold; at that rate he would have to have sold about seventy-five to a hundred million records to be owed that much. Nonetheless, James probably was shorted by Levy in his accountings for sales. When confronted with this information, Levy's response was predictable and so frightening that James's manager quickly dropped his client.[76] James and Levy had a final blow-up over payments in 1972, and Levy finally released him from his contract in 1974.

8

Remainders: 1969–1974

The music business is like a big pie. There are slices for everyone.
You don't f--- with my piece; I don't f--- with yours.
—Morris Levy

By the late sixties Roulette was increasingly becoming merely a front for Levy's silent partners, who were putting pressure on him to produce a return on their investment. Pressures on the Mafia itself, including increased scrutiny by New York and Federal authorities, led to Levy forging new alliances that would in turn bring him increasingly under suspicion. Sometime in the mid- to late sixties, longtime backer Dominic Ciaffone was joined by a new partner, Tommy Eboli, who had a much higher profile in the Mafia world; some sources believed that Eboli had ascended to head the Genovese crime family by this time. Eboli and Levy discovered new ways to make money from the record business that did away with the need to deal with often petulant artists, producers, and songwriters. They entered the business of buying and selling remaindered or overstock records from the major labels, as well as ruthlessly mining Roulette's own back catalog through direct-to-consumer advertising on late-night television.

Levy's relationship with Ciaffone was souring in the mid-sixties as Roulette struggled to make a profit. According to an unnamed FBI informant, Ciaffone was taking a stronger hand in running the label, much to Levy's chagrin. One informant even reported that "on March 19, 1962, [Ciaffone] physically beat up [Levy] in the Roulette office," stating that he did not know the reason for the altercation.[1] In March 1966, another informant stated that "JAMES PLUMERI, also known as 'Jimmy Doyle,' is backing Roulette with CIAFFONE and they are beginning to make money."[2] Doyle was the uncle of Johnny Dio (Dioguardi), and was a captain in the Lucchese crime family, involved with labor racketeering in the trucking and garment businesses. He was murdered during the Mafia wars of 1969–71.

According to a second informant reporting to the FBI in February 1966, Levy was becoming increasingly unhappy under the thumb of Ciaffone: "LEVY is scared to death of CIAFFONE and would like to break away from him but is afraid to do so."[3] Whatever his feelings toward Ciaffone, Levy kept him on Roulette's payroll until the mobster passed way in 1980, and sent money to his widow in 1986 when she needed $1,000 to help pay for surgery.[4]

Financial problems continued to plague Roulette through at least the end of 1966, when an FBI informant reported that Levy and Ciaffone were continuing to "sink 'dough' into [the] company." By early 1967, however, the same informant told the FBI that the company was now "financially sound."[5] FBI files from this period also report that Levy had taken out numerous loans to keep Roulette afloat from commercial banks, notably Bankers Life and Casualty Company in Chicago. The agency reported that while the bank was "not known as either a hoodlum controlled or dominated company . . . the bank . . . is capable of any kind of underhanded dealings which will make money."[6] According to a lawyer who worked with Levy, the ever parsimonious record executive worried over whether to purchase a dollar's worth of gasoline while driving his Rolls Royce to a meeting with the Chicago bank to discuss obtaining a $250,000 loan.[7] FBI sources felt that the total amount Roulette owed various banks had ballooned by the late sixties and early seventies to over $850,000.[8]

Complicating matters during this period was the increasing financial problems of Levy and Ciaffone's other major joint venture, the Roundtable restaurant. In early 1963, the restaurant filed for protection under the Bankruptcy Act; this was quickly followed that May by a claim filed against the restaurant by the US district attorney for unpaid taxes. The case was coming up for trial in spring 1965.[9] To prepare for it, the FBI methodically interviewed all of the club's creditors, including its law firm, food and liquor distributors, and PR agencies. This must have rattled Levy and Ciaffone, who certainly did not enjoy government scrutiny of their operations. As of early 1966, the once swanky East Side restaurant was described by the FBI as a "hangout for shylocks and gamblers."[10] Nonetheless, the restaurant remained open into the early seventies.

These cash problems and his growing unease about working with Ciaffone may have led Levy to seek an outside buyer for his music holdings. In September 1968, the *Wall Street Journal* reported that an agreement in principle had been reached to sell Roulette and Big Seven Music Publishing to Omega Equities Corporation, "a real-estate holding company." The *New York Times* reported that Omega, seeking to diversify its holdings, "took off on an acquisition trek, [acquiring] 10 companies in the music and entertainment, men's clothing, and technology fields" during that year.[11] Omega offered Levy and his partner Morris Gurlek $7.3 million for their holdings in the two companies, which were said to have done $3 million in business during the previous year.

However, by December 1968, Omega reported that the deal was off, due to "the possibility of adverse tax consequences." It was not specified whether it was

Omega or Levy/Gurlek who faced tax problems if the deal went through. Levy claimed to have ended the deal himself, telling *Billboard* at the time that, instead of selling out, he was aggressively expanding his businesses.[12] That same month, sales of Omega's stock were suspended because of Securities and Exchange Commission (SEC) concerns that the firm had offered "incomplete and inaccurate information relating to the company's financial condition, product lines and its acquisition program."[13] The SEC's interest may have been piqued by the amazing rise in Omega's stock price, from about 60 to 70 cents a share in April 1968 to a high of $33–35 in December, perhaps indicating the stock's price was being artificially inflated.[14]

Further information emerged when Roulette and Big Seven sued Omega in early 1969 for $2.5 million, saying that "Omega had announced a merger with them to enhance the value of Omega's stock." Omega responded that Levy and Gurlek were using the lawsuit as a means to avoid repaying a $300,000 loan made by the company to them in anticipation of closing the deal.[15] The sketchy details of this deal raise several tantalizing questions. As Omega was involved in real estate and construction, it may possibly have been a front for organized crime; the rush to invest in Omega's stock during 1968 may have been the result of an attempt to launder profits from other illegal activities.

Roulette's success with Tommy James and the rise of psychedelic rock led the label to sign a number of rock acts in the late sixties and early seventies, most of which failed to make the charts. Among the rock entrepreneurs who attracted Levy's attention was a half-Jewish, half–African American singer/songwriter/ producer/all-around hustler named Artie Wayne (born Wayne Kent). A protégé of teen idol Bobby Darin, Wayne first entered the music business in 1959, and soon was working for the famous Aldon Music operation, before forming his own publishing company. In 1968 he cut a demo record for his own song, "Come and Live with Me," and decided to release it under the nom de disc of Shadow Mann (a pun drawn on the lyrics in which Wayne sings he will "be your shadow, shadow man"). The song features typical late-sixties psychedelic elements, including a semi-shouted vocal, wah-wah guitar, and mountains of echo. Lacking capital to press and promote the record, Wayne went with his producer Ron Haffkine and publishing partner Keili Ross to Morris Levy seeking funding:

> Ronnie puts the music on . . . turns the volume up . . . and I leap onto Morris' desk!! In my black, floppy "Shadow Hat" . . . custom made black suede jacket with a giant red eagle on the back . . . I lip-synch my little heart out!! . . .
>
> Morris can hardly contain himself . . . he makes me perform it over and over for different members of his staff. Then he clears his office . . . leaving only the three of us. Morris slowly lights a cigar . . . and tries not to appear excited.

Then he says, "OK Shadow ... I want to do an album ... I'll even give you and Kelli your own label!! How much cash do you want to get started?" Haffkine chimes in "$25,000" ... at which point Morris reaches under his desk ... pulls out a brown paper bag and hands me $25,000 in cash!!

I look at Morris wide-eyed and say, "Don't you want me to sign anything?," he laughs and says, "Don't worry, I know where you live!"[16] [Ellipses in original]

The company they formed was named Tomorrow's Productions. As its second signing, Wayne brought a young Texas singer to the studio to record a novelty number commenting on John Lennon's recent *Two Virgins* album, with its cover portrait of Lennon and Yoko Ono in the nude. The song was "John You Went Too Far This Time," and the singer was Sissy Spacek, who Wayne gave the name of Rainbo. Wayne and Haffkine coproduced the record, which featured late Beatlesque psychedelic touches including harpsichord-like keyboards, Baroque trumpet licks (lifted from "Penny Lane"), and "I Am the Walrus"–style swirling strings. Both Wayne and Spacek toured in support of their records, but their fame was short-lived and the label ended when Wayne left to pursue opportunities on the West Coast in 1970.

Perhaps in a move to diversify his holdings beyond the music business—or planning for his future retirement—in 1968 Levy began purchasing farmland in Ghent, New York. By 1970 he had consolidated six different properties consisting of about 700 acres; the property eventually expanded to 2,000 acres.[17] He named the property Sunnyview, reportedly placing a plaque on the door to the large mansion he built on the property that said it was "a sunny place for shady characters."[18] In 1969 Levy announced a plan to build an eight-track studio on his property, "complete with living quarters and a cook," hoping to attract artists to record there. He told *Billboard*: "We're already negotiating with a full-time engineer who'll be available day or night at the studio. . . . [a] group will be able to record when they feel productive and not have to try to produce on demand."[19] Despite Levy's investments in the property, an informant told the FBI in 1970 that "the farm ... [c]ould not be self-sustaining and outside income would be necessary for it to function."[20]

At first Levy raised cattle on the property and operated a dairy, then switched to farming hay and corn in the mid-seventies, and finally raising race horses beginning in 1979.[21] Levy encouraged both Mob and music industry figures to invest in his horses. Tommy James—a frequent visitor to the property in the early seventies—reported that Levy kept "an arsenal of hunting rifles, pistols, and shotguns, and walls of ammunition" on the farm, purportedly for sporting purposes.[22] The *New York Times* noted that the complex included "a semi-Southern style mansion, complete with a pool, a bathhouse, a tennis court, and a man made lake."[23]

Levy's entanglement with mobsters seemed to deepen in the late sixties. In one of the most breathtaking scenes in Tommy James's memoirs, he recounts how Levy presented him to a group of his friends and backers following the death of Vito Genovese, the head of a major Mafia family who died in prison of a heart attack in 1969. Genovese's death sent shockwaves not only through the Mob world but also within Roulette, where James reported that all normal business seemed to come to a halt.

Ushered into the inner sanctum of Levy's offices, James was shocked to see a gathering of a veritable Mafia Who's Who:

Morris's office . . . was eerily quiet. Sitting on the L-shaped sofa and some scattered chairs were half a dozen very serious-looking men, with very solemn faces. Morris shut the door, which he never did, and walked me over to a guy sitting on a chair. He was leaning forward, elbow on knee, with his right hand cupping his chin. He had a shock of black hair and wore a white dress shirt opened at the neck and black slacks. "This is Mr. Gigante." I knew this was serious shit. Morris never called anybody "mister." Mr. Gigante shook my hand and said, "Hey." This was Vinnie "the Chin" from the Genovese family. I had just seen him the other night on the news as one of Vito [Genovese]'s possible successors. Morris turned me toward the sofa and said, "This is Mr. Cirillo." Better known as "Quiet Dom" Cirillo. . . . Next was a heavy, bald-headed, scary-looking guy with a cigar sticking out of his mouth. I knew who he was because I had seen him several times on TV. It was "Fat Tony" Salerno from the Jersey wing of the Genovese family. . . . When I went to shake Fat Tony's hand, Mr. Cirillo said, "This is Mr. Holiday." Maybe they were afraid I'd recognize the name.

Next came Mr. Vastola, whom I knew as Sonny Vastola, another member of the Jersey clan. Then Morris said, "And you know Mr. Eboli." . . .

With his hands on my shoulders, Morris said to all of them, "He's a good kid. He's got the number one record this week." They all gave a collective, deep-throated grunt of approval. "It was nice to meet you all," I mumbled. . . . and I left the room.[24]

This rogue's gallery of Mafia talent had deep connections in the music business. Vincent "The Chin" Gigante began his career in the early fifties as a boxer, managed by none other than Tommy Eboli (then going by the name of Tommy Ryan). Eboli also managed the young Dom Cirillo, another aspiring boxer who ended up a key member of the Genovese crime family; Cirillo and Gigante would remain close associates for decades. Gigante gained greater fame in the Mob world in 1957 when he was hired by Genovese to gun down rival Mob boss Frank Costello. When Costello was entering his apartment building, Gigante took a shot at him, but the bullet merely grazed Costello's head and he miraculously survived. In return for not identifying his assailant, Costello was able to "retire" from the Mob, while Gigante was saved from serving prison time. "Fat" Tony Salerno was another Genovese soldier and confidante of Gigante who fronted for Gigante when he became head of the Genovese family in the eighties.

Tommy Eboli became one of Levy's key partners/investors in 1969. He was born in Scisciano, Italy, in 1911, making him sixteen years older than Levy. The Eboli family immigrated to the United States shortly after his birth. Levy said he first met Eboli when he was fourteen years old and working as a hatcheck boy at the Greenwich Village Inn.[25] After working briefly as a boxing promoter, Eboli formed the Tryan [Tommy-Ryan] Cigarette Service company in 1952, leasing vending machines and jukeboxes to bars. Through the fifties and sixties, Eboli rose to be a major player in the Genovese crime family, serving as Vito Genovese's voice to the outside world beginning in 1959 when Genovese was imprisoned on narcotics charges. When Genovese died of heart failure in 1969, Eboli rose to head of the family. That same year, he partnered with Morris Levy in a new business called Promo Records. According to a 1972 government report, Eboli invested $100,000 in the new company for a 50 percent share, and drew a salary of $1,000 a week.[26]

Promo Records' business was based on buying remaindered records, which it would then resell to record stores and other distributors. Major labels often had leftover stock of records that failed to sell to initial expectations or simply was older stock that no longer had an immediate market. Remainder dealers would purchase these records in bulk at a greatly reduced price; the majors would thus clean out their warehouses, saving on inventory charges, while the remainder dealer could resell the product profitably to retailers. There was much room for fraud within this business. A remainder dealer could buy 500 copies of an album and then press several thousand more by simply copying the jacket and making a new master from a copy of the record; the remainder sale then would become a "front" for the more lucrative pirating of the original record.[27] The major labels also could benefit by remaindering albums that still were selling well, because the remaindered items were sold with no royalty obligation to the artist, would free up valuable and costly warehouse space, and the sale could be taken as a tax loss by the label. Some labels even came up with the idea of purposely overprinting records by acts that had little more than local success; the resulting "direct-to-remainder" inventory could help offset the profits on legitimate acts.

The major labels dealt with a small number of large resellers who had the financial means to purchase large quantities of stock; these dealers in turn sold to smaller regional dealers who would then move the inventory through jobbers who handled mom-and-pop record stores, smaller department store chains, and other outlets. At each level, fraud and piracy were rife. One common ploy was to exploit loopholes in distribution contracts. When the Electric Light Orchestra moved the distribution of their Jet label from United Artists to Columbia, Levy's Promo Records snapped up over 1.2 million remaining copies of the group's album *Out of the Blue* from UA's warehouses. CBS and Jet sued, saying that they were the owners of this inventory under the new distribution agreement they had signed; United Artists counterclaimed that it was allowed to sell off the remaining discs under the *same* agreement. Levy countersued CBS for "interfering with business, unfair competition, fraud, libel, etc.," charging his old friend Walter Yetnikoff as well as the label.[28] The group was left holding the bag; with their backlist album now available at a cutout price they obviously could not count on continued income from it.[29]

Another way to work the system was to reimport items sold to foreign distributors; technically these records were not to be sold in the United States, but once they were freely available on the European market, sold to various smaller distributors, there was no way to stop them from dumping records to American resellers who were willing to deal with them. The labels often sublicensed the manufacture of their product to foreign firms; these firms could legitimately press new records (although again these were supposed to be limited to their licensed markets). For these foreign pressing plants, it was tempting to simply press up additional inventory specifically to sell to the American remainder dealers. While not exactly piracy—or illegal—the labels and the artists were deprived of additional income and sales. This is the kind of behavior that—when practiced against Roulette—Levy was quick to discourage through sheer muscle; but that did not keep him from participating in these gray markets when it was to his advantage.

In a 1973 interview with *Billboard* magazine, Levy defended the role that remainder dealers like Promo played in the record business. He blamed the rack jobbers—the middleman distributors who placed the independent labels' releases in retail outlets—for over-ordering albums and then taking advantage of their returns privileges for the remainder problem:

> The rackjobber ... buy[s] the top-selling items, [and] takes the item off the shelf when it no longer sells, and give[s] the product back to the manufacturer on a 100 percent return policy. They take no risk and have no responsibility. The manufacturer ... is faced with either "eating" the returns or selling them as cutouts. You can't expect even the most idealistic manufacturer to "eat" three or four million of these records a year.[30]

Levy's Promo operation forged exclusive deals with many labels to purchase their overstock, including Atlantic and Motown. By making these deals, Levy claimed that Promo was actually "protecting" the major labels through its business operations. By selling product from all the labels, mixing the releases of various labels and various artists, Promo was not flooding the market with discs from any particular producer.[31] Levy even had the nerve to claim that remainder dealers *helped* artists, because the "artist welcomes the exposure and reaches markets he would never reach ordinarily."[32] Naturally, he didn't mention that the artist was deprived of the royalties normally paid on sales. According to Levy, Promo's cutouts retailed for between "33 cents to $1.99." In 1969, its first full year in business, Levy claimed that Promo grossed $1.8 million, and by 1972 the business had grown to $12 million; projected sales for 1973 were $15 million.[33]

Despite the rosy picture that Levy painted of the Promo operation as almost a service industry, he and Eboli jealously protected their turf and made sure smaller operators did not try to poach their business. One smaller dealer, John LaMonte, who worked out of Philadelphia, learned what it meant to try to make an end run around Levy's tight grasp on the market. Unable to purchase remainders directly from Motown because of its deal with Levy, LaMonte approached the label's Puerto Rico licensee, making a deal to purchase product directly from them. When Levy got wind of this, he called LaMonte to New York for a meeting to discuss the situation. According to journalist William Knoedelseder:

> LaMonte went to the meeting because he felt he had no choice—if he didn't go, they'd come after him sooner or later. Besides, he was a cocky young kid in those days and thought he could talk his way out of the situation. "How quick can you come up with $100,000 in cash?" was Levy's opening line. LaMonte's jaw dropped. "You better kill me now," he responded. Levy lowered the figure to $25,000. The threat was unspoken. LaMonte agreed to pay and to stop bringing in the records from Puerto Rico.[34]

This would not be LaMonte's last run-in with Levy.

Another mobster who partnered with Levy in 1969 was Joseph Pagano, who had a long history of loan sharking, extortion, and fraud. Eboli probably brought Pagano into the Roulette world.[35] In late 1968, an informant told the FBI that Pagano was partnering with Levy in a new record label in order to promote "two relatively unknown vocalists."[36] Levy often recorded singers who were managed by his mobster friends, including their various girlfriends. According to a producer who worked at Roulette: "We musta spent $250,000 a year recording big-titted phony blondes and hookers for these guys that Morris was doing favors for, using the best bands and backup you could find."[37]

Eboli partnered with Pagano to open a nightclub called the Camelot Inn in Rockland County featuring a singer who was "developed" by Pagano. An informant told the FBI that the singer allegedly cut a record for Roulette Records and TOMMY EBOLI was allegedly paid for putting [redacted] in touch with Roulette. The informant was asked if this was a routine transaction.

The informant advised that usually an individual who is cutting a record would need financial backing. . . . He stated the cost would be approximately $18,000 and that if the record was a hit then the entertainer, the backer, and the record company made money, and if it was a flop, the backer . . . would be out $18,000.

The information surmised that perhaps EBOLI may have been paid in records for distribution in his juke boxes.[38]

Eboli's taking records in lieu of payment would fulfill several purposes: It would inflate the "sales" numbers of the record itself, pushing it up the charts; it would save Roulette the actual cash, which could pay Eboli his commission in the form of the records that had a higher retail value than what they cost to produce; and it would make the transaction much more difficult to trace. After investigating this deal, it appears that—like many other of Roulette's questionable operations—the FBI concluded this was standard procedure in the often rough-and-tumble world of the record business.[39]

The late sixties and early seventies brought other changes to Levy's operations. Levy lost a major patron and friend in 1970 when Morris Gurlek died. Gurlek had given Levy his start as a hatcheck boy in the mid-forties, and the two had been partners in business from at least the early fifties when they formed M&M Concessions (presumably for Morris and Morris). By most reports, Gurlek was a pleasant, easygoing man in contrast to the often volatile Levy.[40] Gurlek was sixty-eight years old at the time of his death.[41] The FBI files note that Gurlek's holdings in Roulette, Big 7, and the other firms in which he held stock all went to Levy, although it is unclear what financial arrangement—if any—was made with Gurlek's widow and son.[42] Losing Gurlek as a mentor, confidant, and partner must have put additional strain on Levy, who had few longtime close associates by the end of the 1960s.

Another death in 1970 that affected Levy was the unexpected passing of George Goldner. Levy had come to Goldner's aid once again in 1966, purchasing his remaining interests in Red Bird Records, the ill-fated partnership Goldner had formed two years earlier with the songwriters/producers Leiber and Stoller. The songwriters had become dismayed by Goldner's selling the label's hit records through "back door" deals and his close association with mobsters. To rid themselves of this association, in 1965 Leiber and Stoller sold out their stake in the label to Goldner for a token dollar, and Goldner turned around a year later and sold out to Levy.[43] Ever the entrepreneur, Goldner's last attempt to launch a label came in 1970 with Firebird Records, but on April 15 he had a heart attack and died at the age of fifty-two.[44] Although he did not work directly for Levy, Goldner—through his constant need for funding—helped build the Roulette catalog. Every time he failed, Levy was able to scoop up his copyrights and masters.

One earlier partner who was key to Levy's publishing success—Phil Kahl—returned to the fold in 1971. Kahl had left to work with his brother, Joe Kolsky, at Diamond Records, which had a few minor successes in the early sixties. He also established several publishing firms to exploit the label's copyrights. The Kolsky/Kahl team then went to work for the William Morris talent agency in 1968, a leading agency for music acts.[45] A sharp dresser who was always dressed to the nines, Kahl brought a real showbiz mentality to the publishing operation.[46] His return undoubtedly gave Levy's publishing companies a much-needed boost, as he was an able and well-connected manager.

The late sixties and early seventies also was a time of unrest among the Mafia families, with many of Levy's closest associates being targeted by rival families. The *New York Times* reported at least fifteen Mob members killed beginning with the attempted murder of Joseph Columbo Sr. in June 1971 through summer 1972—although some placed the number closer to twenty-seven.[47] Tommy James reports in his autobiography that Levy mysteriously disappeared from the Roulette offices for a period of approximately six months from late 1971 to mid-1972: "The cover story was that Morris and Nate [McCalla, his business partner/bodyguard] had left for Spain. There was a war going on and Morris was on the wrong side. . . . Were there people after Morris who wanted him dead? It was only a few weeks before that Nate had warned me again, 'Don't walk outside with me. I don't know what's going to happen.'"[48] James's lawyer advised him also to leave town until things cooled down, so he went to Nashville to record his next album.[49]

The culmination of this period came when Tommy Eboli was gunned down on July 16, 1972, sometime before 1 a.m., "in traditional gangland fashion," according to the *New York Times*.[50] His body was found outside his girlfriend's apartment lying face down on the streets of Crown Heights, Brooklyn. Eboli had borrowed $4 million from rival gangleader Carlo Gambino to fund a new drug-trafficking operation, but before he could repay the loan the government had shut him down. Gambino purportedly ordered the hit on Eboli, although the murder is officially unsolved to this day. According to Joe Buonanno—a Gambino family capo—Eboli had angered one of his own capos, Vincent Gigante, who resented Eboli's management of Gigante's Greenwich Village crew. Buonanno said that Gigante was present at the hit to "make sure it was done right."[51] Eboli was sixty-one years old at the time of his murder.

Tommy James saw Levy two days after Eboli's shooting, recording a rare moment of vulnerability showing through Levy's tough exterior: "Morris really

Morris Levy posing with Howard Fisher's fraternal twin sons,
Peter and Michael, at their bar mitzvah, February 1973. Photo
courtesy the Fisher family.

looked bad. He was visibly shaken by this. Tommy Eboli was not only Morris's
connection and protection 'downtown,' but they had been pals for a long time."[52]

Not surprisingly, the FBI visited Levy at the Roulette offices soon after the
murder to interview him about Eboli. Taking his usual position, Levy stated he
had no knowledge of Eboli's alleged criminal activities and no idea who would
have wanted him killed: "LEVY said that he knows of EBOLI's reputation in the
underworld, but attributes a large part of this to exaggerated newspaper copy.
LEVY admits to having met such persons as FAT DOM ALONGI, VINCENT
'CHIN' GIGANTE and others in the company of EBOLI, but said any association of EBOLI with alleged crime figures had no relationship or effect on their
business dealings."[53] Levy went on to damn Eboli with faint praise, telling the
FBI agents "although almost illiterate, [he] had a good business head and was an
able worker." Typically, Levy downplayed Eboli's role in his business, both out of
ego and the need to obscure his own knowledge of Eboli's Mob activities. Levy

was considered as a possible suspect in Eboli's murder, but this seems to have been just part of the New York City police's overall investigation of anyone with connections with the Mob leader. Despite Eboli's death, Promo Records continued in business until 1983.

After Eboli's death, Vincent "The Chin" Gigante appears to have increased his role in Levy's life and businesses. Through the seventies, Gigante would tighten his control on Levy and Roulette, and by the early eighties Levy was totally dominated by the mobster, at least according to FBI informants. This had a large impact on Levy's business.

Despite the tumult throughout the early seventies, Levy managed to burnish his own image through supporting various philanthropies, most notably serving on the music division of the United Jewish Appeal (UJA), helping arrange their annual dinners and selecting honorees for it. The music division in turn threw a special dinner in his honor in 1973 that was attended by many of Levy's friends. According to *Billboard*, about twelve hundred people attended, raising "just under 500,000 with additional pledges still uncounted," and the dais was packed with "leading forces in the industry."[54] Held at the ballroom of the New York Hilton, the evening included music from Harry James and Tito Puente, and the crowd was served a lavish buffet. Everyone attending was dressed to the nines, including Levy sporting a tuxedo, accompanied by his eleven-year-old son, Adam.

Joe Smith—who started his career as a Boston deejay and was in attendance at the famous Miami convention that inspired the payola hearings—was master of ceremonies; at the time, he was president of Elektra Records, part of the Warner Bros. Records group. Smith later said that he had arrived on the redeye flight from Los Angeles at the event and had not had time to prepare remarks, so he just improvised.[55] He took potshots at the assembled "legends," pointedly underscoring their unspoken but widely rumored practices including payola, failure to pay artist royalties, and shady bookkeeping. Smith concluded his general comments with the remark, "I will tell you with this group of cut-throats on this dais, every one of you would be safer tonight in Central Park than in this ballroom."[56] The sad truth was that everyone gathered for this meal had made their fortunes without regard to the welfare of the artists who actually created the hits. It took considerable bravery for Smith to point this out; as he quipped at one point, "Either tonight I'm a hit or tomorrow morning I get hit, one or the other."

At the conclusion of his roast, Smith made several jokes about Levy's business practices and alleged Mob ties, ending his presentation by saying "I take this opportunity to extend my own personal best wishes to Moishe, a man I've known for many years, admired, and enjoyed. And I just got word from two of his best friends on the West Coast that my wife and two children have been released!" While the audience laughed with approval, Levy's reputation as the toughest among a group of the most hardened industry veterans was well deserved.

A year after this gala affair, Levy sold off his entire holdings of Latin labels, including Tico and Alegre. The sale was made to Fania Records, which had been founded in 1964 by New York bandleader and power broker Johnny Pacheco—who had a strong hold on Latin artists through his role as agent, manager, concert promoter, and label owner, like the roles Levy himself had played in the jazz world in the fifties. Pacheco had partnered with an ex-cop and lawyer named Jerry Masucci in establishing the label. In a clever marketing scheme, they formed a "super group" in 1968 known as the Fania All-Stars, who helped further popularize Latin-styled music. Beginning in 1971, Masucci began snapping up competing labels by purchasing the Cotique label, and by 1974 Fania's only competitors were owned by Levy. At the time, Levy was cutting back on new recording activity anyway, and may have felt he could no longer compete with Fania. The death of Eboli may have put further pressure on his operation, so he may also have been looking for a quick infusion of cash through selling these assets.

Levy's interest in promoting new recordings and artists was also waning. He expanded his recording empire during the early seventies primarily through new marketing and promotion schemes rather than through artist development—which was never one of his strengths. One new marketing opportunity that Levy leapt on was direct-to-consumer telemarketing of records. He was not the originator of this idea, however. It took a Canadian company called K-Tel to discover the potential for selling records through TV advertisements. K-Tel was founded by Philip Kives in 1962.[57] Kives had gotten his start in business selling cookware door to door; tiring of all the footwork, he tried an inexpensive TV pitch as a way of more effectively reaching his market. By the mid-sixties, he was the king of such legendary late-night wares as the Veg-o-Matic. In 1966 Kives branched out into music by releasing the album 25 *Great Country Artists Singing Their Original Hits*. The country market was an ideal one to reach via TV; many country fans lived far from major record stores, and were used to buying items through mail order. Kives did not know what to expect on releasing his first album, and was pleasantly surprised when sales far surpassed expectations.[58] He began licensing music from the major record labels—including Roulette—building on the original concept of repacking "original hits by the original artists."

Levy had established the idea of selling rock 'n' roll compilation albums through his *Golden Goodies* series as early as 1964. However, though sold at a discount price, these albums were still sold through traditional retailers. The K-Tel model must have been intriguing to Levy, who saw great potential in selling directly to consumers. He launched his first TV marketing efforts in the early seventies with the TeleHouse and Dynamic labels, followed in 1973 by Adam VIII, named for Levy's eldest son. The packaging on these products was minimal at best; the inner sleeves on multi-record sets were left blank, liner notes (if they existed) were minimal, and the covers and record labels themselves looked like they were printed on a Xerox machine in the back of someone's garage. Besides drawing on Roulette's catalog, Levy followed the K-Tel model in licensing material from other label's back catalogs.

In 1972 *Rolling Stone* magazine reported on one successful compilation that Levy released through his Dynamic House label, *The Greatest Rock and Roll Hits, Part I*, a four-record set of early rock hits promoted through TV ads featuring twister Chubby Checker. (Ironically, even though Checker promoted the record, the only version of "The Twist" on the set was the Levy-owned track "The Peppermint Twist" by Joey Dee.) One estimate was that Levy was shipping as much as 14,000 units a day of this set thanks to TV ads in over 300 major markets, "making it the fastest selling $6.98 album in the country over the past two months." However, the article noted that accurate sales figures were nearly impossible to get for the set, raising alarms among music publishers and their representative, the Harry Fox Agency, which suspected that they were not being paid the required publishing royalties on these sales.

Levy countered in typically blunt manner that such claims were "a load of crap." He asserted that the industry standard rate for publishing rights of two cents per song could not be paid on a four-album set that sold for only $6.98, and that he negotiated individual deals with the song's publishers in order to make the set profitable, leaving off any songs that he could not afford. Levy failed to mention that he often was both the publisher and the licensor, as he drew mostly on songs where he owned the publishing rights (and in some cases had cut himself in also as a "co-composer"). What this meant was that Levy could "negotiate" with Levy for a rate of nothing at all, avoiding the need to pay royalties to the publishers. *Rolling Stone* interviewed songwriter Doc Pomus, who had several songs represented on this and other compilation sets issued by Levy. Pomus claimed he had received no royalties; his publisher, Hill and Range Music, filed a complaint with the Fox agency over this issue.[59]

Adam VIII's business fluctuated with the overall economy; most of its customers came from the lower rungs of the economic ladder, and when they were hit by tough times they tended to cut back on their purchases. In late 1974, *Billboard* reported that the sale of recorded music through telemarketing was down 20–40 percent over 1973 due to the recession. Levy reported that Adam VIII was cutting back on its release schedule "from 60 to 70 percent" due to a "30 to 40 percent drop in sales."[60]

As in the past, Levy was happy to form strategic partnerships to expand his telemarketing businesses. In 1976, he formed I&M Teleproducts with Ira

Pittelman, who previously had worked as a Broadway songwriter. Pittelman and Levy struck gold with a compilation produced for them by Casablanca Records called *A Night at Studio 54*; they ended up selling nearly a million units of the compilation, according to Pittelman.[61] Not limiting themselves to telemarketing, Pittelman and Levy founded a separate label, Beckett Records, for new releases to be sold through normal retail outlets. They scored with "I'll Do Anything for You" by Jamaican-born, New York–based reggae artist Denroy Morgan and his group the Black Eagles, which reached #9 on the R&B charts and #7 on the dance charts in 1981. In 1982 Pittelman left I&M to form a partnership with Lawrence Welk Music, resulting in the creation of Heartland Records, a very successful telemarketer.

At the same time Levy was experimenting with telemarketing on his own, he was also licensing Roulette and related label back-catalog product to K-Tel in the early seventies. In a business not known for scrupulous record keeping, it is not surprising that Levy eventually sued K-Tel, citing five different counts including underreporting royalties on certain albums, fraudulently selling off inventory at a price lower than contractually agreed on, and reissuing tracks without properly licensing them from Roulette. That Levy was charging K-Tel of failure to accurately report royalties is ironic in light of the fact that he practiced the same loose accounting for his own telemarketed sets. This lawsuit, filed in early 1973, followed an earlier settlement agreement addressing similar concerns. Totaling the five related claims, Roulette was asking for over $1 million in damages.[62] The suits never made it to court, so presumably Levy came to a settlement with K-Tel.

Along with selling directly to consumers through telemarketing, in 1976 Levy purchased a bankrupt New England–based chain of record stores that he renamed Strawberries Records.[63] Emulating the business model of Sam Goody—the originator of the record store chain that specialized in offering a large selection of bargain-priced LPs—Levy used the chain to sell his own overstock plus the remainders he bought through Promo Records. Strawberries also operated as a "one-stop" (rackjobber), selling independent label product to smaller mom-and-pop record outlets.[64] As with Promo Records, Levy's partners in Strawberries were drawn from the Mob. In secretly recorded tapes, Joe Buonanno stated that "The GIGANTE faction of the Genovese LCN Family owns a share of Levy's . . . Strawberries." He added that one of Gigante's brothers "has a piece of Strawberries on the books" as a means of "getting it that way and also the green"—i.e., the Gigantes planned to take total control of the business and the money it generated.[65]

Strawberries did not get off to a great start. By mid-1977, with four stores open, Levy entered a partnership with James Sutton of Jimmy's Record World to manage the stores and one-stop operation as a test of Sutton's possibly purchasing them. Even *Billboard* labeled Jimmy's as a "lowball operation . . . notorious for its super lowball discounting." Rumors in the industry were that the major labels were underwriting Jimmy's thirty-two-store chain centered in New York and New Jersey as a means of moving current hit product at well below normal retail; Jimmy's was pricing new releases as low as $2.99 for product with a suggested retail price of $6.98. This made it difficult for smaller independents to compete because they would have to sell product at below their wholesale price. (The majors denied any such scheme or that they offered preferential pricing to Jimmy's that other dealers were not given.) Sutton also ran a record distribution company out of Rahway, New Jersey. Whatever the motivation for this deal—Levy's investors in Strawberries may also have had a hold on Sutton's operations and encouraged him to consolidate the two businesses—Jimmy's was out of business by the end of the year, declaring bankruptcy and hastily shutting down all operations. Levy seems to have extricated himself neatly from this situation, as Strawberries was not among the assets that Sutton was forced to sell off in his bankruptcy.[66]

Strawberries grew to be quite successful by the late seventies, with nearly forty outlets. In 1984 Levy said that the chain had been adding "eight to ten stores during the last four years—even during the so-called bad years"[67] and was projecting having sixty-four outlets by year's end. The same year, the chain announced it was aggressively moving into marketing home videos, opening dedicated video sections in its larger stores.[68] Strawberries targeted the suburbs of smaller cities such as Albany, New York, or Hartford, Connecticut, for new locations.[69] It would purchase properties—often next door to major malls—to take advantage of customer traffic generated by the bigger retailers. Thus the chain was more than an outlet for cut-price records; it was a means for Levy and his partners to invest in large swaths of valuable real estate. Through Strawberries, Levy was able to expand his reach well beyond New York City, arranging benefit concerts in the Boston area and befriending local politicians in the process.[70]

The purchase and rehabilitation of properties for the Strawberries chain benefited Gigante and related Mob figures in many other ways as well. The New Jersey Commission of Investigation related how the renovation of a space in Philadelphia in 1986 was farmed out to Mob-controlled businesses. Using an intermediary—Philadelphia deejay Jerry Blavat—Levy contacted Philadelphia-area Mob boss Nicodemo Scarfo, providing blueprints for his planned renovation of a midtown building he had recently purchased for the chain. Blavat carried several messages to the local crime boss, including that: Levy would employ Scarfo's concrete finishing business as part of the renovation; Scarfo was to see that there was "no union involvement in the . . . project . . . to keep construction costs down"; and "Vincent 'The Chin' Gigante was aware of the situation and had approved everything."[71]

Vincent Gigante in the late fifties. Photo courtesy Library of Congress.

Subsequently, Scarfo visited New York to verify with his own contacts that the Chin had approved the project. As it turned out, the work was completed by two Scarfo-owned businesses, without union involvement. Levy typically balked at the total costs and stiffed Scarfo on the final payment of about $5,000 due on the work, angering the local boss. Levy must have had the Chin's tacit approval to do so; it is possible that the final payment went to Gigante as a means of paying for his services.

Levy came up with another idea to make money without actually dealing with artists or even marketing records. He founded a label called Tiger Lily Records around the early to mid-seventies with the express purpose of releasing flops. Like the Broadway financiers in Mel Brooks's film *The Producers*, Levy purposely released material by little-known bands with even less of a chance to be successful. The idea was to press a minimum number of records, leave them in the warehouse, and then destroy them as dead inventory, in order to take a tax writeoff. Tommy James commented:

> Morris used Tiger Lily like a garage sale. He took random recordings that had been accumulating in his vaults and then pressed them up. . . . If they were sent out [to retailers], it was only in tiny shipments meant to give the impression of vast

distribution. Some of the material was by legitimate artists but most of the albums pressed were from kids who had sent crudely made tapes of their songs to Roulette on the million-to-one shot of hitting the big time. . . . Most of the obscure bands on Tiger Lily had no idea an album of their material was even made. Morris would press up a few hundred copies of each album, claim he'd actually pressed up 25,000 or more, and then claim the loss.[72]

Tiger Lily seems to have been active primarily in 1976–77, although much of its source material dated back to sessions from the late sixties and early seventies.[73] Because the LPs were barely sold when new and the bands enjoyed at best local notoriety, some of the releases have become cult classics. It is possible that Levy would throw in Tiger Lily releases in his batches of remainders that he sold through Promo Records, hiding the product among legitimate cutout items.

The best-known performer to appear on the label was Richard Pryor, whose album *LA Jail* was released on it in 1976. The provenance of these recordings has been questioned; two tracks appeared on a previous legitimate release by Pryor, the 1974 LP *Craps (After Hours)*, recorded live at Redd Foxx's nightclub in January 1971. The notes on the Tiger Lily release state that the recordings came from a different venue and year, which may have been an attempt to hide their actual source. Some say Pryor himself supplied the recordings (perhaps hoping to make a quick buck). Levy later admitted to *Variety* that the album was released as a tax shelter, although it is unclear whether it was to benefit Pryor or Levy.[74]

As Levy made deals with various partners in the business, the number of "labels" he ran multiplied. Around 1973 Levy issued an album by the New Orleans band the Meters consisting of material they had previously recorded for the Sansu label (run by Marshall Sehorn and Allen Toussaint) and outtakes from their first Warner Brothers album. The band's road manager, Rupert Surcouf, saw the album in several record stores while they were performing in Philadelphia, and called Sehorn to tell him that they were being bootlegged. Sehorn suggested that Surcouf call Morris Levy:

> So I call Morris Levy and he says, "Who's this? What do you want?"
> "Well, I manage a band called the Meters."
> "Never heard of them."
> "I found a bootleg record of theirs that is on one of your labels."
> "What label is that?"
> "Gemini."[75]
> "I don't have any labels except Roulette."
> "Well I was told this is your label."

Then he says, "Listen and you listen carefully. Just mind your own business. And don't make me find out who you are." And he slammed the phone down.

I realized later that Sehorn set up the whole thing. I'm sure that Sehorn called Levy and told him to scare the shit out of me.[76]

Apparently, Sehorn and Levy had partnered to issue this material without telling the band, pocketing the profits without paying them any royalties.[77]

All of Levy's worst tendencies—his willingness to sue anyone who he thought was infringing on his rights; his appetite to make a big score with a minimal investment; his lack of respect for artists and their rights—but also his charm and ability to make a handshake deal based on his tough-guy persona came together in a bizarre episode in the mid-seventies involving John Lennon. Lennon was going through his own period of disillusionment with the record business, having seen his solo album sales drop well below what he had experienced as a Beatle, plus having to deal with the aftermath of the many less-than-ideal contracts he had signed as a young man over the control of his recordings and compositions. The Beatles' Apple Records—formed to be a new model of cooperative record production—soon was mired in dozens of claims and counterclaims by the Beatles versus the label's distributor, EMI/Capitol Records. If this was not enough, in 1973 Lennon had been given the boot by his wife Yoko Ono and was living in exile in Los Angeles where he embarked on a "lost weekend" of drinking, drugging, and generally outrageous behavior.

Levy first made himself known to Lennon by suing him for copyright infringement for the song "Come Together" (technically a Lennon-McCartney composition, but the two acknowledged that Lennon was its sole author). Lennon had appropriated a line from Chuck Berry's 1950s song "You Can't Catch Me" in the opening line of "Come Together," "Here comes ol' flattop . . . ," and some hear a similarity in the song's chord structure and rhythm to the Berry original. The entire flavor of the recording is quite different, and Lennon's nod to Berry's influence on his own writing and career was undoubtedly meant as an homage and not a ripoff. (It is interesting to note that when Lennon covered "You Can't Catch Me" on his *Rock 'n' Roll* album, he purposely performed in a style that made the connections with "Come Together" more obvious than in the original Berry version; perhaps he was merely ironically commenting through his performance on the fact that all rock artists mimic the sounds and styles of their idols in their performances.) Nonetheless, Levy filed suit around 1971 as the owner of Berry's publishing rights, and the lawsuit was one of many irritants that had been occupying Lennon and his lawyers in the early seventies. Eventually, in 1973 a judge found that Lennon had indeed breached Levy's copyright.[78]

As a settlement to the suit, Lennon's lawyers negotiated with Levy, coming to an unusual agreement. On Lennon's next released album, he agreed to record three of Levy's copyrighted songs. Knowing that back catalogue songs could be given an enormous boost by a current artist covering them, Levy reasoned that having Lennon record three of his songs would give him a bigger payoff than any cash settlement he might be able to negotiate through his lawsuit. Lennon had already been toying with the idea of recording an album of oldies as a way of getting back to his roots, and so in autumn 1973 began working with producer Phil Spector on the album that would become *Rock 'n' Roll*.

The story of the album's troubled initial recording sessions in Los Angeles— in which Lennon would often show up drunk and become increasingly inebriated as the evening went on, and Spector displaying the erratic behavior that would eventually lead to his murder conviction in 2009—has been often told. By the time Lennon sobered up and returned to New York, he had mixed feelings about releasing any of the material. Instead, he quickly recorded an album of new material called *Walls and Bridges*. Perhaps as a sop to Levy—or perhaps as a passive-aggressive acknowledgment that he was failing to deliver the three covers he had promised to record—Lennon included at the end of the album an offhand recording of Levy's copyright song "Ya Ya," featuring John's son Julian (then eleven years old) on drums. Lennon's companion at the time, May Pang, acknowledged that the subpar recording was Lennon's way of sticking a finger in Levy's eye for the trouble his lawsuit had created: "[John] actually put out a version of *Ya Ya* on *Walls and Bridges* as a joke. You can hear John say at the beginning of that one, 'Ok, let's do sitting in the la la and get rid of that' which was a joke to Morris Levy, who was not amused."[79] Indeed, Levy was very angry and immediately threatened to revive his original suit. He insisted on a meeting with Lennon to clear up the matter.

In what would become an infamous meeting at New York's Club Cavallero on October 8, 1974, Lennon and his lawyer Harold Seider; Bernard Brown, who handled some of Lennon's business affairs; and May Pang met with Levy and his partner Phil Kahl.[80] Lennon had a rough tape of the Spector sessions but did not feel the material was good enough to be issued on its own.[81] Spector was holding the tapes hostage, and did not release them until Lennon's label, Capitol Records, paid him $90,000 for his work on the sessions. In addition to being slightly embarrassed by the overall lack of polish of the material, Lennon now also was in the hole for the $90,000 to Capitol. He was undoubtedly looking for a way to retrieve that money and release the tapes without interrupting what was looking like a period of career revival; Lennon had unexpectedly scored a #1 hit that fall with the song "Whatever Gets You Through the Night," recorded with Elton John.

Levy proposed the idea of selling Lennon's new album through a late-night TV promotion. He bragged to the Beatle about the profits he made in this arena. For Lennon, this would be a way to recoup his investment without embarrassing

John Lennon and his companion May Pang in 1974.
Courtesy Photofest.

himself by releasing the record in the normal way. As the judge in the subsequent lawsuit wrote in his opinion: "Lennon was unquestionably interested in [marketing his album through television promotion], because he felt that the delay in completion of the album had somehow diminished its chance of success if it were marketed through normal channels, and because he was attracted to the idea of using a different means of promotion and distribution."[82]

Levy presented Lennon with a plan to release the tapes through his direct-marketing label, Adam VIII. Levy felt Lennon had the right to release the material in this way, based on discussions he had with Allen Klein. Klein—the notorious accountant-manager of the Rolling Stones and late career manager of the Beatles—had found a loophole in Apple Records (a.k.a. the Beatles) contract with Capitol Records for the US distribution of their recordings. Mail-order sales were excluded from the agreement; Capitol argued that this applied to record clubs, which would license popular albums from the major labels and sell them directly to consumers in a "Record of the Month"–style promotion. Levy (and Klein) reasoned that this also applied to direct-mail sales via television promotions.[83] Later, Lennon and his representatives claimed that they rejected this idea, stating they believed Capitol did have mail-order rights to Lennon's recordings, but their immediate actions contradict this.

The day after the October 8 meeting, Lennon played Levy the rough Spector tapes. By this time, Lennon had decided to record new material in New York with his *Walls and Bridges* sidemen, and Levy invited him to come to his farm in Ghent on the weekend of October 18 to rehearse with the group. The following week beginning on Monday, the 21st, Lennon and the group spent several days cutting the remaining tracks for the *Rock 'n' Roll* album in New York City; shortly thereafter, Lennon gave Levy a rough mix of the entire album. The tracks were not all completely remixed and the order was still tentative, but Lennon may have hoped that by giving the tapes to Levy he could show he seriously was trying to fulfill the terms of the original agreement. In mid-November, Levy met with Seider and another Lennon lawyer to discuss the details of the costs of producing the album and how much Lennon would be paid per record sold.[84] That December, Levy invited Lennon, Julian, and May Pang to stay at his Florida apartment for a vacation, including a visit to Disney World.[85]

Things started to unravel when Capitol got wind of the deal in early 1975. Lennon's lawyers had sent a letter to Levy on December 31, 1974, indicating that "Lennon was prepared to go forward with the second phase of the 'Come Together' settlement"; whatever the meaning of this statement, Levy asserted in his response on January 9 that this settlement was now void and that he was proceeding with the new agreement (presumably negotiated on October 8) to release Lennon's *Rock 'n' Roll* album "throughout the world by use of television advertising."[86] That same day Seider met with a Capitol executive and told the label for the first time about the October 8 meeting. According to the United States Court of Appeals, Second Circuit's findings, Capitol:

> thought [the record] had commercial possibilities, and rejected the idea of selling the album on television. Seider advised [Capitol] that they would have to convince Lennon that the album should be released through normal channels. On January 15, 1975, Seider told Levy about the meeting with the Capitol executives and mentioned that they were preparing a marketing program to demonstrate to Lennon that the album should be marketed in the normal retail way.
>
> On January 28, 1975, Capitol personnel convinced Lennon that the album should be sold through normal commercial channels, because selling through television was inappropriate for an artist of his stature and would antagonize record dealers. Lennon then reviewed and approved Capitol's entire merchandising plan....
> On January 30, Seider informed Levy that Lennon would not release the album as a television package through Levy, and Levy thereupon informed Seider that his Adam VIII concern would release the Lennon album nevertheless, using the preliminary tape that had been given him. Seider threatened Levy with an injunction, but none was ever obtained.[87]

Levy rush-released the Adam VIII version based on Lennon's rough album mix in early February 1975; Capitol was forced to respond and put out the Lennon album on the 15th of that month.[88]

Levy's release on Adam VIII was typical of the shoddy production values that marked the label as subpar even by the standards of direct marketing. For the cover, he used a badly cropped image of Lennon taken sometime in the late sixties, tinted brown and printed against a mustard yellow background with the title *John Lennon Sings the Great Rock and Roll Hits* across the top, and the word *Roots* set above a list of the album's tracks (thus it has become known as the "Roots" album). On the back cover, Levy printed advertisements for two other Adam VIII releases, including *Soul Train Super Tracks*. He also brazenly included the legend at the bottom of the back sleeve: "produced from master recordings owned by and with permission of John Lennon and Apple Records, Inc." The sound quality of the rough tapes was poor and the cheap pressing undoubtedly added to the subpar fidelity. Overall, the look and feel of this release was decidedly down-market and cheesy. Television advertisements ran in a few cities for only three days before Capitol telegrammed TV and radio stations and record distributors stating that the album was not authorized. By the time the dust settled, Levy managed to sell a tiny 1,270 copies of his album, "with gross revenues amounting to less than $7,000, not enough to cover Adam VIII's out-of-pocket pressing, printing and advertising costs" through his late-night scheme.[89]

Unfortunately for Levy, when his suit came to trial, the judge failed to accept that any kind of meeting of the minds was reached at the October 8 meeting for Levy to telemarket Lennon's album. Part of this was Levy's doing; in his testimony, Levy had trouble articulating the exact terms of the agreement and seemed to contradict himself.[90] Dismissing the claim of an oral agreement, the judge nonetheless found that Lennon had agreed to record three of Levy's copyrights on his "next album." Although *Walls and Bridges* came chronologically first, the judge found that in speaking of the "next album" all parties were clearly referring to the oldies record that Lennon was recording with Spector. However, the official Capitol release only featured two Levy copyrights, Berry's "You Can't Catch Me," the song that set in motion the entire series of events, and "Ya Ya"; a third recorded Levy song, "Angel Baby," was dropped by Lennon from the final album. Finding that this omission did hurt Levy, the judge awarded his Big Seven publishing company $6,795 for lost royalties.[91]

However, this sum paled in comparison to what was awarded to Lennon. Using a complex formula based on the sales of Lennon's other solo albums, the court found that Capitol would have sold 100,000 more albums if Levy's "Roots" album had never been released; with his royalty rate of sixty-six cents per album, Lennon would have made an additional $66,000. The court also believed that Capitol had to lower the price of Lennon's record from their usual $6.98 retail price to $5.98 to compensate for the fact that Levy had charged only $4.98 for his TV-only release, resulting in a loss of another $43,700 to Lennon (or ten cents per unit). The total thus was $109,700.[92]

On appeal, this number was reduced for two reasons: the Court of Appeals found that, although Capitol had to rush-release its own version of the album, neither their production nor marketing campaign was materially hurt by Levy's release of his Adam VIII version. Further, the computation of average sales of Lennon's solo albums made by the original judge excluded both his best-selling (*Imagine*) and worst-selling (the trio of "avant garde" recordings he issued with Yoko Ono: *Two Virgins*, *Life with the Lions*, and *Wedding Album*) albums. Based on a full computation of all his solo albums, the average sale of Lennon's solo work was actually lower than the total sales Capitol enjoyed with *Rock 'n' Roll*, making the finding that 100,000 sales were lost "clearly erroneous." Limiting themselves to just the average of the sales of the three albums released closest to the date of *Rock 'n' Roll*—*Mind Games, Walls and Bridges*, and the "greatest hits" collection *Shaved Fish*—the appellate court calculated a loss of sales for the rock album of 61,000 units, reducing Lennon's royalty damages to $40,260 less union fees.[93]

The argument that Capitol had to lower its list price for the album from $6.98 to $5.98 due to Levy's prior release of "Roots" was also challenged on appeal. Unfortunately for Lennon, the president of Capitol Records gave a deposition stating that the primary considerations in lowering the price were the general state of record sales in early 1975—the economy was in a slump and sales had been poor—along with the fact that the album consisted of non-original material. Further, he testified that there would have been no loss in sales if the price had been kept at the normal $6.98 level. The appellate judge lowered the amount of damages to one-third of what was originally awarded based on this analysis. Lennon's net recovery was now figured to be $49,912.96, less than half than what was originally awarded.

Writer Joseph Self, who published a comprehensive analysis of the entire affair on the Internet, feels that even this amount was excessive. In his analysis of the case, he wrote:

> I find it very hard to believe that "Rock 'n' Roll" sold 100,000 or even 61,000 less copies because Levy issued his half-baked product and sold a whopping 1,270 copies. The true reason is well known to every fan of the Beatles—this album simply wasn't that good.... The [low] sales of "Mind Games," with only one hit single should have tipped off the court that Lennon was not damaged by Levy's action. "Rock 'n' Roll" had only a cover of "Stand By Me" [as a single], which barely cracked the top twenty in America.[94]

Lennon had also been awarded $35,000 in the original trial for damage to his reputation caused by the shoddy production of the "Roots" album. Levy appealed, saying that Lennon's reputation could hardly be damaged given that he had been arrested for drug possession and had posed naked on the cover of *Two Virgins*. The judge found for Lennon on this count, agreeing that the cover of "Roots" was "cheap looking—if not ugly" and its audio quality "shoddy and fuzzy, with one out-of-tune track and indistinct voices in some places."[95]

For punitive damages, Lennon was awarded $10,000, what he felt was a tiny amount given the fact that Levy flagrantly released the tapes knowing that he had no right to do so. On appeal, however, this amount was upheld. The Appeals Court noted that:

> Lennon and Levy were both looking toward the latter's marketing Lennon's record and Levy provided him hospitality, in the form of rehearsal time, trips and the like, which was gladly accepted by Lennon. Lennon willingly furnished Levy a master tape, even though it was not finally edited, and Lennon did not have the courtesy to reply through counsel or otherwise to Levy's letter of January 9, which claimed that Levy had a contract (which the court later held he did not have). While there may be no excuse for Levy's ultimately issuing the "Roots" album, we think the fault therefore—in a concededly "hustlin'" business—was by no means all his. . . .[96]

The judge further found that Levy's reliance on Klein's statement that the Apple/Capitol contract did not cover mail-order sales "turned out to have been at least partially correct, even if simplistically misplaced." There was no fraud because the performances were actually made by Lennon as advertised, even if he did not authorize their release.

Finally, Levy appealed the finding that his loss was a meager $6,795 from Lennon's failure to include "Angel Baby" on the final album. He pointed to the phenomenal success of the Carpenters' 1970 cover of "Close to You" as an example of a song that earned far more royalties—about two-thirds of its total income, Levy estimated—from covers than from the original recording. However, Lennon's own expert witness was able to counter this argument, pointing out that some songs like "Angel Baby" depend for their success on the style of their original recording, while "Close to You" was open to interpretation by various artists, typical of other Burt Bacharach compositions. The Carpenters cover was issued as a single, whereas the Levy copyright would have been an album track, so it would not have had the same impact. The appeals court upheld the original finding.

Given that Levy must have known that issuing the album would be a provocation that neither Lennon nor Capitol would accept, one wonders why he went ahead and did it. It is consistent with Levy's general modus operandi, however;

to him a handshake deal was a deal, and he felt—rightly or wrongly—that Lennon had agreed to this marketing scheme. He may not have even felt that his issuing the album would affect Capitol's ability to market it through normal retail channels. Levy may have also felt that releasing the album would give him leverage in future litigation with Lennon based on the original settlement of the "Come Together" lawsuit. Finally, he did feel slighted because Lennon failed to live up to his initial bargain to seriously record three of his copyrights, and may have legitimately felt that Lennon's covers would generate renewed interest—and thus new income—from them.

"All I want is for justice to prevail. John lied to me and I feel morally bound to pursue it," Levy told *Rolling Stone* magazine at the time, which estimated that his legal fees alone cost him about $400,000 in addition to the money he lost on the album. *Rolling Stone* further speculated that Levy was using the trials as leverage to get Lennon to record an additional album for him, which Levy denied.[97]

Ironically, because the "Roots" album was withdrawn within days of its being issued, original copies are highly collectible. It also inspired countless bootleg releases—all repeating the ugly album art and terrible sound quality of the original. Levy thus made a permanent mark on Lennon's posthumous career, although the actual loss to Lennon's reputation or the assessment of his overall impact as a recording artist was minimal.

9

Why Do Fools Fall in Love? 1975–1980

Without adversaries, how can you be a winner?
—Chuck Rubin

Levy's quixotic attempt to outsmart John Lennon was a major mistake. Levy ended up losing money while exposing his need to dominate his adversaries through whatever means necessary. Ironically, it was the beginning of a long period of litigation for Levy, Roulette, and his music publishing companies. Perhaps his adversaries finally realized that Levy could not muscle all of his victims; perhaps it was the growing understanding among artists of their financial and moral rights. Many pop artists of the seventies had better management and a keener understanding of their rights than those of earlier eras and were not as easily pushed around. Meanwhile, the music business was rapidly consolidating, with independents like Ahmet Ertegun's Atlantic Records selling out to corporate owners who were less willing or able to tolerate the wheeling and dealing of figures like Levy. His method of doing business was being squeezed from all sides.

Besides losing his court case to Lennon, 1975 was hardly a banner year for Levy. That July he visited the Blue Angel nightclub in New York with a girlfriend and his associate, Nat McCalla. As they left the club, three strangers approached them, one of whom began flirting with Levy's companion. Perhaps not realizing that the man trying to pick up his date was an off-duty policeman, Levy attacked him outside of the club. The police report of the incident stated that McCalla held the officer's hands behind his back while Levy pummeled him, blinding him in his left eye. Strangely, the case was dismissed before it reached court and all records were later expunged; a related civil suit was also settled out of court. In an interview given shortly before his death, Levy asserted that the cops were drunk, which is why the charges were dropped: "They were drunk and riding around in a fucking police car. One of the guys was a fucking police captain. I hired a fucking private detective and we got all the charge receipts from the people in the restaurant who saw it and, one of them was an ambassador, and I was going to subpoena them to testify."[1]

Levy later claimed that he didn't mean to injure the cop: "I didn't know the cop was hurt, I just fought him."[2] Levy noted: "I guess he lost his eye. But did you talk to him? I took care of [the cop]," seeming to justify his action because he paid a private cash settlement to the officer for his pain and suffering.[3] This kind of violent outburst on the part of Levy showed how much pressure he must have been under during the period.[4]

Despite the changes that were transforming the business, Levy continued to run Roulette as he had always done, with little regard for the rights of the artists who created the music. In 1976 Levy was approached by Orville O'Brien, who had recorded two live shows by the jazz singer Betty Carter in 1969. At the time, O'Brien worked as a soundman at various small jazz clubs, and had discussed with Carter the possibility of their forming a record label. Carter was frustrated by her work earlier in the 1960s with major labels who had tried to shape her into a pop singer; she also felt that her live performances were more spontaneous and were superior to any studio recordings she had made. Two shows were recorded and the plan was to issue them on the new label. The deal unraveled when Carter discovered that O'Brien was trying to make a side deal for the recordings. Over the next few years, she was successful in thwarting his efforts to resell the tapes, but was unaware of the deal that O'Brien made with Levy in 1975 to sell all rights to the material for a paltry $500.[5] Ironically, Carter's career was by then on the upswing, with renewed interest in her bop-influenced style leading to new gigs.

Levy issued the tapes on two Roulette albums, *Finally Betty Carter* and *Round Midnight*. Mysteriously, the same material also appeared on the Joy label, a bootleg label that may have been operated by Levy himself as a way of doubling down on his investment. (Levy would undoubtedly have sued anyone who had the nerve to bootleg him!) At about the same time as he was preparing to issue these tapes, Levy approached Carter to invite her to record new material for Roulette. Carter was not happy about the tapes being issued, and told Levy the story about how O'Brien had cheated her. In an apparent settlement, Levy signed Carter to record an album for Roulette and also for her to sign new jazz acts, to help revitalize the once prominent label. Carter told *Down Beat* magazine that she trusted Levy thanks to their long friendship dating back to his days owning Birdland: "Morris Levy and I have a kind of handshake agreement, he respects what I'm about.... I'm personal with the man I'm with, if he says 'no' we fight and holler—he respects me enough to know that I will holler—and I know he'll holler. I've listened to him holler. But that is what I want, I'd much rather have it out in the open, on top, than underneath."[6]

The resulting album, *Now It's My Turn*, was recorded with Carter's working trio, and issued in 1976 along with the two 1969 recordings. However, Levy typically did not credit Carter as the composer of her three original songs on it, and

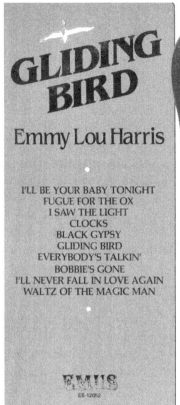

The cover of *Gliding Bird*, the re-release on Levy's budget label Emus of Emmylou Harris's first album, which led to Harris successfully suing him.

assigned them to his own publishing company. Angered, Carter broke off her relationship with Roulette, and disavowed the album, telling fans at one performance not to buy it. In 1979 Carter sued Levy over the purchase of O'Brien's tapes, and in 1981 a settlement was paid by Levy giving him ownership of these recordings.[7]

Having not learned his lesson from his dealings with John Lennon and Betty Carter, in 1979 Levy tried to take advantage of well-known pop star Emmylou Harris. Harris had recorded an album in 1969 for Jubilee Records, a label originally founded in the late forties by Herb Abramson (later a partner in Atlantic Records) and Jerry Blaine. Jubilee was on its last legs when it issued Harris's album, *Gliding Bird*, in 1970. Soon after, its assets were sold to Levy. In 1979, Levy reissued Harris's album on yet another one of his budget labels, Emus Records. (As another example of Levy's black sense of humor, it has been suggested that the name was an anagram inspired by Levy's frequent response to demands for royalty payments: "Su-me"![8] Emus is also the Yiddish word for "truth."[9]) Most of Emus releases were cut-price reissues of old Roulette albums by artists like Count Basie and Joey Dee. As with Lennon, Levy picked up a press photo of Harris—now a major recording star on Reprise Records—to use on the cover, which had a similar "printed in my basement" look to his Adam VIII products.

What Levy failed to take into account was that five of the songs were Harris originals, and the title track was written by her then-husband Tom Slocum. They had the foresight to hold onto their publishing rights. Levy failed to pay any royalties for the use of these copyrighted songs, and in November 1979, Harris successfully sued Levy for copyright infringement.[10] As Harris recalled many years later: "I just wanted to stop him from putting that record back out because I didn't feel it was indicative of the artist that I became, and I didn't think it was fair. The suit was not for the money, it was for principle. . . . he hid behind about 50 different organizations and titles, but we got him on a technicality because he hadn't [cleared] the publishing [rights]."[11] Harris was awarded $60,000 in damages for the use of the copyright compositions and $34,152.97 in legal fees, representing "approximately half of the amount plaintiff's attorneys claim to have earned in this rather extensive litigation."[12]

While he was dealing with the many copyright lawsuits and other legal entanglements Levy's recording and publishing operations were becoming mere shells of what they had once been. Roulette had issued some new material in the mid- to late seventies, mostly items that Levy was able to pick up cheaply, and a few new acts catering to the disco craze. But mostly Levy found opportunities by bankrolling old business friends and associates as a silent partner in their ventures.

Through the mid-seventies, longtime bodyguard/enforcer Nat McCalla continued to operate his own record label and publishing company (called JAMF, which stood for Jive Ass Mother Fucker) out of Levy's offices.[13] When Bob Marley and reggae music suddenly became popular on the charts, McCalla was able to make a deal with Jamaican record producer Clement Dodd, who recorded Marley's band the Wailers from 1963–66. In 1976 Dodd licensed ten Wailers singles to McCalla for release, claiming he selected McCalla because he was "a fellow Jamaican." (McCalla's actual background is unknown; he may have represented himself as Jamaican to Dodd as a way of encouraging him to make a deal.) McCalla gave him a check for $5,000 as an advance on royalties, but Dodd said later that the check bounced. After that Dodd, was unable to collect anything further from McCalla; "Nobody knew where he was," says Dodd of McCalla, "His address was unknown for a couple of years. I couldn't find him."[14] Somehow the masters were passed from McCalla to Columbia Records (*Billboard* reported that "some sources believe it was [Morris] Levy, not McCalla, that cut the deal with Sony."[15]) In May 1977, CBS released the same material that had previously appeared on Calla as a two-record set.[16]

At about the same time, McCalla was involved with staging a rock concert held on July 4, 1977, on Maryland's Eastern Shores. Washington, D.C., deejay Bob "Nighthawk" Terry was the emcee/coproducer of the festival. Local authorities believed that Genovese Mob money was behind the event, and McCalla may have been present to oversee the ticket sales and protect the Mob's investment. Nighthawk had been a popular deejay on Washington's WOL radio station since the mid-sixties, when the station switched to playing all R&B. The station's dee-jays were labeled "Soul Brothers," and even in the years before the Black Power movement came to the forefront, Nighthawk had promoted black artists and encouraged blacks to patronize local, black-owned businesses. During the late sixties through the mid-seventies, he had hosted several concerts that led the FCC to investigate him and the station for supposedly accepting payola from concert promoters.[17]

After the July 4 concert, Nighthawk and his producing partners had a dis-agreement over the exact number of attendees who were at the show. Nighthawk asserted that only 10,000 people came, which resulted in a large loss; his inves-tors believed the count was actually closer to 200,000, which meant that they should have cleared at least $1 million.[18] At least part of this shortfall may have been caused by a pair of counterfeiters named Theodore Brown and Howard McNair, who flooded the market with fake tickets; their bodies were found two days before the event near the festival site. A few months after the concert, both Terry and McCalla also vanished. Terry's body—presuming he was killed—was never found. However, McCalla suffered a worse fate:

> In 1980 McCalla turned up in a rented house in Fort Lauderdale, dead of a gunshot wound in the back of his head, which literally exploded. Police found him slumped in a lounge chair in front of a switched-on television. The rear door was ajar and keys were in the lock. McCalla had been dead for at least a week and was badly decomposed, a process that had been accelerated because someone had sealed the windows and turned on the heater. No suspects were apprehended.[19]

The loss of McCalla was another blow to Levy's operations.

Just as in the sixties Levy had relied on picking the fruit of smaller labels, through the later seventies he continued to draw on his many contacts in the music business to find new material to release on Roulette. Among these people was a producer named Jerry Love, who had previously worked for A&M. Love formed a partnership with Michael Zager, a young musician/arranger who had recently left the band Ten Wheel Drive. Zager was half of the musical brains

Producer Michael Zager in the studio working on a recording by Johnny "Guitar" Watson, 1981. Zager was responsible for a handful of disco hits for Roulette in the mid-seventies. Courtesy Michael Zager.

behind the band, which combined instrumentation inspired by the jazz-rock of Blood, Sweat and Tears and Chicago with the lead vocals of Genya Ravan, whose voice was often compared to Janis Joplin's. The group never really broke through, and by the mid-seventies Zager wanted to get off the road and work in the studio, where he could have more control over his music.[20] Rather than searching for bands to produce, Love and Zager simply assembled studio musicians to create music in a specific commercial style.

The first project the duo brought to Roulette was Love Child's Afro-Cuban Blues Band, a grab bag of a name for a group that performed a grab bag of music, from covers of past Latin jazz hits ("Bang Bang") to mid-seventies funk. Love brought Zager to Levy's office to pitch the idea, and like many others before him Zager noticed a number of "tough looking characters" hanging around the place. Zager was surprised when—after just a short amount of small talk—Levy gave the project a green light. Zager was also impressed that Levy paid all the session costs without question, and never asked for an accounting of the duo's expenses. The group's album was duly issued in 1975 and saw some sales action, but Levy did not show any particular interest in working with Love and Zager to produce a followup. At this point, he was not interested in developing a roster of artists at Roulette so much as profiting quickly from his releases. Working with artists over the long term was too much of a hassle for Levy.

Once the record achieved some sales success, Zager got his first taste of how Levy worked when he phoned his lawyer to enquire about when they might expect to receive a royalty statement. "*You* ask him," Zager's lawyer said, hanging up quickly.[21] The upfront money paid for the session was all that was going to come of the project, and may be the reason that Love and Zager decided to take the band's next recording elsewhere.

Love and Zager worked with Levy one more time on a project that could only have seen the light of day during the seventies disco explosion. The producing partners were always looking for an angle they could exploit to underwrite their studio work. As disco records gained popularity, it became clear that any track with a danceable beat and a reasonably attractive singer had the possibility of gaining popularity in the clubs. Love suggested that the pair combine the attraction of disco music with a commercial slant. The duo worked up a disco song called "Benihana," the Japanese word for "Little Flower," which also happened to be the name of a very successful chain of Japanese steakhouses owned by self-made millionaire Hiroaki "Rocky" Aoki.

Love and Zager made the pilgrimage out to Aoki's palatial home in Teaneck, New Jersey, to convince him to underwrite the recording of "Benihana." The song would not only help advertise his business, but it would also underscore the restaurant as a cultural phenomenon and hopefully bring in disco dancing youngsters to experience the joy of Japanese cuisine. Love and Zager intended to make the recording using a hired singer, preferably a good-looking Japanese woman, but Aoki had other ideas. Among his properties was *Oui* magazine, a soft-core porn publication; one of the magazine's writers had been singing in clubs on the side. "You must hear her," he told the producing duo. The woman's name was Marilyn Chambers. Although Zager had never heard of her, Chambers was already infamous for her performance in the porno films *Behind the Green Door* (1972) and *The Resurrection of Eve* (1973). Seeking a career as a "serious" singer/nightclub performer, she was anxious to appear on record—any record. Aoki would only fund the session if the producers agreed to use her.

The resulting disc sounds suspiciously like Donna Summer's monster hit "Love to Love You Baby" as well as "More, More, More" by ex–porn star Andrea True, right down to the sexualized moaning. *Billboard*'s reviewer acknowledged both Chambers's steamy reputation and the record's debt to Summers and True, but gave the record an overall favorable notice.[22] According to Zager, Chambers became a big draw at deejay conventions, sometimes performing in a body stocking (or topless) to help promote the song. It became a top dance hit and (to Zager and Love's embarrassment) was named a top record of 1977 by none other than *Screw* magazine. Chambers described the record as "sex-rock" to *Billboard*, suggestively saying that it was "a record to which you close your eyes and fantasize."[23] Roulette was able to make a good profit on the single as they had no investment costs beyond pressing the discs; however, Zager and Love never received royalty payments for their work on the record.[24]

Levy must have realized that his independent operation was becoming increasingly outdated in a new era of corporate ownership of the music industry. He expressed his growing frustration with this new world in a nostalgic "commentary" piece he wrote for *Billboard* in 1981. Titled "The Old Timers Knew," Levy specifically targets Gene Froelich, then a vice president at MCA Records and later its CEO. Levy was angered when Froelich refused to waive a late payment fee for bills from his Strawberries Records chain. Froelich even had the nerve to place Strawberries' account on hold. Levy could not understand why Froelich would not extend the courtesy of waiving these fees, something that the "old timers" would do as a matter of principle.

Levy pinned the problems that the industry faced on executives like Froehlich, contrasting their numbers-driven approach with the founders of the fifties independents, the true "visionaries" who launched R&B and rock 'n' roll:

So, who [is] responsible [for the financial problems of the record industry]? I can tell you who it [isn't]. It [isn't] Irving Green [Mercury Records] or Don Robey [Peacock Records] or Randy Wood [Dot Records]. They scuffled, scratched and fought to carve out a place for themselves and their companies. It [isn't] Leonard Chess [Chess Records] or Dave Kapp [Kapp Records] or the Erteguns [Atlantic Records]. All these were men who knew and understood music and people and built a business on the foundation of this knowledge and understanding.

In contrast, we now have Mr. Froelich of MCA who tells us straight out . . . that he as a youngster, "never bought a record." What's more, he "could never figure out why anyone else would."[25]

Levy's mythic vision of the origins of the modern popular music business leaves out some key details. While these men may have held certain values straight out of the Old West, their morality was tinged with a high degree of self-interest if not a downright disregard of the rights of their artists. While varying in the degree of their sometimes unethical practices, producers like Don Robey, Leonard Chess, and even Ahmet Ertegun were known to give their artists short shrift, adding their own names to copyrights and failing to pay royalties. Levy took these common business practices to an extreme and was one of the worst offenders. While their code of ethics meant they would extend credit to each other, these same ethics did not extend to uniformly treating their artists fairly.

Levy is savvy enough to realize that his world *has* changed, so he is careful to temper his comments about the new corporate industry. He recommends that executives like Froelich "go into the field, walk into a radio station with a record to promote, sit in a crowd at a rock concert, visit a one-stop in Detroit, spend some time in retail accounts (including the Strawberries chain, where he would be more than welcome). I think he should get involved, get a feel, 'get his hands dirty', and become a part of the business."

However, it was the "dirty hands" of operators like Levy that could no longer be tolerated in the new corporate music world. What Levy failed to realize was that the Old West was gone, that the new sheriffs in town were executives like Froelich who would bring closer financial scrutiny to a business that was used to storing extra cash in the back of a desk drawer.

Ironically, shortly after Levy's editorial appeared, MCA filed suit against him and his Cambridge Distributors (the one-stop that supplied Strawberries) for a little over $129,000 in unpaid bills from August 1979 to May 1981.[26] Levy believed the lawsuit was filed to harass him based on his unflattering portrayal of Froelich in his *Billboard* editorial.[27]

The bad practices of the fifties-era record business would come back to haunt figures like Levy as artists became more savvy about their right to share in the profits of their works. As the boom in nostalgia for older rock acts from the fifties and early sixties grew, a few entrepreneurs came forward to help these artists gain the recognition—and royalty payments—they were long denied. In this battle, one figure was more than Levy's match in his knowledge both of how the music industry worked and of the rules of a good street fight: Chuck Rubin. During the late seventies and eighties, through Rubin several of Levy's artists were able to gain long-overdue payment and recognition for their recordings and musical works.[28]

Originally a schoolteacher living in North Jersey, in the early sixties Rubin began booking a local group known as the 4 Graduates, a pop-harmony group in the mold of many others, including another New Jersey foursome just getting their start, the 4 Seasons. Rubin hustled to get the Graduates jobs in area clubs, and eventually developed exclusive arrangements with a number of them, enabling him to guarantee regular work for the groups he managed. From this base, Rubin wangled his way into a job as an agent-in-training with New York's General Artists' Corporation, at the time the second biggest talent agency after Hollywood's MCA. Among GAC's clients were most of the top R&B acts of the day, including Chuck Berry, Etta James, and Sam Cooke. In 1963 GAC nabbed a new act that was hoping to make a big splash in the US market: the Beatles. Rubin ended up doing much of the grunt work for the Beatles' first US visit in February 1964. Rubin also continued to work with the 4 Graduates, who eventually took a "hipper" name, the Happenings. Modeling themselves on the

Tokens—who made new vocal arrangements of earlier pop hits—the Happenings scored big with their cover of "See You in September" in 1966. Ironically, once they finally achieved pop stardom the group summarily fired Rubin as their manager.

Within the next few years Rubin went out on his own, ending up managing one-time hitmaker Wilbert Harrison, best known for his 1959 hit "Kansas City." In the late 1960s, Harrison was enjoying a slight career comeback when the popular blues-rock band Canned Heat covered his song, "Let's Work Together." John Fogerty invited Harrison to tour Europe with his popular group Creedence Clearwater Revival, and Rubin went along for the ride. Harrison's renewed success was short lived, but Rubin continued to manage him as best he could through the mid-seventies.

One day Harrison complained to Rubin about never receiving royalties from his song "Kansas City," despite the fact that it appeared on many oldies compilations and on film soundtracks. His longtime lawyer, who had never been able to deliver on his promise to help him get his royalties, had died. Rubin decided to ask around among industry lawyers who he knew, hoping to find someone who could help out. He was universally turned down; most felt the case was too old, and that artists like Harrison would never be able to collect on the flimsy contracts that they originally signed. Frustrated, Rubin finally found a young attorney willing to take on Harrison's case—but only if Rubin did all of the discovery work himself. This was the beginning of Rubin's new life as an artist-advocate.

According to Rubin, it was Harrison who came up with the financial arrangement that he would use as a model going forward: "Wilbert asked me how much a lawyer would charge to take his case. I said, 'I don't know—maybe a third of the judgment plus expenses.' Wilbert said, 'Well, then, you take one-half of what we get.' It was Wilbert who came up with the 50 percent amount."[29]

Rubin wasn't a philanthropist; he had to support himself and underwrite the considerable cost in researching Harrison's claims. Years later, some artists who signed deals with Rubin came to regret giving him 50 percent of all earnings, including future royalties, but that was the deal they made.

After some investigation, Rubin discovered a strange twist in the history of Harrison's recording of "Kansas City." Although it was originally issued by Bobby Robinson's Fury Records, Harrison had actually paid for the session "in order to get out of his contract with Savoy Records in Newark and onto Fury ... so we made a claim that we owned the master."[30] Rubin initially went after Robinson and Fury Records for nonpayment of royalties. However, Robinson told him that he had licensed the recording to Morris Levy with the agreement that Levy would be responsible for the artist royalties. Rubin knew Levy's reputation for being a tough operator, and was also convinced that Levy had shorted Harrison by failing to report any sales to him. In their first meeting, according

Chuck Rubin in his offices ca. 1980. Courtesy Gabin Rubin/Artists Rights Enforcement Corporation.

to Rubin, Levy was surprised that he "couldn't buy him off," as he had done with so many other claimants. Rubin did not want a lump payment; he wanted a full accounting of what was due to Harrison and—more importantly—wanted to set a precedent for ongoing royalty payments for the record. It was not the past primarily that concerned him, but the song's future life. "I realized there was money to be made in the second generation [renewed use] of these songs," Rubin said. Ultimately, Rubin and Harrison prevailed, earning a legal judgment against Levy.[31]

Rubin's success inspired dozens of other fifties-era artists to come forward seeking redress of their claims of nonpayment for the use of their recordings or compositions. Rubin formed the Artists Rights Enforcement Corp. in 1981 to, in the words of the *Washington Post*, "hound, bully or sue record companies that he thought were depriving artists of their earnings."[32] While Levy was not his only target, he was a particularly ripe one, because he had consistently failed to send royalty statements or payments to his artists. Levy fumed, "[Rubin is] a guy who didn't happen in the business, and then created a new business of harassing and suing people. My personal opinion would be he'd sell his mother for a nickel."[33] Of course, Levy was not above selling his mother—or indeed anyone—for the nickels and pennies that came from his massive catalog of songs.

By the early seventies, just as the doowop revival was beginning with nostalgic groups like Sha Na Na and fifties rock was making a comeback led by Elvis in full karate regalia, so too did Levy's back publishing catalog continue to churn out regular income, providing a much needed cushion for his other businesses. According to a 1979 article in *Billboard*, the firm was raking in royalties from major motion pictures and cover versions of its extensive catalog: "With a strong base of rock 'n' roll songs of the '50s and '60s, both soundtracks and individual artist's sessions run heavy with [Levy's] copyrights. The company had seven copyrights in *American Graffiti*, three in *American Hot Wax*, and one each in *Saturday Night Fever* and . . . *Rock 'n' Roll High School* and *The Wanderer*."[34] Just as he had been stingy in paying recording royalties and sought ways to avoid reporting accurate sales to his artists, Levy was less than forthcoming when it came to reporting publishing income to the songwriters whose copyrights he owned.

At the same time Levy's businesses were coasting on his past successes, Rubin was looking for new opportunities to build his young firm. Rubin did not just sit around and wait for a good case to cross his threshold; he actively sought out the musicians and—in the case of those who had passed away—their heirs who might be unaware of their right to be paid for the continued use of their music. One of the saddest cases that Rubin championed was that of Hank Ballard, the originator of such great records as "Work with Me Annie" and "The Twist." Ballard seemed always to be on the edge of making it big, only to see his ideas co-opted by others. Rubin went to work tracing the history of "The Twist," Ballard's most valuable copyright, and discovered that the song had been copyrighted twice; once by Ballard following a 1958 performance in Florida, and the second time by King Records when Ballard's original recording was issued in 1959. The first version featured different lyrics and therefore could be considered a separate composition. Based on the first copyright, Rubin applied for renewal of the song's copyright.[35]

However, Ballard and Rubin faced another wrinkle in the saga of retrieving the rights to "The Twist" and other Ballard compositions. During the mid-seventies, Ballard's career was in serious decline and he was desperate for money to support himself. At the time he sold his copyrights to Morris Levy, who was always willing to "help" a friend in need, in exchange for a "loan" of $25,000, Ballard signed two documents with Levy, one that gave him the right to collect performance royalties from BMI for all of Ballard's compositions until $20,000 of the total loan was repaid; and the second—which seemed to contradict the first—stated that, in exchange for a pittance, just $5,000, Levy was given all rights to twenty of Ballard's original compositions. Either way (or perhaps more accurately, both ways), Levy won. Ballard's lawyer, Paul Walker, characterized this as being confusing to say the least: "Though Levy characterizes the transaction as a sale, rather than a loan, the language in the documents is vague. I still don't think I understand what those documents mean. So how could Hank?"[36]

Because the contract Ballard signed was ambiguous as to whether he had given away all his rights or merely assigned his rights to Levy to act as his agent in collecting royalties on the songs, Ballard eventually won his lawsuits, although by this time Levy had passed away and the rights had been inherited by his son, Adam.

Rubin continued to hunt for fifties artists who might be owed money either for performance or recording rights. This led him to the biggest and most drawn-out battle that he had with Levy. The song that gave Rubin his ammunition was "Why Do Fools Fall in Love?" Having bested Levy several times now, Rubin was girded for battle. "Without adversaries," he mused, "how can you be a winner?"[37] Levy was the ideal adversary.

The authorship credit for "Fools" had a convoluted history. Group members Herman Santiago and Jimmie Merchant claimed that they composed a version of the song for the group before Frankie Lymon joined. However, the original record label listed Santiago, Lymon, and producer George Goldner as the song's authors, although mysteriously Santiago's name was dropped when Goldner actually applied for the copyright. According to their later testimony, Santiago and Merchant agreed that Lymon made some changes to the song "during the time between the [group's] audition [for Goldner] and recording session, which included, among other changes, adjusting the song to suit Lymon's vocal range."[38] However, they also asserted that Goldner was in no way involved in writing the song. Acknowledging Lymon's contribution was important because otherwise the original copyright and its renewal might have been ruled invalid and the song would fall into public domain—and there would be no money to collect.[39]

On June 24, 1965, the chronically short-of-money Goldner sold his authorship and publishing rights in "Fool" to Levy, conveying this information to the US Copyright Office and BMI.[40] Goldner not only disavowed his authorship of "Fools" at the time but also forty-nine other songs, including some of his early Latin recordings.[41] Also sometime in 1965, Lymon—hooked on drugs, in prison in California, and desperate for money—sold his authorship rights to all his songs to Levy for around $1,500.[42] Lymon's then-lawyer Maxwell T. Cohen—who also was employed by Levy, creating an obvious conflict of interest—drew up the agreement.[43]

Levy justified on several counts his collecting royalties on the song as both its publisher and author: "We publish[ed] [the song], one. Two, I bought 'em off Frankie a few times [Laughs]. . . . When I paid him $1500 for his share, that song was earning for six-seven years an average of $60 a year. So it was more than a fair price."[44] Levy also insisted that Goldner and he had made legitimate changes to the song (although he was rather vague as to exactly what their con-tribution was). He also raised the rhetorical question of—if he was able to put his name on every copyright—why his name only appeared on a handful of Lymon's songs: "Frankie Lymon wrote 20–30 songs and [I'm] only [listed as coauthor] on two of them. And if [I] had the power to put [my] name on two of them, [I] had the power to put them on the 30."[45]

Perhaps it was the appearance of "Why Do Fools Fall in Love" on the hit film *American Graffiti*'s soundtrack, or perhaps it was the #1 hit enjoyed by Diana Ross with the song in 1981, that inspired Rubin to try to track down the heirs of the song's (listed) coauthor, Frankie Lymon. Lymon had died of a drug overdose in 1968, so Rubin began a search for his heirs, eventually uncovering his wife, Emira Eagle Lymon, an ex-schoolteacher from Atlanta, Georgia, who wed the singer a year before his death. Originally working with lawyer Richard Bennett, Rubin arranged for her to bring suit against Levy and his record and publish-ing companies. Her complaint charged "fraud, misappropriation and copyright infringement, among other offenses. She is attempting to recover all the royal-ties from the date of the record's release because . . . neither Levy nor his prede-cessor as cowriter [George Goldner] . . . is actually an author."[46]

The lawsuit was based on two theories. First, the original copyright claim was fraudulent insofar as Goldner did not coauthor the original song. Given that, Goldner could not assign his authorship to Levy. Further, after Levy "purchased" Lymon's half of the copyright, he simply notified BMI of the change in author-ship and the publishing society did nothing to verify that Lymon intended to give away his rights.

In 1978 the US copyright laws were amended to introduce a new feature allowing artists what became known as "a second bite of the apple." Under the law, a composition could be copyrighted for twenty-eight years with one renewal, for a total of a fifty-six-year term. Before 1978 the artist could sign away his rights and the publisher could exploit the rights for the full fifty-six years. Under the new law, if the artist signed away his rights for the full two terms but died before the first twenty-eight years had passed, his rights would revert to his heirs for the second term—i.e., they had a chance to get back the song and have a "second bite at the apple," or second chance to exploit it. So it was that twenty-eight years after the original copyright was registered for "Fools"—in 1984—Elmira Lymon as the heir could legally claim back the rights to the song. As Richard Bennett told journalist Calvin Trillin at the time: "Goldner's fatal mistake was that he was a fifty percent thief, and not a hundred percent thief. Lymon's name was there, so the widow could take out a copyright and demand her money."[47] In other words, if Goldner had never listed Lymon as an author at all, his widow would not have had a basis for her claim under the new copyright act.

Levy was not about to let Emira and Rubin claim authorship of "Fools" without a battle. Faced with this lawsuit, the ever-wily Levy pulled an ace out of his sleeve: He challenged Emira's status as the true heir to Lyman's estate by producing not one but two other women who claimed to have been married to Lymon. Reportedly paying them both an advance against future royalties, Levy arranged for them to make counterclaims as Lymon's true heirs and thus entitled to his publishing income. At the time, Levy's lawyer, Leon Borstein, rather disingenuously said that Levy would be happy to settle with the true copyright holder—but now that there was more than one person claiming to be Lymon's legitimate heir, what could the publisher do: "We cannot pay royalties to more than one lawful wife, so the question is, who is the lawful wife?"[48] Levy's canny move delayed further progress of Emira's lawsuit. Two years after the initial filing, the judge suspended Emira's case until it could be determined by a surrogate court which of the three women was in fact the legitimate ex-wife of Lymon.

This was a complicated undertaking, as the other two women's claims were shaky at best. Lymon's first "wife," Elizabeth Waters Lymon, began living with Lymon after meeting him backstage at a performance in 1962. She tried to help him kick his growing dependency on heroin, insisting that he get treatment, and for a while Lymon seemed to improve. She bore him a child who died shortly after its birth in 1963, and the two were wed a year later; unfortunately, Elizabeth's divorce from her first husband was not yet official at the time of her marriage to Lymon, raising questions about its legitimacy.[49] Elizabeth and Frankie lived together for about a year in Philadelphia, with Elizabeth drawn into prostitution and drug use herself.[50]

In 1965 Lymon took off for California, where he formed a relationship with Zola Taylor, ex–lead singer of the 1950s doowop group the Platters. According to Taylor, the two had an affair while the two groups were touring together in the late fifties. During the mid-sixties, Taylor was making a decent living on the oldies circuit, and had a large house where Lymon took up residence. Zola claimed that she took Lymon to Mexico to marry him during this period, but could not produce either proof of her divorce from her second husband or the marriage certificate itself. (Both Zola and Elizabeth made claims of being "common-law" wives because they each lived for a period of time with Lymon.) Leaving Frankie alone in her house in December 1965 in order to tour Japan with the latest version of the Platters, Zola returned in April 1966 to discover that he had failed to keep up with the house payments (she had given him a special account to pay the bills) and disappeared. Back in New York, Lymon returned to Elizabeth and drug use, while claiming that the Mexican marriage to Zola was just a "publicity stunt." Trying to find work, Lymon turned to Chuck Rubin, who phoned some smaller clubs in North Jersey to get them to give Lymon a second chance. Rubin claims that, after he was turned down by one club owner, Lymon asked him to hand him the phone so he could personally make his case. "You remember me," Lymon told the owner, "I used to be Frankie Lymon."[51]

In December 1966, Lymon was drafted into the army and was sent for train-ing to Fort Gordon, Georgia, where he met his third wife, Emira, then a church-going schoolteacher; Rubin claims that Frankie married her as a way to get out of living on base.[52] Emira said that Lymon led a sober life as a soldier, com-muting from her home to the base each day, although by mid- to late 1967 he was discharged from the service for going AWOL. Telling Emira that he was returning to New York to try to renew his career, Lymon went north, where he was soon seeing Elizabeth again (who claimed he never told her that he had remarried). Lymon was staying at his grandmother's apartment when he was found on the morning of February 17, 1968, dead on the bathroom floor from a heroin overdose.[53]

It could not have been easy for the surrogate court to come to a decision about which of these women had the strongest claim to being Lymon's heir. The initial decision came down in favor of Elizabeth, but eventually an appeals court in 1989 acknowledged Emira, the last wife, as the true heir.[54]

Meanwhile, Santiago and Merchant were feeling shortchanged because none of these machinations addressed their claim that they were the actual authors of the song. When Rubin and Emira were first planning to take action against Levy, the duo were asked to testify on Emira's behalf in return for her passing along two-thirds of the moneys that she recovered.[55] However—either because they were not needed to make the case, or because they would eat away at the total take for Emira and Rubin—Rubin subsequently cut them out of the settlement, claiming that there never was any agreement reached to add them to the song's authorship.[56] Rubin's action infuriated Richard Bennett, who in 1987 took on Santiago and Merchant as clients against Emira, Rubin, and Levy. Once Emira was found the true heir, the Merchant-Santiago lawsuit could go forward. Ironi-cally, in this action, Rubin agreed to represent Levy and his publishing company, Big Seven, in defending their mutual rights to the song.

Levy and his codefendants asserted that Goldner in fact helped write the song (and that Santiago and Merchant could produce no evidence that he had not). When deposed during the original lawsuit brought by Emira Lymon, Levy incredibly claimed to have "made some changes in the lyric" to "Fools" even though he was not at the session and did not meet the Teenagers until after the song was released. He further described how he helped "write" songs: "You get together, you get a beat going, and you put the music and words together. I think I would be misleading you if I said I wrote songs, per se, like Chopin."[57] This statement was doubly "misleading" in that Levy did not "get together" with any of the participants to help write this song. It was only through the transfer of copyright from Goldner that he was able to have any claim at all.

The defendants made a second claim for Goldner legitimately claiming authorship to the song. Even if the jury found that the producer had not participated in writing it, he hired and paid for the saxophonist who played on the original recording.[58] That solo was not part of the original song that Merchant and Santiago claimed to have written. Because he paid the musician a flat fee for his work (as a "work-for-hire" performer), the rights to the solo belonged to Goldner.[59]

Both of these claims were rejected by the jury in light of Merchant and Santiago's compelling evidence that they were singing the song before Lymon joined the group. They produced witnesses who said they had heard them singing it on Harlem street corners before they met George Goldner. Ira Greenberg, the trial lawyer defending Levy, noted that it was nearly impossible to disprove these eyewitness accounts:

> Herbie Cox, who was one of the Cleftones, came in and testified—apparently
> the jury believed him—that he was there when Merchant and Santiago cowrote
> [the song]. . . . But who knows? Kids were out singing on streetcorners in various
> neighborhoods, making it up as they go along, and none of them had any musical
> training. So Herbie Cox comes in and he says, "I heard them doing the song on who
> knows what street in Harlem." I mean, how do you prove him wrong?[60]

The "work-for-hire" argument was also rejected by the jury and on appeal; the judge on appeal stated that the sax player did not make a substantial contribution to the song because his "solo was merely an arrangement that followed from the song's chord progression."[61] Further, he was not a full-time employee of Gee Records, so the argument that his contribution was a "work-for-hire" was thin.

However, Santiago and Merchant faced another problem: the statute of limitations. They waited "approximately twenty-six years to pursue their claims"[62] when they first sued Levy in 1987. Under the law, copyright owners have to bring suit within three years of their discovery that their rights are being abused; they cannot come forward decades later and then file a claim. As Ira Greenberg stated at the time of the initial appeals trial in 1992, "Thirty-one years after the fact they show up, after all the witnesses that could dispute them are dead, and say they wrote it. [If they win this case it gives a] major incentive for people to suddenly show up and say they wrote songs."[63]

In their defense, Santiago and Merchant invoked their fear of Levy. Attempts to collect royalties for the recording from Levy in 1969 by Santiago and Sherman Garnes and in 1977 by Merchant and Garnes were unsuccessful. Both stated in court that Levy "threatened [them] with physical violence" or said he "would have them killed" if they continued to try to collect their royalties.[64] They therefore took no further action until 1984, when the duo sued Levy over authorship to an additional Teenagers song, "I Want You to Be My Girl." The jury accepted this argument, and found that their fear of Levy was "reasonable." The jury found that their "fear" began in 1969 when Santiago first confronted Levy through 1984 when they finally brought suit for "I Want You to Be My Girl." Thus Levy et al. owed Santiago and Merchant for back royalties for the period 1969–84 (three years before their claim was made in 1987).

However, the appeals court had some serious questions about Santiago's story that he was intimidated by Levy in 1969 when he attempted to collect royalties due for "Fools":

> Despite several occasions during the course of this litigation when testimony about this threat would have been useful, Santiago failed to testify until trial about this event. Considering the importance of the duress toll to plaintiff's case and the abject fear he felt following the threat, we find it inconceivable that he forgot to mention the incident or that his attorney counseled him not to mention it.[65]

The appeals judge concluded that because of Goldner and Levy "fraudulent[ly] conceal[ing] from plaintiffs the accrual of royalties from *Fools* . . . Considering . . . the jury's finding that plaintiffs co-wrote *Fools* . . . a ruling barring plaintiffs' claims would allow the Levy defendants to profit from their untoward action."[66] Nonetheless, the appeals judge overturned the original verdict that the songwriters were owed back royalties for the period 1969–84, limiting their claim to the three years prior to the initial suit. In 1996 that decision in turn was reversed on appeal so that the original argument that Levy and his codefendants made— that Merchant and Santiago knew that their rights were being abused and therefore had to bring suit within the three-year period stated by the copyright law's statute of limitations—was upheld.[67] In a settlement made with Levy's son, Adam, the songwriters were awarded future royalties for both the recording and the song. While their claim of authorship of one of the century's greatest pop songs was now clear, Merchant and Santiago were unable to collect for the many years that Levy had failed to pay or acknowledge them as authors. Levy, by then six years dead, would have undoubtedly enjoyed his vindication.

10

Levy's Last Scam: 1980–1986

There's only one thief here.
—Fritzy Giovanelli

By the early eighties, Roulette barely existed as a functioning record label. Its offices were threadbare, with aging furnishings. The staff was winnowed down to a few essential figures, notably the label's longtime chief financial officer, Howard Fisher, who was one of Levy's first hires in 1957 when he established Roulette.[1] Most of the label's output was limited to repressings of past albums, while Levy continued to skim off the biggest hits for cut-price collections either sold through stores or directly through late-night TV. The offices served primarily as a receiving address for Levy's various music-related activities, as well as his real estate and other holdings. Levy's office remained untouched since the sixties with its odd collection of framed certificates on the walls, attesting to his charitable work for Jewish and African American causes, photos of Levy with dignitaries, and Levy's famous framed motto, "Oh Lord, Give Me a Bastard with Talent!"[2]

On April 1, 1979, Levy married for the fifth and last time, the former Karen White; she would bear his final two children, Simon Becket (born 1980), and Daniel Zachariah Levy (born 1982). However, just two months after his marriage, Levy suffered a major heart attack.[3] Levy survived this first attack and returned to good health, but it was a sign of the stress of trying to run his various businesses while dealing with his many silent "investors."

By this time, Levy and his businesses were increasingly influenced by outside forces—particularly Mob leader Vincent "The Chin" Gigante, who had steadily increased his interest in both Roulette and Levy's Strawberries operations through the seventies. Levy employed Gigante's mistress, Olympia Esposito, who was mother to three of the mobster's illegitimate children. Levy made Esposito an "officer" of Adam VIII Records,[4] and paid her a regular salary out of this and his other labels—presumably as a means of passing cash along to Gigante. During the period 1980–84, the FBI traced payroll checks and loans made to Esposito by at least five of Levy's many recording and distribution operations,[5]

Levy at his desk in 1969. Notice behind him the sign "O Lord give me a bastard with talent." Photo by William "PoPsie" Randolph, copyright © 2015 Michael Randolph, www.PoPsiePhotos.com.

despite the fact that Esposito never visited the Roulette offices or did any work to justify her salary and bonuses.[6]

In its wiretaps of Esposito's and Levy's phones in the early eighties, the FBI picked up many conversations between the two showing how Levy kowtowed to her, providing her with cash and bonds, as well as passing messages through her to Gigante. On February 27, 1985, Levy called Esposito to inform her, "You just got a bonus of [$]25,000," adding "you keep up the good work." On the following April 9, Levy followed up with a $50,000 bonus; the FBI recorded this flirtatious interchange between the two during which he gave her this news:

ML: I'm giving you a fifty thousand dollar bonus today.

OE: Oh, wonderful.

ML: Ain't that good? Because you worked hard last week.

OE: Fantastic.

ML: If ya be a good girl.

OE: I've been. I've been good. . . .

ML: Well, then you're entitled to buy yourself a nice present with that. . . . That's nice, huh? [Both laugh] . . . Alright, I'll run. I'll talk to you later, Sweetheart. I just wanted to give you the good news.

OE: Okay, Morris.

ML: Be a good girl. There's more coming if ya be good.

OE: I'm, I've been good. Ya haven't been good, but I've been good.[7]

In 1983 Esposito moved into a Federal-era brownstone on New York's Upper East Side. The building had been purchased for $525,000 two years earlier by the 67 East 77th Street Realty Corporation, which not surprisingly operated out of Roulette's offices; Levy was listed as president of the corporation, with Esposito vice-president. When Esposito moved into the property, the corporation sold the building at a $35,000 loss to the Olympia Esposito Realty Corporation—which also operated out of Roulette's offices.[8] After she moved in, Gigante visited the apartment secretly each night after midnight to sleep with Esposito and to stage private meetings with his cohorts.[9] However, after discovering a small pile of plaster dust on the dining room floor, Gigante realized the house was not secure; the FBI had rented an apartment next door and had attempted to plant a bug by drilling through Esposito's ceiling.[10]

A further indication of Gigante's influence over Levy was the fact that Levy "donated" two acres of land next to his upstate farm to Gigante's brother Louis, a Bronx-based priest;[11] Levy was also said to have provided Father Gigante with a 50 percent discount on his mortgage rate, enabling him to build a ranch house on the property where Louis threw parties for his friends.[12] Although Louis was never convicted of any Mafia-related activities, he was a defender of his brother throughout his many trials. Gigante's SEBCO, a non-profit corporation that was formed to build housing in the Bronx for the poor, became the subject of numerous investigations for alleged Mob ties.[13]

Vincent Gigante was so deeply involved with Levy's businesses by the mid-eighties that his approval was required even for small transactions. Philadelphia deejay Jerry Blavat approached Levy about help producing an oldies collection that he hoped to market locally. According to the testimony of a New Jersey mobster, "Levy told Blavat that he could not help him . . . unless Levy had the approval of 'The Chin' Gigante."[14] Blavat subsequently used his local contacts to obtain Gigante's blessing and Levy proceeded to clear the tracks and produce the album for Blavat. Blavat then sold the album primarily through local Mob-controlled unions, "to sell to their memberships as a way of increasing record sales."[15] The profits were shared with Blavat's local Mob friends. Presumably, Gigante was also paid for his "participation" in the deal.

While Levy was not particularly active in signing new acts to Roulette, his tentacles reached far and wide in the record business. Calling his Roulette offices a "clinic" for ailing labels, Levy strategically entered into partnerships with independent producers who were experiencing cashflow problems, often as the first step in taking over their operations entirely or at least maintaining centralized control by moving them to Roulette's offices. These myriad associated labels also enabled Levy to effectively pay his overhead out of his many partners' pockets, as well as to hide income from both the taxman and his investors.

One of the many independent operators who experienced cashflow problems in the early eighties was Florida-based Henry Stone. After World War II, Stone—a fellow Jewish American born in the Bronx—established himself as a distributor and producer of records in the Miami area. Among his early discoveries were Ray Charles and James Brown, who he brought to King Records. Stone established a strong power base through his Tone Distribution Company, handling most of the independent labels through the later sixties when many of his key accounts, like Atlantic, went corporate. In the disco era, Stone hit it big once more with TK Records, scoring major hits with KC and the Sunshine Band and helping establish the 12-inch disco single as a new record format. However, by the late seventies, the disco backlash was beginning to eat into his sales.

At the time, Bud Katzel—who had previously worked for Roulette—was helping Stone run TK and reached out to Levy to help Stone sort out its financial problems. Katzel told *Billboard*: "[Morris] might have been the only person able to talk to the creditors and work out payment plans." Katzel added, in an understatement (as he must have experienced Levy's considerable ability to muscle his way to the top): "Morris is a great negotiator. He's a very strong and powerful man who dominates the discussion all the time. He also has a lot of charisma, and that's what enabled him to get the best deal."[16]

The Levy-Stone partnership was greeted with some skepticism by the music press. One particularly tongue-in-cheek notice appeared in *Musician, Player, and Listener* magazine. The magazine wryly noted: "The Stone-Levy collaboration should be most interesting, though, like a solar eclipse, it should be viewed from a safe distance."[17] The magazine also described Levy as being a poor businessman. Levy may have complained, because in the following issue the magazine ran a retraction (albeit again with tongue firmly in cheek), stating: "Oops! Due to a typo in the Industry News column, entrepreneur Morris Levy was 'derided for his lack of business acumen.' Far from it. Levy is one of the industry's sharpest wheeler dealers. Apologies to Mr. Levy."[18] This mock apology must have irritated Levy even further, who had a thin skin when it came to the press criticizing his operations.

After Levy settled TK's problems, he partnered with Stone to launch a new label, Sunnyview Records, named for Levy's horse farm in upstate New York. Sunnyview rereleased several of TK's better-selling records as well as developed new artists. Levy's role was purely financial, with Stone in charge of signing new artists. With his ear to the ground to new musical styles, Stone signed groups like the band Newcleus, an early hip-hop/electronic dance music band that had a hit in 1984 with "Jam on It."[19] The label also was associated with the beginnings of the Miami Bass dance music style thanks to Stone's ties to the local black music community. In 1983 the pair expanded their partnership to start a new distribution business out of South Florida.[20] However, by 1986, as Levy's legal problems were mounting, Sunnyview ceased operations and Stone returned to operating on his own.[21]

Another old hand in the New York record business who turned to Levy when times got tough was Art Kass, who owned Buddah Records. The label traced its history back to a production partnership called Kama Sutra Productions formed in 1965 by Artie Ripp, Hy Mizrahi, and Phil Steinberg; an unnamed "investor" in the operation was said to be mobster Sonny Franzese of the Colombo crime family.[22] Levy's first encounter with the trio occurred after they oversaw the recording of the Shangri-Las' first hit, "Remember (Walkin' in the Sand)," which hit #5 on the charts. It was released on Red Bird Records, run by George Goldner. After the Shangri-Las hit it big, Levy showed up at Kama Sutra's offices to demand his cut of the action, according to Steinberg. Levy claimed that he owned a piece of the group. According to Michael Franzese (Sonny's son):

> Steinberg felt the muscles in his neck tighten. A burly ex-football player, he suppressed an urge to toss Levy out of his office. That wouldn't have been a wise option . . .
>
> "I'll discuss this with my partners, and we'll get back to you," Steinberg said, forcing a smile. "I'm sure we can work this out to your satisfaction."
>
> "Make some calls. Check around," Levy advised. "I'm confident you'll do the right thing."[23]

Sonny Franzese later visited the offices and was outraged when he heard that Levy had tried to muscle in on the action. Franzese told his partners, "You boys worked too hard to have the likes of Moe Levy shake you down. Don't worry about it." When Steinberg subsequently ran into Levy in a recording studio, "Levy was all handshakes and smiles," and not a word was said about their former encounter.[24]

When Steinberg and his associates decided to launch their own label, Kama Sutra Records, Kass, who had previously worked at MGM as an accountant, was brought in to help manage the operation. Kama Sutra was distributed by MGM and initially scored success with the group the Lovin' Spoonful. In 1968 the trio sold Kama Sutra to the Viewlex Corporation, a company that produced educational slides and projectors as well as owning Bell Sound Studios (a prominent New York studio) and record pressing and tape duplicating companies.[25] They formed a second label, Buddah Records, which became best known for launching "bubblegum" music. Producer Neil Bogart was brought in to help run the operation, and Steinberg left by the early '70s. Bogart left in 1973 to form Casablanca Records, and Buddah struggled on until Viewlex decided to sell out in

1975; Kass then raised the money to repurchase the label as its sole owner. However, the bills continued to mount until the early eighties. Finding himself in the hole to the tune of $10 million, Kass turned to Levy as his savior. Called to the bank after missing a $250,000 interest payment, Kass said, "I felt like maybe I was in jail. You're allowed one phone call. I called Morris."[26]

Kass formed Sutra Records in 1980 with Levy in order to wait out the expiration of a pre-existing distribution deal for Buddah with Arista Records.[27] Eventually, both labels were united as part of Levy's empire. Levy's son Adam—who was about twenty-two years old at the time—was named "national promotion chief" of the joint venture.[28] The Buddah label was shuttered soon after the merger, but Sutra lived on for a few years, featuring mostly R&B, disco, and rap acts. Sutra's most successful signing was a group called the Disco 3, who changed their name to the Fat Boys after they scored a hit with their second Sutra single of the same name.[29] Their three albums on the label were said to sell in the neighborhood of 500,000 to a million units.[30] Levy's old employee Joe Kolsky was enticed out of retirement to help guide the group and promote their initial recordings.[31] According to George Hocutt—Levy's West Coast distributor at the time—Levy laughed when he was asked if he ever notified the Fat Boys about their gold records. "Hell no!" Levy replied. "If you start handing out gold records, they expect royalties!"[32]

Kass would learn—as did many others who had the misfortune to go into business with Levy—that Levy often treated his "partners" as if they were not partners at all. In early 1989, Levy and Olympia Esposito—who was given a piece of Buddah/Sutra by Levy—notified Kass that they were going to hold a meeting of the board of directors of the record company and in effect remove him from being its director. This was despite the fact that Kass claims he purchased all of Levy's and Esposito's stock in the company in July 1987! Kass filed suit in February 1989.[33] A settlement was worked out whereby Levy was paid off for his portion of the firm.

In an interview conducted towards the end of his life, Levy gleefully reported that he had overcharged Kass for his portion of Sutra Records:

> You're fucking right I overcharged him ... I fucking milked him for it. It was ridiculous. He paid so fucking much more than it was worth, what an asshole. He was so set on getting me out, thinking he was going to fuck me ... He comes to me and says he wants to buy me out. I said fine. I came in to help him out. That fucker could ruin a money machine. He was hiding figures on me you see. He had this band ... an all-girl group, the Cover Girls ... and he thought he was going to make it big with them and he didn't need me any longer. ... He wanted me out bad and I made him pay for it. And I'd do it again.[34]

Sylvia Robinson of Sugar Hill Records in a publicity photo from the mid-seventies at the time of her comeback as a disco singer.

Levy's most profitable partnership came in the late seventies through another veteran of the music industry, an African American music promoter named Joe Robinson. Robinson was a classic street hustler. After serving in the navy, he was rumored to have worked as a runner in the Harlem numbers racket but was savvy enough to invest in real estate, including a few apartment buildings and bars. Robinson had the good fortune to meet a young singer named Sylvia Vanderpool in the mid-fifties, who as a teenager had already recorded for Savoy and Jubilee. He soon became her husband and manager. Sylvia had tried to learn the guitar, taking lessons from a local jazz musician named Mickey Baker, but she never mastered the instrument. Joe recognized that partnering Mickey's musical ability with Sylvia's vocal (and sex) appeal was a formula for success. Although Mickey was over a decade older than Sylvia, the duo had a hit in 1957 with Sylvia's adaptation of a Bo Diddley tune that she called "Love is Strange." The record featured Sylvia's playful flirting with Mickey, and many fans assumed they were a couple—although Mickey had nothing but contempt for the pop music that they were peddling. Subsequent records failed to make much of a dent on the charts, and the duo ended when Mickey left the United States to live in France in 1962.

Sylvia was the brains behind Joe's brawn; she had an excellent ear for what would make a hit record, although being a woman she was not given the same opportunities to profit from her work. Even during the heyday of Mickey and Sylvia's popularity, Sylvia had to augment her income by taking a job as a secretary. She tried to make the switch to producing records, overseeing some recordings by singer Joe Jones for Roulette, but was dismayed when she got neither credit nor royalties for her work. This would not be the last time that Levy stiffed her and her husband.

In the late sixties, the couple opened their own label, optimistically named All Platinum Enterprises. They built a studio in their home so they could have complete control over their product. As musical tastes changed, Sylvia was able to adapt, turning out hits in both R&B and disco styles. Sylvia produced and wrote hits for groups like the Moments, including 1970's "Love on a Two-Way Street" (1970), and encouraged fifties star Shirley Goodman (of Shirley & Lee) to come out of retirement; she produced "Shame, Shame, Shame" for her, released as by Shirley and Company. Sylvia had also written a sexy disco song intended for singer Al Green which she ended up recording herself. Called "Pillow Talk," it reached #1 on the pop charts in 1973. The soft-R&B flavored love song was banned by some stations for being too suggestive, perhaps because it was sung by a female who was portrayed as the aggressor in the song. Sylvia's little-girl voice was set against lush strings, while the song ended with her sharp, suggestive intakes of breath and soft moaning that by today's standards is quite tame but was shocking for a female singer of the day.

Using the proceeds from these successes, in 1975 the couple bought the masters of the famous Chicago blues label, Chess Records. They were proud to have this important repository of black musical heritage in their hands, and it would prove to be the single most valuable asset that they would own. But, the glory days for All Platinum were coming to an end. The couple was slow to pay artist royalties and suppliers for records. Like many other small labels, All Platinum had difficulty getting its distributors to pay in a timely manner, and eventually the couple went bankrupt. Joe faced payola charges and was convicted for tax evasion in the later seventies; the label's European distributor, Polygram, tried to seize its assets, including the valuable Chess masters. It looked like the end for the Robinsons as music business entrepreneurs.

Although they lived in Englewood, New Jersey—a middle-class suburb that had already attracted African American musicians like Dizzy Gillespie—the couple still had family in Harlem, and their children regularly attended the city's nightclubs. Sylvia's niece managed a large dance club called Harlem World and invited her aunt to a birthday party there in July 1979. What Sylvia heard would change her life and briefly revive her and husband Joe's careers as R&B magnates. On stage was an MC named Lovebug Starski who was egging the audience on through his rhymed announcing while disco music blasted from the sound system. Sylvia realized that this was something fresh and new and that the crowd was genuinely excited by it. She immediately asked her sons to find her some emcees who could recreate Starski's act.

The only problem was that the All Platinum studios were in disrepair and the Robinsons' bank book was empty. There was no way to achieve Sylvia's vision—unless a backer could be found. Joe Robinson decided to drive up to Levy's house in upstate New York to see if he could get him to invest in this new opportunity. Sylvia was against them partnering with Levy; "He's the devil," she said to Joe.[35] According to Robinson, at the fateful meeting, the wily record executive handed him a wad of bills, some $5,000 in cash, and said "Take care of your obligations. When you're done, come see me. We'll start a new label together."[36] At some point Levy obtained as collateral for his investment the rights to the Chess catalog of recordings. This would come back to haunt Robinson years later.

The new label was dubbed Sugar Hill Records in recognition of the famous Harlem neighborhood.[37] Levy and Robinson were said to each chip in $300 for the creation of the label's first release, "Rapper's Delight" by the Sugar Hill Gang. Sylvia's children had enlisted a group of friends to perform as the rappers, while the backing track—a recreation of the instrumental track of the disco hit "Good Times" by Chic—was created in the studio by a group of local musicians with whom Sylvia had worked before. The record was a phenomenal success, selling an estimated two million units in its first few weeks after its release. As Dan Charnas wrote in his history of rap:

> Suddenly, Joe Robinson had to scramble to keep pace with the demand [for the record] ... manufacturing up to 50,000 copies a day. Demand was so great that bootleggers began pressing counterfeit records and selling them directly to stores.... Nobody in the industry seemed to have ever experienced a single that moved this fast ... "Rapper's Delight" had become the biggest-selling 12-inch single ever.[38]

With Levy's distribution clout—and his ability to collect payments promptly from the vendors and to scare off bootleggers—Sugar Hill Records was off to a strong start.

Despite their success, the Robinsons invested little in the actual Sugar Hill offices. Writer Nelson George visited the "Sugar Hill 'complex'" in 1981 shortly following the success of "Rapper's Delight," to write about the Robinsons. He described their office as "A two-story structure with all the charm of a suburban strip mall. Outside it was completely nondescript. Inside it was lined with base-ment-grade wood paneling and had office furniture of equivalent grace. The lighting was uneven and the carpet thin."[39] George also captured the personali-ties of the couple and the roles they played at Sugar Hill: Joe played the part of the tough street negotiator, with a "pockmarked complexion and a gruff, impa-tient voice," while Sylvia oozed a smooth civility, with a "honeyed way and fake sincerity" that she used to win over journalists and Sugar Hill's stable of young artists.[40] George also observed on the premises a "portly European gent who served in some hard-to-define financial capacity . . . I fantasized that [he] was around to protect Levy's investment, though he didn't say and I didn't ask."[41]

With the success of "Rapper's Delight," the Robinsons were swimming in cash. To build the Sugar Hill empire, Joe was not shy about scooping up as many other local raps groups as possible, raiding smaller competitors for the best tal-ent. Local Harlem record store owner Bobby Robinson (no relation) had been on the scene since the fifties and, recognizing rap's potential, had signed acts like Grandmaster Flash and the Furious Five to his Enjoy label. Joe Robinson paid his competitor $10,000 to release his acts to Sugar Hill. Sylvia and Joe spent their newfound money lavishly, both on the business—pouring half a million dollars into their recording studio—but also personal items like furs, jewelry, and fancy cars. Meanwhile—taking a page from Morris Levy's playbook—they were slow to pay their recording artists, often stonewalling requests for accounting. Not to mention that Sylvia took credit as the "writer" of "Rapper's Delight" when the accompaniment was lifted from Bernard Edwards and Nile Rodgers and the lyr-ics were supplied by the three young rappers who appeared on the recording.

Because the backing track was not actually lifted from the original Chic recording, Rodgers and Edwards could not sue based on its use. They had to instead sue for part of the publishing royalties—and those rights were held by none other than Morris Levy. When they announced their plans to file suit, they were surprised when they received an unusual visit while working at the Power Station studio. As Rodgers relates:

> We were in the middle of a session . . . when the [studio's] owner burst in and yelled, "I have to get my people out of here!" He instantly stopped the session and forced his employees to leave the room. Before we could say "What the fuck," three large well-dressed black men entered the now empty studio, led by a guy who'd years ago unsuccessfully tried to sign Chic to a major label.
>
> The situation was strange, but since we thought of this dude as a friend, we had no reason to be nervous. The mood changed when the fellow we knew introduced the three large dapper strangers to us as his friends. At some point I realized that the biggest of the four dudes was clearly packing. . . . Apparently, our "friend" had heard that we were threatening to sue Sugarhill Records. What followed was a lengthy and

puzzling diatribe about how things were going to play out if we continued pursuing legal recourse. "Even if you win, you'll lose," he concluded.[42]

Exactly who was behind this threat is not known, but clearly the idea was to intimidate the duo and stop them from suing. According to Adam Levy, the Robinsons wanted to "brazen it out, see what happens," rather than settle with the duo. Adam claims that it was his father who pushed for a settlement.[43] Rodgers notes that eventually a settlement was reached in which he and Edwards "got equal billing on the copyright—and a lot of money."

In an ironic footnote to the affair, Levy made a final demand on the duo's lawyer in order to complete the settlement:

> We had to buy Morris two round-trip tickets to Paris on the Concorde and a pair of his-and-hers Rolex watches. When [our lawyer] asked, "Why?," Morris responded with a classic so ridiculous, it was funny even to us. "Come on," he said, "I gotta fuck ya!"
>
> Talk about an offer we couldn't refuse.[44]

In 1981, having snagged Grandmaster Flash from Enjoy, Sylvia realized that his unique turntable art could be represented on record. The result was the major hit "The Adventures of Grandmaster Flash on the Wheels of Steel," the first recording of a deejay plying his trade. Running over seven minutes, it became an audio dictionary of the major deejaying techniques for an entire generation. Sylvia also oversaw the creation of the first rap record to address life in the South Bronx. Based on a demo created by one of her house musicians, and working with Melle Mel, Flash's MC, she crafted a song that was called "The Message." Flash had dismissed the song as being too depressing to appeal to his dance-oriented audience and was angered when Sylvia released the record under his group's name. Eventually, he had to sue to gain freedom from the Robinsons and to regain the legal rights to his performing name.[45]

While Sugar Hill enjoyed success through 1981 and into 1982, Robinson's old patterns of amassing large bills from suppliers and failing to pay royalties to performers were beginning to catch up with him. Also, the record world was changing; even bigger independents like A&M were finding it hard to maintain their own distribution due to the increasing power of the majors. Most independents ended up looking for distribution deals from one of the larger labels so they could focus on artist development and promotion.[46] By 1983 the writing was on the wall, and Robinson was looking for a patron to help Sugar Hill survive.

Looking for someone to help him market Sugar Hill's catalog to the majors, Robinson hooked up with a would-be record executive named Sal Pisello. Pisello had previously worked as an associate of the Gambino crime family, mostly in food-related businesses, often as covers for drug smuggling or other illegal activities.[47] While born in the Bronx like Levy, Pisello had primarily been active in the Los Angeles area through the late seventies, until an ill-fated scheme to import drugs through the city's fish market led to scrutiny from local authorities. Somehow Pisello learned of the sting before actually moving any drugs, and he disappeared from Southern California for a few years in the late seventies and early eighties, perhaps retreating to New York. He resurfaced in 1983 with a new business called Consultants for World Records, which was involved with cutout records much like Levy's earlier Promo Records operation. His silent partners in this operation were Levy, Dominic Canterino, and Federico "Fritzy" Giovanelli, who were two high-ranking figures in Vincent Gigante's organization.[48] It is highly likely that Levy encouraged Robinson to work with Pisello. Through Pisello, Robinson was introduced to MCA Records, and the pair began negotiations with the label in November 1983.

Robinson and Pisello met with Al Bergamo, MCA's head of distribution, who was wary of Robinson, knowing his reputation from his All Platinum days as well as his long association with Levy. Bergamo negotiated a straight distribution and pressing deal for the label. MCA would take a 25 percent fee for its services. Bergamo was careful to stipulate that Sugar Hill would be responsible for returned product from its prior sales, and MCA would not bankroll the label's artistic operations (such as costs of signing and recording artists). He also insisted that Sugar Hill put up its one viable asset—the Chess catalog—as collateral so that if the label failed MCA could collect what was owed to it. The deal was finalized on these terms. However, Pisello failed to mention that the Chess catalog had already been used as collateral for a loan from Morris Levy, who was holding it against a $1 million note that Robinson owed him.[49]

The Sugar Hill deal opened a door for Pisello, who somehow convinced MCA to contract with Consultants for World Records to handle remainder sales for the label. Pisello took an office at MCA Records, even though he was not technically employed by the label but merely working as a "consultant." As part of his contract, he was given free rein to sell as many of MCA's remainders as possible.

Pisello was given a list of MCA albums that he could sell on the remainder market. In late March 1984, he attended the National Association of Record Merchandisers (NARM) meeting in Miami to try to unload this product. Whether he was specifically looking for a fall guy, or whether he could not move the product in any other way, he latched onto a small-time dealer, Out of the Past Records, which was operated out of suburban Philadelphia by John LaMonte. LaMonte was hardly a virgin in the cutouts business; he had previously served a prison term for fraud (based on a charge of selling illegally pirated records) in the late seventies and was rumored to have financial backers in the Philadelphia Mob.[50]

LaMonte was attending the meeting with his partner/employee, Sonny Brocco, who he had met while serving his prison term. Brocco worked for both Out of the Past and a New Jersey videotape distributor, Video Warehouse, which was controlled by his cousin, Tommy Vastola—the same Vastola who had worked with Levy in the fifties.[51] In 1983 Vastola had made a loan of $50,000 to LaMonte at the incredible rate of 2 percent interest per week (or 104 percent for one year), so the two were already in bed together.[52] Brocco introduced LaMonte to Pisello, promoting the deal to LaMonte as an once-in-a-lifetime opportunity to buy directly from a major label, rather than having to work with the usual intermediaries (and paying their markup). Brocco may also have targeted LaMonte as the perfect patsy who—because of his own background as a convicted record counterfeiter—could not complain to either MCA or the authorities if the deal went awry.

On the surface the deal was straightforward: Pisello was looking to move four million remaindered albums. LaMonte was invited to make a bid; supposedly others would also be bidding, and whoever bid the most would get the inventory. LaMonte took a copy of the inventory list from Pisello and asked him for a day to "mark it up"; this would also give LaMonte time to feel out his network of buyers to make sure he could not only cover his costs but make a healthy profit. After examining the list, LaMonte felt he could make a million-dollar offer that he could quickly recoup by flipping the better records; by the time all the material was moved, he estimated his profit would be three quarters of a million dollars.

The first surprise came when LaMonte returned the next day to give his bid to Pisello. Pisello begged off, saying he had to check with his own "consultant" before accepting the offer. And who was this consultant? None other than Morris Levy, who joined the discussion at this point. LaMonte had his own history with Levy and was not happy to hear that he was working with Pisello. He knew that Levy would not hesitate to use whatever force was needed to collect on the deal; further he feared that Levy might "cream" the better records from the sale, leaving him with the hardest-to-sell items, while still expecting full payment to be made.

Thus it was not entirely disappointing when Levy rejected LaMonte's initial bid, saying "What are you trying to do, rob us?"[53] LaMonte returned to his suite to tell Brocco the deal was off. While he was relieved not to have to deal with Levy, he still believed that the deal was a sure moneymaker. It may have been that Levy's initial negative reaction to the bid was only meant to whet LaMonte's appetite further; because within a few days, Pisello was back in touch offering to "sweeten" the deal with approximately 200,000 albums by current artists that would be highly desirable in the marketplace. Recognizing Levy's involvement—and considerable clout—LaMonte sought his own protector. It is not known whether he asked Brocco or Brocco suggested it to him, but Vastola was brought in as their partner. With Vastola's deep Mob ties, LaMonte reasoned, Levy had to play straight with them. What Brocco failed to tell LaMonte was that Vastola had a long-running relationship with Levy. Levy may not have known of Vastola's previous relations with LaMonte either, or of the unpaid loan that bound LaMonte to Vastola.

The parties reconvened, and a deal was put together where LaMonte would pay $1.3 million for the inventory. Levy would "guarantee" LaMonte's payment, because, as Pisello told LaMonte, LaMonte's business was not big enough for MCA to extend standard credit terms to it. However, rather than paying Levy a fee directly, Pisello and Levy put forward an unusual plan. Levy would collect directly from LaMonte a three-cent-per-record fee, to be payable on a monthly basis at $15,000 a week until the total ($120,000) was collected. The balance due was to be paid directly by LaMonte to the label. What LaMonte did not know was that Levy was going to divide his commission with Vastola and another partner, Fritzy Giovanelli.

Why Levy was brought in to "guarantee" the payment to MCA is not clear. Later, after the events unfolded and they were on trial, the prosecution painted a picture of a conspiracy among Pisello, Levy, and Vastola (among others) that began with the selection of LaMonte as the "fall guy" to purchase the inventory. In this argument, Levy was presumably inserted into the deal as a means of skimming additional money out of LaMonte. On the other hand, Levy's lawyers (and Levy himself) insisted that he was merely "doing a favor" for Pisello and Vastola in helping with the deal. Levy made many such arrangements with old "friends," particularly when he saw a way to make an easy profit as part of the bargain. Levy said he signed the guarantee because he thought he could not lose any money in the transaction:

> I knew what they were getting and I knew that I'd get my money back. . . . You see they already had the records sold. They tell me they've got this bootlegger [John LaMonte], and I say, "Don't be dealing with this fucking guy, he's a no good motherfucker." But they felt it was okay and really wanted to do it, so . . . I looked the thing over and saw that, . . . if things went bad I could get the product back and sell the stuff myself . . . so I had control of the deal. I signed the papers knowing that, and this is what I meant later when I said, "I thought [LaMonte] was a controllable cocksucker," because I held the reins, and he knew that I knew about him.

According to Levy, he also had an ace up his sleeve that he did not tell Vastola or Pisello; he was already in negotiation to sell Roulette to MCA, and therefore would have additional leverage with the major label if the deal should go south.[54]

The final papers were signed in Levy's offices at Roulette in June 1994. LaMonte was concerned when he saw the inventory list on Levy's desk with various markings on it indicating that Levy had perhaps already marketed some of the items to other vendors. LaMonte's suspicions were further piqued when he spotted two other major remainder dealers sitting in Roulette's lobby waiting to meet separately with Levy. When they left the office, he asked Vastola if Levy was sharing in any of the profit that they were going to make on the deal; Vastola assured him that Levy's only profit would come out of the loan guarantee and that only Brocco, LaMonte, and Vastola would share in the profits. What Vastola did not know was that Levy was not planning to share any profits he made by "creaming" or preselling the better items to other dealers.

When seventy tractor-trailers showed up at Out of the Past's warehouses with 4.2 million MCA records in mid-July 1984, sure enough the "sweeteners" were mysteriously missing. LaMonte was furious, and immediately asked Brocco to contact Vastola to tell him that they were being screwed by Levy and Pisello. LaMonte was particularly galled when he discovered that another local remainder dealer to whom he had arranged to sell some of the better albums had been able to make his own deal directly with a small Los Angeles–based remainder house, Betaco Industries. Pisello had diverted the sweeteners to Betaco, most likely under the instructions of Levy, although Pisello leaned on Betaco's owner for his own additional kickback on the deal. LaMonte calculated that nearly half of his expected profit from the deal had suddenly disappeared.

LaMonte's suspicions were further aroused when the invoice for his records arrived on his desk not from MCA but from Consultants for World Records. Unaware of Pisello's or Levy's connection to this firm, he was mystified as to who they were. LaMonte then made a decision that would cause all of the parties to scramble: he refused to pay the invoice until he was either supplied with the missing records or credited for the undelivered inventory.

This might have remained an argument among thieves had not two government operations—a special Justice Department taskforce investigation operating out of Newark targeting Vastola's Video Warehouse business, and a federal prosecutor's tax fraud case in Los Angeles focused on Sal Pisello—inadvertently stumbled onto the scheme. It began when Vastola started leaning on Brocco to get LaMonte to pay for the goods; through wiretaps on Video Warehouse's phone lines, beginning in October 1984 investigators picked up conversations about the need to get "John [LaMonte]" to pay up or "Morris [Levy]" would be very unhappy. The Newark investigators were quickly intrigued and were able to obtain warrants for further wiretaps to follow up on these mysterious leads. Meanwhile, Pisello was about to face trial for tax evasion, so his involvement with MCA was beginning to draw scrutiny from federal authorities.

LaMonte's refusal to pay led to a series of desperate maneuvers among all the players as they sought to line their own pockets while avoiding any financial or criminal liability. They worked assiduously to hide their allegiances from each other, so that it was never exactly clear who was going to be left holding the bag. Vastola and Brocco had initiated the deal and thus were being held responsible for its outcome by their other partners, not only by Levy but more seriously by Fritzy Giovanelli. Levy's position was that LaMonte was trying to scam them. He asserted that the records had been delivered to LaMonte and LaMonte was simply holding out either to negotiate a discounted price or to pay nothing at all. However, Levy must have been aware that the sweeteners were never delivered to LaMonte, because he was a silent partner with Pisello, who had diverted the actual records to Betaco. (Levy may not have been aware that Pisello was profiting separately from the Betaco deal, in a sense creaming the cream.)

LaMonte's only ace in the hole was that he was able to get documentation showing that the same records that were supposed to be the "sweeteners" were in fact sold to Betaco and then shipped to another reseller. At a meeting in mid-September 1984 arranged to try to resolve the situation, LaMonte presented this evidence. This was the first meeting attended by Fritzy Giovanelli. To LaMonte, Fritzy seemed to be running the meeting, with Vastola strangely silent throughout the proceedings. After LaMonte presented his evidence, he was asked to leave the room so the partners could come up with a solution. When he returned, Fritzy told him that MCA would make him whole by shipping 300,000 additional units of good material at an additional cost.[55] LaMonte left feeling he had accomplished his goal. Shortly after this meeting, LaMonte also made the first of his cash payments of $30,000 to Levy for guaranteeing the deal. Sitting in Levy's offices, he was surprised when Levy gleefully split up the money with Vastola and Fritzy in front of him.

By December 1984, the pressure was building on Vastola to collect the money for MCA, but LaMonte was still waiting for the shipment of the replacement records. Investigators picked up fragments of conversations indicating that Pisello was scrambling in an effort to convince MCA to ship more records to LaMonte, but nothing came of his effort. A second payment by LaMonte of $30,000 to Levy in the form of a check had bounced, further inflaming the situation. Vastola was growing inpatient, feeling that LaMonte's failure to pay was sullying his name among his fellow gangsters, and perhaps fearing their wrath if the deal somehow exploded. In several phone conversations with his cousin during January 1985, he urged Brocco to put additional pressure on LaMonte to pay up by minimally overseeing every shipment going from Out of the Past and collecting the debt from its receivables:

You gotta get a hold of [LaMonte]. We gotta sit down and talk with him, Sonny. They're holding you responsible, too. . . . They're saying you went down to Florida with him and negotiated this deal, so you're partners. They want you to sit in the fucking joint [i.e., LaMonte's warehouse] and not let a record go in or out until this thing is paid. . . . I'm telling you right now it's important.[56]

A month later, Vastola told his cousin to

Get in your car, go over to Philadelphia, pick up the checks for $629,000. I call this dirty motherfucker, everytime I call they're out. . . . I don't like the way this thing is going with this kid [i.e., LaMonte]. . . . I'm going to be out there tomorrow morning. I'll put him in a bucket (inaudible). . . . I'm going to put him in the fucking hospital. I'm not even going to talk to him. I don't like this motherfucker, what he's doing.[57]

In his replies, Brocco seemed to be making excuses for LaMonte's failure to pay, telling his cousin "It's not as easy as going over there and picking up a check." On a call made little over a month later, Vastola expressed fully his anger with LaMonte: "You know, Sonny, you're going to witness a fucking beating that I'm going to give this kid when this thing is over that you'll never believe it. . . ."[58]

On February 28, Vastola again called Brocco, telling him that Levy was upset because LaMonte had again failed to make a payment. Vastola claimed that Levy told him to "make Sonny go smack this guy right in the mouth" for his failure to pay:

VASTOLA: Do me a favor: Slap—walk in and don't say a word, just slap him in the mouth. . . .
BROCCO: And [tell him] that's from you.
VASTOLA: From me he's going to get the rest.
BROCCO: Oh, alright. Have a good day. I'll talk to you.[59]

Brocco's breezy sign-off ("have a good day") belies the seriousness of their conversation.

It is not exactly clear whether the two were discussing payments on the MCA deal or the $50,000 loan that Vastola made to LaMonte in 1983—or both. Although LaMonte told the FBI he was making his payments on Vastola's original loan, judging from his other actions it is likely that he was not always paying on time—if at all. The FBI reported as of mid-1985 that although LaMonte had paid "in excess of $100,000" to Vastola, this was merely interest on the loan, with the principle still outstanding.[60]

Levy and Vastola kicked around several alternatives to collect their money. They first floated the idea of sending their own men down to LaMonte's business and taking it over, wringing the money owed to MCA out of it as quickly as possible, and then pocketing the rest. While this alternative was being considered, Vastola suggested they first make a trip to the warehouse to see if they could locate the missing "sweeteners." The main players, with various associates, showed up at the warehouse on January 22, 1985, to take a physical inventory of Out of the Past's entire holdings. Again LaMonte protested, showing Fritzy Giovanelli the papers documenting that the missing records never reached his warehouse; a thorough search of the place also failed to yield the missing records. At this point, Levy seemed to be on the hot seat as Fritzy blamed him for shorting LaMonte. Giovanelli addressed LaMonte and the others, specifically pointing the finger at Levy, saying, "There's only one thief here, Morris, and it's you. This kid didn't do anything."[61] What the parties did not know was that the FBI was surveilling the meeting and photographed the assembly as they arrived at the warehouse, each man looking grim and determined.

As the pressure built on LaMonte to pay for the remaining inventory, he began pressing Brocco and company to allow him to return some of the unsold inventory to MCA as a means of lightening his debt burden. Pisello did not want to lose face with MCA or the credit for overseeing a million-dollar-plus deal (and presumably did not want to lose his portion of the Levy-Vastola-Giovanelli arrangement). However, an arrangement was made for LaMonte to return nearly two million records to reduce his debt.

Perhaps out of frustration, fear, or just plain stupidity, LaMonte made a decision to make up for the lost income from the undelivered discs by working with an offshore MCA licensor to import MCA product for resale. He had done business with this Caribbean distributor before, and asked him if he could press several hundred thousand current MCA releases that LaMonte would buy to resell as "remainders" in the states. As it happened, some of these items were not among the licensor's current inventory, so he ended up purchasing US copies, photocopying the covers and labels, and pressing them up to deliver to LaMonte. The results looked so shoddy that it did not take long for federal investigators—working with the Recording Industry Association of America (RIAA) to track counterfeit records—to pick up the scent.

Vastola may have been behind this deal as well; the FBI picked up a phone conversation involving Vastola and his lieutenant Elias "Lou" Saka in which:

Saka said, "If you have a contract to produce tapes for someone, are you counterfeiting if you sell some of their tapes?" They discussed Palmer [a.k.a. Sonny] Brocco's meeting with a "guy in Jamaica" and that they were worried about the "guy in Jamaica" picking them out of a "photo spread." Vastola said, "Possession is nine-tenths of the law." They mentioned selling "50,000 pieces" and the number of records and tapes that they have.[62]

This conversation seems to indicate that it was their plan to sell off the foreign inventory before the Feds could trace it; without the government having evidence that they had the counterfeit material, charges could not be brought against them, Vastola believed.

In mid-March 1985, when LaMonte realized his warehouse might be raided by the Feds, he immediately contacted Vastola to let him know that his entire inventory might be frozen or seized. (This further indicates that Vastola knew of the deal to buy the foreign-pressed material.) If all of his inventory was seized, he *really* could not pay MCA; so he begged Vastola to get MCA to accept a large return shipment before the inventory was locked down. Meanwhile, as further insurance—or perhaps again not thinking through the consequences as clearly as he might have done—LaMonte contacted the FBI agent who had previously helped convict him of counterfeiting records in the late seventies. Explaining his predicament to this agent—and telling him that he was merely trying to protect himself from MCA and its gangster cohorts in making his side deal with the offshore distributor—LaMonte perhaps hoped he could shield himself from his partners by providing information to the government.

A year now having passed since the initial deal was made, Levy decided that he wanted to make one last attempt to sell off some of the inventory himself at the upcoming 1985 NARM gathering to be held in late March. He asked Vastola to get LaMonte to send him an inventory list of the remaining inventory. Again, either boldly or foolishly, LaMonte sent a list covering only half of the albums he actually received, representing the deadest, least sellable of the material sent by MCA. Perhaps he believed that the mobsters would allow him to keep the better material to sell so that he could cover the rest of the bill; but whatever his thoughts, Levy was infuriated by LaMonte's brazen action. He believed that LaMonte had already sold the other two million units and was screwing them all by failing to pay anything on those sales.

Vastola felt the pressure too, as he was likely to be blamed for LaMonte's actions. He told Lew Saka:

They think I'm part of a swindle. They feel if John did that [sold two million cutouts] then someone had to allow him to do it. So it had to be me or Sonny.... Morris called my house the last night and says, "You gotta come down [to LaMonte's warehouse] because this is looking bad for you, nobody else. Because if you got people like this around you and they did this here, it's either no respect for you or you're part of it." This is the way everyone is looking at it.... If [LaMonte] swindled

Sonny [by selling off the records without telling him], then I know he swindled us, there's no two ways about it. . . .[63]

LaMonte was summoned to Levy's hotel room at the NARM meeting to discuss the discrepancies in the list. LaMonte insisted that he still had all four million units, but Levy did not believe him. Levy became so enraged that he threw LaMonte out of his hotel suite, calling him a "motherfucker."[64] This impulsive rage would come back to haunt Levy when he later learned that LaMonte had entered the Federal witness protection program.

In early April, realizing that he stood to be punished by either Vastola or Levy (or perhaps both), LaMonte took all of the invoices he had related to the deal to show Vastola that Pisello's original diversion of the inventory cost them a potential profit of $660,000.[65] Vastola was infuriated, and began plotting revenge against Levy, while still telling him that he was going to go to LaMonte's warehouse and "slap the kid around and get him in line." On April 22, the FBI recorded a phone call between Vastola and Saka:

VASTOLA: That $385,000 they made at the beginning, where did that go?
SAKA: Did they swallow it?
VASTOLA: That's what I'm trying to find out.
SAKA: I'm sure they didn't turn around and pay MCA because that was at the very beginning of the deal.
VASTOLA: Well, where did it go?
SAKA: They [Levy and Pisello] cut it up, I figure. . . .[66]

On April 26, 1985, Vastola had a meeting with Fritzy Giovanelli, Dominic Canterino, and Rudy Farone (an associate of Salvatore Pisello and another partner in Consultants for World Records) in which Vastola said, "Let's put our conniving minds together," in order to deal with both LaMonte and Levy. According to the FBI, Vastola told Brocco that Levy had "admitted he had taken [the missing records] and that it was his fault. VASTOLA . . . called LEVY a 'low-life cocksucker' and that 'one of the reasons I don't kill you right now is (unintelligible).'"[67] As a partner of LaMonte, Vastola was angered by Levy's duplicity; as a partner of Levy, he was angered that he had not been cut in on the additional profits Levy made by scamming LaMonte.

Alarmed by what they were hearing through their wiretaps, the FBI task force believed LaMonte was putting himself in serious danger by refusing to pay Levy and his cohorts. Agents visited LaMonte's home, urging him to join the witness protection program. LaMonte initially turned them down, hoping perhaps to use the FBI's growing knowledge of the deal as an additional bargaining chip with Vastola and his associates.

While angry at Levy, Vastola still had a bone to pick with LaMonte over his own failure to keep up payments both on the MCA deal and the separate loan he had made to him. Vastola suggested to LaMonte that they meet to try to resolve these issues. Perhaps as a means of luring LaMonte into a trap, a "safe" meeting place halfway between New York and Philadelphia was selected, in the parking lot of a small hotel in Hightstown, New Jersey, just off the New Jersey Turnpike, on May 18, 1985. When LaMonte arrived at the meeting, Vastola told him that—accounting for what was already paid and for records that LaMonte had returned to MCA—he still owed $91,000. LaMonte figured that this represented Vastola's "lost" profits on the deal. The FBI reported: "Vastola advised [LaMonte] before he left the meeting that he, Vastola, expected LaMonte to pay $5,000 by June 15, 1985, followed by bi-weekly payments of $5,000 until the $91,000 owed to Vastola was paid."[68] Angered by this final squeeze, LaMonte said to Brocco he would pay up, but "I ain't ever doing business with you people again as long as I live."[69] With that, LaMonte turned to leave when Vastola—long frustrated by LaMonte's refusal to pay—suddenly hit him with a single punch. Although Vastola and his associates later claimed that LaMonte did not suffer a major injury, the record dealer was subsequently hospitalized for a broken jaw.

Vastola's violent act had ripple effects on the investigation, empowering the FBI to obtain further orders for wiretaps of Roulette's offices, Levy's farm in upstate New York, and LaMonte's business. The FBI was shaping a RICO (Racketeer Influenced and Corrupt Organization) case against Vastola and Levy for extortion and other criminal activities. These wiretaps would prove invaluable in establishing the facts of the case.

After the May 18 incident, LaMonte finally got the message that he was not going to be able to handle the situation on his own and agreed to work with the FBI in building a case against Vastola and company. He began wearing a wire to meetings. As additional protection against both the Mob and the FBI, LaMonte contacted *Los Angeles Times* reporter William Knoedelseder and began feeding him information; Knoedelseder had already written a series of articles on Pisello and corruption at MCA Records. His investigations led MCA to try to cover up the entire deal by insisting on the return of all the records plus payment at a different rate from what Pisello originally had quoted to LaMonte:

[LaMonte] had [already] returned 1.9 million records for a total of $629,000 in credit, the balance of the deal, he thought. But now MCA was giving him credit for only $479,000 worth. What's more, the company was saying it never agreed to the $1.25 million purchase price. MCA claimed the deal was originally for $1.57 million. So the company either wanted more records returned or more money, $470,000 to be exact. They were pressuring Levy, threatening to sue if the matter wasn't cleared up quickly. Levy, of course, was claiming that LaMonte was . . . responsible for making up the difference.[70]

Vastola suspected that Levy was trying to pull another fast one, telling his associate Lew Saka, "This guy's going to die a horrible death."[71] These words would prove to be eerily prophetic.

In a conversation between Levy and an MCA vice president, Zach Horowitz, on August 27, 1985, Levy asked if LaMonte could return additional records in lieu of further payment. Horowitz replied, "There's no reason why we wouldn't [accept the records in return]; they're our records." Levy then assured him: "I'm going down there tonight and say, 'You either got to come up with the money or the records.'" Horowitz demanded an immediate payment of $150,000, which Levy covered; Horowitz agreed to hold the money as assurance that more records would be returned.[72]

At the same time Levy was negotiating with MCA, Vastola advised LaMonte to stop returning records until he could have further discussions with Levy. Levy was naturally upset when he heard this, saying he was "getting nervous, and I'm not the nervous type. . . . MCA is getting hot. And they have a right to . . . I don't want them to sue because they can hurt with that other thing. . . . If I have to send them the money I will. I have to pacify them now."[73] Levy was in the middle of negotiating several other business deals, so it is not known exactly what the "other thing" was, but it is clear he wanted to avoid any lawsuit brought by the giant entertainment conglomerate.

To resolve the situation between Levy and Vastola a "sit down" was arranged, to be adjudicated by Dominic Canterino, to settle once and for all who was responsible for the balance due to MCA. The group met at Roulette's offices on September 23, 1985; through their wiretaps, the FBI knew about the meeting in advance, and arranged to install audio and video surveillance at Roulette. Canterino was late, so Levy and Vastola had a chance to air their grievances. In the recorded transcript, it is clear that Vastola, Levy, Sal Pisello, and a fourth party—referred to only as Levy's "partner"—had originally arranged the entire deal for their mutual benefit, selecting LaMonte as their patsy. Vastola said: "I[t; i.e., the deal] was with me, you [Levy], and him [Pisello] and your partner before John [LaMonte] got in. Me, you and him and your partner was in with that six million records. We said we'd cut it up three ways . . . You said to 'get me John.'"[74]

From earlier wiretaps, the FBI identified Levy's "partner" as Vincent Gigante. Vastola's beef was that Pisello had sold the better records that were supposed to be delivered to LaMonte—depriving LaMonte and him of about three-quarters of a million dollars in revenue. To add insult to injury, Levy and Pisello pocketed the profit and did not share any of it with him. Levy countered that the initial sell-off was a separate deal and that Vastola was never meant to be a partner in it.

When Canterino finally arrived, the two sides presented their cases and various figures were batted around as to what was still owed. With Canterino holding all the cards—and the powerful Gigante backing him up—Vastola must have realized that he had no option but to try to wring out the money from LaMonte, either by returning additional inventory or in cash. Although he told Levy that he was "not responsible for John LaMonte or anything pertaining to this deal," Vastola also said:

> I want this thing resolved more than you because I know what it means. I know
> what the problem you're having right now with MCA.... One way or the other John
> LaMonte will pay this money. I don't care ... if [LaMonte] did everything right or
> he did everything wrong.... I just want to end this thing where nobody's hurt from
> it that's all. I don't care if I make six cents and I'm sure ... you [i.e., Levy] don't care,
> nobody cares.[75]

The decision was made to visit Out of the Past's offices the following Friday to confront LaMonte. When the FBI heard this, they decided it was too dangerous to let this meeting take place, given that Vastola had previously dislocated LaMonte's jaw when they met in Hightstown. LaMonte and family were whisked out of their home and placed into the witness protection program; over the following weeks, Levy and company scrambled to locate LaMonte while MCA continued to pressure Levy for payment. He sent an additional $125,000 to Horowitz as further guarantee that LaMonte would return the inventory.[76] Soon after, on October 8, armed with subpoenas, the FBI and police raided Video Warehouse and Vastola's and Brocco's homes, among others. Roulette was not yet hit, but Levy correctly foresaw that he would be their next target, telling his longtime associate Howard Fisher: "It's gonna come. So let 'em come, them cocksuckers."[77]

Levy got his first inkling that the government was behind LaMonte's disappearance when he received a phone call on October 23, 1985, from reporter William Knoedelseder. At first Levy declined to take the call; however, Fisher convinced Levy that he might be able to learn something about the government's case from Knoedelseder by speaking with him.[78] The reporter told Levy that LaMonte had been taken into witness protection and was providing the FBI with information about the deal.[79] Asked to comment on the deal, Levy stated: "I know that I'm clean. I've done nothing wrong."[80]

Knoedelseder questioned Levy as to why he was shown as the customer on the invoice from MCA when John LaMonte was the actual buyer. Levy denied being the customer, saying:

LEVY: I guaranteed payment to the people who were buying it. I signed the
  purchase order from them as Consultants for the World . . . [but] I was not the
  customer. . . .
KNOEDELSEDER: And whose company is that?
LEVY: I don't know. Okay, thank you for calling me.[81]

Levy here explicitly links himself with Pisello's Consultants for World
Records. Perhaps realizing he has said too much, Levy abruptly terminated the
conversation.

Immediately following the phone conversation with Knoedelseder, Levy told
Fisher that he now believed that LaMonte had been caught either selling drugs
or bootlegging records. Levy believed that, using that as leverage, the FBI had
flipped him; that explained why LaMonte had refused to pay for the records for
the last year and a half: "It was a sting, I felt that from day one. . . . This motherfucker John LaMonte . . . never paid, because he was being told by the [FBI] not
to pay to get somebody to threaten him."[82]

Levy added that he didn't "believe I did anything wrong, except once again
[the] publicity will be a motherfucker." He was mostly concerned that the news
might "kill this fuckin' thing," a reference to a deal he had been working on since
April 1985 to arrange a "private placement of 50 percent of his stock in Straw-
berry Records."[83] The goal was to raise $10 million for the opening of thirty new
Strawberries Records stores; he had already bragged about the coming deal to
Olympia Esposito, promising her a $2 million cut on the proceeds.[84]

The next day, Levy phoned his son Adam to tell him the news:

MORRIS LEVY: John LaMonte was a government witness all that time. . . .
ADAM LEVY: Holy shit.
ML: It was all a set up. But I think I could dump [the remaining inventory] myself
  . . . I hope (laughter; sigh).
AL: About every six year, seven years (unintelligible).
ML: Seven year locust, should have seen the (unintelligible).[85]

Adam is perhaps referring to Levy's 1979 heart attack, which was about seven
years prior to Levy's latest problems.

For a while, Levy heard nothing further from the government. Then, in June
1986, Howard Fisher was pressured by the FBI to enter the witness protection
program to testify against Levy and Vastola. Levy later told NBC News reporter
Brian Ross: "[Fisher], who's worked with me for about 30 years, a very mild,
meek person was grabbed in the streets of New York when he left work and
taken to the Essex House hotel by an FBI agent and a policeman, held there for

four hours, told he was going to get killed and he must turn into the witness protection program."[86]

Fisher elaborated in an interview with Knoedelseder: "[The FBI] told me Morris was going away for twenty years, that they had him cold. They said I was the weak link in the operation and that Morris and his Mafia friends were going to kill me. They said if I didn't cooperate I would be indicted and arrested at my home in front of my family and neighbors, which they eventually did."[87] Fisher's lawyer stated that his client was "abducted" by the FBI agents against his will.[88]

Two FBI agents turned up at Roulette's offices on July 21, 1986, to serve two subpoenas on Levy and one of his companies, Sutra Records, related to his real estate dealings with Gigante's girlfriend, Olympia Esposito. The agents advised Levy of "the possibility that his life may be in jeopardy due to the implication of OLYMPIA ESPOSITO and VINCENT "CHIN" GIGANTE in the criminal investigation stemming from the activities of LEVY."[89] Levy typically dismissed any concern for his well-being as well as the FBI's allegations noting that he had been "investigated numerous times in the past without success." The agents underscored that Levy "did have a choice if he felt his safety was in jeopardy," clearly trying to entice him to turn state's evidence against Vastola. The agents reported that "LEVY stated he held no respect for the [witness protection] program because it protected people like JOHN LAMONTE who sells drugs 'to children.'"[90] This appears to have been a last-ditch effort to turn Levy before the indictment against him was handed down.

The hammer finally came down early on the morning of September 24, 1986, about a year after LaMonte's disappearance. The US District Attorney for New Jersey, Thomas R. Greelish, announced the arrest of seventeen individuals associated with what he called "The Vastola Organization."[91] However, of the thirty-one pages of charges listing 117 criminal counts, Levy was only mentioned in three counts involving the MCA/LaMonte deal. Along with Vastola, Dominick Canterino, and Howard Fisher, Levy faced a potential sixty years in prison. While most of the defendants were arrested in New Jersey, Levy was taken in handcuffs from his room at Boston's Ritz Carlton Hotel at 7 a.m.; the arrest was caught on camera by NBC News, which was in the midst of producing a series of reports on corruption in the record business.[92] Within a day of his arrest, Levy was released on $500,000 bail.

Brian Ross, an NBC reporter who had been digging into Levy's involvement with the MCA sale, scored a major coup on the day of Levy's release by landing an interview with him on the popular morning news program, *Today*. Levy appeared in all his unwashed New York glory, in a closeup shot standing in front of a blank wall, wearing a worn-looking business coat with a white, open-collar shirt, and speaking in his gravelly voice of the streets.[93] Ross began the interview by asking Levy what he knew about the connection of criminal elements to the music business; Levy categorically answered "There is no connection between the Mob and the music business." In an interview conducted a few days later with the *Boston Phoenix*, Levy wryly noted: "Let me tell you something about the Mob in the record business. You know who owns the record business? There are only six companies—MCA, RCA, CBS, Warner Brothers, Capitol, and Poly-Gram. Those six own 999 out of the 1000 plus a percentage of the one point that's left. So if there's crime infiltration in the record business, that's where the fuck it's gotta be."[94]

Ross followed up asking Levy if the FBI had asked him to join in the witness protection program; he replied that they did, but he refused for

> Two reasons. One, I don't believe in the entire thing as being constitutional. And the other one is that there's nothing I can tell them about a Mob. And the third [*sic*] is I don't . . . there's nothing I can do, I just wouldn't join 'em, I don't believe it's right. I don't believe people should be paid to testify and then given . . . I don't believe in the whole program. I don't believe it's constitutional.

Ross concluded the interview asking Levy about his association with "Corky" Vastola. Levy admitted to knowing him for forty years but stated:

> I haven't seen too much of him in the last 20, 25 years, but I associate with people I've known for a long time, and I don't believe I was indicted for knowing Corky Vastola. I think the 3 charges against me are the charges that we have to face and one is usury [actually extortion], one is trying to collect money that is owed to me. They say that he got beat up but I'm not involved in that at all, and the other one is conspiracy to do these things. The charges are ludicrous; if I joined the Witness Protection Program there would have been no charges.[95]

Levy may have been sending a message out to Vastola and his fellow mobsters that he was not going to "turn" against them despite facing a long prison term. In a separate interview with *Billboard*, Levy repeated his assertion that no charges would have been leveled against him if he had agreed to turn state's evidence and testify against his mobster-partners.[96]

Levy followed the *Today* show interview with a two-and-a-half hour interview with Knoedelseder held at the Roulette offices that ran in the *Los Angeles Times* on October 1, 1986. Levy oozed on the charm, noting his many charitable acts and his long standing in the record industry. He joked with the reporter: "The only thing I know about organized crime is my five ex-wives. Right now, I don't think I'm in danger from anyone, except maybe the FBI."[97] Levy repeated his assertion that the prosecution was motivated by the government's interest in getting him to join the witness protection program. He gave his standard explanation for how he came to know many alleged mobsters: "I've been on the streets since I was 14 years old, and I know and like a lot of people that some might say are organized crime figures—I worked for them as a kid in night clubs."[98] Once again, Levy denied any knowledge of Vastola's "criminal" activities, telling Knoedelseder, "I have nothing to say on that crap, but the government thinks I know something." Levy clearly wanted Vastola to know that he was not going to testify against him in exchange for leniency from the government.

Ironically, the entire deal—which began with Pisello representing Joe Robinson to MCA—came full circle when Robinson filed an $80 million lawsuit against MCA and Pisello on November 20, 1986. Robinson claimed MCA conspired with Pisello to underreport Sugar Hill's sales and to short him on money he was due, in order to drive Robinson into bankruptcy and force him to sell out to MCA, including the valuable Chess catalog, at far below market price. Knoedelseder speculated that Levy might have encouraged Robinson to press his lawsuit in light of his own indictment to put pressure on Pisello and MCA.[99]

Sometime in late 1987 or early 1988, in another strange twist, the Rev. Al Sharpton and his associate Robert Currington—who had previously worked for Nat McCalla at Calla Records and was twice charged with heroin dealing—stepped forward to serve as intermediaries between MCA and Robinson. In a 2014 interview, Currington stated that Morris Levy was his "rabbi" within the record world, and that both Levy and he "served the same God"—meaning the Mafia.[100] At this time, Currington was serving as a top officer of Sharpton's National Youth Movement. They made a deal to collect a fee from Robinson to help him resolve his problems with MCA. The deal quickly turned sour, with Robinson being visited on several occasions at Sugar Hill's offices by an angry Currington and several associates, including the Gambino family boss Joe Buonanno (with whom Currington at one point ran a record label). Currington later admitted to threatening Robinson and telling him he would burn down Sugar Hill's studios unless he paid up. Robinson, frightened for his life, reported the incident to the Englewood Police Department.[101] In August 1988, Sharpton sent a letter to the police defending his and Currington's actions to try to collect their fee from Robinson: "The abuses [Robinson] accused Mr. Currington of were fabricated with the intent of not meeting his obligation to me or Mr. Currington. . . . Not only did we use our contact[s], time, work, and credibility, we did not pursue other business that would have proved very profitable to us at MCA so our consultation of Mr. Robinson would not be compromised."[102]

Sharpton concluded this decidedly odd letter by stating that he was "prepared to move legally and publically (marches, press conferences) to get my money, Mr. Currington's money, and the movement's money" from Robinson. At the time, Sharpton was at the height of his power, leading several protest marches in New York around the alleged rape of teenager Tawana Brawley—so this was no idle threat. How this dispute was cleared up is unknown, although Robinson had a remarkable ability to avoid paying his debts. Eventually, Robinson settled with MCA out of court in 1991. "No money changed hands," he noted, ruefully adding "I couldn't afford the lawyers no more."[103]

11

Trials, Tribulations, and Last Hurrahs: 1986–1990

That's what I get for being a nice guy.
—Morris Levy

Following his indictment on September 26, 1986, Levy's lawyers tried in several pre-trial motions to delay or ultimately quash the government's case against him and his associates. The charges against Levy consisted of only three of the 117 indictments in the government's case against what it called the "Vastola organization," consisting of twenty-one defendants including Levy. Due to the number of charges and complexity of the case, the judge assigned to oversee the trial—Stanley S. Brotman—divided it into seven separate proceedings. Levy and his codefendants—Dominic Canterino and Roulette's CFO Howard Fisher—would be tried first.[1]

Levy's lawyers' first attempt to derail the government's case used the FBI's own statements. While not affirming their truth, Levy's lawyers drew on the FBI's reports stating that Levy was a pawn of Vincent Gigante and the Genovese crime family to assert that he was acting under duress throughout the LaMonte scheme. Thus, he could not be charged with a crime, because his participation was not voluntary. Levy's lawyers cited an affidavit submitted by FBI agent Gerald E. King titled "The Extortion and Control of Morris Levy" as proof of Levy's domination by the Mob.[2] The information about Levy was derived from conversations between Rev. Al Sharpton and Gambino crime boss Joseph Buonanno. Wearing a wire, Sharpton met with Buonanno during April 1984, who gave a detailed account of how Levy was controlled by Genovese kingpin Vincent Gigante.[3]

King outlined how Levy was under the control of Gigante, who extorted money from him and his businesses to purchase property and as kickbacks for Gigante's services settling disagreements between Levy and other mobsters. In one startling passage, Buonanno detailed how Genovese soldier Joseph Pagano plotted to have Levy murdered after Levy tried to intercede on the behalf of a third party who owed the mobster money: "A 'sit-down' was held, and Levy was ordered to pay Pagano $100,000 in damages. When Pagano proceeded to forgive the debt, GIGANTE took credit for this generosity and told Levy that, in appreciation for GIGANTE'S efforts, Levy was to give GIGANTE $10,000 towards the purchase of a piece of property."[4]

Buonanno added that once when Levy hesitated to follow Gigante's orders to purchase some property for other members of Gigante's crew, he screamed: "You Jew cocksucker, you buy those two pieces of property or I'll bury you." Buonanno believed that Levy was trying to extricate himself from his relationship with Gigante, but told Sharpton that Levy "'has only one way out,' at which point Buonanno gestured like someone pointing a gun and pulling the trigger."[5]

Buonanno, who himself had a long criminal record, may not have been a totally reliable witness, however. Besides the usual Mob-related businesses of loan sharking and drug running, Buonanno had dipped his toe in the music business, running a record label with convicted heroin dealer Robert Currington. He had even partnered with Levy and Tommy Eboli sometime in the early seventies to form a remainder company called MRJ. Among its employees was Buonanno's brother, Ralph, who Levy accused of stealing from the company. Buonanno claims that Levy asked Eboli to have a hit arranged on Ralph and that—because the matter involved two different crime families, the Gambinos and the Geneveses—a special commission meeting was held to discuss the merits of the case. Ultimately, the hit was denied, but it must have left bad blood between Buonanno and Levy.[6]

In an affidavit filed on behalf of Levy and Fisher by Fisher's lawyer Leon Borstein, the lawyer outlined how the FBI had made the case that Levy was controlled by the Mob:

> On July 26, 1986, [FBI agents] visited Levy at Roulette's office and told him . . . that the Gigante LCN crime family was going to kill him. . . . These agents also said that they knew that Levy had a family and that Levy and his family should be in fear of death from the Genovese LCN crime family. . . . These agents further warned Mr. Levy that if he refused to provide information and testimony he would be indicted.[7]

Borstein concluded that the government's own information was enough to provide a "defense of duress" for both Levy and Fisher: "It is clear that the United States Attorney[']s office has information that Levy: (a) was and still is under a threat of death, (b) had and still has a well-grounded fear that the threat will be carried out, and (c) had no reasonable opportunity to escape the threatened harm except by participating in the MCA Records transaction. . . ."[8]

Using this argument, Borstein and Levy's attorney at the time, Fredrick P. Hafetz, sent a letter to Assistant US Attorney Bruce Repetto, who would be prosecuting the case. They requested that the FBI turn over the identities of the "confidential informants" who the Bureau claimed had tied Levy to Gigante.[9]

Reporter William Knoedelseder posited that this was an attempt to get Repetto "to drop the charges rather than risk the lives of [the] cooperating witnesses."[10] On April 1, 1987, Repetto responded, rejecting that Levy was "under duress" during the entire eighteen months that the MCA deal played out, saying that the claim was "preposterous."[11] Ultimately, the two lawyers' requests for the informants' names was denied by Judge Brotman, who accepted the government's assertion that it had already turned over to the defense whatever exculpatory evidence that the cooperating witnesses had.

Unable to get the government to accept the duress argument, Levy's legal team targeted the government's star witness, John LaMonte, in an attempt to discredit him. After he entered the witness protection program, LaMonte continued to operate his remainder business under the new identity of John Lancaster—a fairly thin disguise.[12] In their pre-trial investigations, Levy's legal team uncovered evidence that LaMonte was staying in phone contact with his old employees from his new location. This would indicate at the very least that the FBI was not very vigilant in maintaining LaMonte's new identity or in ensuring that he not return to the semi-legal practices that he employed previously. Levy's investigation showed that an FBI agent had even tried to convince one of LaMonte's previous suppliers to send him album masters and cover art he had used to create bootleg albums for resale so he could print more bootleg copies. In essence, Levy's defense was arguing that, through the FBI, the government was facilitating LaMonte's illegal activities.

Besides continuing to sell illegal product, the defense team gave proof that LaMonte had intimidated witnesses who had been approached to testify on Levy's behalf. They pointed particularly to a remainder dealer named Charles Schlang. Schlang said that LaMonte's brother, Tim, called him to advise him not to testify for Levy. A member of Levy's legal team, Cobert, investigated the issue and reported to the judge:

> Tim . . . told Schlang that should he be subpoenaed, his brother John wanted Schlang to be "sick, positively sick" for his "own good."
>
> Tim . . . further told Schlang that John had discussed Schlang with "the boys," and that John had said that Schlang would "bury himself" should he decide to testify. Tim . . . went on to say that the "boys" had a dossier "a mile long, fifty pages long" about Schlang and that if he testifies Schlang will "probably end up with a jail term."[13]

Schlang's wife—who overheard the call on a speakerphone—was so afraid that she said she "was peeing in her pants" during the phone call and subsequently "wanted to hire someone to escort their fourteen year old son . . . to school."[14] There were several followup calls and meetings with Tim and John LaMonte, all advising Schlang that he would be in "heavy shit" if he testified for Levy. John LaMonte simultaneously threatened that either the FBI, IRS, or the Mob would focus on Schlang's business if he testified. LaMonte continued to profess his innocence to Schlang while threatening him, saying "He [i.e., LaMonte] was a victim and was only a pimple on an ass compared to the other problem Morris was involved in."[15]

Judge Brotman took these charges seriously enough to order that the FBI investigate them. Not surprisingly, when the FBI's report was submitted to the court on April 12, 1988, they found that there was no evidence that they had facilitated LaMonte's breaking the law. If LaMonte had engaged in illegal activity, the FBI stated, he was not doing so as "an Agent of the Federal Government," even though he was a protected witness. Levy's lawyers countered that the investigation was a sham; none of their witnesses were contacted by the FBI to followup on their complaints, according to the defense team.

By arguing in advance that LaMonte was an unreliable witness, the defense may have inadvertently signaled to Repetto the fundamental weakness in his case. LaMonte was a victim of the plot but also, it was becoming clear, a willing participant. By signaling that LaMonte would be their main target in the coming trial, the defense gave Repetto enough warning to change his strategy— which is what happened when the case finally came to court.

The defense also was interested in compelling the government to produce documentary evidence of LaMonte's beating on May 18, 1985. Their argument was that there might be evidence to show that the beating was unrelated to the MCA deal. As Levy's attorney Martin London put it: "If there was in fact a punch, it related exclusively to the loan sharking transaction . . . or it relates to something that had to do with neither [the MCA deal or the outstanding $50,000 loan]. Maybe it was a personal offense. Maybe it was a personal slur. Whatever. But it had nothing to do with MCA."[16]

There is some dispute as to whether the beating was witnessed by the FBI, who knew about the meeting—although they were unclear on its location—and had agents assigned to both Vastola and LaMonte to keep an eye on their movements. The FBI claimed that their agents lost track of Vastola en route to the meeting and somehow also failed to track LaMonte's movements on that day.[17] However, several independent reporters—including Knoedelseder—testified that they were told by at least one FBI agent that photos were taken of the beating. LaMonte himself believed he was being followed and thought he saw someone "perched atop" a utility pole observing the meeting. Levy's lawyers hoped to subpoena these reporters to question them about their knowledge of the incident.

Despite this evidence, Judge Brotman determined that the belief that the beating was photographed was based on "erroneous assumption[s]."[18] Levy's request for a further hearing was denied and the subpoenas of the reporters were quashed. Knoedelseder was particularly relieved that he did not have to testify on Levy's behalf: "I . . . got nervous the day that I answered my front door and I was served a subpoena to testify by Morris Levy. . . . I never did testify. I wouldn't have, it's one of those things where it would have been my opportunity to go to jail in Newark, which I wasn't looking forward to, but it never happened."[19]

Meanwhile, the government continued to put pressure on Howard Fisher to turn state's evidence and testify against Levy. A meeting was arranged by the FBI with Fisher and his wife. According to Fisher's son:

[The agents] off handedly made a protection offer: "Look, tell us what we need to know, and we'll put you in witness protection." [But], he didn't think Morris did anything because he didn't have any knowledge of him doing anything. He said it was a setup, a sting. One thing's for sure—Morris Levy was scary, my mother *is* scarier—if he's telling my mother he didn't know anything, he didn't know.[20]

With all defense motions exhausted, there was no further impediment against the trial beginning, now scheduled for early May 1988. However, there was one more twist in the case that Repetto revealed just a day before the trial was to begin: The government was dropping one of the charges against Levy and his codefendants—that they had extorted John LaMonte—and announced he would not be calling John LaMonte as a witness at the trial. Instead, the government would try the defendants on the more nebulous charges of "conspiracy to extort." To prove their case, they would simply rely on the wiretapped conversations of the defendants themselves. It is clear that Repetto felt LaMonte would be a liability at trial; it is also possible that he waited to drop the conspiracy charge until the last minute still hoping that Fisher would turn on Levy and testify against him. Whatever his motives, the defense would have to scramble to come up with an alternate approach to undermining LaMonte's motives and credibility as a witness. By relying on the tapes alone, Repetto removed LaMonte as a potential target of the defense—and it is not possible to cross-examine a wiretapped recording.

The trial opened on May 12 with the opening statement by Bruce Repetto for the prosecution. He began by making a clear distinction between extortion and conspiracy to extort:

Extortion has been defined in the law as the taking of money or something of value from someone under threat or actual harm to his body, to his reputation, to his financial well-being.

Conspiracy to extort, which is what these defendants are charged with, is an agreement to do those things. . . .

If we were presenting an extortion case, the focus would be on the person [being extorted], what was his state of mind, what fear was he in, but we're presenting evidence on a conspiracy to extort. So the focus on the evidence . . . is on the defendant's state of mind. We focus on them. What did they intend? Did they knowingly and willingly wish to extort someone?[21]

Repetto was laying the groundwork for dealing with the obvious question: "Why isn't the man who was being extorted—John LaMonte—testifying in this case?" After laying out the basic story of the record sale—which Repetto characterized as a "controlled sale" in which LaMonte was "brought in" as the patsy—he addressed directly why LaMonte would not be testifying: "John LaMonte will not be a witness for the government in this case. The reason he will not be a witness is that he is not a witness to those conversations [in which the defendants conspired to force him to pay for the records]. John LaMonte is not a witness to what the defendants were doing. They were doing that among themselves. . . ."[22]

Repetto's opening was followed by Martin London's statement for the defense. He attacked the government on several fronts. First he targeted the validity of the tapes. He noted that the government was entering into evidence only "forty conversations" out of the sum total of "thousands" that the government recorded over "months of surreptitious eavesdropping, phones, homes, offices." The implication is that the government was cherry-picking the most damning conversations and omitting others that might set the case in a different light.[23] He attacked LaMonte as a cooperating witness who was wearing a wire, participating in a government sting to "steer" the conversations "the way he wants." He noted that the conversations on the tapes were often difficult to follow and that the government transcripts of them were often inaccurate and slanted to favor their view of the case.[24]

While the government asserted that LaMonte was the victim of this scheme, London turned this argument on its head, stating that LaMonte, Vastola, and Vastola's partners actually "made out like bandits" while only Levy had suffered an actual loss:

MCA said to Levy, "You're a man of your word, you guaranteed the transaction, there's 120 thousand dollars short that we never got back in money, that we never got back in records, pay." And Levy said . . . "That's what I get for being a nice guy," and he sent [them] a check for 120 thousand dollars. And that's the only evidence in this case that anybody lost a nickel.[25]

To further his argument, London presented a chart in which Vastola, Brocco, Saka, and LaMonte were all placed together as constituting one side of the alleged extortion; he was trying to "wall off" these men as being the true conspirators, with Levy and MCA on the other side. Countering the picture that Levy brought LaMonte into the deal as a patsy, London told how LaMonte met Sonny Brocco in prison and subsequently on their release "Brocco and LaMonte did drug deals together. Nothing like doing a drug deal to cement a relationship . . . ," London quipped. London argued that, following the original purchase of the remaindered records, Brocco advised LaMonte on how to deal with Vastola and Saka when they tried to collect their money. Further, London pointed out that Brocco was Vastola's cousin and partner in Video Warehouse along with Lou Saka, and that Brocco and Vastola "had a lot of business with LaMonte back and forth. LaMonte, on this other non-MCA stuff, was a distributor for the Vastola, Brocco, Saka Warehouse. . . . Brocco sold goods for LaMonte and they bought and sold goods for each other."[26]

Finally, London referred to the $50,000 loan from Vastola to LaMonte, which Brocco was charged with collecting. As London ironically remarked: "So in addition to copying records together, in addition to the MCA venture together, in addition to drug deals, we've got something that sounds like loansharking all in this box here, a nice, little family."[27] London was drawing a box around this "nice, little family" as a gang of schemers whose goal was ultimately to defraud Levy and MCA.

In his concluding remarks, London floated several (sometimes contradictory) theories to support Levy's innocence. There was no intent to extort, he says, and if there was it only involved Vastola and his partners, not Levy. He admits that the parties were angry at LaMonte, but that being "frustrated and flailing their arms and stamping their feet in an unsuccessful effort to get a deadbeat to pay for what he had bought" was not the same as "evidence of extortionate means."[28]

After the drama of the opening statements, the trial was anticlimactic. The witnesses called by Repetto were primarily the FBI agents who oversaw the wiretaps of Levy's and Vastola's businesses to verify the dates and times of the tapes, along with the voices of the participants. The jury then listened to the recordings themselves, while referring to the government-provided transcripts. The entire proceeding took several days.

Closing statements followed the end of the testimony. Repetto began by again linking Levy specifically to the conspiracy to extort money from LaMonte, perhaps seeking to rebut the suggestion made by London in his opening that Levy was a separate party—and in fact a victim—in the scheme. Repetto linked Levy with every step of the deal, beginning with the selection of LaMonte as the "customer," stating: "[LaMonte] was chosen, chosen by Morris Levy and Corky Vastola to be the recipient of this deal. . . . Good choice? They think not later on."[29] Repetto admitted that "the relationships among the defendants and the other co-conspirators in this case shift[ed] during the course of the transaction," but that "one thing that they are united on, and that's what makes the conspiracy to extort very clear, is that John LaMonte . . . is going to pay."[30]

Repetto repeated his assertion that LaMonte was not called as a witness by the government because "he did not offer evidence on the minds of these defendants." He tried to mitigate against the fact that the defense was able to establish that LaMonte himself was a bootlegger and probably involved in selling drugs, among other crimes: "John LaMonte may be the kind of individual that you don't want to have over for a beer. . . . He may be the kind of person that you'd never want to associate with in your life. [However,] this case is about is not the nature of the victim. It's about the arrogance of power, the arrogance of control."[31]

Repetto showed how Vastola began to worry when LaMonte continued to fail to make promised payments, and referred specifically to Levy as the one putting pressure on him to get LaMonte to pay. He pointed out that, when the conspirators decided to send Lew Saka to take over LaMonte's business, Levy gave "explicit directions" to Saka as to how to document LaMonte's operations, including to open all incoming mail and to compile a "complete balance sheet."[32]

The case against the other two defendants was barely made at trial, and Repetto spent little time on them in his summation. He admitted that the evidence against Dominick Canterino was weaker, as his involvement did not begin until much later.[33] Repetto also noted that Howard Fisher was neither "a decision maker" nor "as culpable" as Levy and Canterino, but still claimed that Fisher was "a knowing and willing participant in the conspiracy."[34]

Throughout the trial, Fisher remained mystified as to why Repetto was still pursuing the case against him. To his family, he expressed "a lot of frustration—wondering why—once the trial had started, [he believed] that Repetto would have realized that there was really nothing he could give them. [He'd say,] 'I can't understand why this is going on.'"[35] Indeed, it is a mystery as why Repetto pursued Fisher once the FBI failed to convince him to become a cooperating witness.

Martin London gave Levy's closing statement after Fisher's and Canterino's lawyers spoke. As he had in his opening, London refuted the idea that Levy was in partnership with Vastola, Brocco, or Saka. He suggested instead that Vastola and company were in partnership with LaMonte, and that Levy was the innocent victim of their manipulations. At the same time, he asserted that Levy, Vastola, and their cohorts were only acting as reasonable businessmen in trying to assert control over LaMonte; LaMonte's business was floundering, and in sending Saka and Brocco in to try to manage it, they were only protecting their investment. London tried to both remove Levy from the inner circle of the conspiracy at the same time he was deflating the notion that there was a conspiracy at all.

Finally, London reintroduced the theme that, if anyone was a bad apple in this scheme, it was LaMonte. What do we know about LaMonte, London asked rhetorically:

> We know that he's into loan-sharks, he owes money. We know that he deals drugs. We know ... that he's bootlegging [records] and he expects to be indicted. We know that he's already been to prison once. And we know that he owes a ... substantial part of the one point something million dollar debt to MCA and probably he knows that he already sold off a good chunk of the records and he ain't got the money. So he's got a heap of troubles.[36]

London claimed that LaMonte was unable to dig himself out of this hole until he turned state's evidence, wearing a wire to record his meetings, and "agree[ing] to steer the conversations the way [the FBI] tell him to...."[37] London implied that it was LaMonte's job to get the defendants to implicate themselves through refusing to pay for the records.

London then pointed out that the government dropped the actual charge of extortion at the last minute:

> When all you good people were all chosen on May 2, there were three counts to the indictment and his honor read them to you: Conspiracy, conspiracy, extortion.
>
> The substantive count of taking money or property from John LaMonte by inducing the fear or threat of violence ... the government dropped that charge.
>
> What are we left with? We're left with ... they talked about doing it and we no longer say they did it.[38]

Repetto quickly objected but the judge allowed it, stating to the jury: "The truth is the truth. The government withdrew the count."[39]

London finished by suggesting that the government elected not to call LaMonte because ultimately he would undermine their case: "When there's particular access, when they have control over somebody, when they got him on [their] team and he has pertinent information to give, and [they] don't bring in here, you [i.e., the jury] make an inference that the reason [they] don't bring him is because the things he'd say would not help [their] case."[40]

After the summations, the jury went into deliberations, delivering its verdict before noon the next day, May 25: all three were found guilty on both counts of conspiring to extort. On June 1, 1988, Levy posted a bail bond in the amount of one million dollars for himself and Canterino.[41]

Howard Fisher hugging his daughter Gail, at a party celebrating the overturning of his conviction; his wife is seen in the background on the left. Photo courtesy the Fisher family.

Following their convictions, the Levy defendants requested that the judge overturn them and order a new trial; not surprisingly, this motion was rejected by Brotman. However, on appeal, Levy's accountant Howard Fisher saw his conviction overturned in August 1988. Fisher's lawyer successfully argued that the evidence was not sufficient to support his conviction. As Judge Brotman commented on overturning the verdict:

> None of the evidence relied on by the government to sustain Fisher's conviction establishes his knowledge of the purpose of the conspiracy—to use extortionate means against John LaMonte. . . . Therefore, in light of the government's failure to present evidence at trial sufficient . . . to convict Howard Fisher . . . this court is constrained to enter a judgment of acquittal on behalf of that defendant.[42]

Levy and Canterino lost their appeals and were scheduled for sentencing on October 28, 1988.

Once convicted, the judge would decide on what sentence to impose on Levy and Canterino. Levy's lawyers solicited letters in support of Levy's long career and his charitable work to mitigate against the seriousness of the charges and possible financial penalty and prison term he faced. Repetto, on the other hand, drew up a sentencing recommendation letter that pulled out all the stops in picturing Levy as a bad character who had a long history of Mob involvement.

Rev. Louis Gigante standing in an abandoned lot in the South Bronx where he was planning to build a housing development, ca. 1980. Courtesy Salvatore Gigante.

In making the case that Levy was passing money to Vincent Gigante and his family, Repetto cited the sale of two acres of land on Levy's upstate horse farm to Gigante's brother, the Rev. Louis Gigante, at a below-market price, along with providing him a preferential mortgage rate. Levy's defense team responded with a letter from Louis Gigante documenting that he had made all the mortgage payments and that the deal, while generous, was legitimate. Gigante went further, telling how Levy had convinced him to build the house to aid one of his ailing coworkers:

Morris charitably donated a small parcel of his land and his own know-how and physical labor to build a home for a paralyzed churchworker from my parish . . .

[who] in 1977, at the age of 48 . . . suffered a terrible stroke. . . . Because of her love of the farm, Morris suggested building a house for her there. I insisted that I pay for it, and we began building a modest home suitable for [her] needs. . . . [She] has been living full time at the farm since about 1980. . . . Morris and I visit frequently and I often bring children from the parish to visit and spend time in the country. . . .[43]

This almost Dickensian story strained credulity, as Gigante was known to use the house himself, throwing parties there for his friends and associates. Gigante concluded the sob-story letter with the plea, "I hope and trust Your Honor will give no credence to those who would turn a simple act of charity and love into something evil."

Also in the sentencing letter, Repetto repeated the charge that LaMonte's business had been hurt by the extortion scheme. To counter this argument, Levy's lawyers hired an accountant to analyze all of the transactions in the original deal. He submitted an affidavit showing that in fact LaMonte made a profit on the deal.[44] This repeated what Levy's lawyers had argued at trial—that the only loser in the deal was Levy himself.

Perhaps most damning, Repetto introduced a new wrinkle in his sentencing letter by citing evidence of Levy's involvement with drug dealing. In 1987 the FBI had arrested in Philadelphia a noted drug kingpin named Roland Bartlett. Among his many enterprises, Bartlett had partnered with Levy in Domino Records, which operated out of Roulette's offices. The label's sole hit was a 1986 recording by Philadelphia singer David Ebo called "I'd Rather Be by Myself."[45] The FBI believed that the label was merely a front for Bartlett to launder his drug money.[46]

During the sentencing hearing, Repetto called to the witness stand FBI agent Jeff Dossett, who had interviewed Bartlett following his arrest. Bartlett described how Morris Levy had personally set up purchases of pure heroin for him to distribute in Philadelphia: "[Bartlett] stated that he didn't receive the drugs from Mr. Levy personally, but that Mr. Levy directed him to meet with individuals on the pickup points in Manhattan and, most often, at the Holland Tunnel in New Jersey. . . . He stated that he would deliver the money to Mr. Levy's office in a suitcase. . . ."[47]

These were serious charges with the potential of influencing the judge to give Levy the maximum sentence—twenty years. Judge Brotman was loath to take the word of a convicted drug dealer, however:

I have great problems . . . with a statement made by someone in Mr. Bartlett's position who faced I don't know how many numbers of years and who had entered a plea and said he would cooperate with the Government. . . .

Certainly in the case in which Mr. Levy was involved, that was tried here in this courtroom, there was nothing that could lead me to believe that conclusion as to his being a major supplier of heroin.[48]

Ultimately the judge declined to consider Levy's broader involvement in organized crime or drug dealing in determining his sentence. Despite Levy's lawyers' success in rebutting much of the inflammatory claims from Repetto's sentencing letter, their effort seems to have had little effect on the outcome. Levy was sentenced to ten years in prison and a fine of $200,000, with bail set at $3 million. Levy put up his Sunnyview Farm—with an estimated value of $16 million—as collateral for his bail.[49]

Following his conviction, *Billboard* ran an editorial under the title "Sadly, No Tears for Morris Levy."[50] Although it was rather mild in its assessment of Levy—balancing his philanthropic work and longtime involvement in the music industry with the charges that led to his conviction—the editorial was unusual for a magazine that usually served as a booster of the record industry. The editorial writer admitted that "the ability to wheel and deal are such essential elements of success in . . . the music industry" that "the thin line between unscrupulous and criminal behavior is often obscure and hard to pinpoint." Nonetheless, the writer concluded that "Levy clearly crossed the line." The editorialist was most concerned with the stain that Levy's conviction placed on the rest of the industry: "Levy's sentencing is a warning that music industries had better be careful how they operate. . . . The government is clearly watching the glamour industry, and it would behoove all concerned to avoid even the appearance of links with mob-connected individuals."

Not surprisingly, even this mild reprimand inspired an outcry from Levy's friends and supporters. Levy himself wrote a letter refuting several points raised by *Billboard*'s coverage of the trial, characterizing it as a "shoddy attempt at slanting a story for its crass sensationalism."[51] Perhaps the most surprising aspect of this letter is that Levy wrote it while in the hospital in late November 1988 following surgery to remove a cancerous part of his colon.

Longtime associate Bud Katzel also wrote a long defense of Levy and his business practices:

> I've known Morris Levy for over 30 years. I worked for him for over eight years and was involved in countless business dealings. Tough, stubborn, implacable, unyielding, inflexible are all part of the Levy character, but so is the honest, straightforward, trustworthy, and fiercely loyal part of his makeup. . . . In all the time that I worked with him, I never knew him to intimidate, threaten, or harass anyone. . . . I know of no independent distributor who can claim that they were treated unfairly or lost

money dealing with Morris Levy. And, contrary to rumors, innuendos, and industry back-biting gossip, I never saw him deal with an artist or a manager except in a fair and an equitable manner.

Katzel noted that the music industry was known for its "full share of rogues, knaves, thieves, and disreputable characters," so he wondered why *Billboard* had singled out Levy in "such a cruel and heartless manner."[52]

Finally, industry attorney Sanford R. Ross took the unusual and costly step of placing in *Billboard* a one-page "Open Letter to the Music Industry about Morris Levy." Ross repeated the defense that, despite his toughness, Levy was always true to his word:

> He was street-wise, a tough guy, and a real mensch. "The music business is like a big pie," Morris used to say. "There are slices for everyone. You don't f_ _ _ with my piece; I don't f_ _ _ with yours."
>
> His language was colorful, but his integrity was impeccable. I negotiated numerous deals with him. If Morris agreed to pay 8%, I knew I'd get 8%. HIS WORD WAS HIS BOND. [capitalized and underscored in the original][53]

The indictment, hearings, trial, and ultimate conviction surrounding the remainder deal to LaMonte was in many ways a turning point for Levy. As early as his initial indictment, Levy seems to have decided to cash out of his businesses once and for all. He told *Billboard* that he was going to sell off his recording, publishing, and retail businesses, along with his farm in Ghent, New York, in order to move to Australia after his trial was over.[54] He felt Australia offered a better climate for him: "Society isn't as screwed up there as it is here," he told the *Boston Phoenix*. "They don't have any government witness protection program. I'd be in the music business and have a horse farm, too."[55] However, with the tangled histories of many of his operations, it would take several years for Levy to actually liquidate his holdings. Because of his reputation and past associations, several of these deals left many unanswered questions in their wake.

Even before his indictment, Levy had been trying to unload some of his assets, particularly the Strawberries Records chain. The retail record business was changing rapidly during the eighties, with newcomer superstores like Tower Records and chains like Circuit City undermining smaller operations, including Strawberries, which tended to focus on opening smaller stores in less affluent locations. Even the venerable Sam Goody chain was finding it hard to beat Tower. "Some in Boston's music circles" told *Billboard* that Levy had been shopping the chain since at least late 1982.[56] Still, on his official announcement in 1986 that he planned to sell the chain, Levy told the *Boston Globe*: "It's not a panic sale. If the right customer comes, it's for sale. If I don't get my price, I'll hang on."[57]

Levy may have met his match when it came to selling the Strawberries chain, in an ambitious executive who worked for the Hollywood-based film production company Carolco Entertainment, heading up their video and record distribution business. The executive was the Cuban-born José Menendez, whose family would gain notoriety in the later eighties following the brutal murders of Menendez and his wife.

Menendez had previously worked for RCA Records, eventually becoming head of the label. While there, he gained a reputation for being willing to do just about anything to drive the division to profitability. According to one source at the label, this included the common industry practice of pushing product out the door to inflate initial sales numbers, knowing full well that the label would be hit with disproportionately large returns. By the time RCA was purchased by General Electric in 1986, Menendez's shady practices had caught up with him and he was eased out of his position at the label.

After leaving RCA, Menendez was recruited by Carolco to run its International Video Entertainment Inc. (IVE) video production and distribution subsidiary. (It was later renamed LIVE Entertainment.) As an independent company, IVE had first produced pornographic videos, but then branched out into more mainstream entertainment. The California attorney general believed that the company was originally funded by organized crime.[58] Menendez began buying other distributors to build up the company's presence and revenues. This included the early 1989 purchase of the Strawberries Records chain from Levy. LIVE paid Levy about $40.5 million for the company. One business analyst characterized the deal as a "steal," saying that Menendez took advantage of Levy's legal problems to extract a lowball price for the operation; Levy's lawyer disagreed, stating that the price represented about twelve times earnings, a relatively high amount for a retail operation.[59] *Billboard* estimated the chain's gross income as being $60 million for the fiscal year before the sale.[60]

The deal would probably have attracted little attention outside of the record industry had it not been that, just a few months later in mid-August, Jose and his wife, Mary Louise (a.k.a. Kitty) Menendez, were murdered in their posh Beverly Hills mansion. The rumors surrounding Levy's Mob associations only fueled the mystery around the Menendezes' murders.[61] One police investigator was quoted by the *Los Angeles Times* as saying that the murder "was definitely a message killing. There's no question it's organized crime." On August 30, ten days after the killings, "rumors flooded the New York Stock Exchange ... that former Strawberries owner Morris Levy had been slain by gunfire while sitting in his car in New Jersey. Those rumors ... initiated a volatile plunge in the LIVE stock."[62]

Billboard reported that the firm's acting president, Roger Smith, personally "telephoned Levy then spoke to several analysts to spike the speculation."[63] To further assure the stock market, the firm hired the law firm of Paul, Weiss, Rifkind, Wharton & Garrison—ironically, the same firm that originally had defended Levy in the LaMonte trial—to further review the purchase. LIVE issued a statement that "Given Mr. Levy's previous history, the due diligence was unusually careful and exhaustive. This review did not identify any questionable practices or improprieties at Strawberries."[64]

As it turned out, there was no Mob involvement in the murders; the explanation was more mundane. Menendez's two sons, Lyle and Erik, were arrested for murdering their parents in an attempt to gain control over their estimated $15 million fortune.[65] Strawberries would pass through various hands in the 1990s, including a management-based leveraged buyout, and eventually became a part of Trans World Entertainment, which also owned other low-end record and video retailers.[66] Although Strawberries returned to profitability in the later nineties, all retailers of records and videos faced an uphill battle in the coming decade as the Internet replaced "brick and mortar" retailers as the main source for music and video purchases.

The sale of Levy's music publishing was more straightforward than that of the Strawberries chain. Levy shopped around his music publishing holdings. He came close to making a deal with well-known publisher Freddy Bienstock, who along with his brother Johnny owned the influential Carlin Music publishing company. Bienstock discussed buying Levy's publishing from him but ultimately passed on the opportunity: "I had lunch with [Levy], and he said, 'I want $10 million, but if you're interested, you can have it for nine.' And I should have bought it. . . . But my lawyer said, 'You shouldn't do it because he hasn't been paying the writers and once you take it over you will have nothing but lawsuits.' So I didn't do it. It was a big mistake."[67]

Eventually Levy sold Big Seven and his related publishing companies to Windswept Pacific Music, a Japanese music publisher that was seeking to establish itself in North America. The rumored purchase price was around the $10 million that Levy had told Bienstock he was seeking for the companies.

Levy's publishing holdings would generate good income for the company, but also involved it in a number of complex lawsuits. Levy's many handshake deals to purchase the copyright holdings from many of the label owners and artists who he had known since the fifties—often made when the seller was under duress—opened Windswept to many lawsuits. The "contracts" that Levy made to seal these purchases were, to say the least, often ambiguous, making the terms of each agreement open to wide interpretation.

One of the aggrieved parties who came forward in 1994 was Leslie Glover, representing the estate of her father, Henry Glover. In 1980, when he was short on funds, Glover obtained a $15,000 loan from "Adam R. Levy and Father Enterprises," with his portion of the publishing rights to 109 songs that he "coauthored" used as collateral. The loan was never repaid and when Levy sold his holdings to Windswept Pacific, Glover's songs had been included in the deal. His daughter sued, stating that her father's "security arrangement" with Levy did not mean he was abandoning "his rights to his share of the songs."[68] The Glover estate also sued BMI for failing to pass along his songwriting royalties on these songs. Both Windswept and BMI refuted the claims a month after it was filed in April 1994. The case was subsequently dismissed without prejudice by the US Court, Southern District, New York, in September of that year.[69]

The Glover lawsuit was only one among many that arose out of Levy's dealings, particularly as artists became more savvy about their rights—and Levy was no longer alive to intimidate those who might be tempted to sue. Ten years after purchasing Levy's publishing, Windswept sold most of its holdings to EMI— which already co-owned his master recordings, as we will see—for a reported $200 million in 1999. *Billboard* reported at the time:

> At one time, it appeared that Warner/Chappell Music was close to a deal, but in the last month momentum [shifted] to EMI Music. Interest in the company by the world's two leading publishing companies appeared to center on Windswept Pacific's strong holdings of rock'n'roll copyrights from the '50s, represented by its ownership of the Big Seven Music catalog started by the late Morris Levy.[70]

The value of Levy's publishing had skyrocketed in the years following his death. Or perhaps because the connection with Levy and his operations was now fading, and many settlements had been reached with the various aggrieved parties, it was deemed safe by EMI to invest in the catalog.

Selling the Roulette label was more difficult. None of the major labels were interested because of Levy's reputation for not paying artists and issuing material of dubious provenance. Levy preferred not to work with the "suits," as he called them, anyway, so he sought out smaller, independent buyers. A deal announced in *Variety* and *Billboard* in August 1988 to sell Roulette for $4.5 million to K.B. Entertainment, headed by record producer Kenny Bloom (who produced concert events and did marketing for the major labels), fell through.[71] It took another year to finally sell the label. The offer came from a feisty independent label, Rhino Records, which specialized in reissues of classic rock and pop music, which was not one of the buyers Levy actively pursued.[72]

Rhino was established out of a used record store by partners Richard Foos and Harold Bronson in the mid-seventies. Their initial success was in reissuing classic rock acts like the Turtles and the Monkees, appealing to the nostalgia for fifties and sixties rock among their generation of listeners. As the business grew,

Richard Foos and Howard Branson, co-owners of Rhino Records, at the time they purchased Roulette Records from Morris Levy.

they hired Bob Emmer in 1987 to head their business and legal affairs department. Foos and Bronson realized that, if the label was to grow, it would need to move beyond merely licensing material to reissue to actually owning a significant back catalog of recordings. They asked Emmer to look for independent catalogs that were rich in the kind of material—fifties and sixties pop—that was Rhino's specialty.

Foos and Bronson had attempted to license albums from Levy in the past, but he would only license individual tracks—reasoning that he was still selling his own albums through his budget labels. Easily offended, Levy had cut off Rhino from further licensing deals shortly before Emmer joined the staff. Emmer was able to mend relations with Levy, and broached the topic of buying Roulette's masters from him. Levy was interested, but the price he named was too high for Rhino to meet. Determined to make the deal work, Emmer and Foos were attending a Lakers game when they spotted Jim Fifield, chairman of Capitol Records, sitting courtside along with Joe Smith. Capitol was distributing Rhino's product at the time, so they already had a relationship. At half time, the duo pitched the idea of the bigger label putting up half the cash in return for the rights to Levy's jazz recordings—which were not of interest to Rhino—plus the pop catalogue outside of North America.

With Captiol's blessing, Emmer was able to arrange a meeting in New York for him and representatives of EMI—Capitol's parent company based in London—to be held at Levy's Central Park apartment. When Emmer arrived with the three British executives, Levy was seated in a chair wearing a T-shirt, underwear, and a half-open bathrobe. Suffering from sciatica, he often had to lie down during the discussion. All was going well until Levy took offense at something said by one of the EMI representatives, and he suddenly burst out in anger, "Fuck it! This is over," and threw Emmer and the EMI employees out of his apartment.

The EMI executives were ready to fly home, but Emmer knew that Rhino's future was riding on this deal. Calling Levy that evening, Emmer pleaded with him for a second chance, telling him how much Rhino valued Roulette's catalogue. He guaranteed that they would help guard Levy's legacy as a pioneering record man. Levy finally relented and said they could return in the morning, saying, "OK, you can come back tomorrow, but I'm only fucking talking to you."

The next morning, the EMI representatives and Emmer sat on one sofa facing Levy on another. If one of the EMI execs wanted to ask Levy a question, he turned to Emmer and said, "Ask Mr. Levy whether he is willing to do so and so." Emmer would then pose the question to Levy, who more often than not said, "Tell him, 'Fuck no!'" Emmer would then repeat Levy's reply to the EMI man. The entire situation was surreal, to say the least.

Finally a deal was hammered out, but at the last minute Levy excused himself to take a phone call. On his return, he told the group that he had just received a call from a "third party"—he would not say who—who he also had been negotiating with to sell the label. They were ready to close, according to Levy. However, he said, he was "a man of his word" and would honor the deal they had negotiated if Rhino/EMI were able to have the paperwork completed by Monday morning at 9 a.m.; it was now midday on Thursday. Whether or not this was a ruse on Levy's part, Emmer had little choice but to try to make it work.[73]

Levy allowed them to work in his lawyers' offices and supplied them with a draft 100-page agreement that he said was the basis of his previous negotiations. It was a hot July weekend, so the EMI representatives, lawyers, Emmer, and some paralegals hunkered down to hash out the terms. The office's air conditioning was shut down for the weekend, so by Saturday they were all working in their underwear. On Sunday, Levy called Emmer for a report on their progress. Emmer said they were three-quarters of the way to finishing the work, but could not guarantee they would finish by Monday morning. Impressed, Levy drove down from his farm in Ghent and brought the entire crew Chinese food to eat. ("You know what Sunday is for Jews?" Levy asked Emmer. "It's Chinese food night!")

Before signing the paperwork, Levy insisted that he meet one of Rhino's owners, so Emmer arranged for Richard Foos to come with him to Levy's farm. They had dinner and then Levy left the table, saying he was tired and retiring to his bedroom where they could continue their discussions. When Foos and Emmer came upstairs, they found him ensconced on the bed, propped up on pillows. Despite the fact that Levy was already suffering from cancer, Foos still found him to cut an imposing figure: "He was physically imposing still. I was surprised how young he looked. [Levy was 62 years old at the time.] And he talked like . . . he had the Don Corleone type voice." The final negotiations were completed in Levy's bedroom so he could rest.

During this meeting, Foos was struck by how Levy seemed to have little nostalgia for the label he had run for many decades:

> Levy didn't really have a sense of his legacy. His motive was purely financial at that point. I don't think he had any inherent great love for the music.
>
> [Levy ran Roulette as] a cash-today business, [he] didn't foresee a market in the future for rock and roll. So [he] drain[ed] everything out of the business which is why Roulette wasn't worth very much when we bought it. Morris wasn't very much into artist development. He was sort of an absentee landlord. Roulette was kind of small, he'd [bought] most of the better stuff [from] Gee, Rama. When you think of Roulette itself, it had a hit here and there, but nothing really. . . . Most of what we bought was the Goldner stuff and TK Records which he [had] acquired.[74]

In contrast, Emmer felt that Levy *was* concerned about his legacy. He said Levy was pleased that Rhino would reissue Roulette's catalog with good documentation and careful audio restoration. Emmer strongly bonded with the older label owner. When the deal was done, they exchanged gifts: Emmer gave Levy a twelve-pack of underwear, celebrating both Levy's garb at their initial meeting and the fact that the team had toiled in their underwear to complete the paperwork; and Levy gave Emmer a box of disposable Bic pens.[75]

In the end, EMI and Rhino got Levy's entire catalog of labels for what Foos thought was a bargain price: "We bought his label . . . and probably paid maybe $5 million.[76] Which [is] nothing to sneeze at. But when you think that, here's a guy who was there at the beginning, and had complete control of it, he should [have been] able to sell it for hundreds of millions of dollars. On the one hand he was very successful; on the other hand he was sort of a two-bit operator."[77] Foos blamed Levy's shortsighted operation of his labels as the reason they were ultimately worth so little by the time he had to sell.

Despite the common belief that Levy rarely paid artist royalties on his records, Foos saw evidence that he kept careful track of what was owed on all his releases and was paying the artists. Foos admits that Levy probably did not go out of his way to locate an artist who may have disappeared from the company's books. Nonetheless, when Rhino purchased Roulette, Levy gave the new owners computerized records of current royalty payments along with the artists' addresses. Rhino had to take Levy's word for the various labels that he claimed to own; there was often little in the way of a paper trail indicating his ownership of some of the 50,000 masters that he had. As Foos admits, "Nobody really knows [exactly what Morris owned]. We *think* Morris owned it; nobody ever came out of the woodwork [claiming ownership of any of the recordings that he sold to us]."[78]

All through this period, Levy was battling colon cancer. He initially was diagnosed in late 1988 and had surgery to remove a cancerous growth. This was the beginning of a series of hospitalizations with problems related to his pre-existing heart condition (which led to his first heart attack in 1979) and his battles with cancer. He suffered a setback in September 1989 following a colonoscopy that perforated his small intestine. During surgery to repair the accidental damage, doctors discovered a large aneurysm in his heart. Levy spent the entire month of October in the hospital, only on release to hear the news that his last appeal of his conviction was denied on November 1.

Levy's lawyers quickly filed for "a stay of execution of the sentence imposed upon defendant on the ground that his medical condition renders him presently unfit to surrender."[79] They requested a stay of a minimum of ninety days for Levy, to be further evaluated after a doctor's report. To make matters worse, a week after this motion was filed, Levy learned that his cancer had spread to his liver. Levy spent most of the month of January 1990 in the hospital being treated for both his heart disease and cancers.

A second motion was filed by Levy's lawyer on February 8, 1990; by then his doctors felt that "Mr. Levy has less than a year to live."[80] His physicians began Levy on a program of intensive chemotherapy that required Levy to visit the hospital three times a week over the next year. Despite his deteriorating medical condition, Levy's lawyers filed another petition on his behalf on February 28, 1990. Levy was asking for relief from the bill he had received from his original legal team for their representation of him at his trial. The lawyers' estimate was that the fees and expenses for the trial would be in the range of "$500,000 and $750,000," however Levy was billed "the total sum of $1,922,588.33."[81] In light of his illness, Levy's lawyers offered to have him give videotaped testimony regarding the dispute.

However, time was running out for Levy. His cancer continued to progress through the spring and he passed away on May 21, 1990. About a month later,

Repetto sent a letter to the clerk of the United States District Court in Trenton to release the "recognizances," including the $2 million bond guaranteeing both Levy's and Canterino's appearance following their convictions for sentencing, and a further $5 million (including $3 million for surety) taken on their conviction in November 1988. Levy died without serving any time in prison on his convictions, small consolation considering his final months of suffering.

While Levy continued to play a role in the music industry—particularly through his support of rap music in its earliest days—by the time of his death he had in many ways become a relic of the music industry's past. The days of the small independents operating at the edge of both financial and legal rules were long gone. Levy's greatest insight was to purchase the copyrights to pop hits that most people at the time felt were worthless. Perhaps from his days as a hatcheck concessionaire, he knew that the pennies and nickels from each song eventually would add up to a sizeable income, one that would continue to flow in good times and bad. Levy also had an unerring ability to spot trends in pop music in advance of their mass acceptance. While he was not particularly attuned to what made an individual song a hit, he could identify new musical forms—from bebop through doowop to sixties pop and finally disco and rap—in advance of their mainstream success. Like a keen stock analyst, Levy knew how to read the pop music charts.

What about Levy's ties with the Mob? On one hand, when Levy began as a nightclub operator, there was no way not to deal with the many shady characters who operated in that world. Payoffs to mobsters—and policemen—were part of the cost of doing business. Levy's business code was an extension of the Mafia's family structure; you might screw an artist, but you would never hurt a fellow operator. Levy felt his word was sacred, and expected others to honor their verbal commitments—even those made in the heat of the moment. Eventually, though, Levy's reliance on mobsters for funding and support became a personal and business albatross. He could not simply break off from his benefactors; but while he was beholden to them he could not continue to operate in a music world that was rapidly changing. The old ways simply could not continue. Levy had to "retire"; death was the only route available, and in a way a natural death was preferable to the alternative. As Tommy Eboli and countless others learned, the Mafia retirement plan did not include sunny days of leisure in Florida (or Australia, as Levy dreamed). Facing prison and an uncertain future, Levy succumbed instead to cancer, leaving behind a tangled legacy.

NOTES

Preface

1. Ruth Brown with Andrew Yule, *Miss Rhythm: The Autobiography of Ruth Brown* (New York: Donald I. Fine, 1996).

Chapter 1

1. Fifteenth Census of the United States, 1930, New York, King's County, Brooklyn Borough, Enumeration District 5970 24-33, 12B, accessed via ancestry.com.

2. Petition for Naturalization, U.S. District, Southern District, New York, No. 280956, June 11 1930, filed September 14, 1936; accessed via ancestry.com. The FBI report on Levy's birth certificate gives her name as "Rachel Rodrik"; see Report of Jack Louis Marshall, "Morris Levy: A. Personal History and Background," New York FBI Field Office File No. 92-2015, 8/30/61, 3.

3. Dorothy Wade and Justine Picardie, *Music Man: Ahmet Ertegun, Atlantic Records, and the Triumph of Rock and Roll* (New York: Norton, 1990) 54.

4. Frederic Dannen, *Hit Men* (New York: Vintage, 1991), 48; Wade and Picardie, 54.

5. In 1930 Rachel applied for naturalization as a US citizen, which was granted in 1936; one of the witnesses was named Morris Levy of Brooklyn, New York. Census records show that this Morris Levy was probably the uncle of his namesake; he had emigrated from Greece in 1909 and in the 1930 census was listed as a groceryman, although by 1936 he gave his occupation as "retired" on Rachel's naturalization documents. In 1930 he was sixty years old with four children. Fifteenth Census of the United States, 1930, New York, Kings County, Brooklyn Borough, Enumeration District 5970 24-33, 12B, accessed via ancestry.com.

6. Dannen, 48.

7. Wade and Picardie, 55.

8. U.S. Census, 1940.

9. Marshall, "Morris Levy: A. Personal History and Background," 3.

10. Dannen, 48.

11. Wade and Picardie, 55.

12. In *Broadway: An Encyclopedia* (New York: Routledge, 2003), Ken Bloom cites a young Jewish immigrant Abraham Ellis (1901–1975) as among the originators of the idea. A. J. Liebling (*The Telephone Booth Indian* [New York: Crown, 2008], 182ff) gives credit to a different Jewish entrepreneur, Harry Suskind, for pioneering the business. A 1911 *New York Times* article reporting on abuses in the hatchecking system cited a "German Jew" named Jacob Michaud as yet another possible candidate for this spot; "Hat-Check Pirates Face Strong Revolt," July 30, 1911; accessed online April 5, 2013.

13. "Hat-Check Pirates Face Strong Revolt."

14. Dannen, 35.

15. Wade and Picardie, 55.

16. Jeff Rutledge, unpublished interview with Morris Levy, ca. 1989; transcript courtesy Joel Selvin.

17. Some sources give his name as "Gurlak," but *Billboard* consistently spells it "Gurlek."

18. Fredric Dannen, Unpublished interview with Morris Levy, July 30, 1988; transcript courtesy Joel Selvin.

19. Dannen, p. 35.

20. Karen L. Schnitzspahn, *Jersey Shore Food History* (Charleston, SC: History Press, 2012), 110.

21. Rick Walton, *Bullfrog Pops!* (Layton, UT: Globe Smith, 1999), 93.

22. William H. Sokolic, Robert E. Ruffolo, *Atlantic City Revisited* (Mount Pleasant, SC: Arcadia, 2006), 64.

23. "Philly Nite Belt Gets Look-See," *Billboard*, January 27, 1945, 25; "Philly Dads Asked to Hold Agents to Decency in Shows," *Billboard*, January 19, 1946, 31.

24. Donald L. Barlett and James B. Steele, *Empire: The Life, Legend, and Madness of Howard Hughes* (New York: Norton, 1979), 280.

25. Marshall, "Morris Levy: A. Personal History and Background," 8.

26. Leif Bo Petersen and Theo Rehak, *The Music and Life of Theodore "Fats" Navarro: Infatuation* (Lanham, MD: Scarecrow Press, 2009), 107.

27. For more on 52nd Street's jazz clubs, see Arnold Shaw, *52nd Street: The Street of Jazz* (New York: Da Capo, 1977).

28. Jeremiah's Vanishing New York: Strip Street, posted on January 27, 2011; http://vanishingnewyork.blogspot.co.uk/2011/01/strip-street.html; accessed March 11, 2014.

29. "MANNERS & MORALS: It's Back," *Time*, March 8, 1948; accessed online March 11, 2014.

30. Dannen, 37; other sources say that Levy and Watkins made a deal with Topsy's owners that they would guarantee to pay the lease for six months on the location in return for operating the room; see Robert Sylvester, *No Cover Charge: A Backward Look at the Night Clubs* (New York: Dial Press, 1956), 273.

31. Kastin, David, *Nica's Dream: The Life and Legend of the Jazz Baroness* (New York: Norton, 2011), 70–71; see also interview with Phoebe Jacobs on the website *Old New York Stories*, conducted June 18, 2009; accessed May 14, 2013.

32. Shaw, 215. "B-girls" was contemporary slang for strippers and prostitutes who would encourage patrons to buy drinks and arrange for hookups outside of the clubs. This passage is based largely on an interview with Ralph Watkins by Arnold Shaw in Shaw, 212–20.

33. "52d Street Ops Eye Roosts' Move for Jazz on Main Stem," *Billboard*, February 28, 1948; accessed online December 2, 2010.

34. "Customers Outbop the Boppers; Roost Doesn't Have to Toss in the Towel," *Down Beat*, August 25, 1948, 3.

35. 1930 U.S. census information from Ancestry.com.

36. Shaw, 272.

37. "Customers Outbop the Boppers," 3.

38. Shaw, 215.

39. Dannen, 35–36.

40. "Jazz on B'way Brings Bux Back Alive," *Billboard*, August 7, 1948; accessed online December 3, 2010.

41. "Pob Si Tahw?" *Billboard*, September 25, 1948; accessed online December 2, 2010.

42. "Jazz on B'way Brings Bux Back Alive."

43. Robert Sylvester, 275–76.

44. "Bop City Bows April 14 with La Fitzgerald," *Billboard*, March 5, 1949; accessed online December 2, 2010.

45. Bill Chase, "Bop City Opening Bopsolutely Mad," *New York Age*, April 23, 1949, 8.

46. "Royal Roost Goes Sepian," *New York Age*, April 23, 1949, 8. The article states the club would be managed by Ruby Fox; there is no mention of Levy in this notice.

47. "Bop City Bows April 14 with La Fitzgerald."

Chapter 2

1. Leonard Feather, "The Birdland Story." Liner notes to Roulette SRB-2, n.d. [1961], n.p.

2. A nearby popular Scandinavian nightclub/restaurant named the Iceland also may have been an inspiration.

3. In an interview with Leonard Feather, Levy credited bass played Harry Bugin with the idea for the club's name. Feather, "The Birdland Story."

4. Monte Kay denied he had a financial interest in the club, despite Levy later acknowledging that they were partners in the venture.

5. "City Halts Birdland Debut," *Down Beat*, September 1949; clipping accessed via microfilm.

6. "Birdland Bistro Fails to Open; No Liquor OK," *Billboard*, September 17, 1949, accessed online July 15, 2010.

7. "City Halts Birdland Debut."

8. This passage is based on a videotaped interview with Morris Primack that was made ca. February 1998 and now in the possession of his son, Aurin Primack, along with an interview with Aurin Primack by the author, February 18, 2014. Morris Primack was just shy of his eighty-ninth birthday when he gave the interview to a Delray Beach, Florida, jazz promoter.

9. Ibid.

10. "Birdland Again Sets Opening," *Down Beat*, January 13, 1950, accessed via microfilm. Although the issue was dated January 13, 1950, it must have appeared in early December because the opening night is announced as December 15, 1949. John S. Wilson's review of the first night's performance did not appear until the January 27, 1950 issue.

11. Author interview with Peter Pullman, January 15, 2014.

12. Dannen, 37.

13. Frank Rose, *The Agency: William Morris and the Hidden History of Show Business* (New York: HarperBusiness, 1995), 239.

14. US Treasury Department, Bureau of Narcotics, *Mafia: The Government's Secret File on Organized Crime* (New York: Skyline, 1999), 390.

15. Feather, "The Birdland Story."

16. John S. Wilson, "Birdland Applies Imagination to Jazz," *Down Beat*, January 27, 1950, 3.

17. Dannen, 36. Levy told this same story to Leonard Feather, who recounts it in his liner notes to "The Birdland Story," op. cit.

18. "With Bop City Kaput, Birdland Only Broadway Joint with Bop Format Left," *Down Beat*, December 1, 1950; accessed via microfilm.

19. Marshall, "Morris Levy: A. Personal History and Background," 8–9. Levy said he was charged with bookmaking again in April 1951 but the FBI could find no records of this when they were investigating him in 1961.

20. Ibid., 8.

21. Mariani, Rob, "Lullaby of Birdland," All About Jazz website, August 2002; accessed August 12, 2010.

22. Feather, "The Birdland Story"; such hokey décor was a standard for New York nightclubs of the day. For example, Kelly's Stable featured various Western motifs (wagon wheels and such) on the walls and a hayloft filled with fireproof "hay" (presumably to meet fire codes); Shaw, 218, 219.

23. Feather, "The Birdland Story."

24. Ibid.

25. "Listen to Larry," *New York Age*, August 4, 1951, 8.

26. Video interview with Morris Primack.

27. Author interview with Aurin Primack.

28. "Birdland Waiter Owns Cadillac," *Jet*, December 12, 1954; accessed online July 15, 2010.

29. Evelyn Cunningham, "New York's Famous Birdland," *Pittsburgh Courier*, January 12, 1957, 31.

30. Some sources give his surname as Ciafone, but the FBI consistently spells it with two fs, which I have followed here.

31. "Jazz Baseball Game Pits Bops vs. Swing," *Pittsburgh Courier*, July 23, 1955, 15.

32. John Szwed, *So What? The Life of Miles Davis* (New York: Simon & Schuster, 2002), 92–93. In Miles Davis with Quincy Troupe, *Miles: The Autobiography* (New York: Simon & Schuster, 1989), Davis relates how Gardner sent a message to him through Peewee Marquette inviting him to attend a party with her after his gig (237).

33. For example, *Jet* reported the news that singer Bixie Crawford claimed she was "assaulted [and] spit on" by Count Basie's wife at Birdland, supposedly after Basie's wife discovered love letters from Crawford in the bandleader's pocket; "Singer Slaps Basie's Wife with $25,000 Suit," *Jet*, June 30, 1955, 16.

34. "Girl Addicts Name Places Throughout City Where Narcotics Are Sold," *New York Times*, June 15, 1951, accessed online August 11, 2010.

35. Chase, "Bop City Opening Bopsolutely Mad," 8.

36. "Larry Douglas on Long Island," *New York Age*, May 5, 1951, 8.

37. Bill Crow, *From Birdland to Broadway* (New York: Oxford University Press, 1992), 88.

38. Ibid.

39. Mariani.

40. Quoted in Doug Ramsey, *Take Five: the Public and Private Lives of Paul Desmond* (Seattle: Parkside, 2005).

41. Bobby Hutcherson, interview with Fred Jung, 1999; http://wallofpaul.com/keep-it-short-pee-wee, accessed on December 10, 2010.

Notes

42. Paul Tatara, "Keep It Short, Pee Wee," Wall of Paul website, April 15, 2010; accessed on August 12, 2010. Horace Silver, in his autobiography, also tells this anecdote; Horace Silver, *Let's Get to the Nitty Gritty* (Berkeley: University of California Press, 2006), 49. This quip has been ascribed to various jazz players, including Miles Davis and vocalist Dinah Washington.

43. Will Friedwald, *A Biographical Guide to the Great Jazz and Pop Singers* (New York: Random House, 2010), 433.

44. Feather, "The Birdland Story."

45. "New Remote Trend Hypes Dance Bands," *Billboard*, August 6, 1955, 35, 40.

46. In *On the Road*, Sal Paradise and Dean Moriarty hear Symphony Sid playing "the latest bop" on the radio as they end their odyssey, driving into "the great and final city in America" in the early morning hours. Jack Kerouac, *On the Road* (1957; New York: Penguin, 1991), 247.

47. Ross Russell, *Bird Lives* (New York: Da Capo, 1996), 276.

48. Stokely Carmichael and Michael Thelwell, *Ready for Revolution: The Struggles of Stokely Carmichael* (New York: Scribner, 2003), 98.

49. Ross Russell, *Bird Lives* (New York: Da Capo, 1996), 158.

50. "Hal Jackson Birdland M.C.," *Pittsburgh Courier*, August 8, 1953, 18.

51. "Network's Phones Ring as Record Show Exits," *New York Age*, December 5, 1953, 7. Other notable deejays including Bob Garrity also broadcast from the club.

52. Interview with Bill Crow by the author, June 12, 2013.

53. Crow, 110–11.

54. Dr. William E. Taylor, oral history interview by Mr. Brown and Eugene Holly, November 19, 1993; deposited at the Archives Center, National Museum of American History, Smithsonian Institution, transcript, 107–8.

55. Feather, "The Birdland Story."

56. Goodstein interview with Don Manning, fall 1986, cited in Peter Pullman, *Wail: The Life of Bud Powell* (self-published, 2012), ebook ch. 8, fn1.

57. Maley Daniele Dufty, "The Sound of Truth," Pt. 1, *New York Citizen-Call*, September 29, 1960, 20; clipping in Bud Powell file, Institute of Jazz Studies, Dana Library, Rutgers–Newark. Dufty at the time was the wife of William Dufty, who coauthored Billie Holiday's biography, *Lady Sings the Blues*; she was known as a regular at New York's jazz joints.

58. Cited in Guthrie P. Ramsey, *The Amazing Bud Powell: Black Genius, Jazz History, and the Challenge of Bebop* (Berkeley: University of California Press, 2013), 113.

59. Brian Priestley, *Chasin' the Bird: The Life and Legacy of Charlie Parker*. New York: Oxford University Press, 2005, 82.

60. Jerry Wexler, "Night Club Review: Birdland, July 6, 1950," *Billboard*, July 22, 1950, 43.

61. Billy Taylor with Teresa Reed, *The Jazz Life of Dr. Billy Taylor* (Bloomington: Indiana University Press, 2013); accessed online July 26, 2013.

62. Feather, "The Birdland Story."

63. Ibid.

64. Dorothy Kilgallen, "Voice of Broadway," August 14, 1950; accessed online August 14, 2013.

65. Feather, "The Birdland Story."

66. Ibid.

67. Feather says that the band was playing "Stars Fell on Alabama" while Parker was playing "Stardust"; Leonard Feather, "The Birdland Story." Either way suggests that Parker may have

been using his solo to ironically comment on his unhappiness with the quality of the musicians who were accompanying him.

68. Priestley, 101.

69. Feather, "The Birdland Story."

70. Robert George Reisner, ed., *Bird: The Legend of Charlie Parker* (1962; New York: Da Capo, 1975), 152.

71. "Birdland's Birthday Moves Broadway," *Pittsburgh Courier*, December 18, 1954, 14.

72. "Honors Go to Top Show Biz People," *Pittsburgh Courier*, June 4, 1955, 15.

73. "'Birdland' Is Growing," *Pittsburgh Courier*, July 9, 1955, 14.

74. Feather, "The Birdland Story."

75. Ibid.

76. Chet Falzerano, *Gretsch Drums: The Legacy of "That Great Gretsch Sound"* (Milwaukee: Hal Leonard, 1995), 56.

77. Herm Schoenfeld, "Birdland's 'Brave New Jazz' Policy Pays Off with Five Year Operation," *Variety*, March 17, 1954, 42.

Chapter 3

1. Gleason's article about Levy originally appeared in the *San Francisco Chronicle* on September 29, 1957; however, it gained more notoriety after *Variety* reported on and ran an excerpt of it in their October 30, 1957, issue, 67; clipping in Count Basie file, Institute of Jazz Studies, Dana Library, Rutgers–Newark.

2. Dannen, 34.

3. George Shearing with Alyn Shipton, *Lullabye of Birdland* (New York: Continuum, 2004), 137–38; Levy's partner Morris Primack tells essentially the same story in a video interview made ca. February 1998, courtesy of Aurin Primack.

4. According to Morris Primack, the song was so profitable that Levy and a group of Birdland investors traveled on the *Queen Mary* to Europe in 1956 for an expensive vacation in order to launder the money they had made on the song; Video interview with Morris Primack, October 27, 1997, courtesy of Aurin Primack.

5. "Disney Hires Farrow, Kahl," *Billboard*, February 3, 1951, 12; Harvey Kubernik, *Hollywood Shack Job: Rock Music in Films and on Your Screen* (Albuquerque: University of New Mexico Press, 2006), 34; John Broven, *Record Makers and Breakers* (Champaign: University of Illinois Press, 2009), 244.

6. Dannen, unpublished interview with Morris Levy.

7. "Birdland's Levy Bids for Piece of Gale Agency," *Billboard*, July 15, 1955; accessed online July 15, 2010.

8. Interviews with Irving Siders and unnamed informant (probably Moe Gale), in Report of Jack Louis Marshall, "Morris Levy: A. Personal History and Background," 38, 58.

9. In his liner notes to *The Birdland Story*, Leonard Feather credits Teddy Reig with coming up with the idea of organizing the first Birdland tour. However, Reig does not himself take credit for this idea in his autobiography.

Notes

10. Edward "Sonny" Murrain, "Front and Center," *New York Age*, January 24, 1953, 20.

11. "Duke Scores at Carnegie," *Billboard*, November 22, 1952, 44.

12. Edward (Sonny) Murrain, "Front and Center," *New York Age*, December 12, 1953; accessed online August 17, 2013.

13. "Birdland Show Talent Signed," *Billboard*, November 17, 1954; accessed online September 10, 2010.

14. Feather, "The Birdland Story."

15. Not to be confused with the John Levy who was the manager/lover of Billie Holiday, who badly mistreated the singer.

16. John Levy, *Men, Women and Girl Singers* (New York: Beckham, 2008), 99.

17. Ibid., 98.

18. Ibid.

19. Count Basie, as told to Albert Murray, *Good Morning Blues: The Autobiography of Count Basie* (New York: Random House, 1986), 316.

20. Ibid., 317.

21. Joe Cohen, "Desegregation in Show Biz: Fight on Bans Led by Unions," *Variety*, September 26, 1956, 1, 50.

22. Ibid.

23. Ibid.

24. "'Birdland Stars' Will Not Play Segregated Houses: Ask Music Union to Aid Bias Fight," *Pittsburgh Courier*, October 4, 1956, 20, accessed online August 13, 2013.

25. "Levy Sets Up New Birdland Franchise Op," *Billboard*, March 10, 1956; accessed online September 2, 2010.

26. "Florida's Color Bars Tumble," *Jet*, December 31, 1953, 60–61; accessed online August 12, 2010. Levy also put a rider into his Birdland '57 Tour contracts requiring the shows to be integrated, or the promoters would forfeit a required pre-show bond; see Nadine Cohodas, *Queen: The Life and Music of Dinah Washington* (New York: Pantheon, 2004), 269.

27. Bob Bolontz, "Clubs Jumping Again, Jazz in N.Y. Comeback," *Billboard* [1954], 28; accessed online November 11, 2013.

28. Uncredited liner notes, *At the Embers: Dorothy Donegan*, Roulette R-25010, 1957.

29. Buck Clayton with Nancy Miller Elliott, *Buck Clayton's Jazz World* (New York: Continuum, 1995), 144.

30. Author interview, June 12, 2013.

31. "Birdland's Levy Leases Versailles for Jazz Setup," *Variety*, March 5, 1958, 65.

32. Dannen, 37.

33. See, for example, Dorothy Kilgallen, "Voice of Broadway," syndicated column, October 6, 1959; accessed online December 20, 2013.

34. All citations from Mel Heimer, "My New York," syndicated column, June 2, 1958; accessed online August 17, 2013.

35. Author interview, June 12, 2013. In this recollection, Crow may have confused Morris Gurlek with Morris Primack. In a video interview made ca. February 1998, Primack claims he managed the Embers for a period in the later fifties that corresponds with when this incident occurred.

36. Jack Hooke, a promoter and co-owner of Royal Roost Records, also took credit for introducing the two. See John A. Jackson, *Big Beat Heat: Alan Freed and the Early Years of Rock & Roll* (New York: Schirmer, 1991), 84–85.

37. Ibid., 42.

38. Ibid., 64–65.

39. Ibid., 67.

40. Dannen, 42.

41. Freed's employer station WINS and Freed's Cleveland manager Lew Platt were also cut into the copyright; Jackson, 85.

42. Levy's associates usually referred to him by his Yiddish name, Moishe. Later, when the FBI wiretapped Levy's offices, whoever served as their transcriber apparently did not know Yiddish because they wrote the name as "Mersh."

43. Dannen, 42.

44. Wade and Picardie, 84.

45. Dannen, 37.

46. Vastola told the FBI that he referred to Ciaffone as his uncle, even though they were second cousins; many sources have thus incorrectly stated that Vastola was Ciaffone's nephew. Marshall, "Morris Levy: A. Personal History and Background," 60.

47. Dannen, 37. The story of Tarnopol, Vastola, and Jackie Wilson's professional relationship is told in Tony Douglas, *Jackie Wilson: Lonely Teardrops* (New York: Routledge, 2005).

48. Rutledge, unpublished interview with Morris Levy. In an interview given to the *Boston Phoenix* at about the same time, Levy said that the "rib joint" was run by his brother Irving; Jim Schuh, "Record Heat: Morris Levy's Bad-Rap Rap," *Boston Phoenix*, October 7, 1986, 10; clipping in FBI Memorandum, from SAC, BOSTON (183A-1310) (RUC) to SAC, NEWARK (183A-2061), Subject; PIER II/RICO/OO:NK, date 10/28/86.

49. Jackson, 243.

50. Ibid., 75.

51. Dannen, 42.

52. Jackson, 86.

53. *Cash Box*, January 29, 1955; accessed online May 16, 2013, at www.alanfreed.com/wp/wp-content/uploads/2010/07/1-29-1955-rock-n-roll-ball.jpeg.

54. "Deejay Freed Opens B'klyn Para to Flesh," *Billboard*, February 19, 1955, 25.

55. Dannen, 43.

56. Jackson, 89–90.

57. *Variety* reported the total as $154,693 for the week, a "staggering amount." See Abel Green, "Alan Freed's Rock 'n' Roll Troupe Pulls Spectacular 154G at B'Klyn Par," *Variety*, September 14, 1955, 49.

58. *Cash Box*, "Music," 1955; http://www.alanfreed.com/wp/archives/archives-rocknroll-1951-1959/newspaper-magazine-clippings/, accessed May 16, 2013.

59. Abel Green, 49.

60. "A Question of Questionable Meanings," *Life*, April 18, 1956, 168.

61. Rutledge, unpublished interview with Morris Levy.

62. Edith Evans Asbury, "Rock 'n' Roll Teen-Agers Tie Up the Times Square Area," *New York Times*, February 23, 1957; accessed online May 16, 2013.

63. Ibid.

64. http://www.alanfreed.com/archives/archives-payola-scandal/livestage-brook-para mount/, accessed on October 28, 2014.

65. H.T.T., "Frenzy and Furor at the Paramount," *New York Times*, February 23, 1957; accessed online May 16, 2013.

Chapter 4

1. RCA was not the only path to record making that Levy was pursuing. He was making similar overtures to the fledgling ABC-Paramount label, newly founded by the movie studio/ TV channel to cash in on its music holdings.

2. "Victor Signs Levy to 6-Year Contract," *Billboard*, September 10, 1955; accessed online May 15, 2013.

3. "Birdland LP Is Sleeper for Victor," *Billboard*, January 14, 1956; accessed online June 6, 2013.

4. After establishing Roulette Records, Levy retrieved the rights to the Birdland series releases from Victor, according to columnist Dorothy Kilgallen; see "Voice of Broadway," September 20, 1957; accessed online December 27, 2013.

5. Author interview, May 8, 2013.

6. Mark Schwartz, "Players Club: Memories from the Days of the Mamboniks," *Guilt and Pleasure* Issue 6, Fall 2007; www.guiltandpleasure.com/index.php?site=rebootgp&page=gp_article&id=60; accessed June 28, 2013.

7. The Mamboniks blog, November 1, 2007; http://mamboniks.blogspot.com/search/label/ Art%20Raymond; accessed June 28, 2013. For more on Raymond's involvement with Goldner, see Tony Fletcher, *All Hopped Up and Ready to Go: Music from the Streets of NY, 1927-77* (New York: Norton, 2009), 90ff; *Mambo Gee Gee: The Story of George Goldner and Tico Records*, at www.spectropop.com/tico/TICOpart1.htm.

8. Fletcher, 93.

9. Author interview, anonymous source, June 19, 2013.

10. Dannen, 40.

11. "Teen Agers Demand Music With A Beat, Spur Rhythm-Blues," *Billboard*, April 24, 1954, 14.

12. See Jim Dawson and Steve Propes, *What Was the First Rock 'n' Roll Record?* (Boston: Faber & Faber, 1992), 124–27, for a full discussion of the evolution of this song.

13. Peter A. Grendysa, "Why Do Fools Fall in Love: Frankie Lymon and the Teenagers," in Colin Escott, ed., *All Roots Lead to Rock: Legends of Early Rock 'n' Roll* (New York: Schirmer, 1999), 226.

14. Dawson and Propes, 126–27.

15. Jay Warner, *American Singing Groups: A History from 1940 to Today* (Milwaukee: Hal Leonard, 2006), 138. Melino's Orchestra was known for its novelty numbers, releasing "Mambo a la Strauss," "Tutti Frutti Cha-Cha-Cha," and even an entire album of cowboy songs recorded Mambo-style, titled *Yippee Olé* in 1958.

16. Joel Selvin, *Here Comes the Night: The Dark Soul of Bert Burns* (Berkeley: Counterpoint, 2014), etext location 859–75.

17. "Kolsky Near on Half of Rama Buy," *Billboard*, November 12, 1955, 20.

18. The story of "Why Do Fools Fall in Love?" is told in many sources; see, for example, Warner, 243–44.

19. "Get Your Price and Get Out or Suffer Jazz Complexity," *Billboard*, December 12, 1955; accessed August 12, 2010, and May 15, 2013.

20. Dannen, 40.

21. Jackson, 153.

22. "Birdland Club, Roost Diskery Sign Contract," *Billboard*, June 18, 1955; accessed online September 2, 2010.

23. "Levy Again Wants in on Roost Label," *Billboard*, February 25, 1956; accessed online July 15, 2010.

24. "Roulette Makes Bow," *Billboard*, February 2, 1957, 22. There is no further mention of Joe Derashio's association with the label in any other sources that I could locate.

25. DA Notes of interview with Morris Levy, November 1, 1962; accessed on October 28, 2014, at www.alanfreed.com/archives/archives-payola-scandal/da-people-vs-freed/.

26. Dannen, 43; Wade and Picardie, 84.

27. DA Notes of interview with Morris Levy.

28. "Freed, Levy Come to Parting of the Ways," *Billboard*, March 30, 1957, 31.

29. "Freed Deals Add Up to Hefty Sked," *Billboard*, April 13, 1957, 45–48.

30. Joel Selvin, unpublished interview with Jack Hooke, no date; transcript courtesy Joel Selvin.

31. Rutledge, unpublished interview with Morris Levy.

32. "Freed-Levy Team Back in Harness," *Billboard*, May 27, 1957, 20.

33. Ibid.

34. Tony Fletcher, 117.

35. Dannen, 41.

36. Ibid.

37. Report of Jack Louis Marshall, 43.

38. "Goldner Sells Out to Levy; Stays in Field," *Billboard*, April 6, 1957, 16, 44; "Goldner Debs Own New Disk and Pub Firms," *Billboard*, April 13, 1957, 42, 57.

39. Report of Jack Louis Marshall, 43.

40. Broven, 238.

41. Ibid., 244.

42. Hugo and Luigi, "Voice of Broadway," October 26, 1957; accessed online August 12 and 14, 2013.

43. "Roulette to Reissue Alan Freed LPs for 'Hot Wax' Spinoff Try," *Variety*, April 5, 1978, 78.

44. Hugo and Luigi, "Voice of Broadway," October 26, 1957.

45. Broven, 245.

46. Rutledge, unpublished interview with Morris Levy.

47. Jimmy Bowen and Jim Jerome, *Rough Mix* (New York: Simon and Schuster, 1997), 42–43. Bowen would become a major figure in the music industry from the sixties to the nineties.

48. Broven, 245.

49. Bowen and Jerome, 44.

50. Ibid., 59–60.

51. Ibid., 61.

52. Ibid., 63.

53. Fred Goodman, *Allen Klein: The Man Who Bailed Out the Beatles, Made the Stones, and Transformed Rock & Roll.* (Boston: Houghton Mifflin Harcourt, 2015), 22–23; Bowen and Jerome, 64, 70.

54. Broven, 245–46.

55. Ibid.

56. "Gary James Interview with Jimmie Rodgers," www.classicbands.com/JimmieRodgers Interview.html; accessed on July 19, 2013.

57. Rodgers v. Roulette Records, Inc., 677 F. Supp. 731-Dis. Court, SD New York, 1988.

58. Dannen, unpublished interview with Morris Levy.

59. Author interview with Paul Walker, January 16, 2014.

60. Ronald Cohen, *Rainbow Quest: The Folk Music Revival and American Society* (Amherst: University of Massachusetts Press, 2002), 71.

61. "Richmond Thanks Roulette," *Billboard*, December 16, 1957, 28.

62. "Officers Suspended in Injury to Singer," *Spokane Spokesman-Review*, January 5, 1968, 2.

63. "Officers Cleared of Assault on Singer Jimmie Rodgers," *Tuscaloosa* (Alabama) *News*, March 28, 1968, 28. See also "Gary James Interview with Jimmie Rodgers," www.classicbands .com/JimmieRodgersInterview.html; accessed on July 19, 2013.

64. "Folk Singer Settles Suit for $200,000," UPI wire service story, August 23, 1973; accessed online July 19, 2013.

65. Based on a series of AP and UPI wire stories and newspaper articles from the time found on Google News. In addition to those already cited, these include: "Singer Hospitalized," December 2, 1967, AP; "Show Business," *Milwaukee Journal*, December 22, 1967, 10; "Jimmie Rodgers' Injury Linked to Fall," December 20, 1967, UPI; also an interview with Jimmie Rodgers posted on Youtube as "A Singer Silenced," www.youtube.com/watch?v=aySlePJT-XE#at=339; accessed on July 19, 2013.

66. "Gary James Interview with Jimmie Rodgers."

67. Rodgers v. Roulette Records, Inc., 677 F. Supp. 731-Dis. Court, SD New York, 1988.

Chapter 5

1. "12 Albums on Roulette's Debut LP List," *Billboard*, May 6, 1957, 20, 63.

2. Author interview with Peter Pullman, January 15, 2014.

3. "Roulette Records Advertorial," *Billboard*, February 3, 1958, 15.

4. Ibid.

5. Ibid., 18.

6. Dorothy Kilgallen, "The Voice of Broadway," September 20, 1957 and September 1, 1958; accessed online December 27, 2013.

7. "They Love Basie at Birdland," *Pittsburgh Courier*, October 1, 1955, 14.

8. Video interview with Morris Primack, ca. February 1998.

9. Basie and Murray, 299.

10. Ibid.

11. Author interview, June 12, 2013.

12. "Count Basie's Crew Set for Two Weeks at Birdland," *Pittsburgh Courier*, January 29, 1955, 16.

13. "Count Basie Sets Birdland Record, Now on Tour," *Pittsburgh Courier*, February 19, 1955, 15.

14. "'Eased Out,' Says CBS; 'I Quit,' Counters Basie," *Down Beat*, July 25, 1956; clipping in Count Basie file, Institute of Jazz Studies, Dana Library, Rutgers–Newark.

15. Teddy Reig and Ed Berger, *Reminiscing in Tempo* (Lanham, MD: Scarecrow Press, 1995), 46.

16. Frank Driggs and Chuck Haddiz, *Kansas City Jazz: From Ragtime to Bebop, A History* (New York: Oxford University Press, 2006), 145–46.

17. Transcript of Norman Granz interview with Albert Murray, cited by Ted Hershorn, *Norman Granz: The Man Who Used Jazz for Justice* (Berkeley: University of California Press, 2011), 264.

18. Basie and Murray, 321–22.

19. Levy ran the hatcheck concession at the Royal Roost, not Birdland; and that was in 1948, actually nine years earlier.

20. "Big Wheel & New Disk Deals (Morris Levy, Music Octopus)," *Variety*, October 30, 1957, 67; clipping in Count Basie file, Institute of Jazz Studies, Dana Library, Rutgers–Newark.

21. "Granz Sees No Rivalry with Morris Levy over Jazz Shows on Labels," *Variety*, November 13, 1957, 64.

22. Quincy Jones, *Q: The Autobiography of Quincy Jones* (New York: Doubleday, 2001), chapter 6. Marshal Royal, a member of the band during this period, commented that Basie never played during the rehearsal sessions for the band's Birdland gigs because he was too busy sitting "in the back of the room, trying to figure out what horse was running at Aqueduct," an indirect reference to his gambling habit. See Marshal Royal with Claire P. Gordon, *Marshal Royal: Jazz Survivor* (New York: Continuum, 2001), 101.

23. Broven, 243–44.

24. Tony Bennett, *The Good Life: The Autobiography of Tony Bennett* (New York: Simon & Schuster, 2010), 153. A similar story is given in Bennett's followup book, *Life Is a Gift: The Zen of Bennett* (New York: Harper, 2012). Bennett was no fan of Levy, so his description of Basie's relation to the producer should be taken with a grain of salt.

25. "Izzy Rowe's Notebook," *Pittsburgh Courier*, October 15, 1955, 14.

26. Gary Giddins, *Natural Selection: Gary Giddins on Comedy, Film, Music, and Books* (New York: Oxford University Press, 2006), 244.

27. "Levy Cues New Tape Policy," *Billboard* September 9, 1957, 16; accessed online December 20, 2012.

28. Jones, 300–301.

29. According to the website Measuringworth.com in terms of increase in income value.

30. *Billboard* advertisement, October 3, 1960, 7; accessed online, May 19, 2013.

31. "Discourse from the *Billboard* Sales Department: Count Basie," *Billboard*, October 10, 1960, 33.

32. *Billboard* advertisement, October 31, 1960, 41.

33. "Basie Drops Levy," *Jet*, May 31, 1962, 62.

34. Dorothy Kilgallen, syndicated column, May 13, 1962; accessed online, August 17, 2013.

35. Basie, 343.

36. Ibid., 344.

37. Gene Grove, "A Jazz Man From Red Bank Looks Back over the Years," *New York Post*, March 13, 1962, 40; clipping in Count Basie file, Institute of Jazz Studies, Dana Library, Rutgers–Newark.

38. Author interview with Peter Pullman, January 15, 2014.

39. Nadine Cohodas, 378–79.

40. Report of [Name Redacted], August 21, 1964, FBI Field Office File No. 122-1394, 10.

41. Leslie Gourse, *Sassy: The Life of Sarah Vaughan* (New York: Scribner's, 1983), 104.

42. Unnamed informant; Report of Jack Louis Marshall, 42. Vaughan was interviewed by Marshall on September 21, 1961, and repeated this information; Report of Jack Louis Marshall, New York FBI Field Office File No. 92-2015/Bureau File No. 92-5493, October 25, 1961, 14.

43. Cohodas, 395.

44. Ibid., 400.

45. Ibid., 230.

46. Author interview, anonymous source. According to Cohodas, Lane also quickly settled with Mercury Records, taking a lump-sum payment in lieu of all future royalties.

47. Letter by Nesuhi Ertegun to Teddy Reig, July 28, 1960; cited in Chris DeVito et al., *The John Coltrane Reference* (New York: Routledge, 2008), 207.

48. Tom Percard, *Lee Morgan: His Life, Music, and Culture* (London: Equinox, 2006), 137.

49. Ibid., 158–59.

50. Randy Weston and Willard Jenkins, *African Rhythms: The Autobiography of Randy Weston* (Durham, NC: Duke University Press, 2010), 95, 224.

51. Alan Nahigian and Zoe Anglesey, "Ferguson and Big Band Christen New Birdland," *Down Beat*, January 1977, www.maynardferguson.com/article_christen.html; accessed online April 24, 2013. See also Scott Yanow, ed., *The Trumpet Kings: The Players Who Shaped the Sound of Jazz Trumpet* (Milwaukee: Hal Leonard, 2001), 159.

52. Marc Myers, "Maynard Ferguson on Cameo," Jazz Wax, www.jazzwax.com/2012/02/maynard-ferguson-on-cameo.html; accessed September 10, 2014.

53. "Roulette Drums Up Percussion Promotion," *Billboard*, May 1, 1960, 41.

54. Falzerano, 56, 57.

55. Sylvester, 285–86.

56. Ibid., 286. Levy was a source for Sylvester's book, as was Ralph Watkins, so it is possible that one of them was the unnamed source quoted here.

57. Video interview with Morris Primack, October 27, 1997, courtesy of Aurin Primack.

58. Gene Santoro, *Myself When I Am Real: The Life and Music of Charles Mingus* (New York: Oxford University Press, 2000), 103.

59. Szwed, 92.

60. "Birdland Owner Stabbed to Death," UPI, January 28, 1959; accessed online August 14, 2013.

61. Harvey Aronson, "Cops Search Jazz Haunts for Slayer," *Newsday*, January 27, 1959, 5.

62. "Kin Quizzed in Jazz Killings," *Newsday*, January 29, 1959, 7.

63. "Birdland May Become a 'Siberia,'" *Amsterdam News*, January 31, 1959, 1; "Murder of Morris Levy's Brother; Second Recent Victim at N.Y.'s Birdland," *Variety*, January 28, 1959, 43.

64. Report of Jack Louis Marshall, 16.

65. "New York Couple Held in Stabbing," UPI, January 31, 1959; accessed online August 14, 2013.

66. "Couple Accused in Birdland Case," *New York Times*, January 31, 1959; accessed online December 17, 2010.

67. Not to be confused with Joe Bonanno, a Mafia kingpin who was known as "Joey Bananas."

68. United States District Court, Southern District of New York, "In the Matter of the Application of the United States of America for an Order Authorizing the Interception of Oral Communications Occurring within the Triangle Social Club . . . ," WP-0202/1X, paragraph 52. Posted on www.thesmokinggun.com; accessed April 8, 2014, and following.

69. Levy denied ever visiting Israel in unpublished interviews with both Jeff Rutledge (ca. 1989) and Fredric Dannen (July 30, 1988); both transcripts courtesy Joel Selvin.

70. Earl Wilson, syndicated column, February 3, 1959; accessed online August 12, 2013.

71. Author interview, June 12, 2013.

72. "Slayer Convicted," *New York Times*, November 10, 1959; "Killer is Sentenced," *New York Times*, December 16, 1959; both accessed online December 17, 2010.

73. Fredric Dannen, "The Godfather of Rock & Roll," *Rolling Stone*, November 17, 1988, 23.

74. Tommy James, *Me, the Mob, and the Music: One Helluva Ride with Tommy James & The Shondells* (New York: Simon & Schuster, 2010), 175.

75. Rutledge, unpublished interview with Morris Levy.

76. "Kin Quizzed in Jazz Killings," *Newsday*, January 29, 1959, 7.

77. Dorothy Kilgallen, syndicated column, January 31, 1959; accessed online August 17, 2013.

78. Dorothy Kilgallen, syndicated column, February 19, 1959; accessed online August 17, 2013.

79. Dorothy Kilgallen, syndicated column, March 5, 1959; accessed online August 17, 2013.

80. See, for example, "Jazz Emporium Figure Slain by Hopped-Up Fan," *Eureka Humboldt* (California) *Standard*, January 26, 1959, 1.

81. Bill Butler, "Killing Doesn't Disturb 'Cool' Birdland Tempo," *Newsday*, January 27, 1959, 5.

82. Ibid.

83. "Birdland May Become a 'Siberia,'" 1.

84. Ibid.

85. Davis and Troupe, 238. See also "Miles Davis Seized," *New York Times*, August 26, 1959.

86. Davis and Troupe, 238.

87. "Order Investigation of Miles Davis-Cop Fracas in New York," *Jet*, September 10, 1959; accessed online August 12, 2010.

88. Davis and Troupe, 239.

89. "Davis Arrest Studied," unidentified newspaper clipping, Miles Davis clipping file, Institute for Jazz Studies, Cali Library, Rutgers–Newark.

90. *Amsterdam News*, September 19, 1959, 1, 9; cited in DeVito et al., *The John Coltrane Reference*, 175.

91. "Trumpeter Cleared of Police Assault," *New York Times*, January 12 1960; accessed online August 10, 2010.

92. "Miles Exonerated," typescript labeled "Hoefer News—1," in Miles Davis clipping file, Institute for Jazz Studies, Cali Library, Rutgers–Newark.

93. Author interview with Aurin Primack, February 20, 2014.

94. Video interview with Morris Primack, ca. February 1998, courtesy Aurin Primack.

95. A. Down Katz, "Sounds of an Unusual Night: Blakey, Rich Tiff Over Diplomat's Drums," *Pittsburgh Courier*, May 7, 1960, 8.

96. "Birdland Rocks When Ambassador Plays Hot Drums: Musicians ALMOST Come to Blows," AP, April 22, 1960; accessed online August 15, 2013.

97. George F. Brown, "The Mission of Olatunji and His Drums of Passion," *Pittsburgh Courier*, February 10, 1962, 21. See also Babatunde Olatunji and Akinsola A. Akiwowo, *The Beat of My Drum: An Autobiography* (Philadelphia: Temple University Press, 2005), 195.

98. Video interview with Morris Primack, ca. February 1998.

99. Ibid. Primack's son Aurin recalled that his father also brought in at least one additional investor at about this time to prop up the club's finances, a lawyer from Northern New Jersey. Author interview, February 18, 2014.

100. Video interview with Morris Primack, ca. February 1998; courtesy Aurin Primack.

101. "Bankrupt NY Birdland Reports $103,778 in the Red," *Washington Afro American*, June 30, 1964, 14.

102. "Johnny Gray Rises: From Band Boy, Valet to Birdland Manager," *Pittsburgh Courier*, October 10, 1964, 4.

Chapter 6

1. Broven, 246.

2. Ibid., 246.

3. Ibid., 247.

4. "Roulette to Offer New Stock Issue," *Billboard*, September 7, 1959, 4.

5. *Billboard* reported that Levy's total expenditures on the building's renovation would be half a million dollars, not a million, including the costs of building a new recording studio; see "New Quarters for Roulette," *Billboard*, July 6, 1959, 4.

6. "Izzy Rowe's Notebook," *Pittsburgh Courier*, February 6, 1960, 22.

7. Author interview with Brad Fisher, February 1, 2015.

8. Dorothy Kilgallen, syndicated column, March 25, 1958; accessed online August 12, 2013.

9. "Levy Huddles with Fox on Roulette Sale," *Billboard*, December 9, 1957, 13, 20.

10. Dorothy Kilgallen, syndicated column, September 11, 1960; Earl Wilson, "It Happened Last Night," syndicated column, September 19, 1960; both accessed online August 13, 2013. According to one source, Sinatra wanted a 51 percent holding in Roulette, which Levy refused to grant. Interview with anonymous source, February 24, 2015.

11. "Morris Levy, President, Roulette Records . . . ," FBI New York Case File 122-1394, August 21, 1964, 11.

12. Ibid.

13. Based on IRS interview of Dominic Ciafone on May 22, 1964, reported to the FBI, and included in Morris Levy's files, Field Office File #MM 92-695/Bureau File #92-5493, 2.

14. Wade and Picardie, 82–83.

15. Basie and Murray, 332.

16. Dannen, 47.

17. "Payola Probers Ask Why Record Firms Paid $117,664 Tab," AP, February 11, 1960; accessed online August 12, 2013.

18. "Hotel Records Subpoenaed in Payola Investigation," UPI, February 25, 1960; accessed online August 14, 2013.

19. Wade and Picardie, 88.

20. Earl Wilson, "It Happened Last Night," syndicated column, December 4, 1959; accessed online August 14, 2013.

21. Earl Wilson, "It Happened Last Night," syndicated column, December 3, 1959; accessed online August 14, 2013.

22. George G. Connelly, "Professor at Large," *Berkshire Eagle*, March 7, 1960, 15.

23. Jackson, 264; "Band Leader Tells of Loan to Freed," UPI, December 4, 1959; accessed online August 12, 2013.

24. Jackson, 272.

25. DA Notes of interview with Morris Levy, November 1, 1962, 1–2; accessed October 28, 2014 at www.alanfreed.com/archives/archives-payola-scandal/da-people-vs-freed/.

26. Dannen, 44; see also Jackson, 273.

27. Dannen, 44.

28. Wade and Picardie, 90–91.

29. "Roulette Trying to Line Up Support of Disk Jockeys Vs. FTC Payola Rap," *Variety*, June 1, 1960, 55.

30. Ibid.

31. Federal Trade Commission Decisions, Vol. 59, "In the Matter of Roulette Records, Inc. Et Al., Order, Etc., in Regard to the Alleged Violation of the Trade Commission Act," Docket 7710, Complaint, December 30, 1959—Decision, August 8, 1961, 209–12; see their identical decision in the case against Big Top Records, 230–33. www.ftc.gov/sites/default/files/documents/com mission_decision_volumes/volume-59/ftcd-vol59july-december1961pages201-302.pdf; accessed online March 20, 2014.

32. Henry Stone with Jake Katel, *The Stone Cold Truth on Payola*, Self-published etext, loc. 587 of 867.

33. Alan Freed, letter to Morris Levy, December 2, 1964, www.alanfreed.com/archives/archives-final-years-1962-1965/personal-writings/; accessed October 28, 2014.

34. "Reisman Heads Roulette A&R," *Billboard*, February 9, 1959, 2.

35. "Roulette Bids Nat Tarnopol to A&R Spot," *Billboard*, May 4, 1959, 30.

36. "Roulette Lends 25G to Hanover-Signature in 1st Stage of Takeover," *Variety*, July 27, 1960, 111.

37. "Hanover Label Troubles as Roulette Moves to Foreclose $25,000 Loan," *Variety*, May 31, 1961, 45.

38. Bob Thiele, *What A Wonderful World* (New York: Oxford University Press, 1995), 94.

39. Morris I. Diamond, *The Name Dropper or "People I Schlepped With"* (Albany, GA: Bearmanor, 2011), 132.

40. Ibid., 134.

41. Thiele, 93–94.

42. Ibid., 59.

43. Author interview with anonymous source, June 19, 2013. Information on Johnny Dio came from various sources on the New York Mob.

44. David McGee, web discussion of his book, *B.B. King: There Is Always One More Time*, accessed on March 26, 2014 at www.well.com/conf/inkwell.vue/topics/259/David-McGee-BB -King-There-is-Alw-page04.html.

45. Napier-Bell does not give a date for the meeting, but Harold Bronson believes that it was around 1969–70 based on his knowledge of the duo's visit to the United States; email correspondence with the author, January 27, 2015.

46. Simon Napier-Bell, "The Life and Crimes of the Music Business," from the *Observer*, January 20, 2008, www.simonnapierbell.com/buggered_2.html; accessed September 15, 2014.

47. Author interview with Chuck Stewart, March 21, 2014.

48. Drew Pearson, "Drew Pearson's Merry-go-Round," syndicated column, March 27, 1960; accessed online August 12, 2013.

49. Report of Jack Louis Marshall, 42–43.

50. Ibid., 39.

51. Report of Field Agent [Name Redacted], "Morris Levy," New York Field Office File No. 92-2015/Bureau File No. 92-5493, June 1, 1962, 4.

52. Report of Jack Louis Marshall, 58–59.

53. As of the time of the FBI interview, Levy had kept up with the payments. FBI interview with Joe Kolsky, May 5, 1965, included in Morris Levy's files, Field Office File New York 92-2015/ Bureau File # 92-5493, [p. 4] ,.

54. "Joe Leaves: Planetary Buys Kolsky Interest in Roulette," *Billboard*, August 21, 1961, 3.

55. "Phil Kahl Sells Interests in Pubs, Roulette Diskery," *Billboard*, January 20, 1962, 5; "Joe Kolsky Joins Diamond Records," *Billboard*, January 27, 1962, 8. Note that the headline misstates the contents of the article, which in fact relate to Phil Kahl joining Diamond; Kolsky was already the owner/president of the label.

56. FBI interview with Joe Kolsky, May 5, 1965, included in Morris Levy's files, Field Office File New York 92-2015/Bureau File # 92-5493, 5.

57. For a full story of Grenell and Young People's Records, see David Bonner, *Revolutionizing Children's Records* (Lanham, MD: Scarecrow Press, 2008), 165.

58. Edward Ranzal, "Alleged Loan Shark, Convicted in Tax Case, Held on New Charge," *New York Times*, August 18, 1965, 22.

59. Emanuel Perlmutter, "Loan-Shark War Thought the Cause Of 5 Recent Killings," *New York Times*, July 19, 1977, 36; Arnold H. Lubasch, "Westies Informer Tells How Gang Cut Up Body," *New York Times*, October 22, 1987; "Westies Informer Tells of Links to Gambino Mob," *New York Times*, November 6, 1987. Accessed online, March 30, 2014.

60. Bonner, 162.

61. Thanks to David Bonner for making this draft proposal available to me.

62. This agreement was apparently drawn up before Kolsky had sold his shares in Roulette because it called for, in addition to the loan, Madison to purchase Kolsky's holdings, which the proposal noted amounted to approximately "28-29%" of the company.

63. Bonner, 165.

64. "Roulette Records, Incorporated: Labor Management Relations Act, 1947; Investigative Matter," New York Field Office file 122-1012, January 11, 1963, 7.

65. "Roulette Records, Incorporated, et al.," New York Field Office File #1012/Bureau File #122-304, 1.

66. This section is based personal interview, anonymous source, June 19–20, 2013.

67. "Morris Levy, President, Roulette Records . . . ," New York Case File 122-1394, August 21, 1964, 5.

68. Ibid., cover sheet, 1. Although Ciaffone's name is blacked out in this report, it is clear that he is the union official mentioned through the cross-references to the earlier IRS interview of Dominic Ciaffone on May 22, 1964, included in Morris Levy's files, Field Office File #MM 92-695/Bureau File #92-5493, 2.

69. "Morris Levy, President, Roulette Records . . . ," New York File Number 122-1394/ Bureau File No. 122-4048, October 6, 1964, 1.

70. "Morris Levy, President, Etc. Et Al, LMRA-IM OO: New York," Memorandum to Director, FBI, from SAC, New York, November 2, 1964, 1.

71. Dorothy Kilgallen, syndicated column, October 1, 1956; accessed online August 17, 2013.

72. Dorothy Kilgallen, syndicated column, April 18, 1959; accessed online August 17, 2013.

73. "Our Miss Brooks," *Life*, April 1, 1957, 51.

74. Dorothy Kilgallen, "The Voice of Broadway," syndicated column, November 27, 1961; accessed online August 17, 2013.

75. Earl Wilson, "It Happened Last Night," syndicated column, February 8, 1962; accessed online August 17, 2013.

76. "Roulette Goes Classical Via Forum Line," *Billboard*, August 3, 1959, 3, 50.

77. Ask Mr. Music website: www.digitaldreamdoor.com/pages/mr-music/Ask-Mr-Music -125.html; accessed August 7, 2013. And "Co-Star: The Record Acting Game," Drew Friedman blog, http://drewfriedman.blogspot.com/2011/11/co-star-record-acting-game.html; accessed August 7, 2013.

78. "All the World's A Stage . . . ," Liner notes, Co-Star CS-104, 1958.

79. Levy held these albums in high esteem, and reissued them himself in the late seventies even though there is scant evidence that they were ever very successful. Richard Foos of Rhino Records told me that Levy said that the Co-Star releases were his favorites among all the albums that he released at Roulette; author interview, April 20, 2012.

80. Cami's memoirs were published in an expanded form as John Johnson Jr. and Joel Selvin with Dick Cami, *Peppermint Twist* (New York: St. Martin's Press, 2013). Much of the information about Biello contained here is drawn from that text.

81. Some of this information came from Joey Dee's website, www.joeydee.com, accessed online, various dates in 2012–13 as well as Johnson and Selvin with Cami, op. cit.

82. Johnson and Selvin with Cami, 113–15.

83. "They came, saw, twisted at the Peppermint Lounge . . . ," *Life*, November 24, 1961, 76–77.

84. "New Dance Craze Sweeping New York," AP, October 29, 1961; accessed online August 20, 2013.

85. "Dorothy Kilgallen's Broadway," syndicated column, October 25, 1961; accessed online August 20, 2013.

86. From Joey Dee's website, www.joeydee.com, accessed online August 20, 2013.

87. Dorothy Kilgallen, syndicated column, November 10, 1961; accessed online August 17, 2013.

88. "Music As Written: New York," *Billboard*, October 12, 1959, 20.

89. Dorothy Kilgallen, syndicated column, November 18, 1961; accessed online August 20, 2013.

90. "Levy 'Twisting' Lots of Loot Out of Terp Craze," *Variety*, December 6, 1961, 51.

91. Joey Dee, "Mafia Doowop," YouTube, www.youtube.com/watch?v=swKWWvcdDzU; cited in Kliph Nesteroff, "Mobsters, Scoundrels, Comedians and Rat Finks," posted on WFMU's Beware of the Blog website, http://blog.wfmu.org/freeform/2012/03/mobsters-rat-finks.html; accessed September 17, 2013.

92. Ibid.

93. "Roulette Gets Haley . . . ," *Variety*, March 7, 1962, 47.

94. Johnson and Selvin with Cami, 142.

95. Levon Helm and Stephen Davis, *This Wheel's on Fire: Levon Helm and the Story of the Band*, 2nd ed. (Chicago: Chicago Review Press, 2000), 57.

96. Ibid., 62.

97. "The Record Shop," syndicated column, September 2, 1962; accessed online, December 27, 2013.

98. Report of Jack Louis Marshall, 2.

99. Helm and Davis, 71.

Chapter 7

1. Larry LeBlanc, "In the Hot Seat with Larry LeBlanc: Industry Profile: Tommy LiPuma (Part 1)," in *Encore Access* (internet publication) http://celebrityaccess.com/members/profile.html?id=541&PHPSESSID=btbijjv4dmvf51dhu77vf9b8p4; accessed September 26, 2013.

2. Phil Ramone and Charles L. Granata, *Making Records: The Scenes Behind the Music* (New York: Hyperion, 2007), 23–24.

3. Walter Yetnikoff with David Ritz. *Howling at the Moon* (New York: Broadway Books, 2004), 62. William Knoedelseder gives a similar account, although in his telling the amount was $300,000 and that Levy paid in full when Yetnikoff was in his office; see Knoedelseder, 56–57. Dannen repeats the story, but gives the figure as $400,000; see Dannen, 34. While Yetnikoff's memoirs are not totally reliable, this story seems in keeping with Levy's character, although it is surprising that he would have paid the entire amount due—particularly given the amount of money involved.

4. Unpublished interview with Ira Hertzog and Seymour Strauss by Joel Selvin; courtesy Joel Selvin. Bob Emmer told me that Levy told him a similar story; interview, January 26, 2015. Quincy Jones had a similar experience, saying that Levy told him during one negotiation for his work arranging on a Count Basie session, "You can ask for whatever you want, you're only getting one per cent." Matthew Garrahan, "Keeping Up with My Jones," *FT Magazine*, www.ft.com/intl/cms/s/2/124f89c2-3cd3-11e1-8d38-00144feabdc0.html#axzz3D2TQNcyA; accessed September 11, 2014.

5. Rutledge, unpublished interview with Morris Levy.

6. "The First Family Story—Wow!," *Billboard*, January 26, 1963, 6.

7. Nesteroff, "Mobsters, Scoundrels, Comedians and Rat Finks."

8. Ibid.

9. Ibid.

10. Francis Stilley, "Adult 'Coloring Books' Finding Ready Market," AP, September 29, 1962; accessed online September 17, 2013.

11. Earl Wilson, syndicated column, July 14, 1961; accessed online September 17, 2013.

12. The ownership was 49 percent Kannon and 51 percent Levy; personal interview with anonymous source, June 19, 2013.

13. John S. Wilson, "Rat Fink Club Prospers as Others Lag," *New York Times*, February 24, 1964; accessed online September 17, 2013.

14. Gary P. Gates, "Jackie Kannon Uses 'Rat Fink' to Promote Self," UPI, December 4, 1964; accessed online September 17, 2013.

15. Jean Ater, "In the Spotlight: Modern Art—And Art?" *Amarillo Globe-Times*, January 26, 1966, 30.

16. "John Stewart: Folksy and Tuneful," *Los Angeles Times* (Ventura County edition), December 17, 1992, 16.

17. "Roulette . . . Absorbs Gone and End," *Billboard*, July 7, 1962, 22; "Goldner Goes Independent With Gold Disc," *Billboard*, July 13, 1963, 3.

18. Jason Ankeny, "Joe Jones Biography," All Music Guide, www.allmusic.com/artist/joe -jones-mn0000137424; accessed December 11, 2013.

19. Broven, 353–54.

20. "Gary James' Interview with Lou Christie," 2002, www.classicbands.com/LouChristie Interview.html; accessed September 18, 2013. Also posted at www.storyofthestars.com/lou_ christie.htm.

21. Dan Matovina, *Without You: The Tragic Story of Badfinger* (San Mateo, CA: Frances Glover Books, 1997), 87.

22. "Sam Moore: The Soul Man," *Zani* magazine, 2007, http://www.zani.co.uk/music/39 -sam-moore-the-soul-man; accessed May 4, 2011, and September 18–19, 2013.

23. Unpublished interviews of Ira Hertzog and Seymour Strauss by Joel Selvin.

24. "'Goodies' Off and Running With Help of Browser," *Billboard*, June 15, 1963, 3.

25. Warner, 360.

26. "Roulette Spins Off Another Deal," *Billboard*, February 5, 1966, 4.

27. Joe Conzo with David A. Perez, *Mambo Diablo: My Journey with Tito Puente* (Blooming-ton, IN: AuthorHouse, 2010), 245.

28. Ibid., 180.

29. Aaron Cohen, "Perfection key to Palmieri's success," *Chicago Tribune*, August 30, 2005; accessed online July 11, 2013.

30. Claude Hall, "WWRL 'Format Frontiersmen," *Billboard*, December 21, 1966, 22.

31. "Roulette Buys Mardi Gras," *Billboard*, May 21, 1966, 4.

32. Claude Hall, "Latin's in U.S. Are Starving for Latin Music: Roulette's Levy," *Billboard*, April 27, 1968, 14.

33. Joel Selvin, unpublished interview with Red Schwartz, no date; transcript courtesy Joel Selvin.

34. Claude Hall, "Commentary," www.hollywoodhillsgroup.com/commentaries/ch-04-22 -13/; accessed September 17, 2014.

35. Dan Charnas, *The Big Payback: The History of the Business of Hip Hop* (New York: New American Library, 2010), 28, 30.

36. "Roulette Buys Stock in Calla," *Billboard*, August 13, 1966, 8.

37. David Edwards and Mike Callahan, Calla Albums Discography, www.bsnpubs.com/roulette/calla.html; accessed September 20, 2013.

38. Bettye LaVette and David Ritz, *A Woman Like Me* (New York: Blue Rider/Penguin, 2012), 59.

39. James, 113; Dannen, 50.

40. FBI interview with Morris Levy, April 19, 1965; according to Levy, Phase Music was leasing the theater. The new corporation was 80 percent owned by Roulette and 20 percent by two "entertainers" whose names were redacted out of the FBI report, although one was associated with Motown Records. FBI File 92-5493, report of Edward J. Mallon, August 19, 1968, 7.

41. Soupy Sales with Charles Salzberg, *Soupy Sez! My Zany Life and Times* (New York: M. Evans, 2001), 145.

42. Ibid., 147.

43. Steven Roby and Brad Schreiber, *Becoming Jimi Hendrix* (New York: DaCapo, 2010), 113.

44. Sales with Salzberg, 147–49.

45. Graham Nash, *Wild Tales: A Rock & Roll Life* (New York: Simon & Schuster, 2013), 73.

46. "Levy Says Labels Held Back," *Billboard*, May 22, 1965, 4.

47. "Peretti and Creatore Return to Roulette," *Billboard*, August 8, 1964, 4.

48. FBI Report of SA Arthur S. Hamilton, dated October 19, 1964, 2.

49. "Hugo and Luigi Exit Roulette Records," *Variety*, December 15, 1965, 60.

50. PR postcard, "The Hullabaloos," ca. 1965.

51. FBI Report of SA Don W. Walters dated August 13, 1964, 2.

52. "On the Beat: Roulette for Sale," *Billboard*, August 18, 1965, 6.

53. https://sites.google.com/site/pittsburghmusichistory/pittsburgh-music-story/radio/mad-mike; accessed June 11, 2014.

54. James, 50; the "Mad Mike" story is related in Dan Lewis, "Launched By A Sleeper," syndicated column, November 19, 1966; accessed online September 15, 2013. Chuck Rubin agrees that it was Bobby Mack who discovered the record; author interview, January 17, 2014.

55. Jerry Armstrong, "Platter Chatter," syndicated column, May 7, 1960; accessed online September 15, 2013; James, 50.

56. James, 58–59.

57. Author interview with Chuck Rubin, January 17, 2014.

58. James, 59.

59. Joel Selvin, unpublished interview with Red Schwartz, no date; transcript courtesy Joel Selvin.

60. James, 60.

61. Ibid., 61.

62. Lewis, "Launched By A Sleeper."

63. James, 68–69.

64. Joel Selvin, unpublished interview with Red Schwartz, no date; transcript courtesy Joel Selvin.

65. James, 75-76.

66. Ibid., 88.

67. Ibid., 91.

68. Joel Selvin, unpublished interview with Red Schwartz, no date; transcript courtesy Joel Selvin.

69. Bruce Pollock, By *the Time We Got to Woodstock: The Great Rock 'n' Roll Revolution of 1969* (New York: Backbeat, 2009), 18.

70. James, 92.

71. Ibid., 111–12.

72. Reported to be either $10,000 or $15,000.

73. Dannen, unpublished interview with Morris Levy.

74. James, 180.

75. Ibid., 195–97; for some reason, James consistently misspells his name as "Joel Kulsky."

76. Ibid., 200–202.

Chapter 8

1. Report of Field Agent [name redacted], "Morris Levy," New York Field Office No. 92-2015/Bureau File No. 92-5493, June 1, 1962, 2.

2. FBI Report of SA William David Kane, dated August 16, 1966, 3.

3. Ibid. 2.

4. William Knoedelseder, "Morris Levy: Big Clout in Record Industry: His Behind-the-Scenes Influence Is Felt Throughout the Industry," *Los Angeles Times*, July 20, 1986, accessed online, various dates.

5. Report of Unnamed SA [name redacted], dated July 19, 1967, 4.

6. Report of SA Francis P. Henry, dated June 26, 1972, 2.

7. Author interview with anonymous source, June 29, 2013.

8. Report of SA Francis P. Henry, dated April 10, 1972, 5.

9. Report of SA Arthur S. Hamilton, dated February 26, 1965, 2–4.

10. Report of SA William David Kane, dated August 16, 1966, 4.

11. Isadore Barmash, "And Now: The Mini-Conglomerates," *New York Times*, December 8, 1968, accessed online October 27, 2013.

12. "Big 7 Acquires All of Figure, Snapper Firms," *Billboard*, December 26, 1960, 3.

13. Report of Unnamed SA [name redacted], dated April 8, 1969, 2–3.

14. "Redemption Right on Fund Is Lifted," *New York Times*, December 21, 1968; accessed online October 27, 2013.

15. "Omega Equities Named in Suits; 3 Brokerage Houses Also Cited," *New York Times*, April 30, 1969; accessed online October 27, 2013.

16. Artie Wayne, "Legendary Music Man Morris Levy and 'Shadow' Mann A Legend in His Own Mind," August 6, 2006, Artie Wayne on the Web, http://artiewayne.wordpress.com/2006/08/06legendary-music-man-morris-levy-meets-shadow-morton, accessed May 4, 2011, and subsequent dates.

17. Dannen, 32.

18. Joel Sucher, "Music and the Mob," June 19, 2014, Huffington Post, www.huffingtonpost .com/joel-sucher/music-and-the-mob_b_5509816.html; accessed September 9, 2014.

19. "Roulette's Stepped Up College Try," *Billboard*, August 2, 1969, 6.

20. Report of SA Francis P. Henry, dated December 7, 1970, 1 .

21. Suzanne Daley, "State Purses Encourage Horse Farms," *New York Times*, October 12, 1980; accessed online August 10, 2010.

22. James, 185–86.

23. Suzanne Daley, op. cit.

24. Ibid., 171–72.

25. Unpublished interview with Fredric Dannen, July 30, 1988, courtesy Joel Selvin.

26. After Eboli's death in 1972, Levy told FBI interviewers that Eboli was not a full partner in Promo Records until 1972, when Levy sold to him and an unnamed partner a 50 percent interest in the operation. However, it is clear from FBI surveillance that Eboli was active in Promo at least as early as 1969. See Report of SA Francis P. Henry, dated October 6, 1972, 3, 4.

27. Dannen, 38–39; Knoedelseder, "Morris Levy: Big Clout in Record Industry."

28. "Morris Levy Files Counter-Suits in ELO LP Dispute," *Variety*, February 7, 1979, 95.

29. According to Sharon Osbourne, Levy actually bootlegged the ELO album having been given the artwork and master tapes by Artie Mogull, following a falling-out between Mogull and Osbourne's father Don Arden (born Harry Levy, no relation to Morris), then the manager of ELO. Arden and Mogull had discussed jointly purchasing United Artists Records, but at the last minute Mogull dropped Arden from the deal. In retaliation, Mogull took ELO—UA's biggest selling act—to Columbia; in revenge, Mogull conspired with Levy to flood the market with copies of *Out of the Blue*; see *Sharon Osbourne Extreme: My Autobiography* (New York: Springboard Press, 2006), 98.

30. "Racks Create Cutouts, Says Morris Levy," *Billboard*, February 24, 1973, 1, 6.

31. Ibid., 6.

32. Ibid.

33. Ibid.

34. Knoedelseder, 51.

35. Report of SA Francis P. Henry, dated February 2, 1972, 20.

36. Report of Unnamed SA [name redacted], dated April 8, 1969, 3–4.

37. Knoedelseder, 58.

38. Report of SA Francis P. Henry, dated February 2, 1972, 15, 17, 20–21.

39. The FBI questioned Levy on October 15, 1971, about a $15,000 payment made by Roulette to Eboli. Levy said this was a commission paid to Eboli for bringing a singer to Roulette. This may have been the same singer who Pagano and Eboli were promoting.

40. One anonymous source told me that Gurlek was the only one who could control Levy when he was inclined to act impulsively; interview, conducted February 24, 2015.

41. "Funeral Service for Gurlek," *Billboard*, October 9, 1970, 8.

42. Regarding Planetary Music, one of many companies Levy owned with Gurlek, the FBI stated: "When GURLEK died in 1970, it is reported that any stock reverted to the company, and that MORRIS LEVY is in complete control." By 1972 the FBI believed that Roulette Records was a subsidiary company of Planetary. Report of SA Francis P. Henry, dated April 10, 1972, 3.

Notes

43. The Red Bird story is told by various sources, including Jerry Leiber and Mike Stoller, with David Ritz, *Hound Dog: The Leiber and Stoller Autobiography* (New York: Simon and Schuster, 2009).

44. David Edwards and Mike Callahan, "The George Goldner Story," www.bsnpubs.com/roulette/goldner.html; accessed November 2, 2013.

45. "Kahl Rejoins Levy in Big 7 Music," *Billboard*, December 22, 1971, 51.

46. Author interview with Brad Fisher, February 1, 2015.

47. Emanuel Perlmutter, "A Key Gang Figure Slain in Brooklyn," *New York Times*, July 17, 1972; Eric Pace, "Funerals Aren't What They Used to Be," *New York Times*, July 23, 1972, both accessed online August 2, 2012.

48. James, 197–98.

49. *Billboard* quoted James saying he was acting as a representative of Roulette to establish a studio in Nashville; see "Tommy James Bidding for Roulette Nashville Ofc," *Billboard*, November 20, 1971, 3.

50. Perlmutter, op. cit.

51. William Bastone with Andrew Goldberg and Joseph Jesselli, "Al Sharpton's Secret Work as FBI Informant," posted April 7, 2014, on www.smokinggun.com; accessed April 8, 2014 and following.

52. James, 204.

53. Report of SA Francis P. Henry, dated October 6, 1972, 4.

54. "General News," photo and caption, *Billboard*, November 10, 1973, 13.

55. "A Day in the Life of Joe Smith," *Billboard*, April 3, 1976, 43.

56. All quotes taken from the film *Sliced Steak*, which was made at the event by Richard Perry. The film was never commercially released but has been widely circulated in the music world. Provided to the author by an anonymous source.

57. Actually, the company was not formally incorporated until 1968, but the original business premise remained unchanged beginning with Kives's first TV ad in 1962.

58. "About the Founder: Philip Kives," www.ktel.com/about.php; accessed November 2, 2013.

59. "Where's the Money from TV Oldies?" *Rolling Stone*, November 9, 1972, 16.

60. Ibid.

61. Jim Bessman, "Heartland Music's TV Success," *Billboard*, March 23, 2002, 80.

62. "Roulette Spins Out $1 Million Suit Vs. K-Tel International," *Billboard*, May 12, 1973, 4, 22.

63. Dannen, 33.

64. Irv Lichtman, "Strawberries Mapping New Expansion," *Billboard*, October 9, 1982, 3.

65. United States District Court, Southern District of New York, "In the Matter of the Application of the United States of America for an Order Authorizing the Interception of Oral Communications Occurring within the Triangle Social Club . . . ," paragraphs 51 and 53. Posted on www.thesmokinggun.com; accessed April 8, 2014 and following.

66. John Sippel, "Unique Trial Run for Chain Buyout," *Billboard*, May 21, 1977, 4; see also Is Horowitz, "Jimmy's 'Going Out of Business Sale' OKed," *Billboard*, November 5, 1977, 3, 107.

67. Fred Goodman, "Fruitful Times for Strawberries," *Billboard*, December 15, 1984, 23.

68. Fred Goodman, "Strawberries Commits to Video," *Billboard*, July 31, 1984, accessed online, March 12, 2014.

69. Goodman, "Fruitful Times for Strawberries."

70. Knoedelseder, "Morris Levy: Big Clout in Record Industry."

71. Ileana N. Saros and Michael R. Hoey, Untitled Report on Mafia Infiltration of New Jersey Bars, State of New Jersey, Commission of Investigation, www.state.nj.us/sci/pdf/ocbars .pdf; accessed September 17, 2014.

72. James, 220–21.

73. "Tiger Lily Records Discography," http://forbiddeneye.com/labels/tigerlily.html; accessed November 2, 2013.

74. "Roulette to Reissue Alan Freed LPs for 'Hot Wax' Spinoff Try," *Variety*, April 5, 1978, 78.

75. Surcouf recalled the record as being released on the Gemini label. I have not been able to locate a Gemini label Meters album, but have seen one on the Virgo label, which is listed as a division of Suellen Productions, a shell corporation that Levy was associated with, according to the FBI. The cut-rate graphics of the plain album cover, featuring a stock photo of a parking meter, is typical of Levy's mid-seventies off-price labels, such as Emus and Adam VIII.

76. Author interview with Rupert Surcouf, July 11, 2014.

77. According to Harold Bronson, co-owner of Rhino Records, the Meters were among the few acts who came forward after Rhino purchased Roulette to make a claim for unpaid royalties. Harold Bronson, *The Rhino Records Story: Revenge of the Music Nerds* (New York: SelectBooks, 2013), Kindle ebook loc. 5805. Bob Emmer states that Sehorn convinced Rhino that he owned the masters, and that Levy refunded from the purchase price the amount they had to pay Sehorn in settlement; author interview with Bob Emmer, January 26, 2015; email correspondence, January 30 and 31, 2015.

78. Big Seven Music Corp v. MacLen Music Inc., Northern Songs, Ltd. and Apple Records, Inc. (S.D.N.Y. 70 Civ. 1348).

79. Jean Teeters, "May Pang Talks about John Lennon's Classic Album *Rock 'n' Roll*," http:// articles.absoluteelsewhere.net/Articles/may_pang_rocknroll2.html; accessed November 17, 2013.

80. BIG SEVEN MUSIC CORP and Adam VIII, Ltd., Plaintiffs v. John LENNON et al., Defendants and Morris Levy, Additional Defendant on Counterclaim, No. 75 Civ. 1116, United States District Court, S.D. New York, February 20, 1976, Pt. IV.

81. Ibid., Pt. II.

82. Ibid., Pt. IV.

83. Joseph C. Self, "Lennon v. Levy—The 'Roots' Lawsuit," 4–5, http://abbeyrd.best.vmh.net/ lenlevy.htm; accessed June 28, 2010, and subsequent dates; BIG SEVEN MUSIC CORP and Adam VIII, Ltd., op. cit., Pts. III and V. Self's account is the best and most coherent of various retellings of the Lennon and Levy story. See also William McCoy and Mitch McGeary, "John Lennon: The Roots of Rock 'n' Roll," www.rarebeatles.com/roots/roots.htm; accessed May 4, 2011, and subsequent dates.

84. BIG SEVEN MUSIC CORP and Adam VIII, Ltd., February 20, 1976, Pt. VI.

85. BIG SEVEN MUSIC CORP. and Adam VIII, Ltd., Plaintiffs-Appellants v. John LEN-NON et al., Defendants-Appellees, and Morris Levy, Additional Defendant on Counterclaims-Appellant, Nos. 624, 860, Dockets 76-7454, 76-7480, United States Court of Appeals, Second Circuit. Argued January 27, 1977; Decided April 13, 1977, Pt. I: The Alleged Oral Contract.

86. BIG SEVEN MUSIC CORP and Adam VIII, Ltd., February 20, 1976, Pt. VI ; see also Self, 3.

87. BIG SEVEN MUSIC CORP. and Adam VIII, Ltd., April 13, 1977, Pt. II: Damages Awarded to Lennon; see also BIG SEVEN MUSIC CORP and Adam VIII, Ltd., February 20, 1976, Pt. VI.

88. Self, 4.

89. BIG SEVEN MUSIC CORP. and Adam VIII, Ltd., April 13, 1977, Pt. II Damages Awarded to Lennon. Capitol's version would sell 342,000 copies in the United States.

90. BIG SEVEN MUSIC CORP and Adam VIII, Ltd., February 20, 1976, Pt. V.

91. BIG SEVEN MUSIC CORP. and Adam VIII, Ltd., April 13, 1977.

92. This was reduced later by mutual agreement by $9,400 for union dues that Lennon would have had to pay to the American Federation of Musicians; BIG SEVEN MUSIC CORP. and Adam VIII, Ltd., April 13, 1977, Pt. II: Damages Awarded to Lennon; and Self, Op. cit., 8 of 12.

93. Ibid.

94. Self, Op. cit., 9 of 12.

95. BIG SEVEN MUSIC CORP. and Adam VIII, Ltd., Op cit. April 13 1977, Pt. II: Damages Awarded to Lennon, Part B: Injury to Lennon's Reputation.

96. Ibid., Pt. II: Damages Awarded to Lennon, Part C: Punitive Damages.

97. "Random Notes," *Rolling Stone*, May 15, 1977, and December 12, 1976; accessed online, December 27, 2013.

Chapter 9

1. Rutledge, unpublished interview with Morris Levy.

2. Dannen, 50.

3. Rutledge, unpublished interview with Morris Levy.

4. Dannen, 50; Knoedelseder, 52. The charges were dropped by the grand jury on June 30, 1976; see Supreme Court of the State of New York, County of New York, The People of the State of New York against Morris Levy on Indictment, Assault in the Second Degree, No. 3163-75, filed June 19, 1975, Miscellaneous Certificate No. 5883. Levy later applied for all records in the case to be sealed, which was ordered by Irving Long of the Supreme Court of the State of New York (Order Ind. No. 2867/78).

5. The Bush label story is told in William R. Bauer, *Open the Door: The Life and Music of Betty Carter* (Ann Arbor: University of Michigan Press, 2002), 110–11, 113, 118–19, 135–37.

6. Herb Nolan, "Betty Carter's Declaration of Independence," *Down Beat*, August 12, 1976, 23; cited in Bauer, 136-37,

7. Bauer ,op. cit., 141–42.

8. Joel Sucher, "Music and the Mob," Huffington Post, posted June 19, 2014; www.huffington post.com/joel-sucher/music-and-the-mob_b_5509816.html; accessed September 9, 2014.

9. Email correspondence with Bob Emmer, January 31, 2015.

10. 734 F.2d 1329; 222 U.S.P.Q. 466, 1984 Copr.L.December P 25,665: Emmylou HARRIS, dba Hannah Brown Music and Emmylou Harris, Plaintiffs-Appellees, v. EMUS RECORDS CORPORATION; Roulette Records, Inc.; Suellen Productions, Inc.; Admo Music Corporation; and Promo Records Distributing Company, Defendants-Appellants; and Nos. 81-5753, 82-5613: Emmylou HARRIS, dba Hannah Brown Music Ltd., and Emmylou Harris, Plaintiffs-Appellees,

v. EMUS RECORDS CORPORATION, a New York corporation; Roulette Records, Inc., a New York corporation; Suellen Productions, Inc., a New York corporation; Admo Music Corporation, a New York corporation; and Promo Records distributing Company, a New Jersey corporation, Defendants-Appellants. The two cases were combined on appeal.

11. Interview with Emmylou Harris, *Billboard*, December 4, 1999, 14.

12. 734 F.2d 1329; 222 U.S.P.Q. 466, 1984 Copr.L.December P 25,665, op. cit.; and Nos. 81-5753, 82-5613 op. cit. Argued and Submitted August 4, 1983; Decided May 29, 1984; paragraphs 33 and 36.

13. Dannen, 50.

14. Don Jeffrey, "Ska Compilation Generates Intrigue," *Billboard*, June 18, 1994, 97.

15. Ibid.

16. David Edwards and Mike Callahan report that McCalla formed a separate label in 1976, Shakrat Records, and then made a distribution deal with CBS for its more popular releases, including presumably the Marley albums. "Calla Records Discography," www.bsnpubs.com/roulette/calla.html, accessed February 1, 2014.

17. "Police Fear Foul Play in Case of Missing Deejay," *Afro-American*, September 17, 1977, 7.

18. Timothy S. Robinson and Chris Schauble, "Officials Suspect Disc Jockey Was Victim of Murder," *Washington Post*, May 15, 1978, C1, C9.

19. Dannen, 51.

20. Much of the information in this section is based on author interview with Michael Zager, February 18, 2014.

21. Author interview Michael Zager, February 18, 2014.

22. "Top Single Picks: First Time Around," *Billboard*, February 5, 1977, accessed online March 5, 2014.

23. "Ex-Porn Star Goes Vocal: Strives for Image Change," *Billboard*, April 9, 1977, 4.

24. Author interview Michael Zager, February 18, 2014. He tells a similar story of the making of this record in James Arena, *First Ladies of Disco: 32 Stars Discuss the Era and Their Singing Careers* (Jefferson, NC: McFarland, 2003), 50–51.

25. Morris Levy, "The Old Timers Knew," *Billboard*, August 1, 1981, 16. All of the quotes throughout this passage are from this commentary piece.

26. "Cambridge Sued by MCA Distributing," *Billboard*, August 15, 1981, 3.

27. "Suit Retaliation, Says Levy," *Billboard*, August 29, 1981, 3.

28. The information on Chuck Rubin and his career was largely drawn from an interview with author, January 17, 2014.

29. Author interview, January 17, 2014. Rubin would later face criticism for taking such a large percentage as his fee for recovering both past and future royalties, so his assertion that the idea came from Harrison should be taken with a grain of salt.

30. Stan Soocher, *They Fought the Law: Rock Music Goes to Court* (New York: Schirmer, 1999), 66.

31. Author interview, January 17, 2014.

32. Paula Span, "Three Wives & The Legacy of 'Love'; A Courtroom Clash Over Frankie Lymon's '56 Song," *Washington Post*, March 30, 1988, C1.

33. Soocher, 66–67.

34. Irv Lichtman, "Big 7 Music Expands Subpublishing Ties," *Billboard*, July 14, 1979, 10.

35. The Ballard copyright story is told in Stan Soocher, "The Royalty Recovery Project: How Rock's Pioneers Finally Got a Piece of the Action," *Musician*, January 1, 1988, 39–40, 42, 44–46.

36. Ibid., 45.

37. Author interview, January 17, 2014.

38. Jimmy MERCHANT and Herman Santiago, Plaintiffs, v. Emira LYMON, as Widow and Administratrix of the Estate of Frankie Lymon, Morris Levy, Big Seven Music Corp., Roulette Records, Inc., and Broadcast Music, Inc., Defendants. No. 87 Civ. 7199 (VLB) (NRB) United States District Court, S.D., New York, July 23, 1993, 1054.

39. Author interview with Ira Greenberg, January 15, 2014.

40. Jimmy MERCHANT and Herman Santiago, op. cit., fn. 1.

41. Calvin Trillin, "You Don't Ask, You Don't Get," in *American Lives* (New York: Ticknor & Fields, 1991), 207–8.

42. Span, "Three Wives & The Legacy of 'Love'"; Trillin, 207.

43. Barbara Fagin, "Two Women Claim to be 'Widow' of Famous Singer; In Fight for $1 Million," *Jet*, March 11, 1985, 62.

44. Dannen, unpublished interview with Morris Levy.

45. Ibid.

46. Span, C1.

47. Trillin, 208.

48. Fagin, 62.

49. At the time of the 1984 lawsuit, Elizabeth finally moved to have her original marriage annulled, as both she and her first husband were underage when they wed; Fagin, 61.

50. Rubin later uncovered her rap sheet in Philadelphia, which he claimed stretched "down the entire hall" of the city's office of records; author interview, January 17, 2014.

51. Author interview, January 17, 2014.

52. Ibid.

53. This narrative is based on Paula Span's reporting in the *Washington Post*, op. cit.

54. Trillin, 217.

55. Jimmy MERCHANT and Herman Santiago, Op. cit., fn. 8.

56. Paula Span, "The Long Wait for a Hit to Turn Gold; A Jury Agrees These Men Wrote 'Why Do Fools Fall in Love?' Now They Stand to Get a Cut. Maybe." *Washington Post*, November 27, 1992, B1.

57. Deposition of Morris Levy, April 18, 1985; Emira Lymon v. Morris Levy, U.S. District Court, Southern District of New York; cited in Dannen, 49, and Trillin, 211. Trillin's version slightly differs in wording.

58. Jimmy MERCHANT and Herman Santiago, Op. cit., 1054–55.

59. Ibid.

60. Author interview, January 15, 2014.

61. Jimmy MERCHANT and Herman Santiago, Op. cit., 1058.

62. Ibid., 1055. In footnote 5 to the finding by the court, the judge noted that the plaintiffs were underage when they signed their original agreement so that it was not until they came of age—in 1961—that they would have been required to file claim for their copyright to the song.

63. Span, "The Long Wait for a Hit to Turn Gold."

64. Jimmy MERCHANT and Herman Santiago, Op. cit., 1055.

65. Ibid., fn 15.

66. Ibid., 1063–64.

67. Jimmy MERCHANT and Herman Santiago, Plaintiffs-Appellees-Cross-Appellants, v. Morris LEVY, Big Seven Music Corp., Roulette Records, Inc., Defendants-Appellants-Cross-Appellees, and Windswept Pacific Entertainment Co., Intervenor-Defendant-Appellant-Cross-Appellee. Nos. 1322, 1653, 1768, Dockets 95-7763L, 95-7765CON, 95-7767XAP, United State Court of Appeals, Second Circuit, Argued May 2, 1996, Decided August 7, 1996.

Chapter 10

1. Author interview with Brad Fisher, February 1, 2015.

2. Dannen, 34, among many other sources.

3. Sydney J. Mehl, M.D., Letter submitted to the judge in support of a motion for a stay of execution of Levy's sentence, submitted by Camille M. Kenny on November 28, 1989, to the United States District Court, District of New Jersey, Cr. No. S-86-301.

4. Knoedelseder, 98–99.

5. Lawrence S. Ferreira, United States Court, Southern District of New York, Affidavit in Support of Orders Authorizing the Interception of Wire Communications, August 1985, 25–26.

6. Ibid., 32.

7. Ibid., 34–35.

8. United States District Court, Southern District of New York. "In the Matter of the Application of the United States of America for an Order Authorizing the Interception of Oral Communications Occurring within the Triangle Social Club . . . ," WP-0952/1A and WP-0952/1A. Posted on www.thesmokinggun.com; accessed April 8, 2014, and following.

9. Dannen, 40; and, for example, Philip Lentz, "Officials Say Mobster's Act Belies His Role," *Chicago Tribune*, March 19, 1989; accessed online December 21, 2013.

10. Eleanor Randolph, "N.Y.'s Don Days Warm Up With Trial of 'The Chin,'" *Los Angeles Times*, July 3, 1997; accessed online December 21, 2013.

11. Louis Gigante actually "purchased" the land for a dollar; in a letter to judge Stanley S. Brotman addressing the sale, Gigante stated that the market rate for the land was only $200 an acre at the time; see Louis R. Gigante, Letter to Honorable Stanley S. Brotman, September 20, 1988, part of the trial records of US v. Levy.

12. Bastone with Goldberg and Jesselli, op. cit.

13. Jennifer Redfearn, "Sins of the Father," *Village Voice*, January 16, 2007, www.villagevoice.com/2007-01-16/news/sins-of-the-father/; accessed May 28, 2014; see also, Raab, Selwyn, *Five Families* (New York: St. Martin's Press, 2006), 544–48.

14. Ileana N. Saros and Michael R. Hoey, Untitled Report on Mafia Infiltration of New Jersey Bars, State of NJ, Commission of Investigation, www.state.nj.us/sci/pdf/ocbars.pdf; accessed September 17, 2014.

15. Ibid.

16. Fred Goodman, "Morris Levy Severing Music Industry Ties," *Billboard*, December 20, 1986, 71.

17. "Industry News," *Musician, Player, and Listener* 29 (January 1, 1981): 12.

18. "Correction," *Musician, Player, and Listener* 30 (February 1, 1981): 8.

19. http://jamonproductions.com/newcleus.html; accessed February 2, 2014.

20. "Stone, Levy Team in New Distributorship," *Billboard*, November 9, 1983, 28.

21. Information drawn from Henry Stone's Internet page, www.henrystonemusic.com, and various other sources.

22. Larry Harris, Curt Gooch, Jeff Suhs, *And Party Every Day: The Inside Story of Casablanca Records* (Milwaukee: Hal Leonard/Backbeat, 2009), 6. See also Michael Franzese, *Blood Covenant* (New Kensington, PA: Whittaker House, 2003), 22–25.

23. Franzese, *Blood Covenant*, 22–25.

24. Ibid.

25. "Viewlex Purchase of Kama Sutra and Buddah Completed," *Billboard*, November 30, 1968, 10; and "Viewlex Sells Audio Visual Arm," *Billboard*, December 14, 1974, 8.

26. Dannen.

27. "Kass Starts Sutra Label in New York," *Billboard*, September 13, 1980, 3.

28. Irv Lichtman, "Arista, Buddah Agree on Termination of Distrib Deal," *Billboard*, January 7, 1984, 4.

29. Charnas, *The Big Payback*.

30. Brian Chin, "Fat Boys on New Label," *Billboard*, October 4, 1986, 92.

31. George Lipsitz, *American Studies in a Moment of Danger* (Minneapolis: University of Minnesota Press, 2001), 146.

32. Author interview with George Hocutt, June 27, 2013.

33. "Art Kass Files Suit Against Morris Levy," *Billboard*, February 25, 1989, 84.

34. Rutledge, unpublished interview with Morris Levy.

35. Charnas, 39.

36. Ibid., 37.

37. Ibid., 38–39.

38. Ibid., 43.

39. Nelson George, *Hip Hop America* (New York: Penguin, 2005), 30.

40. Ibid., 31.

41. Ibid., 31–32.

42. Nile Rodgers, *Le Freak: An Upside Down Story of Family, Disco, and Destiny* (New York: Random House, 2011), 174.

43. Abigail T. Dereco, "Illegitimate Media: Gender and Censorship in Digital Remix Culture," diss., Graduate School of Northwestern University, June 2008, 189; Dereco cites an interview with Adam Levy that appeared in Steven Daly, "Hip Hop Happens," *Vanity Fair*, November 2005.

44. Rodgers, 175.

45. Charnas, 87–88.

46. Knoedelseder, 20–21.

47. The story of Sal Pisello is based on reporting by William Knoedelseder; see Knoedelseder, 16ff.

48. Knoedelseder, 85–87; 99.

49. Ibid., 29–31.

50. Author interview with Chuck Rubin, January 17, 2014.

51. Vastola had been convicted in 1962 in a counterfeiting scheme involving Johnny Mathis and Frank Sinatra albums; see *Billboard*, March 20, 1961, 2, and May 19, 1962, 5.

52. This loan was mentioned in the original indictment of Levy and the other defendants in Count 33; by mistake, the federal government linked this loan to Levy, Fisher, and Canterino, when it was in fact made by Vastola alone prior to the remainder sale. This was later amended so the loan was removed from the extortion charges against Levy. See United States of America v. Morris Levy, Dominick Canterino, and Howard Fisher, Indictment filled on March 20, 1987 and then redacted to apply to the three defendants on May 2, 1988.

53. Knoedelseder, 50.

54. No such deal was announced in the trades at the time, while other negotiations to sell Roulette were reported. However, Levy insists that this was the case in several places in this interview. Rutledge, unpublished interview with Morris Levy.

55. Affidavit of Thomas J. Dossett, in the Matter of the Application Authorizing the Interception of Oral Communications Occurring in the Three Executive Offices of the Southwest Wall of Video Warehouse . . . , Originally Filed June 26, 1985, paragraph 20.

56. Knoedelseder, 100–101.

57. The United States of America, Plaintiff, vs. Gaetano Vastola, Larry Martire, et al., Defendants, Criminal No. 86-301SSB, Newark New Jersey, September 24, 1986, Transcript of Proceedings before the Honorable Serena Perretti, direct testimony of John Mahoney, 56–57.

58. Ibid., 59.

59. Ibid., 62–63.

60. Affidavit of Thomas J. Dossett, Op. cit., paragraph 16.

61. Knoedelseder, 112–14.

62. Affidavit of Thomas J. Dossett, Op. cit., paragraph 15.

63. Knoedelseder, 125–26.

64. Transcript of recording made of Morris Levy, Howard Fisher, two unknown males and one unknown female, on October 23, 1985, in Levy's offices at Roulette Records, 5:06 p.m.; Exhibit E, submitted as part of an Affidavit by Martin London in the case of United States of America, Plaintiff, against Morris Levy, Howard Fisher and Dominick Canterino, Defendants, April 20, 1988.

65. Knoedelseder, 129–30.

66. Ibid., 139.

67. Lawrence S. Ferreira, 20.

68. Affidavit of Thomas J. Dossett, Op. cit., paragraph 23.

69. Knoedelseder, 156.

70. Ibid., 164.

71. Ibid.

72. Ibid., 165.

73. Lawrence S. Ferreira, 22.

74. Knoedelseder, 171.

75. Wiretap conversation reported in United States of America, Plaintiff v. Morris LEVY, Howard Fisher, and Dominick Canterino, Defendants. Crim. No. 86-301, United State District Court, D. New Jersey, August 23, 1988, Pt. 1, "Levy and Canterino," 3.

76. Knoedelseder, 174–75.

77. Ibid., 176.

78. Cited in United States of America, Plaintiff v. Morris LEVY, Howard Fisher, and Dominick Canterino, Defendants. Crim. No. 86-301, United State District Court, D. New Jersey, August 23, 1988, Pt. 2, "Fisher," 6.

79. FBI transcript of intercepted phone call, October 23, 1985, 4:54 p.m., between William Knoedelseder and Morris Levy.

80. Ibid.

81. Ibid.

82. Transcript of meeting at Roulette Records office, October 23, 1985, 5:06 p.m., SD New York #1077; submitted as Defendant's Exhibit D142.1(a).

83. Charles E. Beaudoin, United States District Court, Southern District of New York, In the Matter of the Application of the United States of America for an Order Authorizing the Interception of Wire Communications with the Premises Known as Roulette Records, Second Extension, 11.

84. Lawrence S. Ferreira, Op. cit., August 1986, 35–36. See also William J. Confrey, United States District Court, Southern District of New York, In the Matter of the Application of the United States of America for an Order Authorizing the Interception of Wire Communications Occurring Over Telephone Number (212) 744-6324, Subscribed to By Olympia Esposito . . . , October 1985, paragraph 67.

85. Charles E. Beaudoin, Op. cit., 16–17.

86. Transcription of *Today* show interview of Morris Levy by Brian Ross; www.youtube .com/watch?v=DCdMCWzmMXQ; accessed February 10, 2013.

87. William Knoedelseder, op. cit., October 1, 1986: 1; also cited in Knoedelseder, 263.

88. Leon Baer Borstein, "Affidavit in Support of Defendants Morris Levy and Horris Fisher . . . ," United States District Court for the District of New Jersey, CR No. 86-301 (SSB), filed April 24, 1987, B: The Death Threat Warnings, 1: The Warnings to Fisher, 18. Fisher's son, Brad, said that his father told him that the FBI agents would not let him leave; author interview, February 1, 2015.

89. Federal Bureau of Investigation, Investigation on 7/21/86 at New York, New York; File # New York 183-3066 by SA Stephen F. Steinhauser and SA William J. Confrey, Date Dictated 7/29/86, date of transcription 8/11/86.

90. Ibid.

91. Cited in Knoedelseder, 259.

92. When the agents who arrested Levy inventoried the items on his person, among the usual things (driver's license; credit card; etc.), they found a calling card for "JEB S. MAGRUDER, Committee for the re-election of the President." Apparently Magruder had applied for a job at Roulette, which is why Levy may have been carrying his card. FD-302, Regarding arrest of MORRIS (nmn) LEVY at Boston, Massachusetts, on 9/23/86, 3; author interview with Brad Fisher, February 1, 2015.

93. Levy apparently suffered from polyps which, along with his thick Bronx accent and his intense manner, added to the impact of his voice. Author interview with Brad Fisher, February 1, 2015.

94. Jim Schuh, "Record Heat: Morris Levy's Bad-Rap Rap," *Boston Phoenix*, October 7, 1986, 10; clipping in FBI Memorandum, from SAC, BOSTON (183A-1310) (RUC) to SAC, NEWARK (183A-2061), Subject; PIER II/RICO/OO:NK, date 10/28/86.

95. Transcription of *Today Show* interview of Morris Levy by Brian Ross, op. cit.

96. Jim Bessman, "N.J. Jury Issues Indictments in Cutouts Probe," *Billboard*, October 4, 1986, 91.

97. When Bob Emmer visited Levy's farm, he was surprised to see all the family photos on the walls had the heads of Levy's ex-wives razored out. "I love my family but I hate my ex-wives," Levy commented; author interview, January 26, 2015.

98. Knoedelseder, October 1, 1986, 1.

99. Knoedelseder, 269–71.

100. Bastone with Goldberg and Jesselli, op. cit.

101. Ibid.

102. Letter to Detective Sergeant Edwards Stempinski from Rev. Al Sharpton, August 23, 1988; published on www.thesmokinggun.com April 7, 2014; accessed April 8, 2014, and following.

103. Knoedelseder, 464.

Chapter 11

1. Knoedelseder, 397.

2. United States District Court, Southern District of New York. "In the Matter of the Application of the United States of America for an Order Authorizing the Interception of Oral Communications Occurring within the Triangle Social Club . . . ," Affidavit in Support of an Order Authorizing the Interception of Oral Communications, WP-0202/1X, Posted on www .thesmokinggun.com; accessed April 8, 2014, and following.

3. Bastone with Goldberg and Jesselli, op. cit.

4. Gerald E. King, United States District Court, Southern District of New York. "In the Matter of the Application of the United States of America for an Order Authorizing the Interception of Oral Communications Occurring within the Triangle Social Club . . . ," Affidavit in Support of an Order Authorizing the Interception of Oral Communications, February 1985, WP-0202/1X, paragraph 52. Posted on www.thesmokinggun.com; accessed April 8, 2014, and following.

5. Ibid.

6. Ibid.

7. Leon Baer Borstein, op. cit., filed April 24, 1987, 19–20.

8. Ibid., 21.

9. Letter dated February 10, 1987 to Bruce Repetto Esq. from Leon Borstein and Frederick P. Hafetz, included as an attachment to Leon Baer Borstein, op. cit., filed April 24, 1987. Actually it turned out there was only one informant, Al Sharpton. In the various FBI affidavits submitted to Levy's defense, Sharpton was referred to as both "CI-7" and "CI-8" by mistake, leading Levy's attorneys to believe there were multiple informants involved; see Bastone with Goldberg and Jesselli, op. cit.

10. Knoedelseder, 310.

11. Letter dated April 1, 1987, to Frederick P. Hafetz from Bruce Repetto, included as an attachment to Leon Baer Borstein, op. cit., filed April 24, 1987.

12. Author interview with Richard Foos, June 20, 2012. Foos also said that he visited LaMonte's warehouse before he went into witness protection and saw workers printing record covers for bootleg records on the premises.

13. Stuart M. Cobert, United States District Court, District of New Jersey, United States of America, Plaintiff, against Dominick Canterino, Morris Levy, Howard Fisher, Defendants. CR. No. S-86-301 (SSB), Notice of Motion, Dated April 13, 1988, 3.

14. Martin London, The United States of America vs. Morris Levy, Howard Fisher, Dominick Canterino, Defendants, Criminal Action No. 86-301, Motions of Defendant, April 29, 1988, 7.

15. See memos from John E. McNally Investigations, Inc., to Leon Borstein, Esq., dated June 21, 1987, and Office Memorandum, dated March 23, 1988, Diary No. 11006-001 to Files from Stuart Cobert; attached to Stuart M. Cobert, United States of District Court, District of New Jersey, United States of America, Plaintiff, against Dominick Canterino, Morris Levy, Howard Fisher, Defendants. CR. No. S-86-301 (SSB), Notice of Motion, Dated April 13, 1988.

16. Martin London, The United States of America vs. Gaetano Vastola, Et Al. Defendants. Motion by Defendants for Production of Documents and to Take Testimony, February 25, 1988, 3–4.

17. United States of America v. Gaetano VASTOLA, et al., Defendants. Crim. A. No. 86-301(SSB). United States District Court, D. New Jersey, May 6, 1988, III. Discussion, B. The Evidence Presented at the Brady Hearing, 922; see also Knoedelseder, 155.

18. Ibid., 923.

19. Trevor McShane, "Interview with LA Times Journalist and Author: Bill Knoedelseder," posted August 2, 2010, http://trevormcshanemusic.wordpress.com/2010/08/02/billknoedel seder/; accessed February 8, 2014.

20. Author interview with Brad Fisher, February 1, 2015.

21. Opening statement of Bruce Repetto, United States of America vs. Morris Levy, Howard Fisher, Dominick Canterino, Defendants, Criminal Action No. 86-301, May 11, 1988, trial transcript 27.

22. Ibid., 37–38.

23. Ibid., 41–42.

24. Opening statement of Martin London, United States of America vs. Morris Levy, Howard Fisher, Dominick Canterino, Defendants, Criminal Action No. 86-301, May 11, 1988, trial transcript 45–48.

25. Ibid., 54–55.

26. Ibid., 58.

27. Ibid., 59.

28. Ibid., 67.

29. Closing statement of Bruce Repetto, United States of America vs. Morris Levy, Howard Fisher, Dominick Canterino, Defendants, Criminal Action No. 86-301, May 23, 1988, trial transcript 1102.

30. Ibid., 1103.

31. Ibid., 1105.

32. Ibid., 1119.

33. Ibid., 1151.

34. Ibid., 1151–52.

35. Ibid.

36. Closing statement of Martin London, United States of America vs. Morris Levy, Howard Fisher, Dominick Canterino, Defendants, Criminal Action No. 86-301, May 24, 1988, trial transcript 1312–13.

37. Ibid., 1313.

38. Ibid., 1316.

39. Ibid.

40. Ibid., 1319, 1320.

41. Supreme Court, County of Columbia, Index No. 3449-88, United States of America against Morris Levy, Affidavit of Confession of Judgment, June 1, 1988.

42. United States of America, Plaintiff, v. Morris LEVY, Howard Fisher, and Dominick Canterino, Defendants, Crim. No. 86-301, United States District Court, D., New Jersey, August 23, 1988, OPINION, BROTMAN, District Judge.

43. Louis R. Gigante, Letter to Honorable Stanley S. Brotman, September 20, 1988, found in the trial records of United States Government v. Levy et al.

44. United States of America, vs. Morris Levy, United States District Court, District of New Jersey, Cr. No. S-86-301 (SSB), Affidavit of Richard P. Shanley, September 23, 1988.

45. Jim Nicholson, "David Ebo, 43; Sang With The 'Blue Notes,'" *Philadelphia Daily News*, December 3, 1993; accessed online April 20, 2014.

46. Kitty Caparella, "The Big One Raids Crack Roland Bartlett's Drug Empire, Officials Say," *Philadelphia Daily News*, March 11, 1987; accessed online January 11, 2014.

47. Knoedelseder, 421.

48. The United States of America vs. Morris Levy, Howard Fisher, Dominick Canterino, Defendants, Criminal Action No. 86-301, transcript, October 28, 1988, 91–93.

49. Knoedelseder, 424.

50. *Billboard*, November 19, 1988, 13.

51. "Commentary: Levy, Boosters Score *Billboard* Coverage," *Billboard*, December 3, 1988, 9.

52. Ibid.

53. "An Open Letter to the Music Industry About Morris Levy," *Billboard*, January 7, 1989, 5.

54. Fred Goodman, "Morris Levy Severing Music Business Ties," *Billboard*, December 20, 1986, 1, 71.

55. Ian MacKay, "News Diary," *The Age*, January 14, 1987, 2.

56. Ibid.

57. "Indicted Strawberries Boss; Will Sell For The Right Price," *Boston Globe*, December 18, 1986, 58.

58. John R. Emshwiller and Kathleen A. Hughes, "Live's Choice of Paul Weiss to Conduct Probe Draws Conflict-of-Interest Charge," *Wall Street Journal* (Eastern edition), September 5, 1989, 1.

59. Ronald L. Soble, "Jose Menendez's Conflict and Controversy," *Los Angeles Times*, August 25, 1989, 1. This article is the source for much of the biographical information on Menendez.

60. Geoff Mayfield, "Few Changes at Sound Warehouse, Strawberries," *Billboard*, February 4, 1989, 54.

61. Ronald L. Soble, op. cit. Bob Emmer, in an interview with the author on January 26, 2015, said he was called by the FBI shortly after the Menendez murder because he had just

completed the deal to purchase Roulette's masters from Levy. The FBI grilled him about Levy's involvement with Strawberries. The encounter was sobering to Emmer, who luckily was able to convince the FBI that he had no knowledge of the Strawberries deal.

62. "LIVE Reviews its Purchase of Strawberries," *Billboard*, September 16, 1989, 1, 101.

63. Ibid.

64. Ibid.

65. John Johnson and Ronald L. Soble, "The Menendez Brothers: Jose Menendez Gave His Sons Everything. Maybe Even a Motive for Murder," *Los Angeles Times*, July 22, 1990, http://articles.latimes.com/1990-07-22/magazine/tm-930_1_jose-menendez/1; accessed online March 21, 2014.

66. Chris Reidy, "Getting back in a groove," *Boston Globe*, July 8, 1998, C1.

67. Broven, 269.

68. "Newsline . . . Suit," *Billboard*, June 11, 1994, 4.

69. www.legalmetric.com/cases/copyright/nysd/nysd_194cv02410.html#s10; accessed online April 4, 2014.

70. Irv Lichtman, "Newsline . . . ," *Billboard*, July 31, 1999, 95.

71. Irv Lichtmann, "Roulette Agrees to $4.5 Mil Sale to KB Communications," *Billboard*, August 20, 1988, 6, 77; "KB May Acquire Roulette Records," *Variety*, August 10, 1988, 53.

72. This narrative is based on author interviews with Bob Emmer, January 26, 2015, and Richard Foos, June 20, 2012; email correspondence with Harold Bronson, January 23 and 26, 2015; Bronson, *The Rhino Records Story*.

73. Emmer says that in fact the third party was Windswept Entertainment, which had already purchased Levy's publishing; author interview, January 26, 2015.

74. Author interview with Richard Foos, June 20, 2012.

75. Author interview with Bob Emmer, January 26, 2015.

76. Foos said $10–12 million, but Harold Bronson and Bob Emmer assert that the figure was actually $5–7 million; Bronson, *The Rhino Records Story*, Kindle ebook loc. 5775; author interview with Bob Emmer, January 26, 2015.

77. Author interview with Richard Foos, June 20, 2012.

78. Actually, there was at least one instance where Levy's ownership of a master was disputed, according to Harold Bronson; email to the author, January 30, 2015.

79. United States of America, Plaintiff, against Morris Levy, Howard Fisher and Dominick Canterino, Defendants, Cr. No. S-86-301 (SSB), Notice of Motion to Stay Execution of Sentence, Filed November 28, 1989.

80. United States of America, Plaintiff, against Morris Levy, Howard Fisher and Dominick Canterino, Defendants, Cr. No. S-86-301 (SSB), Certificate of Camille M. Kenny, February 8, 1990.

81. United States of America, Plaintiff, against Morris Levy, Howard Fisher and Dominick Canterino, Defendants, Cr. No. S-86-301 (SSB), Petition, Filed February 28, 1990.

INDEX

Index

Index